The Wallace: Selections

Middle English Texts

General Editor

Russell A. Peck
University of Rochester

Associate Editor

Alan Lupack
University of Rochester

Assistant Editor

Dana M. Symons
University of Rochester

Advisory Board

Rita Copeland
University of Pennsylvania

Thomas G. Hahn
University of Rochester

Lisa Kiser
Ohio State University

R. A. Shoaf
University of Florida

Bonnie Wheeler
Southern Methodist University

The Middle English Texts Series is designed for classroom use. Its goal is to make available to teachers and students texts that occupy an important place in the literary and cultural canon but have not been readily available in student editions. The series does not include those authors, such as Chaucer, Langland, or Malory, whose English works are normally in print in good student editions. The focus is, instead, upon Middle English literature adjacent to those authors that teachers need in compiling the syllabuses they wish to teach. The editions maintain the linguistic integrity of the original work but within the parameters of modern reading conventions. The texts are printed in the modern alphabet and follow the practices of modern capitalization, word formation, and punctuation. Manuscript abbreviations are silently expanded, and *u/v* and *j/i* spellings are regularized according to modern orthography. Yogh is transcribed as *g*, *gh*, *y*, or *s*, according to the letter in modern English spelling to which it corresponds. Distinction between the second person pronoun and the definite article is made by spelling the one *thee* and the other *the*, and final *-e* that receives full syllabic value is accented (e.g., *charité*). Hard words, difficult phrases, and unusual idioms are glossed on the page, either in the right margin or at the foot of the page. Explanatory and textual notes appear at the end of the text, along with a glossary. The editions include short introductions on the history of the work, its merits and points of topical interest, and also contain briefly annotated bibliographies.

The Wallace: Selections

Edited by
Anne McKim

Published for TEAMS
(The Consortium for the Teaching of the Middle Ages)
in Association with the University of Rochester

by

MEDIEVAL INSTITUTE PUBLICATIONS
College of Arts and Sciences
Western Michigan University
Kalamazoo, Michigan
2003

Library of Congress Cataloging-in-Publication Data

Henry, the Minstrel, fl. 1470-1492.
  [Wallace. Selections]
  The Wallace : selections / edited by Anne McKim.
Includes bibliographical references.
  ISBN 1-58044-076-2 (pbk. : alk. paper)
 1. Wallace, William, Sir, d. 1305--Poetry. 2. Scotland--History--Wallace's Rising, 1297-1304--Poetry. 3. Revolutionaries--Poetry. 4. Nationalists--Poetry. 5. Guerrillas--Poetry. I. McKim, Anne, 1953- II. Title.
  PR1989.H6A7 2003
  821'.2--dc21

                                                            2003010365

ISBN 1-58044-076-2

Copyright 2003 by the Board of Trustees of Western Michigan University

Printed in the United States of America

Cover design by Linda K. Judy

Contents

Acknowledgments	vii
Introduction	1
Select Bibliography	9
The Wallace	13
Explanatory Notes	217
Textual Notes	265
Glossary	279

Acknowledgments

I am grateful to the former School of Humanities at the University of Waikato for a research grant for this project. My thanks are also due to the Trustees of the National Library of Scotland for permission to use Advocates MS 19.2.2, and to Michelle Keown and Simone Marshall for research assistance.

I very much appreciate the generous editorial advice provided by Russell A. Peck, the assistance with formatting from John Sutton and Michael Livingston, and the careful supervision and final proofreading undertaken by Dana M. Symons, who also printed the camera-ready copy. Michael Livingston read the manuscript against a photocopy of the Advocates MS 19.2.2., adding numerous textual notes and assisting with the regularization of *w* to *u*, *v*, and *w*. Rhiannon Purdie made helpful suggestions toward establishing the orthography of the volume, and the Robbins Library at the University of Rochester provided superb resources for checking details. At Kalamazoo, the staff of Medieval Institute Publications saw the volume through the press. We are all grateful to the National Endowment for the Humanities for its generous financial support in the preparation of the volume.

My greatest debt is to my family, especially my husband Ian.

The Wallace

Introduction

One of the very first books printed in Scotland, *The Wallace* is a verse biography, composed c. 1471–79, of the celebrated Scottish national hero, William Wallace. Written more than a century and a half after his subject's death (1305),[1] Hary's largely imaginative account of this real historical personage's role in the Scottish Wars of Independence has nevertheless exerted an enormous influence on representations of Wallace right down to the present day, including the hugely successful recent film *Braveheart*.

The Wallace story had become the stuff of legend long before Hary memorialized his hero. Although Hary claims as his authority an eye-witness account written in Latin by Wallace's chaplain and former schoolmate, John Blair (5.537–41; 12.1410–15), no such text survives nor is its existence attested by any other records. The earliest Scottish account of William Wallace is preserved in brief annals by John of Fordun (*Gesta Annalia* caps. 98–103), later included in his *Chronica Gentis Scotorum* (c. 1380), which was a primary source for the fifteenth-century chroniclers Andrew of Wyntoun (c. 1420) and Walter Bower (c. 1440), whose fuller accounts of Wallace, one written in the vernacular, the other in Latin, Hary almost certainly knew. Like his predecessors, Hary also drew on traditional tales of Wallace's exploits, including perhaps some of the "gret gestis" Wyntoun mentions as circulating in the early fifteenth century (*Orygynale Cronykil of Scotland* 8.2300).

The single most important model and, ironically, the "source" for Hary's composition is a fourteenth-century vernacular verse biography of the other most renowned Scottish national hero, Robert the Bruce. Hary refers to *The Bruce* (1375) and its author, John Barbour, a long-serving archdeacon of Aberdeen, a number of times in *The Wallace* and in such a way as to convey his respect for Barbour's biography of the king. If imitation is indeed the sincerest form of flattery, Hary pays Barbour a considerable compliment by going so far as to "borrow" several episodes from the archdeacon's account of Bruce's military career — in which Wallace is not once mentioned — and assigning them to Wallace! As Lord Hailes so memorably put

---

[1] The date and place of his birth remain the subject of considerable debate. A recent biographer argues for 1272 or 1273 in Ellerslie, Ayrshire, although a number of traditions associate him with Elderslie, Renfrewshire. For a recent biography, see James Mackay, *William Wallace: Brave Heart* (Edinburgh: Mainstream, 1995).

The Wallace

it, Hary "celebrated the actions which Wallace did not perform, as well as those which he did."[2] Early in his poem, Hary reveals his belief that Wallace merits comparison with Bruce, and, while he qualifies this with the acknowledgment that Bruce was the legitimate "heir" of the kingdom, his preference for Wallace is evident in his claim that the latter was the greater hero because he was braver and more patriotic, as witnessed by the number of times he rescued Scotland from the English and even challenged the enemy on their own ground:

All worthi men that has gud witt to waille,	*at command*
Bewar that yhe with mys deyme nocht my taille.	*you do not find fault*
Perchance yhe say that Bruce he was none sik.	*such*
He was als gud quhat deid was to assaill	*as; action; attempt*
As of his handis and bauldar in battaill,	*bolder*
Bot Bruce was knawin weyll ayr of this kynrik;	*heir; kingdom*
For he had rycht we call no man him lik.	
Bot Wallace thris this kynrik conquest haile,	
In Ingland fer socht battaill on that rik.	*far; realm*
(2.351–59)	

Appropriately enough, the only surviving manuscript of *The Wallace*, copied in 1488, is preserved and bound along with one of only two extant manuscripts of *The Bruce*, copied in 1489 (National Library of Scotland MS Advocates 19.2.2). The handwriting and separate colophons at the end of each poem proclaim them to be the work of the same scribe, John Ramsay, whom Neilson identifies as a cleric and notary of St. Andrews' diocese (p. 86). Whether they were commissioned by the same patron, which might suggest early recognition of the affinity between the two works, cannot be established. We do know from one of the colophons that the copy of *The Bruce* was made at the request of Sir Symon Lochmalony, vicar of Auchtermoonzie in Fife.

   Like Barbour, Hary's purpose was commemorative and eulogistic. As well as encouraging his readers to honor worthy ancestors, he begins his account of the already renowned Wallace (1.17) with a brief genealogical sketch (1.21–38) in which Wallace's ancestry is traced back through the Crawford line on his mother's side, and on his father's side to the first "gud Wallace" (1.30), whom Hary, following Barbour's lost Genealogy of the Royal House of Stewart (referred to as "The Stewartis Originall" by Wyntoun), identifies as the companion of Walter, the first Scottish Stewart. Introducing his hero in this way is entirely conventional, but Hary also aims to establish beyond doubt Wallace's noble Scottish lineage. In doing so he repudiated received depictions of Wallace as a common thief, rebel, and traitor found in the English records and, at the same

---

[2] See "Bannatyne Poems" in *Ancient Scottish Poems*, ed. Sir David Dalrymple, Lord Hailes (Edinburgh: A. Murray and J. Cochran, 1770), pp. 271–72.

Introduction

time, challenged any lingering perception in Scotland that, because of his inferior rank, Wallace had never commanded the full support of the Scottish nobles.

It is above all for his "nobille worthi deid" (1.2) in defense of his country that Hary celebrates Wallace. He portrays him as a great national liberator, "the reskew of Scotland" (1.38), a hero on a mission that is divinely sanctioned — "he fred it weyle throu grace" (1.40). Early in the narrative the famous seer Thomas the Rhymer prophesies that Wallace will liberate Scotland from English domination and restore peace three times (2.346–50). Later Wallace himself is granted a vision in which St. Andrew, Scotland's patron saint, and the Virgin Mary present him with an avenging sword, a parti-coloured wand, and a precious book, interpreted by his chaplain John Blair as confirmation of his divinely ordained mission (7.65–152). As Brown and McDiarmid have noted, while the suggestion for the prophetic dream probably came from *The Alliterative Morte Arthure* in which King Arthur is visited by Lady Fortune in a dream, the religious interpretation does not (Brown, p. 38; McDiarmid 2.200). Indeed there are a number of explicit allusions to Arthur in Hary's poem, including the claim that "Wallace of hand sen Arthour had na mak" (8.845) which, along with allusions to Hector, Alexander the Great, Julius Caesar, Roland, and Godfrey of Boulogne, strongly suggest that Hary wished Wallace to be added as a kind of tenth "noble" or "worthy" to the illustrious "Nine Worthies" celebrated in literature, art, and architecture in the Middle Ages.

As well as ensuring Wallace's place in the house of fame, Hary both rallies and rebukes his contemporaries in a way that has convinced a number of critics of his propagandist purposes. From the beginning of the poem, there is no mistaking his anti-English feeling for "Our ald ennemys cummyn of Saxonys blud, / That nevyr yeit to Scotland wald do gud" (1.7–8). Blaming "sleuthfulnes" (1.3) for the all too prevalent tendency to forget the debt and respect due to ancestors may be a standard *topos* in medieval historiography, but Hary's criticism of those who perversely "honour ennymyis" (1.5) and proffer them "gret kyndnes" (1.10) has been interpreted as referring specifically to contemporary politics of the 1480s (Neilson, pp. 109–10) or the 1470s (McDiarmid, pp. xiv–xxvi). Certainly internal evidence supports McDiarmid's belief that the poem was written sometime in the 1470s, that is, between 1471 — when the two contemporaries, Sir William Wallace of Craigie and Sir James Liddale of Halkerston, to whom Hary refers at the end of his work as persuading him to deviate a little from Blair's account, were knighted — and 1479, when Sir William is known to have died. These were also years in which James III's policy of matrimonial alliances with England may explain Hary's criticism of the misguided friendliness shown to England expressed in the poem's opening lines (lines 5–10). McDiarmid speculates that Hary's patrons were probably those southern magnates most opposed to James' pro-English foreign policy, including the king's brother Alexander, duke of Albany, to whom Sir James Liddale was steward.

Nevertheless, Hary presents himself as a disinterested as well as a patriotic writer. Although he appeals to fellow patriots — at one point calling on "Yhe nobill men that ar of Scottis kind" (7.235) to avenge atrocities that he alleges the English have committed — he claims that he was not commissioned by "king nor othir lord" (12.1435) to write the book, and that he was not prompted by the prospect of any reward (12.1434). The historian John Major writing in the early sixteenth century informs us that Hary recited his poem in the presence of princes.[3] Whether he ever entertained the king in this way we do not now know, although the royal treasury records reveal that he received gifts of money from James IV on five separate occasions at Linlithgow Palace between 1490 and 1492, indicating that he had connections with the royal court, though in what capacity is not specified.

Indeed, we know very little about the author of *The Wallace*: his name as well as his identity remains something of a mystery. On the authority of John Major (1518) he is said to have been called Henry or Hary, though whether this was his first or last name is not clear. McDiarmid notes that the surname Hare or Henry (with variants such as Henrison) was quite common in the Linlithgow area in the second half of the fifteenth century and ventures the opinion that the writer was born there or thereabouts around 1440, citing in support what he considers to be evidence in *The Wallace* of the author's detailed regional knowledge of Stirlingshire and Perthshire (pp. xxvii–xxviii). Others believe that the name Hary, or Blind Harry as he is often called, was an alias or nickname (Schofield, p.12; Balaban, p. 247). The poet William Dunbar simultaneously attested and perpetuated the currency of the name "blind Hary" when he registered his recent death in the poem best known as "The Lament for the Makars" (c. 1505).

Hary's blindness is confirmed both by the royal records and by John Major, although the latter's claim that the poet was blind from birth has more recently been challenged, particularly by readers who are convinced that only a sighted person could have written the graphic descriptions and detailed topographical accounts which distinguish *The Wallace* (Neilson, p. 85; McDiarmid, pp. xxxiv–xxxvii). The richly allusive and highly literary quality of Hary's writing indicates a widely read man, while a strong respect for reading is also conveyed right from the start of the poem in his references to what readers can learn from books and in his injunctions to his readers to go and read certain books (1.1, 17, 34, 37; see also 7.613, 1293).

Like many other medieval poets, Hary expresses feigned anxiety about the reception of his "nobill buk" (12.1451) which some may dismiss as the "rurall dyt" (12.1431) of a self-confessed rustic or "burel man" (12.1461). In the event, *The Wallace* was an immediate and lasting success. By 1488 it had been copied by John Ramsay, probably as a commission, and — after the first Scottish printing press was set up in Edinburgh in 1507–08 — it was one of the first books printed, almost certainly by Chepman and Myllar. The bibliographer John Miller notes that at least twenty-two other editions were printed before 1707. Adaptations of Hary's work, from the selective revisions of the Protestant printer Lekpreuik (1570) catering to the tastes of a post-Reformation readership to the complete "modernisation" of William Hamilton of Gilbertfield (1722), ensured that *The Wallace* always found an audience. Some

---

[3] *Historia Majoris Britanniae*, ed. Robert Freebairn (Edinburgh: R. Freebairn, 1740), 4.15.

Introduction

readers were more critical than others. Early sixteenth-century Scottish historians tended to be skeptical about Hary's reliability even as they drew heavily on his account as a source for Wallace's career. Major was particularly influential in developing the tradition of the blind minstrel dependent for his livelihood on pleasing wealthy patrons by regaling them with stories drawn from popular sources.

Hary himself locates his work within a learned literary tradition when he purports to translate from a Latin life of Wallace; when he cites and recommends particular books to his readers; and again when he alludes to chronicle sources. His primary model as we have seen is Barbour's *Bruce,* which was evidently respected by fifteenth-century chroniclers, and which provided Hary with a suitable structure to emulate — a sequence of linked episodes describing the heroic actions and incidents in the life of a national hero. While the formal ordering of the narrative into twelve books can be clearly detected from Ramsay's transcription (even though he overlooked the start and end of Book 9 with the result that his manuscript has only eleven books), *The Wallace* is essentially structured according to the protagonist's threefold "rescues" of Scotland from English domination, a narrative strategy complemented by a range of rhetorical strategies, including repetition with variation of *motifs*, many of them also deployed by Barbour. Recent scholarship has highlighted the use of traditional material, including folklore, by even respectable medieval historians like Andrew Wyntoun and Walter Bower, so it is not at all surprising to find that Hary too drew on folklore, most strikingly in the Fawdoun episode in which Wallace encounters the ghost of a man he has beheaded. It is the "conscious blending of folk-myth and Chaucerian literary conventions" that perhaps makes *The Wallace* such an interesting work (Balaban, p. 250). Although Hary's knowledge of Chaucer's poetry — which was quite widely available in fifteenth-century Scotland — has long been noted (Skeat, Neilson, Scheps [1970], Harward) with specific echoes of The General Prologue to *The Canterbury Tales*, The Knight's Tale, The Franklin's Tale, *Troilus and Criseyde*, and *The Legend of Good Women* (all noticed in the explanatory notes section of this edition), critical appreciation of the literary merits of *The Wallace* has come only quite recently.

Familiarity with the great medieval romance cycles of Arthur and Alexander, Scottish translations and derivatives of which were composed and circulated in the fifteenth century, is evident in Hary's poem, particularly in his depiction of Wallace as an exemplary warrior and "chyftayne in wer" (5.842). As well as being handsome, strong, brave, and wise (1.184), as a military leader he inspires loyalty and admiration by his personal prowess, his prudence (e.g., in avoiding open battle when seriously outnumbered), his sound military strategy and tactics, and his generosity to his followers (6.784–86). Wallace, "the flour of armys" (6.56), is almost invariably chivalrous in his treatment of noncombatants, and we are repeatedly told that he refused to harm women, children, and priests. Off the battlefield, he is "curtas, and benyng" (1.202), but because *The Wallace* is so centrally concerned with war, these particular attributes are more stated than demonstrated. Nevertheless, Hary conveys his appreciation of the value that attaches to *courtoisie* when he takes the trouble to praise the son of John Ramsay, one of

The Wallace

Wallace's allies, as the "flour of courtlyness" (7.900) and when he stages a completely unhistorical meeting and conversation between the English queen and his hero in which courtly decorum is displayed (8.1215–1466).

The conflicting claims of war and love exercise the young Wallace (5.611–48) when he is smitten by a young woman in Lanark. Apparently aware of the philosophy that love can spur a warrior on to great feats of prowess, Wallace declares to his friend Kerle that the case is rather different when the liberation of his country is at stake. As a champion of such a cause, he believes love will only distract him from his mission:

. . . he that thinkis on his luff to speid,	*prosper*
He may do weill, haiff he fortoun and grace.	*if he has*
Bot this standis all in ane othir cas:	*things stand differently in this case*
A gret kynryk with feill fayis ourset.	*kingdom [is] with many enemies overrun*
Rycht hard it is amendis for to get	*to obtain amends [from them]*
At anys of thaim and wyrk the observance	*And at the same time perform the duties*
Quhilk langis luff and all his frevill chance.	*belong [to]; fickle fortune*
(5.640–46)	

He also knows from experience how dangerous a distraction love can be, since an earlier liaison with a paramour in Perth had very nearly cost him his life and endangered his men. But despite his asseveration that love is "[n]othing bot folychnes" (5.631), like Troilus, he finds the power of love irresistible once it has made its "prent" (5.606) on his heart. Unlike Troilus, he marries his beloved and comes to regret this only because it costs her her life.

Wallace's personal bereavement serves to deepen his resolve against his enemies, as righteous anger and desire for vengeance unite his personal and political motives:

The saklace slauchtir of hir blith and brycht,	*innocent*
That I avow to the Makar of mycht,	
That of that nacioune I sall nevir forber	*spare*
Yhong nor ald that abill is to wer.	*old; is fit to fight*
(6.215–18)	

He proceeds to kill the sheriff and English inhabitants of Lanark, and his personally motivated reprisal marks the beginning of Scotland's recovery, as Scots who flock to his lead recognize:

Quhen Scottis hard thir fyne tithingis of new	*heard this excellent news*
Out of all part to Wallace fast thai drew,	*From all over*
Plenyst the toun quhilk was thar heretage.	*Settled*
Thus Wallace straiff agayne that gret barnage.	*strove against; barons*
Sa he begane with strenth and stalwart hand	*So*

Introduction

> To chewys agayne sum rowmys of Scotland.   *recover; parts*
> The worthi Scottis that semblit till him thar   *flocked to*
> Chesit him for cheyff, thar chyftayne and ledar.   *Chose*
> (6.265–72)

Hary never lets his readers forget that his hero is a man moved by "pitté" (1.182) for his country and "ire of wrang" (6.224) or the righteous anger caused by wrongs that must be redressed. Provocation ranges from the scorn and insults the young Wallace regularly encounters as he attempts to go about his everyday business in occupied Scotland, to the killing of his kin, which in the course of the narrative includes his father, elder brother, and uncle, as well as his wife. Wallace reacts to these provocations by cutting throats, dashing out brains, shattering bones, striking out eyes and tongues, and beheading others in an orgy of violence described with a relish some readers have found distasteful. Hary's frequently emotive language seems designed not only to express Wallace's rage and Hary's antipathy but also to incite hatred of the English in his readers.

The Wallace catalogues the sheer brutality of war. We are regaled with such detailed accounts of the sacking of towns and the burning down of buildings full of screaming inhabitants that the smells and sounds, as well as the terrible sights of war, are graphically conveyed. The hero may spare women but he gives the severed head of Fitzhugh, Edward I's nephew, to his wife and sends her with it to the English king.

If Hary dwells on the bloodshed in a way that leaves him open to the charge of glorifying slaughter, there is nevertheless a surprising amount of humor in the poem. Much of it, of course, is at the expense of the English. For example, when Edward's drunk and insensible soldiers are burned to death as they sleep in barns outside Ayr, Hary offers an early example of typically Scottish understatement: "Till slepand men that walkand [waking] was nocht soft" (7.440). On other occasions the humor derives from the improbability of the hero successfully passing himself off as a woman to elude capture. Pursued after he kills the constable of Dundee early in his career, Wallace quickly dons a woman's gown, headscarf, and hat, and swaps his bloody knife for a spinning "rok" (1.244), prompting the poet to comment:

> . . . thai socht him beselye
> Bot he sat still and span full conandly,   *skillfully*
> As of his tym, for he nocht leryt lang.   *Considering his [short learning] time; learned*
> (1.247–9)

Hary also gives Wallace a sense of humor as well as a keen sense of injustice. When the captain of Lochmabon scornfully has the tails of Scottish horses docked, Wallace proffers a "[r]eward" (5.756) introducing himself as "a barbour of the best" who has come from the west "[t]o cutt and schaiff" and "lat blud" (5.758–60), before he dispatches the captain and a

The Wallace

companion with his sword. Indeed much of the humor of *The Wallace* is found in the many verbal exchanges that frequently precede physical encounters between the hero and his English enemies, where the jokes are shared with the reader, as when, for example, challenged by the gatekeeper at Perth, Wallace gives his name as "Will Malcomsone" (4.368), which of course he is (Will, son of Malcolm). On another occasion, irreverent humor and witty wordplay are enjoyed by Wallace and his uncle Auchinleck as they prepare to mount a front- and rearguard attack on an army led by Bishop Bek near Glasgow:

"Uncle," he said, "be besy into wer.	*prepare for battle*
Quhethir will yhe the byschoppys taill upber,	*Whether; carry*
Or pas befor and tak his benysone?"	*in front; blessing*
He ansuerd hym with rycht schort provision,	*little hesitation*
"Unbyschoppyt yeit forsuth I trow ye be.	*Not yet blessed by a bishop; believe*
Yourselff sall fyrst his blyssyng tak for me,	
For sekyrly ye servit it best the nycht.	*surely; deserved; tonight*
To ber his taill we sall in all our mycht."	*carry; with all our might*
(7.545–52)	

Wallace may show little respect for an English bishop, but his devoutness is nevertheless illustrated a number of times in the poem when he attends mass, offers up prayers, and finally endures torture by steadfastly reading the psalter he has, we are told, kept on his person since childhood. (Hary adds an ironic touch when he makes the bishop of Canterbury defy Edward I by hearing the last confession of this "rebell.") His execution, following betrayal by a trusted associate and the father of his godchildren, is presented as a martyrdom (12.1305–08) — as it was by Andrew Wyntoun — and divine approbation is conferred through the spirit of an elderly monk who appears in a vision to confirm that Wallace, "a gret slaar of men" and "defendour of Scotland" (12.1278, 1285), will be honored in heaven.

The Wallace has the distinction of being the first extant Middle Scots poem to use the decasyllabic couplet (Scheps, *Studies in Scottish Literature*, 1969). Hary also employs a nine-line decasyllabic stanza rhyming *aabaabbab* (2.171–359), first used by Chaucer in *Anelida and Arcite* and later by all the major Middle Scots poets, Robert Henryson (*The Testament of Cresseid*, lines 407–69), William Dunbar (*The Goldyn Targe*), and Gavin Douglas (*Palise of Honour*, Prologue and Parts 1 and 2); and a decasyllabic eight-line stanza rhyming *ababbcbc* (6.1–104), employed by Chaucer in The Monk's Tale and by Dunbar in a number of poems.

This edition of *The Wallace* provides substantial selections from Hary's narrative, which runs to over 11,000 lines. The key episodes are presented and their place in the unfolding account of Wallace's career until his death is preserved by the inclusion of prose summaries of omitted sections. The division into twelve books, found in Lekpreuik's 1570 edition, is adopted here, and only one book (9), which deals with Wallace's first visit to France, is left

Introduction

out, while several books (1, 2, 7, and 8) are presented in their entirety. Like Matthew P. McDiarmid's complete edition for the Scottish Text Society (1968–69), this edition of selections is based on the sole surviving manuscript, Advocates 19.2.2. Occasionally missing lines and improved readings are supplied from the remaining fragments of the first printed edition (1507–08), preserved in the National Library of Scotland, and its derivative printed by Lekpreuik in 1570. Emendations are recorded in the textual notes, as are different readings from McDiarmid. Spellings have been normalized in accordance with the conventions of the Middle English Texts Series, as stated in the front of each volume: e.g., scribal yogh is transcribed as *y* or *g*; *u/v* and *i/j* have been normalized; final *-e*, if a long vowel with full syllable value, is marked with an accent (e.g., *charité*). Occasionally, the scribe uses *ff* where we would use *f*; if the *ff* indicates a capital, I have rendered it *F*; I have also changed *ff* to *f* in cases where *of* would be confused with *off*, since the pronunciation of the passage remains unchanged. The scribe regularly uses *w* where we would use *w*, *v*, or *u*. I have followed the practice of modern editors and transcribed such words with the modern vowel. Thus *ws* becomes *us*; *trawaill* becomes *travaill*; and *waill* when it means "weal" or "the good" remains *waill*, while *waill* in the sense of "avail" or "help" becomes *vaill*. Occasionally final *-r* and *-s* have a curl, which I have treated as a mere flourish. Contractions in the manuscript have been silently expanded, and capitalization, word formation, and punctuation follow modern practice.

Select Bibliography

Manuscript

National Library of Scotland MS Advocates 19.2.2, fols. 79r–194r. [Bound along with *The Bruce*, the two parts have been transposed in the binding, so that *The Wallace*, copied in 1488, forms the second part and *The Bruce*, copied in 1489, forms the first. *The Wallace* is written on 124 vellum leaves, in single columns, distributed into 6 quires.]

Early Printed Editions

The Actis and Deidis of the Illuster and Vailʒeand Campioun, Schir William Wallace, Knicht of Ellerslie. Edinburgh: Robert Lekpreuik, 1570. British Museum.

The Actis and Deidis of Schir William Wallace. Ed. William Craigie. Scottish Text Society third ser. 12. New York: Scholars' Facsimiles and Reprints, 1940 (for 1938). [Facsimile of Robert Lekpreuik's 1570 edition, above.]

The Wallace

Fragments of an edition in the type of Chepman and Myllar (Edinburgh, 1507/8). National Library of Scotland. [Printed in an appendix to Craigie's facsimile edition of Lekpreuik above.]

The Lyfe and Actis of the Maist Illvster and Vailzeand Campiovn William Wallace, Knicht of Ellerslie, Mainteiner and defender of the libertie of Scotland. Edinburgh: Henry Charteris, 1594. [Title page, preface, and table of contents printed as an appendix to Craigie's facsimile edition.]

Modern Editions

Jamieson, John, ed. *Wallace, or, The Life and Acts of Sir William Wallace of Ellerslie.* By Henry the Minstrel. Glasgow: Maurice Ogle & Co., 1869.

McDiarmid, Matthew P., ed. *Hary's Wallace.* 2 vols. Scottish Text Society fourth ser. 4–5. Edinburgh: William Blackwood and Sons, 1968–69.

Moir, James, ed. *The Actis and Deidis of the Illustere and Vailʒeand Campioun Schir William Wallace Knicht of Ellerslie by Henry the Minstrel Commonly Known as Blind Harry.* Scottish Text Society 6, 7, 17. Edinburgh: William Blackwood and Sons, 1889 (for 1884–89).

Bibliographical Sources

Aldis, Harry Gidney. *A List of Books Printed in Scotland before 1700, Including Those Printed furth of the Realm for Scottish Booksellers, with Brief Notes on the Printers and Stationers.* New York: B. Franklin, [1970].

Geddie, William. *A Bibliography of Middle Scots Poets.* Scottish Text Society 61. Edinburgh: William Blackwood and Sons, 1912.

Miller, John F. *Records of the Glasgow Bibliographical Society.* Glasgow: Glasgow Bibliographical Society, 1913–. [See vol. 3, Part I (1915), pp. 1–25, for an account of the MS and text; see vol. 6 (1918), pp. 20–38, for the editions.]

Introduction

Sources and Analogues

Andrew of Wyntoun. *The Orygynale Cronykil of Scotland*. See entry for Laing, below.

Barbour, John. *Barbour's Bruce*. See entry for McDiarmid and Stevenson, below.

Bower, Walter. *Scotichronicon*. Ed. D. E. R. Watt et al. 9 vols. Aberdeen: Aberdeen University Press, 1987–98.

Selected Criticism

Balaban, John. "Blind Harry and *The Wallace*." *The Chaucer Review* 8 (1974), 241–51.

Barrow, G. W. S. *The Kingdom of the Scots*. London: Edward Arnold, 1973.

———. *Robert Bruce and the Community of the Realm of Scotland*. Third ed. Edinburgh: Edinburgh University Press, 1988.

Brown, J. T. T. *The Wallace and The Bruce Restudied*. Bonner Beiträge zur Anglistik 6. Bonn: P. Hanstein, 1900.

Goldstein, R. James. "Blind Hary's Myth of Blood: The Ideological Closure of *The Wallace*." *Studies in Scottish Literature* 25 (1990), 70–82.

———. *The Matter of Scotland: Historical Narrative in Medieval Scotland*. Lincoln: University of Nebraska Press, 1993.

Harward, Vernon. "Hary's *Wallace* and Chaucer's *Troilus and Criseyde*." *Studies in Scottish Literature* 10 (1972), 48–50.

Laing, David, ed. *The Orygynale Cronykil of Scotland by Andrew of Wyntoun*. 3 vols. The Historians of Scotland 2, 3, 9. Edinburgh: Edmonston and Douglas, 1872–79.

McDiarmid, Matthew P., and James A. C. Stevenson, eds. *Barbour's Bruce: A Fredome is a Noble Thing!* 3 vols. Scottish Text Society fourth ser. 12–13, 15. Edinburgh: Scottish Text Society, 1980–85.

McKim, Anne. "Scottish National Heroes and the Limits of Violence." *A Great Effusion of Blood? Interpreting Medieval Violence*. Ed. Mark Meyers and Daniel Thiery. Toronto: University of Toronto Press, forthcoming.

Neilson, George. "On Blind Harry's *Wallace*." *Essays & Studies* 1 (1910), 85–112.

Roberts, John. *Lost Kingdoms: Celtic Scotland and the Middle Ages*. Edinburgh: Edinburgh University Press, 1997.

Scheps, Walter. "Possible Sources for Two Instances of Historical Inaccuracy in Blind Harry's *Wallace*." *Notes & Queries* 16 (1969), 125–26.

———. "William Wallace and His 'Buke': Some Instances of Their Influence on Subsequent Literature." *Studies in Scottish Literature* 6 (1969), 220–37.

———. "Middle English Poetic Usage and Blind Harry's *Wallace*." *The Chaucer Review* 4 (1970), 291–302.

———. "Barbour's *Bruce* and Harry's *Wallace*: The Question of Influence." *Tennesee Studies in Literature* 17 (1972), 19–24.

Schofield, William Henry. *Mythical Bards and the Life of William Wallace*. Cambridge, MA: Harvard University Press, 1920.

Skeat, W. W. "Blind Harry and Chaucer." *Modern Language Quarterly* 1 (November 1897), 49–50.

Walker, Ian. "Barbour, Blind Harry, and Sir William Craigie." *Studies in Scottish Literature* 1 (1964), 202–06.

Walsh, Elizabeth. "Hary's *Wallace*: The Evolution of a Hero." *Scottish Literary Journal* 11.1 (May 1984), 5–19.

Watson, Fiona. *Under the Hammer: Edward I and Scotland, 1286–1306*. East Linton: Tuckwell Press, 1998.

Wilson, Grace. "Barbour's *Bruce* and Hary's *Wallace*: Complements, Compensations and Conventions." *Studies in Scottish Literature* 25 (1990), 189–201.

The Wallace

Book 1

	Our antecessowris that we suld of reide	*ancestors; should; read*
	And hald in mynde thar nobille worthi deid,	*hold*
	We lat ourslide throw verray sleuthfulnes,	*bypass through very sloth*
	And castis us evir till uthir besynes.	*turn ourselves; other*
5	Till honour ennymyis is our haile entent:	*To; whole intention*
	It has beyne seyne in thir tymys bywent.	*been seen; past*
	Our ald ennemys cummyn of Saxonys blud,	*old*
	That nevyr yeit to Scotland wald do gud	
	Bot evir on fors and contrar haile thar will,	
10	Quhow gret kyndnes thar has beyne kyth thaim till.	*How; shown to them*
	It is weyle knawyne on mony divers syde	
	How thai haff wrocht into thar mychty pryde	*in*
	To hald Scotlande at undyr evirmar,	*perpetually in subjection*
	Bot God abuff has maid thar mycht to par.	*above; diminish*
15	Yhit we suld thynk one our bearis befor;	*Yet; on; forebears*
	Of thar parablys as now I say no mor.	*teachings*
	We reide of ane rycht famous of renowne,	*one [person]*
	Of worthi blude that ryngis in this regioune,	*rules (reigns)*
	And hensfurth I will my proces hald	*narrative*
20	Of Wilyham Wallas yhe haf hard beyne tald.	*I have heard*
	His forbearis, quha likis till understand,	*who*
	Of hale lynage and trew lyne of Scotland,	*good lineage*
	Schir Ranald Crawfurd, rycht schirreff of Ayr,	*Sir; rightful sheriff*
	So in hys tyme he had a dochtir fayr,	*daughter*
25	And yonge Schir Ranald, schirreff of that toune;	
	His systir fair of gud fame and ranoune,	
	Malcom Wallas hir gat in mariage,	
	That Elrisle than had in heretage,	
	Auchinbothe and othir syndry place;	
30	The secund o he was of gud Wallace,	*grandson*
	The quhilk Wallas full worthely at wrocht	*which; acted*

The Wallace

	Quhen Waltyr hyr of Waillis fra Warayn socht.	*When; heir*
	Quha likis till haif mar knawlage in that part	*Who; to have more*
	Go reid the rycht lyne of the fyrst Stewart.	*authentic lineage*
35	Bot Malcom gat upon this lady brycht	
	Schir Malcom Wallas, a full gentill knycht,	
	And Wilyame als, as cornyklis beris on hand,	*chronicles tell*
	Quhilk efftir was the reskew of Scotland.	*Who*
	Quhen it was lost with tresoune and falsnas,	*by treason*
40	Ourset be fais, he fred it weyle throu grace.	*Overrun; foes; freed*
	Quhen Alexander our worthi king had lorn	*lost*
	Be aventur his liff besid Kyngorn.	*By chance; Kinghorn*
	Thre yer in pes the realm stude desolate.	*stood*
	Quharfor thair rais a full grevous debate.	*grievous*
45	Our Prynce Davy, the erle of Huntyntoun,	
	Thre dochtrys had that war of gret ranoun,	
	Of quhilk thre com Bruce, Balyoune, and Hastyng.	*Balliol*
	Twa of the thre desyryt to be kyng.	
	Balyoune clamyt of fyrst gre lynialy,	*as lineal heir by first degree*
50	And Bruce fyrst male of the secund gre by.	*by the second degree*
	To Paryse than and in Ingland thai send	
	Of this gret striff how thai suld haif ane end.	
	Foly it was forsuth it happynnyt sa,	*truly it so happened*
	Succour to sek of thar alde mortale fa.	*seek; foe*
55	Eduuarde Langschankis had new begune his wer	*war*
	Apon Gaskone fell awfull in effer.	*Gascony very fearful in array*
	Thai landis thane he clamde as heretage	
	Fra tyme that he had semblit his barnage	*assembled; baronage*
	And herd tell weyle Scotland stude in sic cace.	*such [a] state*
60	He thocht till hym to mak it playn conquace.	*conquest*
	Till Noram kirk he come withoutyn mar;	*To; without delay*
	The consell than of Scotland mett hym thar.	*representatives*
	Full sutailly he chargit thaim in bandoune	*commanded; subjection*
	As thar ourlord till hald of hym the croun.	*their overlord*
65	Byschope Robert in his tyme full worthi	
	Of Glaskow lord, he said that we deny	
	Ony ourlord bot the gret God abuff.	*Any; except*
	The king was wrath and maid hym to ramuff.	*depart*
	Covatus Balyoune folowid on hym fast.	
70	Till hald of hym he granttyt at the last.	*hold [land as an inferior]*

Book 1

	In contrar rycht a king he maid hym thar	*Against just practice*
	Quhar throuch Scotland rapentyt syne full sar.	*repented afterwards sorely*
	To Balyoune yhit our lordis wald nocht consent.	*yet; would*
	Eduuard past south and gert sett his parliment.	*arranged*
75	He callyt Balyoune till ansuer for Scotland.	
	The wys lordis gert hym sone brek that band.	*caused; bond*
	Ane abbot past and gaif our this legiance.	*handed over; allegiance*
	King Eduuard than it tuk in gret grevance.	*displeasure*
	His ost he rasd and come to Werk on Twede	*host (army); raised*
80	Bot for to fecht as than he had gret drede.	*fight*
	To Corspatryk of Dunbar sone he send,	
	His consell ast for he the contré kend	*counsel asked; countryside knew*
	And he was brocht in presence to the king.	
	Be sutalle band thai cordyt of this thing.	*secret agreement; accorded*
85	Erle Patrik than till Berweik couth persew;	*went*
	Ressawide he was and trastyt verray trew.	*Received; believed [to be] very loyal*
	The king folowid with his host of ranoun;	*army*
	Efftir mydnycht at rest wes all the toun.	
	Corspatrik rais, the keyis weile he knew,	*arose*
90	Leit breggis doun and portcules thai drew,	*bridges; portcullis; drew [up]*
	Sett up gettis, syne couth his baner schaw;	*Opened gates, then displayed his banner*
	The ost was war and towart hym thai draw.	*aware*
	Eduuard entrit and gert sla hastely	*killed*
	Of man and wiff sevyn thousand and fyfty,	*men and women*
95	And barnys als, be this fals aventur	*children also; bad luck*
	Of trew Scottis chapyt na creatur.	*escaped*
	A captayne thair this fals Eduuard maid.	*appointed*
	Towart Dunbar without restyng thai raid	*rode*
	Quhar gaderyt was gret power of Scotland,	*gathered; forces*
100	Agayne Eduuard in bataill thocht to stand.	
	Thir four erllis was entrit in that place	
	Of Mar, Menteith, Adell, Ros upon cace.	*by chance*
	In that castell the erle gert hald thaim in,	*prepared for siege*
	At to thar men without thai mycht nocht wyn,	*[So] that to their; outside; get to*
105	Na thai to thaim suppleying for to ma.	*Nor; to bring relief*
	The battaillis than togiddyr fast thai ga.	*battalions then; go*
	Full gret slauchtyr at pitté was to se	*slaughter*
	Of trew Scottis oursett with sutelté.	*cunning*
	Erle Patrik than quhen fechtyng was fellast	*fiercest*

The Wallace

110	Till our fa turnd and harmyng did us mast:	*did us most harm*
	Is nayne in warld at scaithis ma do mar	*none; injuries*
	Than weile trastyt in born familiar.	*well trusted [associates] in a familiar place*
	Our men was slayne withoutyn redempcioune;	*ransoming*
	Throuch thar dedis all tynt was this regioune.	*lost*
115	King Eduuard past and Corspatrik to Scune	*Scone*
	And thar he gat homage of Scotland sune,	*soon*
	For nane was left the realme for to defend.	
	For Jhon the Balyoune to Munros than he send	
	And putt hym doune forevir of this kynrik.	*kingdom*
120	Than Eduuarde self was callit a roy full ryk.	*king; mighty*
	The croune he tuk apon that sammyne stane	*same stone [of destiny]*
	At Gadalos send with his sone fra Spane,	*from*
	Quhen Iber Scot fyrst intill Irland come;	*When Hibernian Scots (i.e., Irish)*
	At Canmor syne King Fergus has it nome,	*That; after; taken*
125	Brocht it till Scune and stapill maid it thar,	*established*
	Quhar kingis was cround eight hundyr yer and mar	
	Befor the tyme at King Eduuard it fand.	*found*
	This jowell he gert turs intill Ingland,	*treasure; had [it] packed off to*
	In Lund it sett till witnes of this thing,	*London*
130	Be conquest than of Scotland cald hym king.	*himself*
	Quhar that stayne is Scottis suld mastir be.	*should*
	God ches the tyme Margretis ayr till see!	*heir*
	Sevyn scor thai led of the gretast that thai fand	
	Of ayris with thaim, and Bruce, out of Scotland.	*heirs*
135	Eduuard gayf hym his fadris heretage	
	Bot he thocht ay till hald hym in thrillage.	*subjection*
	Baith Blacok Mur was his and Huntyntoun.	
	Till Erle Patrik thai gaif full gret gardoun.	*reward*
	For the frendschipe King Eduuard wyth hym fand,	
140	Protector haile he maid hym of Scotland.	
	That office than he brukyt bot schort tyme.	*enjoyed but*
	I may nocht now putt all thar deid in ryme.	*deeds*
	Of cornikle quhat suld I tary lang?	*Why should I tarry long over general history*
	To Wallace agayne now breiffly will I gange.	*go*
145	Scotland was lost quhen he was bot a child	*youth*
	And ourset throuch with our ennemys wilde.	*overthrown through*
	His fadyr Malcom in the Lennox fled;	
	His eldest sone thedir he with hym led.	

Book 1

  His modyr fled wyth hym fra Elrisle,
150 Till Gowry past and duelt in Kilspynde.
  The knycht hir fadir thedyr he thaim sent
  Till his uncle that with full gud entent   *good intentions*
  In Gowry duelt and had gud levyng thar,   *good livelihood*
  Ane agyt man the quhilk resavyt thaim far.   *aged*
155 Intill Dundé Wallace to scule thai send   *Dundee*
  Quhill he of witt full worthely was kend.   *learning; taught*
  Thus he conteynde intill his tendyr age,   *continued*
  In armys syne did mony hie vaslage   *many feats of prowess*
  Quhen Saxons blud into this realm cummyng,
160 Wyrkand the will of Eduuard, that fals king.   *Working*
  Mony gret wrang thai wrocht in this regioune:
  Distroyed our lordys and brak thar byggynys doun;   *buildings*
  Both wiffis, wedowis thai tuk all at thar will,
  Nonnys, madyns, quham thai likit to spill.   *despoil*
165 King Herodis part thai playit into Scotland
  Of yong childyr that thai befor thaim fand.   *children*
  The byschoprykis that war of gretast waile   *bishoprics; importance*
  Thai tuk in hand of thar archybyschops haile.   *took over completely from*
  No for the pape thai wald no kyrkis forber   *Nor; would they spare any churches*
170 Bot gryppyt all be violence of wer.   *seized by violence; war*
  Glaskow thai gaif, as it our weile was kend,   *Glasgow; very well was known*
  To dyocye in Duram to commend.   *diocese; in commendation*
  Small benifice that wald thai nocht persew.
  And for the richt full worthy clerkis thai slew,
175 Hangitt barrownnys and wrocht full mekill cayr.   *caused great suffering*
  It was weylle knawyn in the bernys of Ayr,   *barns*
  Eighteen score putt to that dispitfull dede.   *cruel death*
  Bot God abowyn has send us sum ramede: *above; remedy*
  The remenbrance is forthir in the taile.   *story (i.e., in Book 7)*
180 I will folow apon my proces haile.   *go on with; narrative*
  Willyham Wallace or he was man of armys   *before*
  Gret pitté thocht that Scotland tuk sic harmys.   *such*
  Mekill dolour it did hym in hys mynd,   *Much distress; caused*
  For he was wys, rycht worthy, wicht, and kynd.   *bold*
185 In Gowry duelt still with this worthy man.
  As he encressyt and witt haboundyt than   *knowledge abounded*
  Intill his hart he had full mekill cayr.

The Wallace

	He saw the Sothroun multipliand mayr,	*English multiplying further*
	And to hymself offt wald he mak his mayne.	*lament*
190	Of his gud kyne thai had slane mony ane.	*kinsmen; many [a] one*
	Yhit he was than semly, stark, and bauld,	*seemly; strong; bold*
	And he of age was bot eighteen yer auld.	
	Wapynnys he bur, outhir gud suerd or knyff,	*bore, either*
	For he with thaim hapnyt rycht offt in stryff.	*often*
195	Quhar he fand ane withoutyn othir presance	*one alone*
	Eftir to Scottis that did no mor grevance.	*that [one]; injury*
	To cutt his thrott or steik hym sodanlye	*stab*
	He wayndyt nocht, fand he thaim savely.	*hesitated; [if] he found [he could do it] safely*
	Syndry wayntyt, bot nane wyst be quhat way,	*Many were missing; know by*
200	For all to him thar couth na man thaim say.	*attribute*
	Sad of contenance he was bathe auld and ying,	*Serious; young*
	Litill of spech, wys, curtas, and benyng.	*[A man] of few words; kind*
	Upon a day to Dundé he was send;	
	Of cruelnes full litill thai him kend.	*Of his warlike nature; knew*
205	The constable, a felloun man of wer,	*fierce*
	That to the Scottis he did full mekill der,	*great harm*
	Selbye he hecht, dispitfull and owtrage.	*was called, cruel; violent*
	A sone he had ner twenty yer of age,	
	Into the toun he usyt evirilk day.	*was wont [to go]*
210	Thre men or four thar went with him to play,	*to amuse themselves*
	A hely schrew, wanton in his entent.	*complete wretch, unrestrained*
	Wallace he saw and towart him he went.	
	Likle he was, rycht byge and weyle beseyne	*Well-made; well-dressed*
	Intill a gyde of gudly ganand greyne.	*garment; fine green*
215	He callyt on hym and said, "Thow Scot, abyde.	
	Quha devill thee grathis in so gay a gyde?	*dresses*
	Ane Ersche mantill it war thi kynd to wer,	*Irish cloak; nature*
	A Scottis thewtill undyr thi belt to ber,	*knife*
	Rouch rewlyngis apon thi harlot fete.	*Rough brogues; worthless feet*
220	Gyff me thi knyff. Quhat dois thi ger so mete?"	*Why do you dress so smartly?*
	Till him he yeid his knyff to tak him fra.	*To; went*
	Fast by the collar Wallace couth him ta.	*seized him*
	Undyr his hand the knyff he bradit owt,	*drew*
	For all his men that semblyt him about,	*gathered*
225	Bot help himselff he wyst of no remede.	*Unless [he] helped; knew*
	Without reskew he stekyt him to dede.	*stabbed him to death*

Book 1

	The squier fell, of him thar was na mar.	
	His men folowid on Wallace wondir sar.	*pursued; intently*
	The pres was thik and cummirit thaim full fast.	*hand to hand fighting; thick; hindered*
230	Wallace was spedy and gretlye als agast,	*quick and also very terrified*
	The bludy knyff bar drawin in his hand;	
	He sparyt nane that he befor him fand.	
	He knew the hous his eyme had lugit in;	*uncle; lodged*
	Thedir he fled for owt he mycht nocht wyn.	*out; get*
235	The gude wyff than within the clos saw he	*mistress of the house; courtyard*
	And "help!" he cryit, "for him that deit on Tre.	*(i.e., Jesus); Cross*
	The yong captane has fallyn with me at stryff."	*got into a fight with me*
	In at the dure he went with this gud wiff.	*door*
	A roussat goun of hir awn scho him gaif	*russet; she gave him*
240	Apon his weyd at coveryt all the layff,	*[Put on] over his clothes; rest*
	A soudly courche our hed and nek leit fall;	*dirty headdress (kerchief) over*
	A wovyn quhyt hatt scho brassit on withall,	*woven white hat; clasped*
	For thai suld nocht lang tary at that in;	*house*
	Gaiff him a rok, syn set him doun to spyn.	*spinning wheel, then*
245	The Sothroun socht quhar Wallace was in drede.	*Englishmen; danger*
	Thai wyst nocht weylle at quhat gett he in yeide.	*knew; gate; went in*
	In that same hous thai socht him beselye	
	Bot he sat still and span full conandly,	*skillfully*
	As of his tym, for he nocht leryt lang.	*Considering his [short learning] time; learned*
250	Thai left him swa and furth thar gait can gang	*so; thus went their way*
	With hevy cheyr and sorowfull in thocht.	*sad expression; melancholy*
	Mar witt of him as than get couth thai nocht.	*More knowledge*
	The Inglismen all thus in barrat boune	*prepared for a hostile encounter*
	Bade byrn all Scottis that war into that toun.	*Ordered [that they] burn*
255	Yhit this gud wiff held Wallace till the nycht,	*kept*
	Maid him gud cher, syne put hym out with slycht.	*Made him welcome, then; stealth*
	Throw a dyrk garth scho gydyt him furth fast;	*dark garden; led; out*
	In covart went and up the watter past,	*[He] went into hiding; river*
	Forbure the gate for wachis that war thar.	*Avoided; sentries*
260	His modyr bade intill a gret dispar.	*waited*
	Quhen scho him saw scho thankit hevynnis queyn	*heaven's queen (i.e., Mary)*
	And said, "Der sone, this lang quhar has thow beyne?"	*long [while] where*
	He tald his modyr of his sodane cas.	*misfortune*
	Than wepyt scho and said full oft, "Allas!	
265	Or that thow cess thow will be slayne withall."	*Unless; stop*

The Wallace

	"Modyr," he said, "God reuller is of all.	
	Unsoverable ar thir pepille of Ingland.	*Insufferable*
	Part of thar ire me think we suld gaynstand."	*oppose*
	His eme wist weyle that he the squier slew;	*uncle knew*
270	For dreid tharof in gret languor he grew.	*distress*
	This passit our quhill divers dayis war gane.	*continued until many*
	That gud man dred or Wallace suld be tane,	*lest; taken*
	For Suthroun ar full sutaille evirilk man.	*Englishmen; cunning*
	A gret dyttay for Scottis thai ordand than.	*indictment*
275	Be the lawdayis in Dundé set ane ayr.	*days for holding trials; justice-ayre*
	Than Wallace wald na langar sojorne thar.	
	His modyr graithit hir in pilgrame weid;	*dressed in pilgrim's clothes*
	Hym disgysyt, syne glaidlye with hir yeid,	*then; went*
	A schort swerd undyr his weid prevalé.	*clothing; secretly*
280	In all that land full mony fays had he.	*foes*
	Baith on thar fute, with thaim may tuk thai nocht.	*Both on foot; they took no more*
	Quha sperd, scho said to Sanct Margret thai socht:	*Whoever asked; went*
	Quha servit hir, full gret frendschipe thai fand	*Whoever worshiped*
	With Sothroun folk, for scho was of Ingland.	*English*
285	Besyd Landoris the ferrye our thai past,	*ferry they crossed*
	Syn throw the Ochtell sped thaim wonder fast.	*Ochil [Hills]*
	In Dunfermlyn thai lugyt all that nycht.	*lodged*
	Apon the morn quhen that the day was brycht,	
	With gentill wemen hapnyt thaim to pas,	*go*
290	Of Ingland born, in Lithquhow wounnand was.	*[who were] dwelling in Linlithgow*
	The captans wiff, in pilgramage had beyne,	
	Fra scho thaim mett and had yong Wallace sene,	
	Gud cher thaim maid, for he was wondyr fayr,	
	Nocht large of tong, weille taucht and debonayr.	*too free of speech; courteous*
295	Furth tawkand thus of materis that was wrocht	*things that had been done*
	Quhill south our Forth with hyr son scho thaim brocht,[1]	
	Into Lithkow. Thai wald nocht tary lang.	
	Thar leyff thai tuk, to Dunypace couth gang;	*leave; went*
	Thar duelt his eyme, a man of gret riches.	*uncle; wealth*
300	This mychty persone, hecht to name Wallas,	*parson, was named*
	Maid thaim gud cher and was a full kynd man,	

---

[1] *Until south across [the River] Forth she brought them with her right away*

Book 1

      Welcummyt thaim fair and to thaim tald he than,
      Dide him to witt, the land was all on ster;   *Made him (Wallace) understand; in turmoil*
      Trettyt thaim weyle, and said, "My sone so der,
305 Thi modir and thow rycht heir with me sall bide   *here; shall stay*
      Quhill better be, for chance at may betyde."   *Until [things] improve*
      Wallace ansuerd, said, "Westirmar we will.   *Further west we will [go]*
      Our kyne ar slayne and that me likis ill,   *kinsfolk*
      And othir worthi mony in that art.   *many other worthy [people] in that area*
310 Will God I leiffe, we sall us wreke on part."   *live; avenge in part*
      The persone sicht and said, "My sone so fre,   *parson sighed; noble*
      I can nocht witt how that radres may be."   *know; revenge*
      Quhat suld I spek of fruster? As this tid   *needlessly? At this time*
      For gyft of gud with him he wald nocht bide.
315 His modyr and he till Elrisle thai went.
      Upon the morn scho for hir brothir sent,
      In Corsby duelt and schirreff was of Ayr.   *sheriff*
      Hyr fadyr was dede, a lang tyme leyffyt had thar.   *had lived*
      Hyr husband als at Lowdon Hill was slayn.
320 Hyr eldest son that mekill was of mayn,   *very strong*
      Schir Malcom Wallas was his nayme but less,   *truly*
      His houch senons thai cuttyt in that press.   *tough sinews [i.e., behind the knee]*
      On kneis he faucht, felle Inglismen he slew.   *many*
      Till hym thar socht may fechtaris than anew,   *more than enough fighters*
325 On athyr side with speris bar him doun.   *either; bore*
      Thar stekit thai that gud knycht of renoun.   *stabbed*
      On to my taile I left. At Elrisle   *story*
      Schir Ranald come son till his sistir fre,   *noble*
      Welcummyt thaim hayme and sperd of hir entent.   *home; asked*
330 Scho prayde he wald to the lord Persye went,   *She; Percy*
      So yrk of wer scho couth no forthir fle   *weary of war*
      To purches pes in rest at scho mycht be.[1]
      Schyr Ranald had the Perseys proteccioune,
      As for all part to tak the remissioune.   *pardon*
335 He gert wrytt ane till his systir that tyde.   *had one written for his sister*
      In that respyt Wallas wald nocht abyde;   *reprieve*
      Hys modyr kyst; scho wepyt with hart sar;   *kissed; heavy heart*

---

[1] *To obtain a pardon so that she might be at peace*

The Wallace

	His leyff he tuk, syne with his eyme couth far.	leave; then; uncle made his way
	Yonge he was and to Sothroun rycht savage.	[the] English; fierce
340	Gret rowme thai had, dispitfull and owtrage.	power; cruel and violent
	Schir Ranald weylle durst nocht hald Wallas thar	keep
	For gret perell he wyst apperand war.	was
	For thai had haile the strenthis of Scotland;	completely occupied the strongholds
	Quhat thai wald do durst few agayne thaim stand.	Whatever
345	Schyrreff he was and usyt thaim amang.	used [to go] among them
	Full sar he dred or Wallas suld tak wrang,	Greatly he dreaded lest; suffer harm
	For he and thai couth nevir weyle accord.	
	He gat a blaw, thocht he war lad or lord,	servant
	That profferyt him ony lychtlynes.	offered; insult
350	Bot thai raparyt our mekill to that place.	frequented too much
	Als Inglis clerkis in prophecys thai fand	found in prophecies
	How a Wallace suld putt thaim of Scotland.	[out] of
	Schir Ranald knew weill a mar quiet sted	more quiet place
	Quhar Wilyham mycht be better fra thar fede	hostility
355	With his uncle Wallas of Ricardtoun.	
	Schir Richart hecht that gud knycht of renoun;	was called
	Thai landis hayle than was his heretage.	All these lands
	Bot blynd he was — so hapnyt throw curage,	
	Be Inglismen that dois us mekill der;	who cause us much injury
360	In his rysyng he worthi was in wer —	early career; war
	Throuch hurt of vaynys and mystymit of blude;[1]	
	Yeit he was wis and of his conseill gud.	
	In Feviryer Wallas was to him send;	February
	In Aperill fra him he bownd to wend.	prepared to go
365	Bot gud service he dide him with plesance	gladly
	As in that place was worthi to avance.	praise
	So on a tym he desyrit to play.	
	In Aperill the twenty-third day	
	Till Erevyn Watter fysche to tak he went;	[the] Irvine River
370	Sic fantasye fell in his entent.	Such [a] notion (whim) came into his mind
	To leide his net a child furth with him yeid,	went
	Bot he or nowne was in a felloune dreid.	before noon; terrible danger
	His suerd he left, so did he nevir agayne;	he did so

---

[1] Pierced through the veins and unlucky [in loss] of blood

Book 1

	It dide him gud suppos he sufferyt payne.	
375	Of that labour as than he was nocht sle;	*then; skilled*
	Happy he was, tuk fysche haboundanlé.	*in plenty*
	Or of the day ten houris our couth pas,	*Before ten o'clock*
	Ridand thar com ner by quhar Wallace was	
	The lorde Persye, was captane than of Ayr.	*Percy*
380	Fra thine he turnde and couth to Glaskow fair.	*thence; went*
	Part of the court had Wallace labour seyne.	
	Till him raid five cled into ganand greyne,	*To; rode; clad in suitable green*
	And said sone, "Scot, Martyns fysche we wald have."	
	Wallace meklye agayne ansuer him gave:	*mildly*
385	"It war resone me think yhe suld haif part.	*right*
	Waith suld be delt in all place with fre hart."	*[Fishing] spoils; divided; generous*
	He bade his child, "Gyff thaim of our waithyng."	*ordered; spoils*
	The Sothroun said, "As now of thi delyng	*dealing*
	We will nocht tak; thow wald giff us our small."	*would give us too little*
390	He lychtyt doun and fra the child tuk all.	*alighted*
	Wallas said than, "Gentill men gif ye be,	*if*
	Leiff us sum part, we pray, for cheryté.	
	Ane agyt knycht servis our lady today.	
	Gud frend, leiff part and tak nocht all away."	
395	"Thow sall haiff leiff to fysche and tak thee ma;	*more*
	All this forsuth sall in our flytting ga.	*we shall remove*
	We serff a lord. Thir fysche sall till him gang."	*These*
	Wallace ansuerd, said, "Thow art in the wrang."	
	"Quham dowis thow Scot? In faith thow servis a blaw."	*do you [serve]; you deserve*
400	Till him he ran and out a suerd can draw.	
	Willyham was wa he had na wapynnis thar	*grieved*
	Bot the poustaff, the quhilk in hand he bar.	*fishing pole, which*
	Wallas with it fast on the cheik him tuk	*struck*
	Wyth so gud will quhill of his feit he schuk.	*until off his feet; reeled*
405	The suerd flaw fra him a fur breid on the land.	*flew; furrow breadth*
	Wallas was glaid and hynt it sone in hand,	*caught*
	And with the swerd ane awkwart straik him gave,	*crosswise stroke*
	Undyr the hat his crage in sondir drave.	*neck asunder struck*
	Be that the layff lychtyt about Wallas.	*By that [time]; rest dismounted*
410	He had no helpe, only bot Goddis grace.	*except*
	On athir side full fast on him thai dange;	*struck blows*
	Gret perell was giff thai had lestyt lang.	*if*

The Wallace

     Apone the hede in gret ire he strak ane;
     The scherand suerd glaid to the colar bane.   *cutting; glided; bone*
415 Ane othir on the arme he hitt so hardely   *vigorously*
     Quhill hand and suerd bathe on the feld can ly.   *Until; lay*
     The tothir twa fled to thar hors agayne.   *other two*
     He stekit him was last apon the playne.   *stabbed*
     Thre slew he thar, twa fled with all thar mycht
420 Eftir thar lord, bot he was out of sicht   *until*
     Takand the mure or he and thai couth twyne.   *Reaching; moor before; part*
     Till him thai raid onon or thai wald blyne.   *at once before; stop*
     And cryit, "Lord abide, your men ar martirit doun   *cut down*
     Rycht cruelly her in this fals regioun.
425 Five of our court her at the wattir baid   *retinue; waited*
     Fysche for to bryng, thocht it na profyt maid.
     We ar chapyt, bot in feyld slayne ar thre."   *have escaped*
     The lord speryt, "How mony mycht thai be?"   *asked*
     "We saw bot ane that has discumfyst us all."   *discomfited (overcome)*
430 Than lewch he lowde and said, "Foule mot yow fall,[1]
     Sen ane yow all has putt to confusioun.   *Since one [person]*
     Quha menys it maist the devyll of hell him droun!   *Who laments*
     This day for me in faith he beis nocht socht."
     Quhen Wallace thus this worthi werk had wrocht,
435 Thar hors he tuk and ger that levyt was thar,   *weapons (gear); left*
     Gaif our that crafft, he yeid to fysche no mar;   *Gave up; occupation; went*
     Went till his eyme and tauld him of this drede,   *uncle; fearful situation*
     And he for wo weyle ner worthit to weide;   *nearly went mad*
     And said, "Sone, thir tithingis syttis me sor,   *Son; grieve me*
440 And be it knawin thow may tak scaith tharfor."   *harm*
     "Uncle," he said, "I will no langar bide.
     Thir southland hors latt se gif I can ride."   *English horse*
     Than bot a child him service for to mak,   *[with] only*
     Hys emys sonnys he wald nocht with him tak.   *uncle's sons (i.e., cousins)*
445 This gud knycht said, "Deyr cusyng, pray I thee,   *Dear cousin*
     Quhen thow wanttis gud cum fech ynewch fra me."   *good [men] come fetch enough*

---

[1] *Then laughed he loudly and said, "May ill befall you["]*

Book 2

Sylvir and gold he gert onto him geyff,	*had given to him*
Wallace inclynys and gudely tuk his leyff.	*bowed; graciously*

Explicit liber primus
& Incipit secundus

Book 2

	Yong Wallace, fulfillit of hie curage,	*full of noble courage*
	In prys of armys desyrous and savage,	*Eager for renown in arms and fierce*
	Thi vaslage may nevir be forlorn,	*courage (vassalage); lost*
	Thi deidis ar knawin thocht that the warld had suorn;	*though; sworn [to the contrary]*
5	For thi haile mynde, labour and besynes,	
	Was set in wer and verray rychtwisnes,	*war; true*
	And felloune los of thi deyr worthi kyn.	*grievous loss*
	The rancour more remaynde his mynd within.	
	It was his lyff and maist part of his fude,	*sustenance*
10	To se thaim sched the byrnand Sothroun blude.	*burning English blood*
	Till Auchincruff withoutyn mar he raid,	*without more [delay]*
	And bot schort tyme in pes at he thar baid.	*only [a]; stayed*
	Thar duelt a Wallas welcummyt him full weill,	
	Thocht Inglismen tharof had litill feille.	*knowledge*
15	Bathe meite and drynk at his will he had thar,	*as he wished*
	In Laglyne Wode quhen that he maid repayr.	*Laglyn Wood; went*
	This gentill man was full oft his resett,	*very often; refuge*
	With stuff of houshald strestely he thaim bett.[1]	
	So he desirit the toune of Air to se.	
20	His child with him as than na ma had he.	*more*
	Ay next the wode Wallace gert leiff his hors,	*Always; wood; did leave*
	Syne on his feit yeid to the merkat cors.	*Then on foot [he] went; market cross*
	The Persye was in the castell of Ayr	*Percy*
	With Inglismen, gret nowmer and repayr.	*number and concourse [of people]*
25	Our all the toune rewlyng on thar awne wis	*Over; ruling; own way*
	Till mony Scot thai did full gret suppris.	*To many; injury*
	Aboundandely Wallace amang thaim yeid.	*Boldly; went*

---

[1] *With household provisions diligently he supplied them*

The Wallace

	The rage of youth maid him to haif no dreid.	
	A churll thai had that felloune byrdyngis bar.	*heavy burdens*
30	Excedandlye he wald lyft mekill mar	*Surpassingly; lift much more*
	Than ony twa that thai amang thaim fand,	*any two*
	And als be us a sport he tuk on hand.	*by custom*
	He bar a sasteing in a boustous poille;	*bucket on a strong pole*
	On his braid bak of ony wald he thoille	*broad back; endure*
35	Bot for a grot, als fast as he mycht draw.	*Only; groat; strike*
	Quhen Wallas herd spek of that mery saw,	*claim*
	He likit weill at that mercat to be	*market*
	And for a strak he bad him grottis thre.	*blow; offered*
	The churll grantyt, of that proffir was fayn.	*offer; glad*
40	To pay the silvir Wallas was full bayne.	*ready*
	Wallas that steing tuk up intill his hand.	*pole*
	Full sturdely he coud befor him stand.	
	Wallace with that apon the bak him gaif	*struck*
	Till his ryg bayne he all in sondyr draif.	*Until; backbone*
45	The carll wes dede. Of him I spek no mar.	*fellow*
	The Inglismen semblit on Wallace thair,	*gathered around*
	Feill on the feld of frekis fechtand fast,	*Many; men fighting hard*
	He unabasyt and nocht gretlie agast.	*undaunted; frightened*
	Upon the hed ane with the steing hitt he,	*pole*
50	Till bayn and brayn he gert in pecis fle.	*Until bone; shattered*
	Ane othir he straik on a basnat of steille	*helmet; steel*
	The tre toraiff and fruschit eviredeille.	*wood snapped in two; broke completely*
	His steyng was tynt, the Inglisman was dede,	*pole; ruined*
	For his crag bayne was brokyn in that stede.	*neck bone; instantaneously*
55	He drew a suerd at helpit him at neide.	*sword that*
	Throuchoute the thikest of the pres he yeid	*press*
	And at his hors full fayne he wald haif beyne.	*glad*
	Twa sarde him maist that cruell war and keyne.	*Two vexed; most; fierce were; warlike*
	Wallace raturned as man of mekyll mayne	*strength*
60	And at a straik the formast has he slayne.	*one blow; foremost*
	The tothir fled and durst him nocht abide.	
	Bot a rycht straik Wallas him gat that tyd.	*well-aimed stroke; dealt; moment*
	In at the guschet brymly he him bar;	*[armhole] gusset fiercely; struck*
	The grounden suerd throuchout his cost it schar.	*sharp; rib it sliced*
65	Five slew he thar or that he left the toune.	*before*
	He gat his hors, to Laglyne maid him boune,	*bound*

Book 2

	Kepyt his child and leyt him nocht abide.	*Defended*
	In saufté thus onto the wod can ride,	
	Feille folowit him on hors and eik on futte	*Many; also*
70	To tak Wallace, bot than it was no butte.	*to no avail*
	Covert of treis savit him full weille,	*Hiding in woods protected*
	Bot thar to bid than coude he nocht adeille.	*stay (abide); at all*
	Gud ordinance that serd for his estate	*provisions; were fitting for his position*
	His cusyng maid at all tyme ayr and late.	*kinsman; whatever the time of day*
75	The squier Wallace in Auchincruff that was	
	Baith bed and meite he maid for thaim to pas	
	As for that tyme that he remanyt thar.	
	Bot sar he langit to se the toune of Ayr.	*sorely; longed*
	Thedyr he past apon the mercate day.	*market*
80	Gret God gif he as than had beyne away!	*if [only]; at this time*
	His emys servand to by him fysche was send,	*uncle's servant; buy*
	Schir Ranald Craufurd, schirreff than was kend.	*known*
	Quhen he had tane of sic gud as he bocht,	*taken; such goods*
	The Perseys stuart sadly till him socht	*steward sternly went up to him*
85	And said, "Thow Scot, to quhom takis thow this thing?"	
	"To the schirreff," he said. "Be hevynnys king,	
	My lord sall haiff it and syne go seke thee mar."	*then you go seek more*
	Wallace on gaite ner by was walkand thar.	*on a nearby street*
	Till him he yeid and said, "Gud freynd, pray I thee,	*went*
90	The schireffis servand thow wald let him be."	
	A hetfull man the stuart was of blude	*hot-tempered*
	And thocht Wallace chargyt him in termys rude.	*challenged*
	"Go hens, thow Scot, the mekill devill thee speid.	*mighty devil speed you*
	At thi schrewed us thow wenys me to leid."	*wicked will; think*
95	A huntyn staff intill his hand he bar;	*in his hand he carried*
	Thar with he smat on Willyam Wallace thair.	*struck*
	Bot for his tre litill sonyhe he maid,	*Because of his wooden staff; hesitation*
	Bot be the coler claucht him withoutyn baid	*caught; delay*
	A felloun knyff fast till his hart straik he,	*fatal*
100	Syn fra him dede schot him doun sodanlé.	*he fell down suddenly*
	Catour sen syne he was but weyr no mar.[1]	
	Men of armes on Wallace semblit thar;	*surrounded Wallace*

---

[1] *Supplier of food thereafter he was certainly no more*

The Wallace

	Four scor was sett in armys buskyt boun	*ready-prepared*
	On the merket day for Scottis to kepe the toun,	*from; defend*
105	Bot Wallace bauldlye drew a suerd of wer.	
	Into the byrneis the formast can he ber,	*breast-plate; did he strike*
	Throuchout the body stekit him to dede	*stabbed; death*
	And syndry ma or he past of that stede.	*many more before; place*
	Ane othir aukwart a sarye straik tuk thar,	*backhanded [blow]; sorry blow*
110	Abown the kne the bayne in sondir schar.	*Above; shattered*
	The thrid he straik throuch his pissand of maile	*gorget*
	The crag in twa, no weidis mycht him vaill.	*armor; avail*
	Thus Wallace ferd als fers as a lyoun.	*acted as fierce*
	Than Inglismen that war in bargane boun	*battle ready*
115	To kepe the gait with speris rud and lang,	*strong*
	For dynt of suerd thai durst nocht till hym gang.	*sword; proceed against him*
	Wallace was harnest in his body weyle;	*armed*
	Till him thai socht with hedis scharp of steyle	*sharp steel [spear] heads*
	And fra his strenth enveronde him about.	*on his strong [ground] encircled*
120	Bot throu the pres on a side he went out	*throng*
	Intill a wall that stude by the se syde;	*[Up] to; sea*
	For weyle or wo thar most he nedis abide,	*await [them]*
	And of thar speris in pecis part he schar.	*cut*
	Than fra the castell othir help come mar.	*(i.e., Ayr Castle)*
125	Atour the dike thai yeid on athir side,	*Over; dike (wall)*
	Schott doun the wall; no socour was that tyde.	
	Than wist he nocht of no help bot to de.	*knew; die*
	To venge his dede amang thaim lous yeid he,	*death; freely*
	On athyr part in gret ire hewand fast.	*either side; anger hacking*
130	Hys byrnyst brand to-byrstyt at the last,	*burnished sword shattered*
	Brak in the heltis, away the blaid it flaw.	*Broke; hilts; blade; flew*
	He wyst na wayne bot out his knyff can draw.	*knew no profit*
	The fyrst he slew that him in hand has hynt	*laid hold of*
	And othir twa he stekit with his dynt.	*stabbed; blow*
135	The ramanand with speris to him socht,	*remainder; fell on him*
	Bar him to ground, than forthir mycht he nocht.	
	The lordis bad that thai suld nocht him sla.	*ordered; kill*
	To pyne him mar thai chargyt him to ga.	*torment; commanded; proceed*
	Thus in thar armys suppos that he had suorn,	*sworn [to the contrary]*
140	Out of the garth be fors thai haff him born.	*enclosure by force; borne away*
	Thus gud Wallace with Inglismen was tane	*taken*

28

Book 2

	In falt of helpe for he was him allayne.	*For want; alone*
	He coud nocht cheys, sic curage so hym bar.	*had no choice, such*
	Frevill Fortoun thus brocht him in the suar,	*Fickle; snare*
145	And fals invye ay contrar rychtwisnes,	*malice (envy) always; virtue*
	That violent god full of doubilnes,	*deceit*
	Thai fenyeit goddis Wallace nevir knew.	*Those false*
	Gret rychtwisnes him ay to mercy drew.	*virtue; always*
	His kyn mycht nocht him get for na kyn thing,	*kinsfolk; get [back]; no kind [of]*
150	Mycht thai have payit the ransoune of a king.	
	The more thai bad, the more it was in vayne.	*offered (bid); vain*
	Of thar best men that day sevyn has he slayne.	
	Thai gert set him intill a presoune fell,	*had him placed; cruel prison*
	Of his turment gret payne it war to tell.	*torture*
155	Ill meyt and drynk thai gert ontill him giff.	*Bad food*
	Gret mervaille was lang tyme gif he mycht leyff;	*marvel; live*
	And ek tharto he was in presoune law	*also; dungeon deep*
	Quhill thai thocht tyme on him to hald the law.	*Until; carry out the law*
	Leyff I him thar into that paynfull sted.	*Leave; place*
160	Gret God above till him send sum ramede!	*help*
	The playne compleynt, the pittows wementyng,	*loud lamenting; wretched mourning*
	The wofull wepyng that was for his takyng,	*arrest*
	The tormentyng of every creatur!	
	"Alas," thai said, "how suld our lyff endur?	
165	The flour of youth intill his tendir age	*flower*
	Be fortoun armes has left him in thrillage,	*thraldom*
	Lefand as now a chifftane had we nane	*Living at this time*
	Durst tak on hand bot young Wallace alane.	*undertake; except*
	This land is lost, he caucht is in the swar.	*snare*
170	Prophesye out, Scotland is lost in cayr."	*Declare everywhere; despair*

	Barrell heryng and wattir thai him gave	*Salted herring*
	Quhar he was set into that ugly cave.	*placed*
	Sic fude for him was febill to comend.	*Such; poor (insufficient); praise*
	Than said he thus, "All weildand God resave	*powerful; receive*
175	My petows spreit and sawle amange the law.	*wretched spirit; soul; humble*
	My carneill lyff I may nocht thus defend.	*carnal*
	Our few Sothroune onto the dede I drawe.	*Too; death*
	Quhen so Thow will out of this warld I wend,	
	Giff I suld now in presoune mak ane end.	*If*

The Wallace

180	Eternaile God, quhy suld I thus wayis de,	*die*
	Syne my beleiff all haile remanys in Thee,	*wholly*
	At Thin awn will full worthely was wrocht?	*That*
	Bot Thow rademe, na liff thai ordand me.	*redeem; decreed for*
	Gastlye Fadyr that deit apon the Tre,	*Spiritual; died; Cross*
185	Fra hellis presoune with Thi blud us bocht,	*redeemed*
	Quhi will Thow giff Thi handewerk for nocht,	
	And mony worthy into gret payne we se,	
	For of my lyff ellys nothing I roucht?	*life otherwise; cared*

	O wareide suerd, of tempyr nevir trew!	*accursed*
190	Thi fruschand blaid in presoune sone me threw	*breaking*
	And Inglismen our litill harme has tane.	*too little; suffered*
	Of us thai haiff undoyne may than ynew!	*more than enough*
	My faithfull fadyr dispitfully thai slew,	*mercilessly*
	My brothir als and gud men mony ane.	*also; many [a] one*
195	Is this thi dait? Sall thai ourcum ilk ane?	*appointed time; every one*
	On our kynrent, deyr God, quhen will Thow rew,	*kinsfolk; have pity*
	Sen my pouir thus sodandlye is gane?	*power*

	All worthi Scottis, allmichty God yow leid,	
	Sen I no mor in vyage may you speid.	*expedition; help*
200	In presoune heir me worthis to myscheyff.	*here I must die*
	Sely Scotland that of help has gret neide,	*Defenseless*
	Thy nacioune all standis in a felloun dreid.	*an extreme danger*
	Of warldlynes all thus I tak my leiff.	*From worldly things; leave*
	Of thir paynys God lat yow nevir preiff,	*experience*
205	Thocht for wo all out of witt suld weid.	*Though; should be driven mad*
	Now othir gyft I may none to yow gyff."	

	O der Wallace, umquhill was stark and stur,	*[who] once was strong; vigorous*
	Thow most o neide in presoune till endur.	*to*
	Thi worthi kyn may nocht thee saiff for sold.	*save with money*
210	Ladys wepyt that was bathe myld and mur,	*gentle*
	In fureous payne the modyr that thee bur,	*bore*
	For thou till hir was fer derer than gold.	
	Hyr most desyr was to be undyr mold.	*under ground (i.e., buried)*
	In warldlynes quhi suld ony ensur,	*should anyone trust*
215	For thow was formyt forsye on the fold!	*strong in life (lit., on earth)*

Book 2

	Compleyn, sanctis, thus as your sedull tellis;	*petition*
	Compleyn to hevyn with wordis that nocht fell is;	*heaven; cruel*
	Compleyne your voice unto the God abuffe;	*above*
	Compleyne for him into that sitfull sellis;	*[who is] in that sorrowful cell*
220	Compleyne his payne in dolour thus that duellis,	*suffering*
	In langour lyis for losyng of thar luff.	*distress*
	His fureous payne was felloune for to pruff.	*fierce suffering; cruel; endure*
	Compleyne also yhe birdis blyth as bellis;	*you maidens cheerful*
	Sum happy chance may fall for your behuff.	*benefit*
225	Compleyne lordys, compleyne yhe ladyis brycht,	*fair (lovely)*
	Compleyne for him that worthi was and wycht,	*bold*
	Of Saxons sonnys sufferyt full mekill der;	*At the hands of the English; great harm*
	Compleyne for him was thus in presone dicht	*condemned*
	And for na caus, bot Scotland for thi richt.	*rights*
230	Compleyne also yhe worthi men of wer;	*you; war*
	Compleyn for hym that was your aspersper	*champion (lit., sharp spear)*
	And to the dede fell Sothron yeit he dicht;	*death many English yet; sent*
	Compleyne for him your triumphe had to ber.	*victory*
	Celinus was maist his geyeler now.	*Mercury; jailer*
235	In Inglismen, allace, quhi sud we trow,	*trust*
	Our worthy kyn has payned on this wys?	*injured*
	Sic reulle be rycht is litill till allow.	*Such rule by; cannot be allowed*
	Me think we suld in barrat mak thaim bow	
	At our power, and so we do feill sys.[1]	
240	Of thar danger God mak us for to rys,	*From*
	That weill has wrocht befor thir termys and now,	*these times*
	For thai wyrk ay to wayt us with supprys.	*always to lie in wait to surprise us*
	Quhat suld I mor of Wallace turment tell?	
	The flux he tuk into thar presoune fell.	*dysentery; in their terrible prison*
245	Ner to the dede he was likly to drawe.	
	Thai chargyt the geyler nocht on him to duell,	*jailer; lose time*
	Bot bryng him up out of that ugly sell	*loathsome cell*
	To jugisment, quhar he suld thoill the law.	*trial; endure*

---

[1] Lines 238–39: *I think we should make them feel our strength in combat, and so we do many times*

The Wallace

This man went doun and sodanlye he saw,
250   As to his sycht, dede had him swappyt snell,
Syn said to thaim, "He has payit at he aw."[1]

    Quhen thai presumyt he suld be verray ded,   *dead for certain*
    Thai gart servandys withoutyn langer pleid,   *further argument*
    Wyth schort awis onto the wall him bar.   *Without delay*
255   Thai kest him our out of that bailfull steid —   *threw him over; woeful place*
    Of him thai trowit suld be no mor ramede —   *For; believed; remedy*
    In a draff myddyn quhar he remaynit thar.   *refuse dunghill*
    His fyrst norys, of the Newtoun of Ayr,   *nurse*
    Till him scho come, quhilk was full will of reid,   *troubled*
260   And thyggyt leiff away with him to fayr.   *begged leave; to take him away*

    Into gret ire thai grantyt hir to go.
    Scho tuk him up withoutin wordis mo
    And on a caar unlikly thai him cast;   *a rough cart*
    Atour the wattir led him with gret woo   *Over; river*
265   Till hyr awn hous withoutyn ony hoo.   *delay*
    Scho warmyt wattir, and hir servandis fast   *quickly*
    His body wousche quhill filth was of hym past.   *washed until the filth was removed*
    His hart was wicht and flykeryt to and fro,   *strong; flickered spasmodically*
    Also his twa eyne he kest up at the last.   *opened*

270   His fostir modyr loved him our the laiff,   *loved; above the rest*
    Did mylk to warme, his liff giff scho mycht saiff,   *Had milk warmed; if*
    And with a spoyn gret kyndnes to him kyth.   *spoon; showed*
    Hyr dochtir had of twelve wokkis ald a knayff: *daughter had a twelve-week-old boy*
    Hir childis pape in Wallace mouth scho gaiff.[2]
275   The womannys mylk recomford him full swyth.   *revived; quickly*
    Syn in a bed thai brocht him fair and lyth,   *Then; kindly and gently*
    Rycht covertly thai kepe him in that caiff,   *secretly; hiding place*
    Him for to save so secretlye thai mycht.   *protect as . . . [as]*

---

[1] Lines 250–51: *So it appeared to him, death had seized him quickly, / Then said to them, "He has paid what he owed [to Nature]" (i.e., he has died)*

[2] *She offered her milk-filled breast to Wallace*

Book 2

	In thar chawmyr thai kepyt him that tide.	*chamber; for a time*
280	Scho gert graith up a burd be the hous side	*had set up a board*
	Wyth carpettis cled and honowryt with gret lycht;	*Covered with woolen cloth*
	And for the voice in eviry place suld bide	*word*
	At he was ded, out throw the land so wide,	*That; [spread] throughout*
	On presence ay scho wepyt undyr slycht.	*company she always pretended to weep*
285	Bot gudely meytis scho graithit him at hir mycht.	*food; prepared; the best she could*
	And so befell into that sammyn tid	*in the meanwhile*
	Quhill forthirmar at Wallas worthit wycht.	*Until later on; grew strong*

	Thomas Rimour into the Faile was than	*Fail [Monastery]*
	With the mynystir, quhilk was a worthi man.	*head of the monastery, who*
290	He usyt offt to that religious place.	*often frequented*
	The peple demyt of witt mekill he can;	*believed he knew a great many things*
	And so he told, thocht at thai blis or ban,	*whether they blessed or cursed [him]*
	Quhilk hapnyt suth in mony divers cace,	*Which turned out to be true*
	I can nocht say be wrang or rychtwisnas,	*through wrong or right*
295	In rewlle of wer quhethir thai tynt or wan.	*lost or won*
	It may be demyt be divisioun of grace.	*deemed by gift*

	Thar man that day had in the merket bene;	*Their*
	On Wallace knew this cairfull cas so kene.	*painful; grievous*
	His mastir speryt quhat tithingis at he saw.	*asked what tidings*
300	This man ansuerd, "Of litill hard I meyn."	*heard I say*
	The mynister said, "It has bene seildyn seyn	*seldom seen*
	Quhar Scottis and Inglis semblit bene on raw	*have been gathered together*
	Was nevir yit als fer as we coud knaw,	*as far as we know*
	Bot othir a Scot wald do a Sothroun teyn	*either; harm*
305	Or he till him, for aventur mycht faw."	*[whatever] chance might befall*

	"Wallas," he said, "ye wist tayne in that steid,	*you know [was] taken; place*
	Out our the wall I saw thaim cast him deide,	*over*
	In thar presoune famyst for fawt of fude."	*starved for want*
	The mynister said with hart hevy as leid,	*lead*
310	"Sic deid to thaim me think suld foster feid,	*Such [a] deed; feud*
	For he was wicht and cummyn of gentill blud."	*strong (bold); noble*
	Thomas ansuerd, "Thir tithingis ar noucht gud.	*These tidings*
	And that be suth myself sall nevir eit breid,	*If that be true*
	For all my witt her schortlye I conclud."	

The Wallace

315	"A woman syne of the Newtoun of Ayr	*then*
	Till him scho went fra he was fallyn thar	
	And on hir kneis rycht lawly thaim besocht	*lowly*
	To purches leiff scho mycht thin with him fayr.	*obtain leave [so]; thence; go*
	In lychtlynes tyll hyr thai grant to fayr.	*scorn; proceed*
320	Our the wattir ontill hir hous him brocht	*to her*
	To berys him als gudlye as scho mocht."	*bury; might*
	Yhit Thomas said, "Than sall I leiff na mar	*shall; live*
	Gyff that be trew, be God that all has wrocht!"	*If*
	The mynister herd quhat Thomas said in playne.	*plainly*
325	He chargyt him, "Than go speid thee fast agayn	*ordered him (the servant)*
	To that sammyn hous and verraly aspye."	*same; see for certain*
	The man went furth at byddyng was full bayn.	*ready*
	To the Newtoun to pas he did his payn	*exerted himself*
	To that ilk hous and went in sodanlye.	*same*
330	About he blent onto the burd him bye.	*glanced; slab*
	This woman rais. In hart scho was nocht fayn.	*arose; glad*
	"Quha aw this lik?" he bad hir nocht deny.	*Whose body is this?*
	"Wallace," scho said, "that full worthy has beyne."	
	Than wepyt scho that peté was to seyne.	
335	The man thartill gret credens gaif he nocht.	*thereto*
	Towart the burd he bowned as he war teyne.	*went quickly as [if]; angry*
	On kneis scho felle and cryit, "For Marye scheyne	*glorious*
	Lat sklandyr be and flemyt out of your thocht."	*blame; banished*
	This man hir suour, "Be Hym that all has wrocht,	*swore*
340	Mycht I on lyff him anys se with myn eyn	*once*
	He suld be saiff thocht Ingland had him socht!"	*though*
	Scho had him up to Wallace be the des.	*brought; by the dais*
	He spak with him, syne fast agayne can pres	*then hurried back again*
	With glaid bodword thar myrthis till amend.	*message; high spirits to improve*
345	He told to thaim the fyrst tithingis was les.	*lies*
	Than Thomas said, "Forsuth, or he deces	*before he dies*
	Mony thousand in feild sall mak thar end.	
	Of this regioune he sall the Sothroun send	*[Out] of*
	And Scotlande thris he sall bryng to the pes;	*thrice*
350	So gud of hand agayne sall nevir be kend."	*known*

Book 2

	All worthi men that has gud witt to waille,	*at command*
	Bewar that yhe with mys deyme nocht my taille.	*you do not find fault*
	Perchance yhe say that Bruce he was none sik.	*such*
	He was als gud quhat deid was to assaill	*as; action; attempt*
355	As of his handis and bauldar in battaill,	*bolder*
	Bot Bruce was knawin weyll ayr of this kynrik;	*heir; kingdom*
	For he had rycht we call no man him lik.	
	Bot Wallace thris this kynrik conquest haile,	
	In Ingland fer socht battaill on that rik.	*far; realm*
360	I will ratorn to my mater agayne.	*return; subject*
	Quhen Wallace was ralesched of his payn,	*released from*
	The contré demyd haile at he was dede;	*completely believed that*
	His derrest kyn nocht wist of his ramede	*knew not; recovery*
	Bot haile he was likly to gang and ryd.	
365	Into that place he wald no langar byde.	
	His trew kepar he send to Elrisle.	*loyal keeper (i.e., the nurse)*
	Eftir him thar he durst nocht lat thaim be.	*Behind*
	Hir dochtir als, thar servand and hir child,	
	He gart thaim pas onto his modyr myld.	
370	Quhen thai war gayne na wapynnys thar he saw	*gone*
	To helpe him with quhat aventur mycht befaw.	*befall*
	A rousty suerd in a noik he saw stand	*corner*
	Withoutyn belt, but bos, bukler, or band.	*without boss, shield*
	Lang tyme befor it had beyne in that steid;	
375	Ane agyt man it left quhen he was dede.	
	He drew the blaid: he fand it wald bitt weill;	*cut*
	Thocht it was foule, nobill it was of steyll.	*in bad condition (rusty); steel*
	"God helpis his man, for thou sall go with me	
	Quhill bettir cum, will God, full sone may be!"	*Until [a] better [sword]*
380	To Schir Ranald as than he wald nocht fair.	*go*
	In that passage offt Sothroun maid repar.	*frequented*
	At Rycardtoun full fayn he wald have beyne	
	To get him hors and part of armour scheyne.	*shining*
	On thedirwart as he bownyt to fair	*In that direction; prepared to go*
385	Thre Inglismen he met, ridand till Ayr,	
	In thair viage at Glaskow furth had beyne.	*traveling*
	Ane Longcastell, that cruell was and keyne,	*fierce*
	A bauld squier, with him gud yemen twa.	*bold; retainers two*

35

The Wallace

	Wallace drew by and wald haiff lattyn thaim ga.	*drew to the side; let*
390	Till him he raid and said dispitfully,	
	"Thow Scot abide. I trow thow be sum spy,	
	Or ellis a theyff, fra presens wald thee hid."	*presence [of others]*
	Than Wallace said with sobyr wordis that tid,	*time*
	"Schir, I am seik. For Goddis luff latt me ga!"	
395	Longcastell said, "Forsuth it beis nocht sa.	
	A felloune freik thow semys in thi fair.	*fighting man; bearing*
	Quhill men thee knaw thow sall with me till Ayr."[1]	
	Hynt out his suerd that was of nobill hew.	*[He] pulled*
	Wallace with that at his lychtyn him drew,	*dismounting*
400	Apon the crag with his suerd has him tayne,	*neck; struck*
	Throw brayne and seyne in sondir straik the bayne.	*brawn; sinew; bone*
	Be he was fallyn, the twa than lichtyt doun,	*Once; alighted*
	To veng his dede to Wallace maid thaim boun.	*avenge; death*
	The tayne of thaim apon the hed he gaiff,	*The one; hit*
405	The rousty blaid to the schulderis him claiff.	*shoulders; cleaved*
	The tothir fled and durst no langar bide;	
	With a rud step Wallace coud eftir glide.	*powerful stride; go easily*
	Our thourch his rybbis a seker straik drewe he,	*Up through; sure stroke he delivered*
	Quhill levir and lounggis men mycht all redy se.	*So that liver; lungs*
410	Thar hors he tuk, bathe wapynnys and armour,	
	Syne thankit God with gud hart in that stour.	*Then; fight*
	Sylvir thai had, all with him has he tayne	
	Him to support, for spendyng had he nayne.	*spending [money]*
	Into gret haist he raid to Ricardtoun.	
415	A blyth semblay was at his lychtin doun	*A happy reunion; dismounting*
	Quhen Wallace mett with Schir Richart the knicht,	
	For him had murnit quhill feblit was his mycht.	*[Who] had grieved for him; enfeebled*
	His thre sonnys of Wallace was full fayne;	
	Thai held him lost, yit God him savth agayne.	*saved*
420	His eyme, Schir Ranald, to Rycardtoun come fast;	*uncle*
	The wemen told by Corsby as thai past	*women*
	Of Wallace eschaipe, syne thar viage yeid.[2]	
	Schyr Ranald yit was in a felloune dreid:	*terrible fear*

---

[1] *Until we know who you are you shall [come] with me to Ayr*

[2] *Of Wallace's escape, then continued on their way*

Book 3

	Quhill he him saw in hart he thocht full lang;	*Until; was downcast*
425	Than sodanlye in armys he coud him thrang.	*embrace*
	He mycht nocht spek, bot kyst him tendirlye;	
	The knychtis spreit was in ane extasye.	*spirit*
	The blyth teris tho bryst fro his eyne two	*happy; then burst*
	Or that he spak, a lang tyme held him so,	*Before*
430	And at the last rycht freindfully said he,	*kindly*
	"Welcum nevo, welcum, deir sone to me.	*nephew*
	Thankit be He that all this warld has wrocht,	
	Thus fairlye thee has out of presoune brocht!"	*wonderfully*
	His modyr come and othir freyndis enew	*enough*
435	With full glaid will to feill thai tithingis trew.	*learn*
	Gud Robert Boyd, that worthi was and wicht,	*strong*
	Wald nocht thaim trow quhill he him saw with sicht.	*believe until; with his own eyes*
	Fra syndry part thai socht to Ricardtoun,	*From diverse places; went*
	Feille worthi folk that war of gret renoun.	*Many*
440	Thus leiff I thaim in mirth, blys, and plesance,	*leave*
	Thankand gret God of his fre happy chance.	*for; magnanimous good fortune*

Explicit liber Secundus
Incipit Tertius

Book 3

	In joyows Julii, quhen the flouris suete	*joyful July*
	Degesteable, engenered throu the heet,	*Were made to bloom, engendered by*
	Baith erbe and froyte, busk and bewis, braid	*herb; fruit, bush and boughs, grew*
	Haboundandlye in eviry slonk and slaid;	*Abundantly; hollow and valley*
5	Als bestiall thar rycht cours till endur,	*Also beasts; proper; maintain*
	Weyle helpyt ar be wyrkyn of natur,	*working*
	On fute and weynge ascendand to the hycht,	*coming to full growth*
	Conserved weill be the Makar of mycht	*Preserved (tended); by*
	Fyscheis in flude refeckit rialye	*river revived royally*
10	Till mannys fude the warld suld occupye;	*busy itself*
	Bot Scotland sa was waistit mony day,	*laid waste*
	Throw wer sic skaith at labour was away.	*war such harm that work was useless*
	Victaill worth scant or August coud apper,	*Provisions became; before; arrived*
	Throu all the land that fude was hapnyt der.	*became dear*

The Wallace

15	Bot Inglismen, that riches wantyt nayne,	*lacked none*
	Be caryage brocht thar victaill full gud wayne;	*By baggage; food in good quantity*
	Stuffit housis with wyn and gud wernage	*Supplied castles; wine; malmsey*
	Demaynde this land as thar awne heretage;	*Governed*
	The kynryk haile thai rewllyt at thar will.	*Whole kingdom; ruled*
20	Messyngeris than sic tithingis brocht thaim till,	
	And tald Persye that Wallace leffand war,	*was [still] alive*
	Of his eschaip fra thar presoune in Ayr.	*escape; prison*
	Thai trowit rycht weill he passit was that steid	*place*
	For Longcastell and his twa men was deid.	*were dead*
25	Thai waryit the chance that Wallace so was past.	*cursed the [lost] opportunity*
	In ilka part thai war gretlye agast	*On every side*
	Throw prophesye that thai had herd befor.	
	Lord Persye said, "Quhat nedis wordis mor?	
	Bot he be cest he sall do gret mervaill.	*Unless; stopped; wonders*
30	It war the best for King Eduuardis availl	*advantage*
	Mycht he him get to be his steidfast man,	
	For gold or land his conquest mycht lest than.	*last*
	Me think beforce he may nocht gottyn be.	*by force*
	Wys men the suth be his eschaip may se."	*by*
35	Thus deyme thai him in mony divers cas;	*they consider; diverse points of view*
	We leiff thaim her and spek furth of Wallas.	
	In Rycardtoun he wald no langar byde,	
	For freindis consaill nor thing that mycht betide;	
	And quhen thai saw that it availlit nocht,	
40	His purpos was to venge him at he mocht	*avenge himself; might*
	On Sothron blud quhilk has his eldris slayne,	
	Thai latt him wyrk his awn will into playne.	*plainly*

[*Wallace, accompanied by Adam, the eldest of Sir Richard Wallace's sons, Robert Boyd, Kneland, and Edward Litill, leaves Riccarton for "Mawchtlyne Mur" (line 60), which McDiarmid (2.150) renders as Mauchline Moor in Ayrshire, to await the reported arrival of Fenwick with supplies for the English. (Lines 43–66)*]

	Towart Lowdoun thai bownyt thaim to ride	*prepared*
	And in a schaw a litill thar besyde	*wood*
	Thai lugyt thaim, for it was nere the nycht,	*camped*
70	To wache the way als besyly as thai mycht.	*vigilantly*
	A trew Scot quhilk hosteler hous thair held	*who [an] innkeeper's house occupied there*

Book 3

	Under Lowdoun, as myn autor me teld,	*Below*
	He saw thar com, syne went to thaim in hye.	*coming, then; quickly*
	Baithe meite and drynk he brocht full prevalye	*secretly*
75	And to thaim tald the cariage into playn.	*told them [about]*
	Thair for-rydar was past till Ayr agayne,	*advance rider*
	Left thaim to cum with pouer of gret vaille.	*company of great advantage (avail)*
	Thai trowit be than thai war in Awendaille.	*believed*
	Wallace than said, "We will nocht sojorne her,	
80	Nor change no weid bot our ilk dayis ger."	*clothes; everyday garments*
	At Corssencon the gait was spilt that tide,	*road; destroyed; time*
	Forthi that way behovid thaim for to ride.	*Therefore*
	Ay fra the tyme that he of presoune four	*Ever since; [out] of prison went*
	Gude sovir weide dayly on him he wour:	*trusty armor*
85	Gude lycht harnes fra that tyme usyt he evir,	*armor*
	For sodeyn stryff fra it he wald nocht sevir	*In case of surprise attack; never without it*
	A habergione undir his goune he war,	*breast-plate*
	A steylle capleyne in his bonet but mar,	*cap; hat; more*
	And glovis of plait in claith war coverit weill,[1]	
90	In his doublet a clos coler of steyle.	*jerkin a fitted collar*
	His face he kepit for it was evir bar,	*guarded; bare*
	With his twa handis the quhilk full worthi war.	
	Into his weid and he come in a thrang	*[Dressed] in his armor; battle*
	Was na man than on fute mycht with him gang.	*compete*
95	So growane in pith, of pouer stark and stur,	*grown in strength; strong; sturdy*
	His terryble dyntis war awfull till endur.	*blows; daunting*
	Thai trastyt mar in Wallace him allane	
	Than in a hundreth mycht be of Ingland tane.	*taken*
	The worthi Scottis maid thar no sojornyng,	
100	To Lowdoun Hill past in the gray dawyng,	*dawning*
	Devysyt the place and putt thair hors thaim fra	*Surveyed*
	And thocht to wyn or nevir thin to ga:	*go from there*
	Send twa skowrrouris to vesy weyll the playne,	*[They] sent two scouts; reconnoiter*
	Bot thai rycht sone raturnde in agayne,	*quickly*
105	To Wallace tald that thai war cummand fast.	*coming*
	Than thai to grounde all kneland at the last	*Then*
	With humyll hartis prayit with all thar mycht	*humble hearts*

---

[1] *And gloves of plate-armor were covered well with cloth*

The Wallace

	To God abowne to help thaim in thar rycht.	*above*
	Than graithit thai thaim till harnes hastely.	*they equipped themselves with armor*
110	Thar sonyeit nane of that gud chevalrye.	*none hesitated; band of knights*
	Than Wallace said, "Her was my fadir slayne,	
	My brothir als, quhilk dois me mekill payne;	*much pain*
	So sall myselff, or vengit be but dreid.	*avenged be without doubt*
	The traytour is her, caus was of that deid."	
115	Than hecht thai all to bide with hartlye will.	*vowed; heartfelt*
	Be that the power was takand Lowdoun Hill.[1]	
	The knycht Fenweik convoide the caryage;	*escorted*
	He had on Scottis maid mony schrewide viage.	*against; accursed excursions*
	The sone was rysyne our landis schenand brycht.	*sun; over*
120	The Inglismen so thai come to the hycht;	*hill*
	Ner thaim he raid and sone the Scottis saw.	
	He tald his men and said to thaim on raw,	*together*
	"Yhonne is Wallace that chapit our presoune.	*escaped [from] our prison*
	He sall agayne and be drawyn throu the toune.	*And he shall again be*
125	His hede mycht mar, I wait, weill ples the king	*more, I think, well*
	Than gold or land or ony warldly thing."	
	He gart servandis bide with the cariage still.	
	Thai thocht to dawntyt the Scottis at thar will.	*subdue*
	Nyne scor he led in harnes burnyst brycht,	*armor*
130	And fyfty was with Wallace in the rycht.	
	Unraboytyt the Sothroun was in wer	*Undaunted*
	And fast thai come, fell awfull in affer.	*very; appearance*
	A maner dyk of stanys thai had maid,	*A sort of stone wall*
	Narrowyt the way quhar throuch thai thikar raid.	*through which they crowded*
135	The Scottis on fute tuk the feld thaim befor;	
	The Sothroun saw: thar curage was the mor.	
	In prydefull ire thai thoucht our thaim to ryde,	*thought to ride over them*
	Bot othirwys it hapnyt in that tide.	
	On athir side togidder fast thai glaid;	*went easily*
140	The Scottis on fute gret rowme about thaim maide,	
	With ponyeand speris throuch platis prest of steylle.	*piercing*
	The Inglismen that thocht to veng thaim weylle,	
	The harnest hors about thaim rudely raide,	*harnessed; roughly*

---

[1] *By that time the [English] force was making its way to Loudoun Hill*

Book 3

	That with unes upone thar feit thai baid.	*difficulty upon; stayed*
145	Wallace the formast in the byrney bar;	*breastplate struck*
	The grounden sper throuch his body schar.	*sharp; cut*
	The schafft to-schonkit offe the fruschand tre;	*shaft broke off; splintering wood*
	Devoydyde sone sen na better mycht be,	*Split; since*
	Drew suerdis syne, bathe hevy, scharp and lang.	*then*
150	On athyr syd full cruelly thai dang,	*struck*
	Fechtand at anys into that felloune dout.	*cruel danger*
	Than Inglismen enveround thaim about,	*encircled*
	Be force etlyt throuchout thaim for to ryde.	*By force aimed*
	The Scottis on fute that baldly couth abyde	*boldly*
155	With suerdis schar throuch habergeons full gude,	*pierced; breastplates*
	Upon the flouris schot the schonkan blude	*flowers; spouting blood*
	Fra hors and men throw harnes burnyst beyne.	*polished armor spurting*
	A sayr sailye forsuth thar mycht be seyne.	*pitiful assault*
	Thai traistyt na liff bot the lettir end.	*expected; except the latter end (i.e., death)*
160	Of sa few folk gret nobilnes was kend,	*For; shown*
	Togydder baid defendand thaim full fast;	*stood defending themselves*
	Durst nane sevir quhill the maist pres was past.[1]	
	The Inglismen that besye was in wer	*who were trained in warfare*
	Be fors ordand in sondir thaim to ber.	*Planned by force to drive them asunder*
165	Thair cheyff chyftan feryt als fers as fyr,	*charged (fared) as fierce*
	Throw matelent and verray propyr ire,	*rage; pure anger*
	On a gret hors intill his glitterand ger	*[equipped] in his glittering armor*
	In fewtir kest a fellone aspre sper.	*fewter (socket) placed a cruel sharp spear*
	The knycht Fenweik that cruell was and keyne,	*fierce; merciless*
170	He had at dede of Wallace fadir beyne,	*at the death of*
	And his brodyr, that douchty was and der.	*who courageous; dearly loved*
	Quhen Wallace saw that fals knycht was so ner	
	His corage grew in ire as a lyoune;	
	Till him he ran and fell frekis bar he doune.	*many men he struck down*
175	As he glaid by aukwart he couth him ta,	*agilely passed crosswise; take*
	The and arsone in sondir gart he ga.	*Thigh; saddlebow he sliced through*
	Fra the coursour he fell on the fer syd.	*steed*
	With a staff suerd Boyd stekit him that tyde.	*strong sword; stabbed*
	Or he was dede the gret pres come so fast	*Before*

---

[1] *None dared separate until the press to battle was past*

The Wallace

180	Our him to grounde thai bur Boyde at the last.	*Over; bore*
	Wallace was ner and ratornde agayne	
	Him to reskew, till that he rais of payne,	*rose with difficulty*
	Wichtly him wor quhill he a suerd had tayne.	*Bravely defended him until*
	Throuout the stour thir twa in feyr ar gayne.	*fighting these two together*
185	The ramanand apon thaim folowit fast;	*remainder*
	In thar passage fell Sothron maid agast.	*many Englishmen were terrified*
	Adam Wallace, the ayr of Ricardtoun,	*heir*
	Straik ane Bewmound, a squier of renoun,	*one*
	On the pyssan with his brand burnyst bar.	*gorget; sword*
190	The thrusande blaid his hals in sonder schayr.	*cutting; neck sheared asunder*
	The Inglismen, thocht thar chyftayn was slayne,	*although*
	Bauldly thai baid as men mekill of mayn.	*Boldly they stood their ground; stalwart*
	Reth hors rependе rouschede frekis undir feit;	*Fierce horses trampled men underfoot*
	The Scottis on fute gert mony lois the suete.	*made many lose their lives*
195	Wicht men lichtyt thaimselff for to defend;	*Bold; dismounted*
	Quhar Wallace come thar deide was litill kend.	*deeds amounted to little*
	The Sothroune part so frusched was that tide	*The English side; crushed; time*
	That in the stour thai mycht no langar bide.	*battle*
	Wallace in deide he wrocht so worthely,	
200	The squier Boid and all thar chevalry,	*band of knights*
	Litill, Kneland, gert of thar ennymys de.	*caused their enemies to die*
	The Inglismen tuk playnly part to fle.	
	On hors sum part to strenthis can thame found	*castles; went*
	To socour thaim, with mony werkand wound.	*save themselves; painful*
205	A hundreth dede in feild was levyt thar,	*dead; were left there*
	And thre yemen that Wallace menyde fer mar;	*mourned*
	Twa was of Kyle, and ane of Conyngayme	
	With Robert Boide to Wallace com fra hayme.	*[had] come from home*
	Four scor fled that chapyt on the south syde.	*escaped*
210	The Scottis in place that bauldly couth abyde	
	Spoilyeid the feld, gat gold and othir ger,	*Plundered*
	Harnes and hors, quhilk thai mysteryt in wer.	*Armor; needed in warfare*
	The Inglis knavis thai gart thar caryage leid[1]	
	To Clidis Forest; quhen thai war out of dreid	*danger*
215	Thai band thaim fast with wedeis sad and sar,	*withes (twisted bark) firm; painful*

---

[1] *English serving men (knaves) they made their baggage transport*

Book 4

	On bowand treis hangyt thaim rycht thar.	*bending; hanged*
	He sparyt nane that abill was to wer,	*spared; were able to fight*
	Bot wemen and preystis he gart thaim ay forber.	*women; priests; always spared them*
	Quhen this was doyne to thar dyner thai went	
220	Of stuff and wyne that God had to thaim sent.	*food*

[*The English flee to Ayr and report to Percy the losses incurred. Percy has cause to regret that Wallace escaped from prison, and resolves that in future supplies will have to be brought in by sea. While Wallace enjoys the English setback, Percy holds a council in Glasgow at which Sir Amer de Valence, incorrectly identified as a Scot and therefore a traitor, counsels a truce and cleverly suggests that Sir Ranald be made the instrument for bringing this about, on pain of losing his lands. With Percy's personal promise that Wallace and his kinsfolk will not be harmed unless the English are attacked by the Scots, Sir Ranald yields to pressure and signs an agreement with him. On the advice of his supporters, Wallace accepts the truce arrangement (for 10 months) that his uncle presents to him. Wallace then returns to his uncle's home in Crosbie. On a visit to Ayr one day, Wallace responds to a challenge to fence and kills his challenger, which results in his party of sixteen, including his uncle, being surrounded by over a hundred English. In the ensuing skirmish many English are killed but when reinforcements from the castle appear Wallace makes a tactical withdrawal to Laglyn Wood. Percy charges Ranald to keep Wallace at home, away from the town.* (Lines 221–444)]

Book 4

	In September, the humyll moneth suette,	*humble*
	Quhen passyt by the hycht was of the hette,	*height; heat*
	Victaill and froyte ar rypyt in aboundance	*Harvestable food; fruit; ripened*
	As God ordans to mannys governance.	*ordains*
5	Sagittarius with his aspre bow,	*cruel*
	Be the ilk syng veryté ye may know	*By the same sign truth*
	The changing cours quhilk makis gret deference;	*difference*
	And levys had lost thair colouris of plesence.	*leaves*
	All warldly thing has nocht bot a sesoune,	
10	Both erbe and froyte mon fra hevyn cum doun.	*must from heaven*
	In thys ilk tyme a gret consell was sett	
	Into Glaskow, quhar mony maisteris mett	*chiefs*
	Of Inglis lordis to statute this cuntré.	*rule*
	Than chargyt thai all schirreffis thar to be.	*sheriffs*

The Wallace

15	Schir Ranald Crawfurd behovide that tyme be thar[1]	
	For he throw rycht was born schirreff of Ayr.	
	His der nevo that tyme with hym he tuk,	*nephew*
	Willyham Wallace, as witnes beris the buk,	*book*
	For he na tyme suld far be fra his sicht;	
20	He luffyt him with hart and all his mycht.	
	Thai graith thaim weill without langar abaid.	*prepared themselves; delay*
	Wallace sum part befor the court furth raid,	*in advance of the retinue rode forth*
	With him twa men that douchtye war in deid,	*bold*
	Ourtuk the child Schir Ranaldis sowme couth leid.	*Overtook; young man; baggage*
25	Softlye thai raid quhill thai the court suld knaw.	*Easily; until; retinue; see*
	So sodeynly that Hesilden he saw	*at Hazelden*
	The Perseys sowme, in quhilk gret riches was.	*baggage*
	The hors was tyryt and mycht no forthir pas.	*tired*
	Fyve men was chargit to keipe it weill all sid;	*[on] all sides*
30	Twa was on fute, and thre on hors couth ride.	
	The maister man at thar servandis can sper,	*their (Sir Ranald's); inquired*
	"Quha aw this sowme? The suth thou to me ler."	*owns; Tell me the truth*
	The man ansuerd withoutyn wordis mar,	
	"My lordis," he said, "quhilk schirreff is of Ayr."	
35	"Sen it is his, this hors sall with us gang	*Since; shall go with us*
	To serve our lord, or ellis me think gret wrang.	
	Thocht a subjet in deid wald pas his lord,	*deeds*
	It is nocht lewyt be na rychtwis racord."	*permitted; opinion*
	Thai cut the brays and leyt the harnes faw.	*straps; gear fall*
40	Wallace was ner. Quhen he sic revere saw,	*robbery*
	He spak to thaim with manly contenance;	
	In fayr afforme he said but variance,	*manner; firmly*
	"Ye do us wrang, and it in tyme of pes.	*truce*
	Of sic rubry war suffisance to ces."	*such robbery; right (proper)*
45	The Sothron schrew in ire ansuerd him to:	*scoundrel*
	"It sall be wrocht as thow may se us do.	
	Thow gettis no mendis. Quhat wald thou wordis mar?"	*amends*
	Sadly avisit, Wallace remembrith him thar	*Firmly resolved*
	On the promys he maid his eyme befor.	*uncle*
50	Resoun him rewllyt; as than he did no mor.	*ruled; for the time being*

---

[1] *Sir Ranald Crawford was obliged to be there at that time*

Book 4

	The hors thai tuk for aventur mycht befall,	*whatever might happen*
	Laid on thar sowme, syne furth the way couth call.	*baggage, then; drove*
	Thar tyryt sowmir so left thai into playne.	*tired pack horse unburdened*
	Wallace raturnd towart the court agayne.	*returned; retinue*
55	On the mur syde sone with his eyme he mett	*moor; uncle*
	And tauld how thai the way for his man sett:	*blocked*
	"And war noucht I was bonde in my legiance,	*honor-bound*
	We partyt noucht thus for all the gold in France.	
	The hors thai reft quhilk suld your harnes ber."	*took; equipment*
60	Schir Ranald said, "That is bot litill der.	*only a small matter*
	We may get hors and othir gud in playne;	*soon enough*
	And men be lost, we get nevir agayne."	*[But] if*
	Wallace than said, "Als wisly God me save,	
	Of this gret mys I sall amendis have	*wrong*
65	And nothir latt for pes na your plesance.	*neither refrain; pleasure*
	With witnes her I gif up my legiance,	*In front of witnesses here; allegiance*
	For cowardly ye lik to tyne your rycht.	*lose*
	Yourselff sone syne to dede thai think to dycht."	*then; kill*
	In wraith tharwith away fra him he went.	*anger*
70	Schyr Ranald was wis and kest in his entent,	*considered carefully*
	And said, "I will byde at the Mernys all nycht.	
	So Inglismen may deyme us no unrycht	*judge us [guilty of] no offense*
	Gyff ony be deide befor us upon cas,	*If any happen to be dead*
	That we in law may bide the rychtwisnas."	*truth*
75	His luging tuk, still at the Mernys baid.	*lodging; waited*
	Full gret murnyng he for his nevo maid,	*grieving*
	Bot all for nocht; quhat mycht it him availl?	
	As intill wer he wrocht nocht his consaill.[1]	
	Wallace raid furth, with him twa yemen past;	
80	The sowmir man he folowid wondyr fast.	*baggage man*
	Be est Cathcart he ourhyede thaim agayne.	*By; overtook*
	Than knew thai weille that it was he in playne,	*for sure (plainly)*
	Be hors and weide, that argownd thaim befor.	*By; dress, who challenged*
	The fyve to thaim retornde withoutyn mor.	*turned back*
85	Wallace to ground fra his courser can glide;	*steed; descended*
	A burnyst brand he bradyt out that tyde.	*polished sword he drew*

---

[1] *In matters of war he did not follow his counsel*

The Wallace

	The maistir man with sa gud will straik he,	*such force*
	Bathe hatt and hede he gert in sondir fle;	*helmet and head; caused*
	Ane othir fast apon the face he gaiff,	*hard; hit*
90	Till dede to ground but mercy he him draiff;	*Until; dashed*
	The thrid he hyt with gret ire in that steid;	*place*
	Fey on the fold he has him left for deid.	*Doomed in life*
	Wallace slew thre; be that his yemen wicht	*strong*
	The tothir twa derfly to dede thai dycht.	*violently killed*
95	Syne spoilyeid thai the harnais or thai wend	*Then they plundered the gear before*
	Of silvir and gold aboundandlye to spend.	
	Jowellis thai tuk, the best was chosyn thar,	*Valuables*
	Gud hors and geyr, syne on thar wayis can fayr.	*weapons, then; went*

[*As Percy holds his Glasgow council, news reaches him of the death of his baggage men and the loss of treasure. Meanwhile, Wallace and his men, resting at an inn in the Lennox, hear that a warrant has been issued for his arrest and that Scots, including his uncle, have been warned not to befriend and aid him. Supporters flock to Wallace in Lennox, including Stephen of Ireland, men of Argyll and others, and Earl Malcolm makes him chieftain of his men. Fawdoun (first mention) too offers allegiance. Wallace's lack of interest in personal riches and his readiness to dispense any amongst poor and rich are praised. Wallace and sixty men move on to Stirlingshire, where they attack and then occupy a stockade at Gargunnock, above Leckie, after Wallace's superhuman effort removes the bar across the gate. They then cross the Forth and move on to Kincardine and Strathearn, killing any Englishmen they encounter. (Lines 99–322)*]

	Thir werlik Scottis all with one assent	*These war-like*
	Northt so our Ern throuchout the land thai went,	*North across [the River] Earn*
325	In Meffan Woode thar lugyng tuk that nycht.	*Methven*
	Upon the morn quhen it was dayis lycht	
	Wallace rais up, went to the forest side,	
	Quhar that he sawe full feill bestis abide,	*a great many*
	Of wylde and tayme, walkand haboundandlye.	*roaming freely (with abandon)*
330	Than Wallace said, "This contré likis me.	
	Wermen may do with fud at thai suld haiff,	*Warriors; perform*
	Bot want thai meit thai rak nocht of the laiff."	*If; care nothing about the rest*
	Of dyet fayr Wallace tuk nevir kepe	*food; heed*
	Bot as it come welcum was meit and sleip.	*food*
335	Sum quhill he had gret sufficience within;	*Sometimes*
	Now want, now has, now los, now can wyn;	

Book 4

	Now lycht, now sadd, now blisfull, now in baill;	*glad; happy; sorrow*
	In haist, now hurt; now sorouffull, now haill;	*healthy*
	Nowe weildand weyle, now calde weddir, now hett;[1]	
340	Nowe moist, now drowth, now waverand wynd, now wett.	*dry (drought)*
	So ferd with him for Scotlandis rycht full evyn	*fared; evenly*
	In feyle debait six yeris and monethis sevyn.	*great strife*
	Quhen he wan pees and left Scotland in playne,	*openly*
	The Inglismen maid new conquest agayne.	
345	In frustir termys I will nocht tary lang.	*In pointless words*
	Wallace agayne unto his men can gang	*went*
	And said, "Her is a land of gret boundance.	*plenty*
	Thankit be God of his hye purvyans!	*providence*
	Sevyn of yow feris graith sone and ga with me.	*companions prepare*
350	Rycht sor I long Sanct Jhonstoun for to se.	*(i.e., Perth)*
	Stevyn of Irland, als God of hevyn thee saiff,	
	Maistir leiddar I mak thee of the laiff.	*Chief leader; rest*
	Kepe weill my men; latt nane out of thi sycht	*sight*
	Quhill I agayn sall cum with all my mycht.	*Until*
355	Byde me sevyn dayis in this forest strang.	*Wait [for]*
	Yhe may get fude, suppos I duell so lang.	
	Sum part yhe haiff, and God will send us mair."	
	Thus turnyt he and to the toun couth fair.	*went*
	The mar kepyt the port of that village;	*officer in charge of the gate*
360	Wallace knew weill and send him his message.	
	The mar was brocht, saw him a gudlye man,	
	Rycht reverandlye he has resavyt thaim than.	*respectfully*
	At him he speryt all Scottis gyff thai be.	*if*
	Wallace said, "Ya, and it is pees trow we."	*peace time*
365	"I grant," he said, "that likis us wondir weill.	
	Trew men of pees may ay sum frendschipe feill.	*feel*
	Quhat is your nayme? I pray yow tell me it."	
	"Will Malcomsone," he said, "sen ye wald witt.	*know*
	In Atryk Forest has my wonnyng beyne.	*Ettrick; dwelling*
370	Thar I was born amang the schawis scheyne.	*fair woods*
	Now I desyr this north land for to se,	
	Quhar I mycht fynd better duellyng for me."	

---

[1] *Now enjoying good [fortune], now cold weather, now hot*

The Wallace

	The mar said, "Schir, I sper nocht for nane ille,	*ask*
	Bot feill tithingis oft syis is brocht us till	*many tidings oftentimes*
375	Of ane Wallace, was born into the west.	
	Our kingis men he haldis at gret unrest,	*distress*
	Martiris thaim doun, gret peté is to se.	*Slaughters*
	Out of the trewis, forsuth, we trow he be."	*Breaking the truce; believe*
	Wallace than said, "I her spek of that man.	*hear speak*
380	Tithingis of him to you nane tell I can."	
	For him he gert ane innys graithit be	*dwelling-place prepared*
	Quhar nane suld cum bot his awne men and he.	
	Hys stuart Kerlye brocht thaim in fusioun	*abundance*
	Gude thing eneuch quhat was into the toun.	*Enough good provisions*
385	Als Inglismen to drynkyn wald him call	*Also*
	And commownly he delt nocht tharwithall.	*had no dealings with them*
	In thar presence he spendyt resonably,	
	Yheit for himself he payit ay boundandlye.	*abundantly*
	On Scottis men he spendyt mekill gud	
390	Bot nocht his thankis upon the Sothren blud.	*willingly*
	Son he consavyt in his witt prevalye	*Soon; understood; secretly*
	Into that land quha was of maist party.	*most power*
	Schir Jamys Butler, ane agit, cruell knycht,	*fierce*
	Kepyt Kynclevyn, a castell wondyr wycht.	*Kinclaven; very strong*
395	His sone Schir Jhon than duelt into the toun,	
	Under capteyn to Schir Garraid Heroun.	
	The wemen als he uysyt at the last;	*(Wallace) visited*
	And so on ane hys eyne he can to cast,	*one*
	In the south gait, of fassoun fresche and fayr.	*street; appearance*
400	Wallace to hir maid prevalye repair.	*secret visits*
	So fell it thus, of the toun or he past,	*before*
	At ane accorde thai hapnyt at the last.	
	Wallace with hyr in secré maid him glaid;	*secret*
	Sotheren wist nocht that he sic plesance haid.	*Englishmen; pleasure*
405	Offt on the nycht he wald say to himsell,	*himself*
	"This is fer war than ony payn of hell,	*far worse; any*
	At thus with wrang thir devillis suld bruk our land,	*possess*
	And we with force may nocht agayne thaim stand.	*against*
	To tak this toun my pouer is to small;	*too*
410	Gret perell als on myself may fall.	
	Set we it in fyr it will undo mysell,	*[If] we set it on fire; myself*

Book 4

Or los my men; thar is no mor to tell.
Yhettis ar clos, the dykis depe withall;   *Gates; shut; ditches deep*
Thocht I wald swyme, forsuth so can nocht all.   *Though*
415 This mater now herfor I will ourslyde,   *put aside*
Bot in this toun I may no langar byde."
Als men tald him quhen the captayne wald pas   *Also*
Hayme to Kynclevyn, quharoff rycht glaid he was.   *Home*
His leiff he tuk at heris of the toun;   *leave; lords*
420 To Meffane Wode rycht glaidly maid him boun.   *bound*
His horn he hynt and bauldly loud can blaw;   *seized; boldly*
His men him hard and tharto sone couth draw.   *heard; drew*
Rycht blyth he was for thai war all in feyr;   *in array*
Mony tithingis at him thai wald nocht speyr.   *find out*
425 He thaim commaunde to mak thaim redy fast;
In gud array out of the woode thai past.
Towart Kynclevyn thai bownyt thaim that tid,   *headed; time*
Syn in a vaill that ner was thar besid,   *Then; valley*
Fast on to Tay his buschement can he draw.   *[the River] Tay; ambush*
430 In a dern woode thai stellit thaim full law,   *dark; crept stealthily; low*
Set skouriouris furth the contré to aspye.   *scouts; spy*
Be ane our nowne thre for rydaris went bye.   *By one past noon; advance riders*
The wach turned in to witt quhat was his will.   *watch returned; know*
He thaim commaund in covert to bide still.   *hiding; wait*
435 "And we call feyr the hous knawlage will haiff   *If we give warning (call "fire")*
And that may sone be warnyng to the laiff.   *rest*
All fors in wer do nocht but governance."   *warlike action; without discretion*
Wallace was few bot happy ordinance   *had few [men]; fortunate provision*
Maid him fell syis his adversouris to wyn.[1]
440 Be that the court of Inglismen com in,   *retinue*
Four scoyr and ten weill graithit in thar ger,   *equipped; armor*
Harnest on hors, all likly men of wer.   *Armed; promising*
Wallace saw weill his nowmir was na ma;   *more*
He thankit God and syne the feild couth ta.   *battlefield*
445 The Inglismen merveild quhat thai suld be,
Bot fra thai saw thai maid thaim for melle.   *from [when]; prepared to do battle*

---

[1] *Caused him many times to triumph over his adversaries*

The Wallace

	In fewtir thai kest scharpe speris at that tide;[1]	
	In ire thai thoucht atour the Scottis to ryd.	around
	Wallace and his went cruelly thaim agayne;	fiercely; against
450	At the fyrst rusche feill Inglismen war slayne.	attack many
	Wallace straik ane with his gude sper of steill	
	Throwout the cost; the schafft to-brak ilk deyll.[2]	
	A burnyst brand in haist he hyntis out;	burnished sword; pulled
	Thrys apon fute he thrang throuch all the rout.	pressed; throng
455	Stern hors thai steik suld men of armys ber;	Strong; stab should
	Sone undir feit fulyeid was men of wer.	trampled
	Butler lychtyt himself for to defend	alighted
	Witht men of armys quhilk war full worthi kend.	reputed
	On athyr syde feill frekis was fechtand fast.	many men were fighting
460	The captayne baid thocht he war sor agast.	withstood; was terrified
	Part of the Scottis be worthines thai slew;	valor
	Wallace was wa, and towart him he drew.	melancholy
	His men dred for the Butler bauld and keyn.	dreaded; bold; fierce
	On him he socht in ire and propyr teyn;	pure rage
465	Upon the hed him straik in matelent,	furiously
	The burnyst blaid throuout his basnett went.	helmet
	Bathe bayne and brayn he byrst throw all the weid.	bone; flesh; burst; armor
	Thus Wallace hand deliverit thaim of dreid.	Wallace's hand; from danger
	Yeitt feill on fold was fechtand cruelly;	on earth (alive)
470	Stevyn of Irland and all the chevalry	horsemen
	Into the stour did cruelly and weill;	battle; fiercely
	And Kerle als with his gud staff of steill.	sword
	The Inglismen, fra thar cheftayne was slayne,	once
	Thai left the feild and fled in all thar mayn.	force
475	Thre scoyr war slayne or thai wald leif that steid.	before; place
	The fleande folk, that wist of no rameid	fleeing; remedy
	Bot to the hous, thai fled in all thar mycht;	castle
	The Scottis folowit that worthi war and wycht.	were valiant and bold
	Few men of fens was left that place to kepe.	defense; guard
480	Wemen and preistis upon Wallace can wepe,	
	For weill thai wend the flearis was thar lord;	they knew well those fleeing; lords

---

[1] *From their lance supports [attached to the saddle] they threw sharp spears at that time*

[2] *Right through the rib; the shaft broke completely*

Book 4

	To tak him in thai maid thaim redy ford,	*prepared themselves*
	Leit doun the bryg, kest up the gettis wide.	*bridge, cast open*
	The frayit folk entrit and durst nocht byde;	*frightened; dared; stay*
485	Gud Wallace evir he folowit thaim so fast	*always*
	Quhill in the hous he entryt at the last.	*Until; castle*
	The gett he wor quhill cumin was all the rout.	*defended until; troops*
	Of Inglis and Scottis he held no man tharout.	*kept none out*
	The Inglismen that won war in that steid,	*were captured*
490	Withoutyn grace thai bertnyt thaim to deid.	*mercy; put them to death*
	The capteynis wiff, wemen and preistis twa,	*(i.e., Lady Butler)*
	And yong childir, forsuth thai savyt no ma,	*truly; spared no more*
	Held thaim in clos eftir this sodeyn cas	*Shut them in*
	Or Sothron men suld sege him in that place;	*Before English; besiege him (Wallace)*
495	Tuk up the bryg and closyt gettis fast.	*quickly*
	The dede bodyes out of sicht he gart cast,	*He had the dead bodies cast out of sight*
	Baith in the hous and without at war dede;	*Both [those] in and outside the castle*
	Five of his awne to berynis he gart leid.	*own [men]; burial*
	In that castell thar sevyn dayis baide he.	*stayed*
500	On ilka nycht thai spoilyeid besylé,	*each; plundered diligently*
	To Schortwode Schaw leide victaill and wyn wicht,[1]	
	Houshald and ger, baithe gold and silvir brycht.	*Furnishings and equipment*
	Women and thai that he had grantyt grace,	*mercy*
	Quhen him thoucht tyme thai put out of that place.	
505	Quhen thai had tayne quhat he likit to haiff,	
	Straik doun the gettis and set in fyr the laiff,	*Demolished; rest [of the castle]*
	Out of wyndowis stanssouris all thai drew,	*stanchions (i.e., supports)*
	Full gret irn wark into the watter threw;	*work; moat*
	Burdyn duris and lokis in thair ire,	*Doors made of boards; locks*
510	All werk of tre, thai brynt up in a fyr;	*wood*
	Spylt at thai mycht, brak brig and bulwark doun.	*Destroyed what they could, broke*

[*Wallace's company of 50 men heads for Shortwood Forest. Meanwhile the captain's wife goes to Perth and relates what has happened to Sir Garraid, who musters 1,000 men and proceeds to surround Shortwood Forest. Wallace is injured in the neck by an archer, and, while his prowess scares the archers off, the Scots are greatly outnumbered. Wallace succeeds in killing one of the leaders, Sir William Loran, before escaping with his men from the wood.*]

---

[1] *To Shortwood Forest removed food and strong wine*

The Wallace

He makes for Cargill Wood, having lost seven men, and the English many more. (Lines 512–694)]

695	The secunde nycht the Scottis couth thaim draw	
	Rycht prevaly agayne to Schortwod Schaw;	*secretly; Forest*
	Tuk up thar gud quhilk was put owt of sicht,	*Picked up; belongings*
	Cleithing and stuff, bathe gold and silvir brycht;	*Clothing; army provisions*
	Upon thar fute, for horsis was thaim fra,	*On foot, because they had no horses*
700	Or the son rais to Meffen Wood can ga.	*Before; sun rose; went*
	Thai twa dayis our thar lugyng still thai maid.	
	On the thrid nycht thai movit but mar abaid,	*moved without further delay*
	Till Elkok Park full sodeynly thai went;	*quickly*
	Thar in that strentht to bide was his entent.	*stronghold; wait; intention*
705	Than Wallas said he wald go to the toun,	
	Arayit him weill intill a preistlik goun.	*Dressed; priest-like*
	In Sanct Johnstoun disgysyt can he fair	*disguised he went*
	Till this woman the quhilk I spak of ayr.	*before*
	Of his presence scho rycht rejosit was	*pleased*
710	And sor adred how he away suld pas.	*sorely afraid*
	He sojornyt thair fra nowne was of the day	*noon*
	Quhill ner the nycht or that he went away.	*Until almost night before*
	He trystyt hyr quhen he wald cum agayne	*arranged with her; back*
	On the thrid day; than was scho wondyr fayne.	*very happy*
715	Yeitt he was seyn with enemys as he yeid.	*by; left*
	To Schir Garraid thai tald of all his deid,	
	And to Butler that wald haiff wrokyn beyne.	*have been avenged*
	Than thai gart tak that woman brycht and scheyne	*caused to be taken; fair*
	Accusyt hir sar of resset in that cas.	*angrily; sheltering an outlaw*
720	Feyll syis scho suour that scho knew nocht Wallas.	*Many times; swore*
	Than Butler said, "We wait weyle it was he	*know well*
	And bot thou tell in bayle fyr sall thou de.	*unless; by burning; die*
	Giff thou will help to bryng yon rebell doun,	*If*
	We sall thee mak a lady of renoun."	
725	Thai gaiff till hyr baith gold and silvir brycht,	
	And said scho suld be weddyt with ane knycht,	
	Quham scho desirit, that was but mariage.	*Whomever; unmarried*
	Thus tempt thai hir throu consaill and gret wage,	*counsel; reward*
	That scho thaim tald quhat tyme he wald be thar.	
730	Than war thai glaid, for thai desirit no mar	

Book 4

     Of all Scotland bot Wallace at thar will.
     Thus ordaynyt thai this poyntment to fullfill. — *arranged; appointment*
     Feyle men of armes thai graithit hastelye — *Many; got ready*
     To kepe the gettis, wicht Wallas till aspye. — *guard; gates, bold*
735 At the set trist he entrit in the toun, — *meeting-time*
     Wittand nothing of all this fals tresoune. — *Knowing*
     Till hir chawmer he went but mair abaid; — *To; chamber; without further delay*
     Scho welcummyt him and full gret plesance maid. — *pleasure showed*
     Quhat at thai wrocht I can nocht graithly say, — *readily*
740 Rycht unperfyt I am of Venus play; — *imperfect*
     Bot hastelye he graithit him to gang. — *prepared; go*
     Than scho him tuk and speryt giff he thocht lang. — *Then; took hold; asked if; wearied*
     Scho askit him that nycht with hir to bid. — *stay*
     Sone he said, "Nay, for chance that may betide. — *Soon; for [fear of any evil] chance*
745 My men ar left all at mysrewill for me. — *in disorder because of*
     I may nocht sleipe this nycht quhill I thaim se." — *until*
     Than wepyt scho and said full oft, "Allace
     That I was maide! Wa worthe the courssit cas! — *born! Alas the accursed case*
     Now haiff I lost the best man leiffand is. — *living*
750 O feble mynd to do so foull a mys! — *offense*
     O waryit witt, wykkyt and variance, — *cursed knowledge; fickle*
     That me has brocht into this myschefull chance! — *evil*
     Allace!" scho said, "in warld that I was wrocht! — *created*
     Giff all this payne on myself mycht be brocht! — *If*
755 I haiff servit to be brynt in a gleid." — *deserved; to an ember*
     Quhen Wallace saw scho ner of witt couth weid, — *was nearly driven mad*
     In his armes he caucht hir sobrely — *gently*
     And said, "Der hart, quha has mysdoyn ocht? I?" — *done something wrong?*
     "Nay, I," quod scho, "has falslye wrocht this trayn. — *deception*
760 I haiff you sald. Rycht now yhe will be slayn." — *betrayed*
     Scho tauld to him hir tresoun till ane end, — *treachery from start to finish*
     As I haiff said. Quhat nedis mair legend? — *What need is there to write more?*
     At hir he speryt giff scho forthocht it sar. — *sorely repented it*
     "Wa, ya," scho said, "and sall do evirmar. — *Alas, yes*
765 My waryed werd in warld I mon fullfill; — *cursed fate; must*
     To mend this mys I wald byrne on a hill." — *amend; wrong; burn*
     He comfort hir and baide hir haiff no dreide. — *told her to have no fear*
     "I will," he said, "haiff sum part of thi weid." — *clothing*
     Hir goun he tuk on hym and courches als. — *head scarves*

53

The Wallace

770	"Will God I sall eschape this tresoune fals.	
	I thee forgyff." Withoutyn wordis mair	
	He kissyt hir, syne tuk his leiff to fayr.	go
	His burly brand that helpyt him offt in neid,	large sword
	Rycht prevalye he hid it undir that weid.	secretly
775	To the south gett the gaynest way he drew,	gate; nearest
	Quhar that he fand of armyt men enew.	enough
	To thaim he tald, dissemblyt contenance,	under this false appearance
	To the chawmer quhar he was upon chance.	[To go] to the chamber
	"Speid fast," he said, "Wallace is lokit in."	locked
780	Fra him thai socht withoutyn noyis or dyn,	From; went
	To that sammyn hous about thai can thaim cast.	look
	Out at the gett Wallas gat full fast,	
	Rycht glaid in hart; quhen that he was without,	outside
	Rycht fast he yeide a stour pais and a stout.	went [at] a strong and sturdy pace
785	Twa him beheld and said, "We will go se.	see
	A stalwart queyne, forsuth, yon semys to be."	woman
	Thai folowit him throwe the South Inche thai twa.	park area south of town
	Quhen Wallace saw with thaim thar come na ma,	
	Agayne he turnede and has the formast slayn.	He turned back
790	The tothir fled. Than Wallace with gret mayn	force
	Upon the hed with his suerd has him tayne;	struck
	Left thaim bathe dede, syne to the strenth is gayne.	then; stronghold went
	His men he gat, rycht glaid quhen thai him saw.	found
	Till thair defence in haist he gart thaim draw;	To their defense [position]; made
795	Devoydyde him sone of the womannys weid.	Divested himself; clothes
	Thus chapyt he out of that felloun dreid.	he escaped; terrible danger

Explicit liber quarta &
Incipit quintus

Book 5

[*The English, with the aid of a bloodhound, pursue Wallace to Methven Wood and, although heavily outnumbered, he and his men escape to the banks of the Tay, but because half his men cannot swim he decides they should all stand their ground and take their (better) chances with the English. (Lines 1–63)*]

Book 5

	Thus fend thai lang into that stalwart stour.	*defend; a long time; valiant fight*
65	The Scottis chyftayne was yong and in a rage,	*spirited*
	Usyt in wer and fechtis with curage.	*Practiced in war; fights*
	He saw his men of Sothroun tak gret wrang.	*[the] English; suffer*
	Thaim to raveng all dreidles can he gang,	*avenge; fearless he proceeded*
	For mony of thaim war bledand wondir sar.	*many; bleeding profusely*
70	He couth nocht se no help apperand thar	
	Bot thar chyftayne war putt out of thair gait,	*Unless; way*
	The bryme Butler so bauldlye maid debait.	*fierce; [who] so boldly resisted*
	Throu the gret preys Wallace to him socht;	*press [of folk]; sought him*
	His awfull deid he eschewit as he mocht.	*deeds; avoided; might*
75	Undir ane ayk wycht men about him set,	*oak bold men*
	Wallace mycht nocht a graith straik on him get.	*direct blow*
	Yeit schede he thaim; a full royd slope was maide.	*he parted them; wide breach*
	The Scottis went out, no langar thar abaid.	*no longer stayed there*
	Stevyn of Irland quhilk hardy was and wicht,	*bold*
80	To helpe Wallace he did gret preys and mycht,	*great and mighty deeds*
	With trew Kerle douchty in mony deid.	*valiant; actions*
	Upon the grounde feill Sothroun gert thai bleid.	*many English they caused to bleed*
	Sexty war slayne of Inglismen in that place	
	And nine of Scottis thair tynt was throuch that cace.	*lost*
85	Butleris men so stroyit war that tide	*destroyed; time*
	Into the stour he wald no langar bide.	*fighting; remain*
	To get supplé he socht onto the staill.	*reinforcements; main body of the army*
	Thus lost he thar a hundreth of gret vaill.	*a hundred [men] of great worth*
	As thai war best arayand Butleris rout	*Butler's company was preparing*
90	Betuex parteys than Wallace ischit out.[1]	
	Sixteen with him thai graithit thaim to ga;	*readied themselves to go*
	Of all his men he had levyt no ma.	*left*
	The Inglismen, has myssyt him, in hy	*missing him; haste*
	The hund thai tuk and folowit haistely.	*hound*
95	At the Gask Woode full fayne he wald haiff beyne,	*gladly*
	Bot this sloth brache, quhilk sekyr was and keyne,[2]	
	On Wallace fute folowit so felloune fast,	*track; extremely*
	Quhill in thar sicht that prochit at the last.	*Until [they had him] in sight; approached*

---

[1] *Between the two parties (i.e., the English armies) Wallace then sallied out*

[2] *But the [female] sleuth hound, which was reliable and fierce*

The Wallace

	Thar hors war wicht had sojorned weill and lang.	*strong; lasted*
100	To the next woode twa myil thai had to gang	*two miles; go*
	Of upwith erde thai yeid with all thar mycht.	*Up rising ground; went*
	Gud hope thai had for it was ner the nycht.	
	Fawdoun tyryt and said he mycht nocht gang.	*not go [further]*
	Wallace was wa to leyff him in that thrang.	*loath; leave; danger*
105	He bade him ga and said the strenth was ner,[1]	
	Bot he tharfor wald nocht fastir him ster.	*move*
	Wallace in ire on the crag can him ta	*struck him on the neck*
	With his gud suerd and straik the hed him fra.	*cut*
	Dreidles to ground derfly he duschit dede.	*Without a doubt; fell violently*
110	Fra him he lap and left him in that stede.	*leapt back; place*
	Sum demys it to ill and othir sum to gud,	*consider*
	And I say her into thir termys rude,	*here; unpolished words*
	Bettir it was he did, as thinkis me.	
	Fyrst to the hunde it mycht gret stoppyn be;	*means of stopping*
115	Als Fawdoun was haldyn at suspicioun	*Also; held in*
	For he was haldyn of brokill complexioun.	*reputed [to be] of fickle character*
	Rycht stark he was and had bot litill gayne.	*strong; traveled*
	Thus Wallace wist had he beyne left allayne,	*knew*
	And he war fals to enemys he wald ga,	
120	Gyff he war trew the Sothroun wald him sla.	*If; loyal; English; kill*
	Mycht he do ocht bot tyne him as it was?	*anything other than let him perish*
	Fra this questioun now schortlye will I pas.	*From*
	Deyme as yhe lest, ye that best can and may,	*Judge; please*
	I bott rahers as my autour will say.	*only recite*

[*The Scots disperse, and while Wallace and the rest move on, Stephen and Kerle, unbeknownst to him, hide near Dupplyn Castle. When the sleuth hound comes across Fawdoun's body, it refuses to go any further. Stephen and Kerle then pass themselves off as Englishmen and mingle with the enemy; as Heroun stands over the dead Fawdoun, Kerle quietly stabs him to death and in the ensuing fuss he and Stephen slip away towards Loch Earn. Meanwhile Wallace, the number of his men reduced to thirteen, rests at the Gask Hall and worries about the fate of the missing Kerle and Stephen. (Lines 125–173)*]

---

[1] *He ordered him to go on and said the stronghold (i.e., Gask Hall) was near*

Book 5

	Thirteen war left with him, no ma had he;	
175	In the Gask Hall thair lugyng haif thai tayne.	*lodging; taken*
	Fyr gat thai sone, bot meyt than had thai nayne.	*soon; food; none*
	Twa scheipe thai tuk besid thaim of a fauld,	*sheep; from a fold*
	Ordanyt to soupe into that sembly hauld,	*Prepared to sup; fine stronghold*
	Graithit in haist sum fude for thaim to dycht.	*Made ready; cook*
180	So hard thai blaw rude hornys upon hycht.	*Just then heard; rough; loudly*
	Twa sende he furth to luk quhat it mycht be.	
	Thai baid rycht lang and no tithingis herd he,	*were away a long time; news*
	Bot boustous noyis so brymly blew and fast.	*loud; fiercely*
	So othir twa into the woode furth past;	*two others*
185	Nane come agayne, bot boustously can blaw.[1]	
	Into gret ire he send thaim furth on raw.	*Angrily; out altogether*
	Quhen that allayne Wallace was levyt thar	*alone; left*
	The awfull blast aboundyt mekill mayr.	*increased much more*
	Than trowit he weill thai had his lugyng seyne.	*believed*
190	His suerd he drew of nobill mettall keyne,	*sharp*
	Syn furth he went quhar at he hard the horn.	*Then; heard*
	Without the dur Fawdoun was him beforn,	*Outside the door*
	As till his sycht his awne hed in his hand.	*As it appeared; own head*
	A croys he maid quhen he saw him so stand.	*He crossed himself*
195	At Wallace in the hed he swaket thar	*He flung the head in at Wallace*
	And he in haist sone hynt it by the hair,	*immediately seized*
	Syne out agayne at him he couth it cast.	*Then*
	Intill his hart he was gretlye agast.	
	Rycht weill he trowit that was no spreit of man;	*believed; spirit*
200	It was sum devill at sic malice began.	*devil that such*
	He wyst no vaill thar langar for to bide:	*knew no advantage*
	Up throuch the hall thus wicht Wallace can glid	*went quickly*
	Till a clos stair, the burdis raiff in twyne;[2]	
	Fifteen fute large he lap out of that in.	*feet high; leapt; dwelling*
205	Up the wattir sodeynlye he couth fair;	*quickly he went*
	Agayne he blent quhat perance he sawe thar.	*looked [at]; appearance*
	Him thocht he saw Faudoun that hugly syr,	*horrid man*

---

[1] *None came back, but [the horn] continued to blow harshly*

[2] *To a stair leading to a close, the boards [he] smashed in two*

The Wallace

	That haill hall he had set in a fyr:	*whole; set on fire*
	A gret raftre he had intill his hand.	*rafter*
210	Wallace as than no langar walde he stand.	
	Of his gud men full gret mervaill had he	*wonder*
	How thai war tynt throuch his feyle fantasé.	*lost; terrible folly*
	Traistis rycht weill all this was suth indeide,	*Be assured; true indeed*
	Suppos that it no poynt be of the Creide.	*Although; part; [Apostles'] Creed*
215	Power thai had witht Lucifer that fell,	
	The tyme quhen he partyt fra hevyn to hell.	*departed from heaven*
	Be sic myscheiff giff his men mycht be lost,	*By such evil if*
	Drownyt or slayne amang the Inglis ost,	*host*
	Or quhat it was in liknes of Faudoun	*in the likeness of*
220	Quhilk brocht his men to suddand confusioun;	*sudden destruction*
	Or gif the man endyt in evill entent,	*if; evil disposition*
	Sum wikkit spreit agayne for him present;	*spirit appearing again for him*
	I can nocht spek of sic divinité,	*such theology*
	To clerkis I will lat all sic materis be.	*leave*
225	Bot of Wallace furth I will yow tell.	*further*
	Quhen he was went of that perell fell	*out of that terrible danger*
	Yeit glaid wes he that he had chapyt swa,	*escaped so*
	Bot for his men gret murnyng can he ma,	*make*
	Flayt by himself to the Makar ofbuffe	*Complained; above*
230	Quhy He sufferyt he suld sic paynys pruff.	*allowed [that]; endure*
	He wyst nocht weill giff it wes Goddis will	*knew; if*
	Rycht or wrang his fortoun to fullfill.	
	Hade he plesd God he trowit it mycht nocht be	
	He suld him thoill in sic perplexité;	*suffer*
235	Bot gret curage in his mynd evir draiff,	*desire; drove [him]*
	Of Inglismen thinkand amendis to haiff.	*have*

[*Wallace is spotted by Butler on Earnside. A confrontation follows, and Wallace kills Butler, so the second English "chieftain" is now dead. Wallace seizes Butler's horse and rides to Dalreach, escaping all attempts to remove him from his mount. At a ford he successfully fends off more attackers but eventually kills the horse, which is too exhausted to carry on, and proceeds on foot until he comes to the Forth, across which he wades to make his way to the Torwood. Fed and sheltered by a sympathetic widow who also assigns two of her sons to him, Wallace sends a woman and child to check whether any of his men are still at Gask Hall. Meanwhile his uncle from Dunipace is fetched and re-united with Wallace, who proceeds to recount his recent experiences.* (Lines 237–376)]

Book 5

      "This nycht," he said, "I was left me allayne,
      In feyle debait with enemys mony ane.   *fierce conflict; many [a] one*
      God at His will my liff did ay to kepe: *It was God's will; always preserve*
380 Our Forth I swame that awfull is and depe.   *Across [the River] Forth*
      Quhat I haiff had in wer befor this day,   *war*
      Presoune and payne to this nycht was bot play,   *suffering*
      So bett I am with strakis sad and sar.   *beaten; blows grave; sore*
      The cheyle wattir urned me mekill mar,   *chill; afflicted; much more*
385 Eftir gret blud throu heit in cauld was brocht,   *blood; heat; cold*
      That of my lyff almost nothing I roucht.   *cared*
      I meyn fer mar the tynsell of my men   *lament far more; loss*
      Na for myselff, mycht I suffir sic ten."   *Than; harm*
      The persone said, "Der sone, thow may se weyll   *parson*
390 Langar to stryff it helpis nocht adeyll.   *contend; at all*
      Thi men are lost and nayne will with thee rys,   *none; rise [up]*
      For Goddis saik wyrk as I sall devys.   *do; shall advise*
      Tak a lordschipe quhar on at thow may liff;   *Accept; on which; live*
      King Eduuard wald gret landis to thee giff."   *give*
395 "Uncle," he said, "of sic wordis no mar.   *more*
      This is nothing bot eking of my car.   *[an] increasing of my care*
      I lik bettir to se the Sothren de   *see; die*
      Than gold or land that thai can giff to me.
      Trastis rycht weyll, of wer I will nocht ces   *Believe me; war; cease*
400 Quhill tyme that I bryng Scotland into pes,   *Until [the] time; peace*
      Or de tharfor in playne to understand."   *die for that cause plainly*
      So come Kerle and gud Stevyn of Irland.   *So [then] came*
      The wedowis sone to Wallace he thaim brocht.
      Fra thai him saw of na sadnes thai roucht,   *From [the time]; cared*
405 For perfyt joy thai wepe with all thar eyne.   *wept*
      To ground thai fell and thankit hevynnys queyn.
      Als he was glaid for reskew of thaim twa;   *Also; about [the] rescue*
      Of thair feris leyffand was left no ma.   *their companions no more were left alive*
      Thai tald him that Schir Garrat wes dede;
410 How thai had weyll eschapyt of that stede.   *fortunately; from that place*

[*Kerle and his companions recount their adventures since separating from Wallace, and when the woman sent to Gask Hall returns she tells Wallace that she found Gask Hall standing empty but came across no news of his men. Newly equipped and with the widow's sons, Wallace leaves, still mourning the men he presumes dead or lost, and heads for Dundaff Moor,*

The Wallace

Stirlingshire, where the elder Sir John Graham and his son of the same name pay tribute to him. After a short rest, Wallace moves to Bothwell Moor and then to the Gilbank in Clydesdale, where he meets up with his uncle Auchinleck. (Lines 411–464)]

465	In Bothwell Mur that nycht remaynyt he	*Bothwell Moor*
	With ane Craufurd that lugyt him prevalé.	*one [of the] Crawfords who sheltered*
	Upon the morn to the Gilbank he went,	
	Rasavit was with mony glaid entent,	*Welcomed*
	For his der eyme yong Auchinlek duelt thar;	*dear uncle*
470	Brothyr he was to the schireff of Ayr.	
	Quhen auld Schir Ranald till his dede wes dycht,	*killed*
	Than Awchinlek weddyt that lady brycht	*fair*
	And childir gat, as storyes will record,	*children; histories*
	Of Lesmahago, for he held of that lord.	*held [land as a vassal]*
475	Bot he wes slayne, gret peté wes the mar,	
	With Perscys men into the toun of Ayr.	
	His sone duelt still, than nineteen yeris of age,	*lived there*
	And brokit haille his fadris heretage.	*enjoyed possession of*
	Tribute he payit for all his landis braid	*wide*
480	To Lord Persie, as his brodir had maid.	
	I leyff Wallace with his der uncle still;	*leave*
	Of Inglismen yeit sumthing spek I will.	
	A messynger sone throw the contré yeid.	
	To Lord Persie thai tald this fellone deid;	*cruel deed*
485	Kynclevyn was brynt, brokyn and castyn doun,	*burnt*
	The captayn dede of it and Saynt Jhonstoun;	
	The Loran als at Schortwod Schawis scheyn.	
	"Into that land gret sorow has beyne seyn	
	Throuch wicht Wallace that all this deid has done.	*bold*
490	The toune he spyit and that forthocht we sone.	*regretted; right away*
	Butler is slayne with douchty men and deyr."	*[along] with brave and loved men*
	In aspre spech the Persye than can speyr:	*sharp; asked*
	"Quhat worth of him, I pray you graithlye tell."	*became of him; promptly*
	"My lord," he said, "rycht thus the cas befell.	
495	We knaw for treuth he was left him allayne,	*We know for a fact; alone*
	And as he fled he slew full mony ayne.	*many [a] one*
	The hors we fand that him that gait couth ber,	*way carried him*
	Bot of hymself no othir word we her.	*hear*
	At Stirlyng Bryg we wait he passit nocht:	*Bridge; know*

60

Book 5

500	To dede in Forth he may for us be brocht."	[the River] Forth
	Lorde Persye said, "Now suthlye that war syne.	would be [a] sin
	So gud of hand is nayne this warld within.	(i.e., valiant in combat); none
	Had he tayne pes and beyne our kingis man	accepted a truce
	The haill empyr he mycht haiff conquest than.	whole; have conquered then
505	Gret harme it is our knychtis that ar ded;	that [so many of] our knights are dead
	We mon ger se for othir in that sted.	must arrange for others to take their place
	I trow nocht yeit at Wallace losyt be:	I do not believe yet that Wallace is dead
	Our clerkys sayis he sall ger mony de."	cause many to die
	The messynger said, "All that suth has beyne.	truly has come to pass
510	Mony hundreth that cruell war and keyne	Many hundreds; fierce; bold
	Sene he begane ar lost without ramede."[1]	
	The Persye said, "Forsuth he is nocht ded.	dead
	The crukis of Forth he knawis wondyr weylle.	windings of [the River] Forth
	He is on lyff that sall our nacioune feill.	alive; know
515	Quhen he is strest than can he swym at will.	hard pressed then
	Gret strenth he has, bathe wyt and grace thartill."	both skill; thereto
	A messynger the lord chargyt to wend	ordered to go
	And this commaunde in wryt with him he send.	writing
	Schir Jhone Sewart gret schirreff than he maid	grand sheriff
520	Of Sanct Jhonstoun and all thai landis braid.	wide
	Intill Kynclevyn thar duelt nayne agayne:	In; none again
	Thar was left nocht bot brokyn wallis in playne.	nothing
	Leiff I thaim thus reulland the landis thar	Leave
	And spek I will of Wallace glaid weillfar.	welfare
525	He send Kerle to Schir Ranald the knycht,	
	Till Boyd and Blayr that worthi war and wicht	strong
	And Adam als, his cusyng gud Wallace;	cousin
	To thaim declarde of all this paynfull cas,	made known
	Of his eschaipe out of that cumpany,	escape
530	Rycht wondir glaid was this gud chevalry;	Extremely glad; band of knights
	Fra tyme thai wyst that Wallace leiffand was,	living
	Gude expensis till him thai maid to pas.	supplies of money to
	Maister Jhone Blayr was offt in that message,	the messenger employed in that errand
	A worthy clerk bath wys and rycht savage.	bold
535	Levyt he was befor in Parys toune	He lived [alone]

---

[1] *Since he began [his rebellion] are lost beyond help (i.e., fatally wounded)*

The Wallace

	Amang maisteris in science and renoune.	
	Wallace and he at hayme in scule had beyne.	home (Scotland); school
	Sone eftirwart, as verité is seyne,	
	He was the man that pryncipall undirtuk,	chiefly
540	That fyrst compild in dyt the Latyne buk	writing
	Of Wallace lyff, rycht famous of renoun,	
	And Thomas Gray persone of Libertoune.	parson
	With him thai war and put in storyall,	narrative form
	Offt ane or bath mekill of his travaill,	Often one or both; struggle
545	And tharfor her I mak of thaim mencioune.	here
	Master Jhone Blayr to Wallace maid him boune;	bound
	To se his heyle his comfort was the mor,	[good] health was all the more comforting
	As thai full oft togyddyr war befor.	frequently
	Sylvir and gold thai gaiff him for to spend;	
550	Sa dyde he thaim frely quhen God it send.	[to] them generously
	Of gud weylfayr as than he wantyt nane.	lacked none
	Inglismen wyst he was left him allane.	
	Quhar he suld be was nayne of thaim couth say,	Where he could be; could
	Drownyt or slayne, or eschapyt away,	
555	Tharfor of him thai tuk bot litill heid.	heed
	Thai knew him nocht, the les he was in dreid.[1]	
	All trew Scottis gret favour till him gaiff,	
	Quhat gude thai had he mysterit nocht to craiff.	goods; he had no need to ask
	The pes lestyt that Schir Ranald had tayne.	truce lasted; accepted
560	Thai four monethis it suld nocht be out gane.	[For] those; months; trespassed against
	This Crystismes Wallace ramaynyt thar,	Christmas [season]; remained there
	In Laynrik oft till sport he maid repayr.	Lanark
	Quhen that he went fra Gilbank to the toune,	from
	And he fand men was of that fals nacioune,	If; found
565	To Scotland thai dyde nevir grevance mar.	never more caused injury
	Sum stekyt thai, sum throttis in sondir schar.[2]	
	Feill war sone dede, bot nane wyst quha it was.	Many; none knew who was responsible
	Quham he handlyt he leyt no forthir pas.	Whomever he dealt with; let
	Thar Hesylryg duelt, that curssyt knycht to vaill;	in respect of worth
570	Schyrreff he was of all the landis haill,	entirely

---

[1] *They did not recognize him, [therefore] he was the less in danger*

[2] *Some were stabbed, some had their throats cut*

Book 5

	Felloune, owtrage, dispitfull in his deid;	*Fierce, violent, cruel; deeds*
	Mony of him tharfor had mekill dreid.	*great fear*
	Mervell he thocht quha durst his peple sla;	*[A] marvel; dared*
	Without the toune he gert gret nowmir ga.	*Out of; gathered a great company [to] go*
575	Quhen Wallace saw that thai war ma than he,	*more*
	Than did he nocht bot salust curtaslé.	*nothing except give greeting*
	All his four men bar thaim quietlik,	*held; quietly*
	Na Sotheron couth deme thaim mys, pur no rik.[1]	
	In Lanryk duelt a gentill woman thar,	*noble*
580	A madyn myld as my buk will declar,	*gentle maiden; book*
	Of eighteen yeris ald or litill mor of age:	
	Als born scho was till part of heretage.	*Also; [a] portion of [an] inheritance*
	Hyr fadyr was of worschipe and renoune,	
	And Hew Braidfute he hecht of Lammyngtoune,	*was called*
585	As feylle othir was in the contré cald;	*many others; region called*
	Befor tyme thai gentill men war of ald.	*Formerly; old*
	Bot this gud man and als his wiff wes ded.	
	The madyn than wyst of no othir rede,	*knew; course [of action]*
	Bot still scho duelt on trewbute in the toune	*tribute*
590	And purchest had King Eduuardis protectiounne.	
	Servandys with hyr, of freyndis at hyr will,	*servants; ready at hand*
	Thus leyffyt scho without desyr of ill;	*lived; wishing ill [of anyone]*
	A quiet hous as scho mycht hald in wer,	
	For Hesylryg had done hyr mekill der,	*her great injury*
595	Slayne hyr brodyr, quhilk eldast wes and ayr.	*heir*
	All sufferyt scho and rycht lawly hyr bar.	*meekly carried herself*
	Amyabill, so benyng, war and wys,	*Agreeable; gracious, prudent*
	Curtas and swete, fulfillyt of gentrys,	*accomplished in noble conduct*
	Weyll rewllyt of tong, rycht haill of contenance,	*Discreet in speech; fresh*
600	Of vertuous scho was worthy till avance;	*In virtues she was praiseworthy*
	Hummylly hyr led and purchest a gud name,	*Humbly she led [her life]; obtained*
	Of ilkyn wicht scho kepyt hyr fra blame.	*She took care to give no one cause for blame*
	Trew rychtwys folk a gret favour hir lent.	*virtuous; granted*
	Apon a day to the kyrk as scho went,	
605	Wallace hyr saw as he his eyne can cast.	*looked around*
	The prent of luff him punyeit at the last	*love; pierced*

---

[1] *No English [man] could find fault with them, poor nor rich*

The Wallace

	So asprely, throuch bewté of that brycht,	*sharply; fair [lady]*
	With gret unes in presence bid he mycht.	*difficulty in [her] presence remain*
	He knew full weyll hyr kynrent and hyr blud	*kinsfolk; lineage*
610	And how scho was in honest oys and gud.	*lived an honorable and good life*
	Quhill wald he think to luff hyr our the laiff,	*Sometimes; resolve; above all others*
	And othir quhill he thocht on his dissaiff,	*other times; remembered his betrayal*
	How that hys men was brocht to confusioun	*destruction*
	Throw his last luff he had in Saynct Jhonstoun.	*the last lady he loved*
615	Than wald he think to leiff and lat our slyd,	*resolved to leave and forget [her]*
	Bot that thocht lang in his mynd mycht nocht byd.	*stay*
	He tauld Kerle of his new lusty baille,	*pleasant suffering*
	Syne askit him of his trew best consaill.	*Then; loyal [and] best counsel*
	"Maister," he said, "als fer as I haiff feyll,	*as far as I know [about love]*
620	Of lyklynes it may be wondir weill.	*In all likelihood; very well*
	Sen ye sa luff, tak hir in mariage.	*Since*
	Gudlye scho is, and als has heretage.	*She is handsome; [an] inheritance*
	Suppos at yhe in luffyng feill amys,	*Although you were wronged in love*
	Gret God forbede it suld be so with this!"	
625	"To mary thus I can nocht yeit attend:	*marry; expect*
	I wald of wer fyrst se a finaill end.	*war*
	I will no mor allayne to my luff gang.	*alone; go*
	Tak tent to me or dreid we suffer wrang.	*Heed me; fear*
	To proffer luff thus sone I wald nocht preffe;	*propose marriage; soon; try*
630	Mycht I leyff off, in wer I lik to leyff.	*leave; war; live*
	Quhat is this luff? Nothing bot folychnes.	*love; foolishness*
	It may reiff men bathe witt and stedfastnes."	*deprive men [of]*
	Than said he thus: "This will nocht graithly be,	*readily*
	Amors and wer at anys to ryng in me.	*Love and war; once; rule*
635	Rycht suth it is, stude I in blis of luffe,	*true; [if] I enjoyed the happiness*
	Quhar dedis war I suld the bettir pruff.	*I should the better succeed in feats of arms*
	Bot weyle I wait quhar gret ernyst is in thocht	*know; the mind is anxious*
	It lattis wer in the wysest wys be wrocht,	*prevents war; fought*
	Les gyf it be bot only till a deid;	*Unless; one deed*
640	Than he that thinkis on his luff to speid,	*prosper*
	He may do weill, haiff he fortoun and grace.	*if he has*
	Bot this standis all in ane othir cas:	*things stand differently in this case*
	A gret kynryk with feill fayis ourset.	*kingdom [is] with many enemies overrun*
	Rycht hard it is amendis for to get	*to obtain amends [from them]*
645	At anys of thaim and wyrk the observance	*And at the same time perform the duties*

Book 5

	Quhilk langis luff and all his frevill chance.	belong [to]; fickle fortune
	Sampill I haif; this me forthinkis sar;	Experience; I sorely regret this
	I trow to God it sall be so no mar.	
	The trewth I knaw of this and hyr lynage.	
650	I knew nocht hyr, tharfor I lost a gage."	her (the maid in St. Johnstone); pledge
	To Kerle he thus argownd in this kynd,	debated; manner
	Bot gret desyr remaynyt intill his mynd	
	For to behald that frely of fassoun.	behold; lovely lady
	A quhill he left and come nocht in the toun;	desisted; came
655	On othir thing he maid his witt to walk,	He kept his thoughts on other things
	Prefand giff he mycht of that langour slak.	Endeavoring if; distress slake
	Quhen Kerle saw he sufferit payne forthi,	on account of this
	"Der schir," he said, "ye leiff in slogardy.	you live in idleness
	Go se youre luf, than sall yhe get comfort."	beloved
660	At his consaill he walkit for to sport,	went out; play
	Onto the kyrke quhar scho maid residence.	lingered
	Scho knew him weill, bot as of eloquence	speech
	Scho durst nocht weill in presens till him kyth.	disclose her mind in his presence
	Full sor scho dred or Sotheron wald him myth,	feared [the] English; observe
665	For Hesilryg had a mater new begone	begun
	And hyr desirde in mariage till his sone.	son
	With hir madyn thus Wallace scho besocht	beseeched
	To dyne with hyr and prevaly hym brocht	secretly
	Throuch a garden scho had gart wyrk of new,	had had made recently
670	So Inglismen nocht of thar metyng knew.	
	Than kissit he this gudlé with plesance,	comely [lady]; pleasure
	Syne hyr besocht rycht hartly of quentance.	beseeched ardently; friendship
	Scho ansuerd hym with humyll wordis wise:	humble
	"War my quentance rycht worthi for till pryse	were; friendship; prize
675	Yhe sall it haiff, als God me saiff in saille;	as God save my soul
	Bot Inglismen gerris our power faill	cause; [to] fail
	Throuch violence of thaim and thar barnage,	baronage
	At has weill ner destroyt our lynage."	That; lineage
	Quhen Wallace hard hyr plenye petously	lament pitifully
680	Agrevit he was in hart rycht gretumly.	Grief-stricken; greatly
	Bathe ire and luff him set intill a rage,	Both; passion
	Bot nocht forthi he soberyt his curage.	nevertheless; moderated; feelings
	Of his mater he tald as I said ayr	concerns; earlier
	To that gudlye, how luff him strenyeit sar.	love constrained him grievously

65

The Wallace

685	Scho ansuerd him rycht resonably agayne	back
	And said: "I sall to your service be bayne	I shall be ready to serve you
	With all plesance in honest causis haill;	wholly
	And I trast yhe wald nocht set till assaill,	trust; attempt to
	For yhoure worschipe, to do me dyshonour,	Because of your honor
690	And I a maid and standis in mony stour	struggles
	Fra Inglismen to saiff my womanheid,	preserve my womanly honor
	And cost has maid to kepe me fra thar dreid.	incurred expense; protect; danger
	With my gud wyll I wyll no lemman be	paramour
	To no man born, tharfor me think suld yhe	
695	Desyr me nocht bot intill gudlynas.	honorably
	Perchance ye think I war to law purchas	Perhaps; would be too low a prize
	For tyll attend to be your rychtwys wyff.	To expect; lawful
	In your service I wald oys all my lyff.	work
	Her I beseik for your worschipe in armys,	appeal to your
700	Yhe charge me nocht with no ungudly harmys,	do not subject me to unseemly
	Bot me defend for worschipe of your blude."	
	Quhen Wallace weyll hyr trew tayll understud,	honest speech
	As in a part hym thocht it was resoun	right
	Of hyr desir, tharfor till conclusioun	[To accede to] her wish
705	He thankit hyr, and said, "Gif it mycht be	If
	Throuch Goddis will that our kynryk war fre,	kingdom was
	I wald yow wed with all hartlie plesance;	heartfelt joy
	Bot as this tym I may nocht tak sic chance,	
	And for this caus, none othir, now I crayff;	
710	A man in wer may nocht all plesance haiff."	at war
	Of thar talk than I can tell yow no mar	more
	To my purpos, quhat band that thai maid thar.	agreement
	Conclud thai thus and syne to dyner went.	then
	The sayr grevans ramaynyt in his entent,	He remained sorely distressed [by] grievance
715	Los of his men and lusty payne of luff.	[Caused by] loss; pleasant
	His leiff he tuk at that tyme to ramuff,	leave; depart
	Syne to Gilbank he past or it was nycht.	before
	Apon the morn with his four men him dycht;	prepared
	To the Corhed without restyng he raid,	Corehead (near Moffat); rode
720	Quhar his nevo Thom Haliday him baid,	nephew; awaited him
	And Litill als, Eduuard his cusyng der,	dear cousin
	Quhilk was full blyth quhen he wyst him so ner,	knew; close
	Thankand gret God that send him saiff agayne,	safe

Book 5

	For mony demyt he was in Strathern slayn.	*believed*
725	Gud cher thai maid all out thai dayis thre.	*They feasted*
	Than Wallace said that he desirde to se	
	Lowmaban toun and Ynglismen that was thar.	*Lochmaben*
	On the ferd day thai bownyt thaim to far;	*fourth; prepared to go*
	Sixteen he was of gudlé chevalré;	*fine knights*
730	In the Knokwood he levyt all bot thre.	*left*
	Thom Halyday went with him to the toun;	
	Eduuard Litill and Kerle maid thaim boun.	*ready*
	Till ane ostrye Thom Halyday led thaim rycht,	*To an inn; straight*
	And gaiff commaund thar dyner suld be dycht.	*prepared*
735	Till her a mes in gud entent thai yeid;	*To hear a mass with good intent; went*
	Of Inglismen thai trowit thar was no dreid.	*believed; danger*
	Ane Clyffurd come, was emys sone to the lord,	*uncle's son (i.e., cousin)*
	And four with him, the trewth for to record.	*to tell the truth*
	Quha awcht thai hors in gret heithing he ast.	*owned; derision; asked*
740	He was full sle and ek had mony cast.	*sly; also; tricked*
	The gud wyff said, till applessyt him best,	*mistress of the house; please*
	"Four gentill men is cummyn out of the west."	*[who] come from*
	"Quha devill thaim maid so galy for to ryd?	*Who [the] devil; handsomely; ride*
	In faith with me a wed thar most abide.	*pledge; must*
745	Thir lewit Scottis has leryt litill gud:	*These ignorant; have learned*
	Lo! all thar hors ar schent for faut of blud."	*ruined because of defective lineage*
	Into gret scorn withoutyn wordis mayr	*more*
	The taillis all of thai four hors thai schayr.	*sheared*
	The gud wyff cryede and petuously couth gret	*wept*
750	So Wallace come and couth the captayne mete.	*met the captain*
	A woman tald how thai his hors had schent.	*injured*
	For propyr ire he grew in matelent.	*pure; rage*
	He folowid fast and said, "Gud freynd abid,	*wait*
	Service to tak for thi craft in this tyde.	*Payment; occupation; time*
755	Marschell thou art without commaund of me;	*Blacksmith; instruction from*
	Reward agayne me think I suld pay thee.	
	Sen I of laitt now come owt of the west	*Since I recently*
	In this contré, a barbour of the best	*region; barber*
	To cutt and schaiff, and that a wondir gude,	*shave; marvelously well*
760	Now thow sall feyll how I oys to lat blud."	*am accustomed; let*
	With his gud suerd the captayn has he tayn,	*sword; struck*

The Wallace

      Quhill hors agayne he marscheld nevir nayn;[1]
      Anothir sone apon the hed strak he, — *Another soon*
      Quhill chaftis and cheyk upon the gait can fle. — *So that; street; flew*
765 Be that his men the tothir twa had slayne. — *By that [time]; other two*
      Thar hors thai tuk and graithit thaim full bayne
      Out of the toun; for dyner baid thai nayne.[2]
      The wyff he payit that maid so petuous mayne. — *woman; piteous lament*
      Than Inglismen fra that chyftayne wes dede — *once; was dead*
770 To Wallace socht fra mony syndry stede. — *sought*
      Of the castell come cruell men and keyne. — *From; bold; fierce*
      Quhen Wallace has thar sodand semlé seyne — *quick assembly seen*
      Towart sum strenth he bownyt him to ryd, — *stronghold; prepared*
      For than him thocht it was no tyme to byd. — *wait*
775 Thar hors bled fast, that gert him dredyng haiff; — *heavily; made him fearful*
      Of his gud men he wald haif had the laiff. — *rest*
      To the Knokwoode withowtyn mor thai raid, — *without delay*
      Bot intill it no sojornyng he maid; — *tarrying*
      That wood as than was nothir thik no lang. — *neither dense nor*
780 His men he gat, syn lychtyt for to gang — *then dismounted; go*
      Towart a hicht and led thar hors a quhill. — *hill; while*
      The Inglismen was than within a myill,
      On fresche hors rydand full hastely;
      Sevyn scor and ma was in thar chevalry. — *company of horsemen*
785 The Scottis lap on quhen thai thar power saw, — *leapt on [horseback]; army*
      Frawart the south thaim thocht it best to draw. — *Away from*
      Than Wallace said, "It is no witt in wer — *skill*
      With our power to byd thaim bargane her.[3]
      Yon ar gud men, tharfor I rede that we — *counsel*
790 Evirmar seik quhill God send sum supplé." — *press on until; help*
      Halyday said, "We sall do your consaille,
      Bot sayr I dreid or thir hurt hors will fayll." — *sorely; fear; these*
      The Inglismen in burnyst armour cler — *burnished; bright*
      Be than to thaim approchyt wondir ner. — *By then; very near*

---

[1] *So that he never again marshaled any horses*

[2] Lines 766–67: *Their horses they took and promptly made themselves ready to leave / The town; they did not stay for dinner*

[3] *With our [smaller] force to wait to [give] them battle here*

Book 5

795	Horssyt archaris schot fast and wald nocht spar;	*Archers on horseback shot; spare*
	Of Wallace men thai woundyt twa full sar.	*grievously*
	In ir he grew quhen that he saw thaim bleid;	*anger he (Wallace)*
	Himself retornde and on thaim sone he yeid,	*turned back; soon; advanced*
	Sixteen with him that worthi was in wer.	*war*
800	Of thai formast rycht freschly doun thai ber.	*vigorously; bore*
	At that retorn fifteen in feild war slayne;	*counter-attack*
	The laiff fled fast to thar power agayne.	*rest; army*
	Wallace folowid with his gud chevalrye.	*company of mounted knights*
	Thom Halyday in wer was full besye,	*fighting; very busy*
805	A buschement saw that cruell was to ken,	*An ambush; fierce; indeed*
	Twa hundreth haill of weill gerit Inglismen.	*well-armed*
	"Uncle," he said, "our power is to smaw;	
	Of this playne feild I consaill yow to draw.	*From open battlefield; advise; withdraw*
	To few we ar agayne yon fellone staill."	*Too; fierce armed party*
810	Wallace relevit full sone at his consaill.	*rallied [his men] quickly on*
	At the Corheid full fayne thai wald haif beyne,	*gladly they would have been*
	Bot Inglismen weyll has thar purpos seyne.	
	In playne battaill thai folowid hardely;	
	In danger thus thai held thaim awfully.	*formidably*
815	Hew of Morland on Wallace folowid fast;	
	He had befor maid mony Scottis agast.	*terrified*
	Haldyn he was of wer the worthiast man	
	In north Ingland, with thaim was leiffand than.	*living then*
	In his armour weill forgyt of fyne steill	
820	A nobill cursour bur him bath fast and weill.	*steed carried*
	Wallace retorned besyd a burly ayk	*turned round; strong oak*
	And on him set a fellone sekyr straik;	*grievous firm blow*
	Baith cannell bayne and schulder blaid in twa,	*[Cutting] both collar-bones*
	Throuch the myd cost the gud suerd gert he ga.	*rib; sword caused*
825	His speyr he wan and als the coursour wicht,	*spear; captured; strong*
	Syne left his awn for he had lost his mycht;	*Then; own; become feeble*
	For lak of blud he mycht no forthir gang.	*go*
	Wallace on hors the Sotheron men amang,	*English*
	His men relevit, that douchty was in deid,	*relieved; valiant; deed*
830	Him to reskew out of that felloune dreid.	*terrible danger*
	Cruell strakis forsuth thar mycht be seyne	*Fierce strokes truly*
	On athir side quhill blud ran on the greyne.	*either; green (i.e., grass)*
	Rycht peralous the semlay was to se:	*encounter*

The Wallace

	Hardy and hat contenyt the fell melle,	*heated continued the fierce fighting*
835	Skew and reskew of Scottis and Inglis als.	*Rescue and rescue again*
	Sum kervyt bran in sondir, sum the hals,	*flesh; neck*
	Sum hurt, sum hynt, sum derffly dong to dede;	*wounded; captured; violently killed*
	The hardy Scottis so steryt in that sted,	*bestirred themselves; place*
	With Halyday on fute bauldly that baid,	*foot boldly; withstood*
840	Amang Sotheron a full gret rowme thai maid.	*breach*
	Wallas on hors, in hand a nobill sper,	*spear*
	Out throuch thaim raid as gud chyftayne in wer.	*rode; war*
	Thre slew he thar or that his sper was gayn,	*before*
	Than his gud suerd in hand sone has tayne,	*sword; soon*
845	Hewyt on hard with dyntis sad and sar;	*Hacked vigorously; blows heavy; grievous*
	Quhat ane he hyt grevyt the Scottis no mar.	*Whomever he struck annoyed; more*
	Fra Sotheron men be naturall resone knew	*Once English*
	How with a straik a man evir he slew,	*blow; every [time]*
	Than merveld thai he wes so mekill of mayne;	*marveled; mightily strong*
850	For thar best man in that kynd he had slayne,	*manner*
	That his gret strenth agayne him helpyt nocht	
	Nor nayne othir in contrar Wallace socht.	*no other against*
	Than said thai all, "Lest he in strenth untayne	*If he continues; uncaptured*
	This haill kynryk he wyll wyn him allayne."	*whole kingdom; win back; alone*
855	Thai left the feild syne to thar power fled	*then*
	And tald thar lord how evill the formest sped.	*ill; succeeded*

[*Wallace and his men leave the field, having sustained no losses. He stays at the rear defending his retreating men until his horse gives out near Queensberry Hill. Wallace is joined by Kirkpatrick and his twenty men and by Sir John Graham and thirty followers just as the English are gaining on him, and together they win the day. He proceeds to take Lochmaben Castle with the help of his nephew, Thom Halliday, and Crawford Castle with aid of Edward Litill.* (Lines 857–1140)]

Book 6

	Than passit was utas of Feviryher	*octaves*
	And part of Marche of rycht degestioune;	*by*
	Apperyd than the last moneth of wer,	*spring (i.e., April)*
	The syng of somir with his suet sessoun,	*sign; sweet season*
5	Be that Wallace of Dundaff maid him boune;	*from; ready [to leave]*

Book 6

	His leyff he tuk and to Gilbank can fair.	*went*
	The rewmour rais throuch Scotland up and doun,	*alarm*
	With Inglismen, that Wallace leiffand war.	*Among Englishmen; was living*
	In Aperill quhen cleithit is but veyne	*clothed; without doubt*
10	The abill ground be wyrking of natur,	*fertile; by*
	And woddis has won thar worthy weid of greyne;	*woods; got; covering of green*
	Quhen Nympheus in beldyn of his bour	*Nymphs; shelter; bower*
	With oyle and balm fullfillit of suet odour,	*sweet*
	Faunis maceris, as thai war wount to gang,	*Faunis' macers; accustomed*
15	Walkyn thar cours in eviry casuall hour	*Follow*
	To glaid the huntar with thar merye sang.	*gladden; song*
	In this samyn tyme to him approchit new	*returned*
	His lusty payne, the quhilk I spak of ayr.	*pleasurable pain; earlier*
	Be luffis cas he thocht for to persew	*According to love's chance; follow*
20	In Laynryk toune and thiddir he can fayr;	*went*
	At residence a quhill ramaynit thair	*lingered there awhile*
	In hyr presence as I said of befor.	*her*
	Thocht Inglismen was grevyt at his repayr,	*[Even] though; displeased; repairing there*
	Yeit he desyrd the thing that sat him sor.	*troubled him extremely*
25	The feyr of wer rewllyt him on sic wis	*fire of spring; such [a] way*
	He likit weyll with that gudlye to be.	*comely [one]*
	Quhill wald he think of danger for to rys	*At times he would; on account of*
	And othir quhill out of hir presens fle.	*times*
	"To ces of wer it war the best for me.	*war*
30	Thus wyn I nocht bot sadnes on all syde.	*gain I nothing except*
	Sall nevir man thus cowartys in me se!	*cowardice*
	To wer I will for chance that may betyd!	*war*
	Qwhat is this luff? It is bot gret myschance	*misfortune*
	That me wald bryng fra armes utterly.	*would distract me from*
35	I will nocht los my worschip for plesance;	*lose; honor*
	In wer I think my tyme till occupy.	*war*
	Yeit hyr to luff I will nocht lat forthy;	*to love her; cease for that reason*
	Mor sall I desyr hyr frendschip to reserve	*keep*
	Fra this day furth than evir befor did I,	
40	In fer of wer quhethir I leiff or sterve."	*state of war; live or die*

The Wallace

	Qwhat suld I say? Wallace was playnly set	*should; determined*
	To luff hyr best in all this warld so wid,	*wide*
	Thinkand he suld of his desyr to get;	
	And so befell be concord in a tid	*agreement; while*
45	That scho was maid at his commaund to bid;	*undertook; obey*
	And thus began the styntyn of this stryff,	*ending; debate*
	Begynnyng band with graith witnes besyd.[1]	
	Myn auctor sais scho was his rychtwys wyff.	*rightful*
	Now leiff in pees, now leiff in gud concord,	*live*
50	Now leyff in blys, now leiff in haill plesance,	*happiness; complete joy*
	For scho be chos has bath hyr luff and lord.	*by choice*
	He thinkis als luff did him hye avance,	*exalt high*
	So evynly held be favour the ballance,	*evenly*
	Sen he at will may lap hyr in his armys.	*wrap her (embrace)*
55	Scho thankit God of hir fre happy chance	*great good fortune*
	For in his tyme he was the flour of armys.	*flower*
	Fortoun him schawit hyr fygowrt doubill face.	*marked*
	Feyll sys or than he had beyne set abuff;	*Many times before then; elevated*
	In presoune now, delyverit now throw grace,	
60	Now at unes, now into rest and ruff;	*in distress; quiet*
	Now weyll at wyll weyldand his plesand luff,	*in gladness enjoying his pleasing love*
	As thocht himselff out of adversité;	*[he] thought himself free from*
	Desyring ay his manheid for to pruff,	*always; prove*
	In curage set apon the stagis hye.	*placed; high [on Fortune's wheel]*
65	The verray treuth I can nocht graithly tell	*full; readily*
	Into this lyff how lang at thai had beyne;	*How long they enjoyed this [married] life*
	Throuch naturall cours of generacioune befell	*it happened*
	A child was chevyt thir twa luffaris betuene,	*conceived these two lovers*
	Quhilk gudly was, a maydyn brycht and schene.	*comely; fair*
70	So forthyr furth be evyn tyme of hyr age	*later on when she was the right age*
	A Squier Schaw, as that full weyll was seyne,	
	This lyflat man hyr gat in mariage.	*wealthy; got her*

---

[1] *[A] beginning made by agreement before ready witnesses*

Book 6

    Rycht gudlye men come of this lady ying. — *are descended from; young*
    Forthyr as now of hyr I spek no mar.
75 Bot Wallace furth intill his wer can ryng; — *went on with his war*
    He mycht nocht ces, gret curage so him bar; — *cease; carried forward*
    Sotheroun to sla for dreid he wald nocht spar, — *Englishmen; spare*
    And thai oft sys feill causis till hym wrocht, — *very often provoked him*
    Fra that tyme furth quhilk movit hym fer mar, — *From; moved*
80 That never in warld out of his mynd was brocht.

    Now leiff thi myrth, now leiff thi haill plesance, — *leave; great pleasure*
    Now leiff thi blis, now leiff thi childis age, — *childhood*
    Now leiff thi youth, now folow thi hard chance,
    Now leyff thi lust, now leiff thi mariage, — *desire*
85 Now leiff thi luff, for thow sall los a gage — *love; lose a pledge*
    Quhilk nevir in erd sall be redemyt agayne. — *earth; redeemed*
    Folow Fortoun and all hir fers owtrage. — *violence*
    Go leiff in wer, go leiff in cruell payne. — *live; war; fierce*

    Fy on Fortoun, fy on thi frevall quheyll, — *fickle wheel*
90 Fy on thi traist, for her it has no lest; — *[good] faith; here; lasting*
    Thow transfigowryt Wallace out of his weill — *completely changed; [good] fortune*
    Quhen he traistyt for till haiff lestyt best. — *continued [enjoying] the best [fortune]*
    His plesance her till him was bot a gest; — *happiness here; jest*
    Throw thi fers cours that has na hap to ho, — *fierce*
95 Him thow ourthrew out of his likand rest. — *pleasing*
    Fra gret plesance in wer, travaill and wo. — *From great favor in war, [to] suffering*

    Quhat is Fortoune? Quha dryffis the dett so fast? — *hastens; destiny*
    We wait thar is bathe weill and wykit chance, — *good and evil*
    Bot this fals warld with mony doubill cast, — *double dealing (i.e., tricks)*
100 In it is nocht bot verray variance;
    It is nothing till hevynly governance. — *to*
    Than pray we all to the Makar abov, — *above*
    Quhilk has in hand of justry the ballance, — *justice*
    That he us grant of his der lestand love. — *everlasting love*

105 Herof as now forthyr I spek no mar, — *On this for now*
    Bot to my purpos schortly will I fayr. — *go*
    Tuelff hundreth yer tharto nynté and sevyn — *1297*

The Wallace

      Fra Cryst wes born the rychtwis king of hevyn,
      Wilyham Wallace into gud liking gais   *happily goes*
110 In Laynrik toun amang his mortaill fais.   *enemies*
      The Inglismen that evir fals has beyne,
      With Hesilryg, quhilk cruell was and keyn,   *ruthless*
      And Robert Thorn, a felloune, sutell knycht,   *fierce, cunning*
      Has founde the way be quhat meyn best thai mycht,   *means*
115 How that thai suld mak contrar to Wallace
      Be argument, as he come upon cace   *circumstance*
      On fra the kyrk that was without the toun,
      Quhill thar power mycht be in harnes boun.   *force; armor ready*
      Schyr Jhon the Grayme, bathe hardy, wys, and trew,
120 To Laynrik come, gud Wallace to persew   *seek*
      Of his weyllfayr, as he full oft had seyne.
      Gud men he had in cumpany fifteen
      And Wallace nine, thai war na feris ma.   *companions*
      Upon the morn unto the mes thai ga,   *they attended mass*
125 Thai and thar men graithit in gudly greyn,   *dressed in fine green [clothing]*
      For the sesson sic oys full lang has beyne.   *such practice*
      Quhen sadly thai had said thar devocioune,   *solemnly; their prayers*
      Ane argunde thaim as thai went throuch the toun,   *One [of the English] challenged*
      The starkast man that Hesylryg than knew,   *strongest*
130 And als he had of lychly wordis ynew.   *contemptuous; enough*
      He salust thaim as it war bot in scorn: *saluted; only*
      "Dewgar, gud day, bone senyhour and gud morn."   *God preserve you; good gentleman*
      "Quhom scornys thow?" quod Wallace, "Quha lerd thee?"[1]
      "Quhy, schir," he said, "come yhe nocht new our se?   *recently from overseas*
135 Pardown me than, for I wend ye had beyne   *thought*
      Ane inbasset to bryng ane uncouth queyne."   *ambassador; foreign*
      Wallace ansuerd, "Sic pardoune as we haiff
      In oys to gyff thi part thow sall nocht craiff."   *Habitually; crave*
      "Sen ye ar Scottis yeit salust sall ye be: *yet you shall be given a greeting*
140 Gude deyn, dawch lard, bach lowch, banyoch a de."
      Ma Sotheroune men to thaim assemblit ner.   *More English; near*
      Wallace as than was laith to mak a ster.   *loath; stir*

---

[1] *"Whom do you scorn?" said Wallace. "Who taught you?"*

Book 6

	Ane maid a scrip and tyt at his lang suorde.[1]	
	"Hald still thi hand," quod he, "and spek thi word."	
145	"With thi lang suerd thow makis mekill bost."	
	"Tharoff," quod he, "thi deme maid litill cost."	lady uttered little [on your account]
	"Quhat caus has thow to wer that gudlye greyne?"	wear; handsome green
	"My maist caus is bot for to mak thee teyne."	greatest reason is only; angry
	"Quhat suld a Scot do with so fair a knyff?"	dagger (penis)
150	"Sa said the prest that last janglyt thi wyff.	priest; lay with
	That woman lang has tillit him so fair	served
	Quhill that his child worthit to be thine ayr."	Until; grew; heir
	"Me think," quod he, "thow dryvys me to scorn."	
	"Thi deme has beyne japyt or thow was born."	mother; tricked before
155	The power than assemblyt thaim about,	armed company
	Twa hundreth men that stalwart war and stout.	brave were; bold
	The Scottis saw thar power was cummand,	army; coming
	Schir Robert Thorn and Hesilryg at hand,	close by
	The multitude wyth wapynnys burnist beyne.	burnished well
160	The worthi Scottis, quhilk cruell was and keyne,	fierce; bold
	Amang Sotherone sic dyntis gaiff that tyd	[the] English such blows; time
	Quhill blud on breid byrstyt fra woundis wyd.	Until; spurted everywhere from; wide
	Wallace in stour wes cruelly fechtand;	combat; fiercely fighting
	Fra a Sotheroune he smat off the rycht hand,	an Englishman; severed
165	And quhen that carle of fechtyng mycht no mar,	fellow; fighting; more
	With the left hand in ire held a buklar;	shield
	Than fra the stowmpe the blud out spurgyt fast,	stump; gushed
	In Wallace face aboundandlye can out cast;	splattered across Wallace's face
	Into gret part it merryt of his sicht.	It spoiled his sight a great deal
170	Schyr Jhone the Grayme a straik has tayne him rycht	blow; delivered
	With his gud suerd upon the Sotherone syr,	English man
	Derffly to ded draiff him into that ire.	Killed him outright in his rage
	The perell was rycht awfull, hard, and strang,	frightening
	The stour enduryt mervalusly and lang.	fighting; long
175	The Inglismen gaderit fellone fast;	extremely
	The worthi Scottis the gait left at the last.	street
	Quhen thai had slayne and woundyt mony man,	many men

---

[1] *One made an obscene gesture and pulled at his long sword (penis)*

The Wallace

	Till Wallace in the gaynest way thai can	*To; nearest*
	Thai passit sune, defendand tham richt weill.	*soon*
180	He and Schir Jhone with suerdis stiff of steill	*swords; steel*
	Behind thar men, quhill thai the gett had tayne.[1]	
	The woman than, quhilk was full will of vayne,	*in despair*
	The perell saw with fellone noyis and dyne,	*terrible; din*
	Gat up the gett and leit thaim entir in.	*Raised the gate*
185	Throuch till a strenth thai passit of that steid.	*to a stronghold; from; place*
	Fifty Sotheroun upon the gait wes dede.	*Englishmen; street*
	This fair woman did besines and hir mycht	*everything in her power*
	The Inglismen to tary with a slycht,	*delay; stratagem*
	Quhill that Wallace onto the wood wes past;	*While; slipped away to the wood*
190	Than Cartlane Craggis thai persewit full fast.	*made their way*
	Quhen Sotheroun saw that chapyt wes Wallace	*escaped*
	Agayne thai turnyt, the woman tuk on cace,	*returned; arrested the woman*
	Put hir to dede, I can nocht tell yow how;	*death*
	Of sic mater I may nocht tary now.	*On such [a] subject*
195	Quhar gret dulle is but rademyng agayne	*grief; without remedy*
	Newyn of it is bot ekyng of payne.	*Renewing; increase*
	A trew woman, had servit hir full lang,	*loyal; [who] had served*
	Out of the toun the gaynest way can gang,	*nearest; went*
	Till Wallace tald how all this deid was done.	*To; deed*
200	The paynfull wo socht till his hart full sone;	*went straight to his heart*
	War nocht for schayme he had socht to the ground	*shame; fallen*
	For bytter baill that in his breyst was bound.	*sorrow; kept fast*
	Schir Jhone the Grayme, bath wys, gentill, and fre,	*noble, and generous*
	Gret murnynge maid that peté was to se,	*mourning*
205	And als the laiff that was assemblit thar	*also the rest*
	For pur sorou wepyt with hart full sar.	*pure; sorely*
	Quhen Wallace feld thar curage was so small	*sensed*
	He fenyeit him for to comfort thaim all.	*concealed his feelings*
	"Ces men," he said, "this is a butlas payne.	*Cease; unavailing (bootless)*
210	We can nocht now chewys hyr lyff agayne."	*bring her back to life*
	Unes a word he mycht bryng out for teyne;	*Scarcely; utter; suffering*
	The bailfull teris bryst braithly fra his eyne.	*woeful; burst suddenly from; eyes*
	Sichand he said, "Sall nevir man me se	*Sighing*

---

[1] *[Remained] behind their men until they reached the gate*

Book 6

	Rest intill eys quhill this deid wrokyn be,	*at ease until; be avenged*
215	The saklace slauchtir of hir blith and brycht,	*innocent*
	That I avow to the Makar of mycht,	
	That of that nacioune I sall nevir forber	*spare*
	Yhong nor ald that abill is to wer.	*old; is fit to fight*
	Preystis no wemen I think nocht for to sla	*Priests nor; slay*
220	In my defaut, bot thai me causing ma.	*Wrongfully, unless they give me cause*
	Schir Jhon," he said, "lat all this murnyng be,	*mourning*
	And for hir saik thar sall ten thousand de.	*die*
	Quhar men may weipe thar curage is the les;	*Whenever; less*
	It slakis ire of wrang thai suld radres."	*lessens anger [provoked] by wrongs; redress*
225	Of thar complaynt as now I say no mar.	*lament; more*
	Gud Awchinlek of Gilbank, duelyt thar,	*who dwelt there*
	Quhen he hard tell of Wallace vexacioune,	*heard*
	To Cartlane Wood with ten men maid him boune.	*made his way*
	Wallace he fand sum part within the nycht;	
230	To Laynryk toun in all haist thai thaim dycht.	*set out*
	The wache of thaim as than had litill heid;	*sentries; heed*
	Partyt thar men and divers gatis yeid.	*Divided; ways went*
	Schir Jhone the Grayme and his gud cumpany	
	To Schir Robert of Thorn full fast thai hy.	*hasten*
235	Wallace and his to Hesilrige sone past	
	In a heich hous quhar he was slepand fast,	*high; sound asleep*
	Straik at the dure with his fute hardely	*Kicked the door*
	Quhill bar and brais in the flair he gart ly.	*Until; floor; made*
	The schirreff criyt, "Quha makis that gret deray?"	*Who; din*
240	"Wallace," he said, "that thow has socht all day.	
	The womannis dede, will God, thow sall der by."	*woman's death, God willing; pay for*
	Hesilrige thocht it was na tyme to ly;	*lie [in bed]*
	Out of that hous full fayne he wald haiff beyne.	*gladly*
	The nycht was myrk yeit Wallace has him seyne,	*dark yet*
245	Freschly him straik as he come in gret ire,	*Vigorously; in a rage*
	Apon the heid birstit throuch bayne and lyr.	*head broke; bone and flesh*
	The scherand suerd glaid till his coler bayne,	*cutting; went smoothly*
	Out our the stayr amang thaim is he gayne.	*over*
	Gude Awchinlek trowit nocht that he was dede,	*did not believe*
250	Thrys with a knyff stekit him in that stede.	*Thrice; stabbed; place*
	The scry about rais rudly on the streyt;	*noise; rose loudly; street*
	Feyll of the layff war fulyeit undir feyt.	*Many; rest; trampled*

The Wallace

	Yong Hesilryg and wicht Wallace is met;	*bold*
	A sekyr strak Wilyham has on him set,	*sure blow*
255	Derffly to dede off the stair dang him doun.	*Violently to death; struck; down*
	Mony thai slew that nycht in Laynrik toune,	
	Sum grecis lap and sum stekit within.	*leapt up the flight of stairs; stabbed*
	A-ferd thai war with hidwis noyis and dyne.	*Frightened; were; hideous; din*
	Schir Jhone the Grayme had set the hous in fyr	
260	Quhar Robert Thorn was brynt up bayne and lyr.	*burnt up bone and flesh*
	Twelve scor thai slew that wes of Ingland born;	
	Wemen thai levit and preistis on the morn	
	To pas thar way, of blys and gudis bar,	
	And swor that thai agayne suld cum no mar.	
265	Quhen Scottis hard thir fyne tithingis of new	*heard this excellent news*
	Out of all part to Wallace fast thai drew,	*From all over*
	Plenyst the toun quhilk was thar heretage.	*Settled*
	Thus Wallace straiff agayne that gret barnage.	*strove against; barons*
	Sa he begane with strenth and stalwart hand	*So*
270	To chewys agayne sum rowmys of Scotland.	*recover; parts*
	The worthi Scottis that semblit till him thar	*flocked to*
	Chesit him for cheyff, thar chyftayne and ledar.	*Chose*
	Amer Wallang, a suttell terand knycht,	*cunning tyrant*
	In Bothwell duelt, King Eduuardis man full rycht.	*completely*
275	Murray was out, thocht he was rychtwis lord	*exiled, though*
	Of all that land, as trew men will racord;	
	Intill Aran he was duelland that tyd,	*dwelling; time*
	And othir ma, in this land durst nocht bide.	*many others; dared; stay*
	Bot this fals knycht in Bothwell wonnand was.	*(i.e., Wallang); dwelling*
280	A man he gert sone to King Eduuard pas	*made*
	And tald him haill of Wallace ordinance,	*Wallace's actions*
	How he had put his pepill to myschance	*people; misfortune*
	And playnly was ryssyn agayne to ryng.	*had risen; power*
	Grevit tharat rycht gretly wes the king;	*Vexed*
285	Throuch all Ingland he gart his doaris cry	*agents proclaim*
	Power to get, and said he wald planly	*A call to arms; openly*
	In Scotland pas that rewme to statut new.	*realm; rule anew*
	Feill men of wer till him full fast thai drew.	*Many; war*
	The queyne feld weill how that his purpos was;	*perceived; what he intended*
290	Till him scho went, on kneis syne can him as	*To; then asked him*
	He wald resist and nocht in Scotland gang;	*stop; go*

Book 6

	He suld haiff dreid to wyrk so felloune wrang.	*fear; grievous wrong*
	"Crystyne thai ar, yone is thar heretage;	*Christians*
	To reyff that croune that is a gret owtrage."	*steal*
295	For hyr consaill at hayme he wald nocht byde;	*her counsel; home; stay*
	His lordis hym set in Scotland for to ryde.	*He arranged for his lords*
	A Scottis man, than duellyt with Eduuard,	
	Quhen he hard tell that Wallace tuk sic part,	*took such [a] position (i.e., had rebelled)*
	He staw fra thaim als prevalé as he may.	*stole [away]*
300	Into Scotland he come apon a day,	*came*
	Sekand Wallace he maid him reddy boune.	*Seeking; ready to go*
	This Scot was born at Kyle in Rycardtoune;	*Riccarton*
	All Ingland cost he knew it wondir weill,	*England's coast*
	Fra Hull about to Brysto evirilk deill,	*Bristol*
305	Fra Carleill throuch Sandwich that ryoll stede,	*royal place*
	Fra Dover our onto Sanct Beis Hede.	*St. Bee's Head*
	In Pykarté and Flandrys he hade beyne,	*Picardy*
	All Normondé and Frans haill he had seyne;	
	A pursiwant till King Eduuard in wer,	*war*
310	Bot he couth nevir gar him his armes ber.	*make him wear his coat of arms*
	Of gret statur and sum part gray wes he;	*size*
	The Inglismen cald him bot Grymmysbé.	*simply called him*
	To Wallace come and into Kile him fand;	*found*
	He tald him haill the tithandis of Ingland.	*news from*
315	Thai turnyt his name fra tyme thai him knew	*changed*
	And cald him Jop; of ingen he wes trew;	*nature; loyal*
	In all his tyme gud service in him fand;	
	Gaiff him to ber the armes of Scotland.	*bear; [coat of] arms*
	Wallace agayne in Cliddisdaill sone raid	*soon rode*
320	And his power semblit withoutyn baid.	*assembled; delay*
	He gart commaund quha that his pees wald tak,	*decreed*
	A fre remyt he suld ger to thaim mak	*pardon; arrange*
	For alkyn deid that thai had doyne beforn.	*every kind; done*
	The Perseys pees and Schir Ranaldis wes worn.	*had lapsed*
325	Feill till him drew that bauldly durst abid	*Many to; boldly dared to withstand*
	Of Wallace kyn fra mony divers sid.	*kinsfolk*
	Schir Ranald than send him his power haill;	*entire army*
	Himselff durst nocht be knawine in battaill	*known*
	Agayne Sotheroun, for he had made a band	*Against [the] English; bond*
330	Lang tyme befor to hald of thaim his land.	*[A] long time; hold from*

The Wallace

	Adam Wallace past out of Ricardtoun,	
	And Robert Boid with gud men of renoun.	
	Of Cunyngayme and Kille come men of vaill,	*From; Kyle; worth*
	To Laynrik socht on hors, a thousand haill.[1]	
335	Schyr Jhone the Grayme and his gud chevalré,	*band of knights*
	Schir Jhone of Tynto with men that he mycht be,	
	Gud Awchinlek, that Wallace uncle was,	
	Mony trew Scot with that chyftayne couth pas.	*traveled*
	Thre thousand haill of likly men in wer	*in all; men fit for war*
340	And feill on fute quhilk wantyt hors and ger.	*many; lacked; weapons*
	The tyme be this has cummand apon hand,	*By this time; come*
	The awfull ost with Eduuard of Ingland	*awesome army*
	To Beggar come, with sexté thousand men,	
	In wer wedis that cruell war to ken.	*armor; fierce; see*
345	Thai playntyt thar feild with tentis and pailyonis,	*planted*
	Quhar claryowns blew full mony mychty sonis;	*clarions; sounds*
	Plenyst that place with gud vittaill and wyne,	*Supplied; food*
	In cartis brocht thar purviance devyne.	*God-sent provisions*
	The awfull king gert twa harroldis be brocht,	*awesome; made; heralds*
350	Gaiff thaim commaund in all the haist thai mocht	*Ordered; might*
	To charge Wallace, that he sulde cum him till	*command; come to him*
	Withtout promys and put him in his will:	*Unconditionally; submit*
	"Becaus we wait he is a gentill man,	*know; noble*
	Cum in my grace and I sall saiff him than.	*[If he] comes; save*
355	As for his lyff I will apon me tak,	*For [the rest of] his life*
	And efftir this gyff he couth service mak,	*after; if he serves me*
	He sall haiff wage that may him weill suffice.	*payment*
	That rebald wenys for he has done supprice	*rebel is proud; has caused injury*
	To my pepill oft apon aventur.	*by chance*
360	Aganys me he may nocht lang endur:	*Against*
	To this proffyr gaynstandand giff he be,	*If he resists this offer*
	Her I avow he sall be hyngyt hye."	*Here; vow; hanged high*
	A yong squier, was brothir to Fehew,	*Fitzhugh*
	He thocht he wald dysgysit to persew	*disguise himself*
365	Wallace to se that tuk so hie a part;	*undertook so much*
	Born sistir sone he was to King Eduuart.	*He was Edward's nephew (sister's son)*

---

[1] *To Lanark made their way on horses, a thousand in all*

Book 6

	A cot of armes he tuk on him but baid,	*without delay*
	With the harroldis full prevaly he raid	
	To Tynto Hill withoutyn residens,	*waiting*
370	Quhar Wallace lay with his folk at defence.	
	A likly ost as of so few thai fand;	*impressive army for so few; found*
	Till hym thai socht and wald no langar stand.	*They made their way directly to Wallace*
	"Gyff ye be he that rewllis all this thing,[1]	
	Credence we haiff brocht fra our worthi king."	*Credentials*
375	Than Wallace gert thre knychtis till him call,	*summoned*
	Syne red the wryt in presens of thaim all.	*read; writ*
	To thaim he said, "Ansuer ye sall nocht craiff.	*You will not want for an answer*
	Be wryt or word, quhilk likis yow best till haiff?"	*In writing or verbally, which*
	"In wryt," thai said, "it war the liklyast."	*most fitting*
380	Than Wallace thus began to dyt in hast:	*compose a reply hastily*
	"Thow, reyffar-king, chargis me throw cas[2]	
	That I suld cum and put me in thi grace.	
	Gyff I gaynstand thow hechtis till hyng me.	*If I oppose; vow; hang*
	I vow to God and evir I may tak thee	*if ever*
385	Thow sall be hangyt, ane exempill to geiff	*provide*
	To kingis of reyff als lang as I may leiff.	*of [the consequences of] plunder; long; live*
	Thow profferis me thi wage for till haiff.	
	I thee defy power, and all the laiff	*repudiate your power [to rule here]; others*
	At helpis thee her of thi fals nacioun.	*That; here*
390	Will God thow sall be put of this regioune,	*expelled from*
	Or de tharfor, contrar thocht thow had suorn	*even though you had sworn the contrary*
	Thow sall us se or nine houris to morn	*see us before nine o'clock in the morning*
	Battaill to gyff magra of all thi kyn,	*Ready for battle in spite of; countrymen*
	For falsly thow sekis our rewme within."	*to occupy our realm*
395	This wryt he gaiff to the harraldis but mar,	*at once*
	And gud reward he gart delyvir thaim thar.	*had handed to them*
	Bot Jop knew weyll the squier yong Fehew	*young*
	And tald Wallace, for he wes evir trew.	*loyal*
	Than he command that thai suld sone thaim tak.	*seize them immediately*
400	Himselff began a sair cusyng to mak.	*severe accusation*
	"Squier," he said, "sen thow has fenyeit armys,	*falsely assumed [heraldic] arms*

---

[1] *If you are the leader of all this thing (rebellion)*

[2] *You, robber-king, charge me because of a mere circumstance*

The Wallace

	On thee sall fall the fyrst part of thir harmys,	these injuries
	Sampill to geyff till all thi fals nacioune."	Example; make
	Apon the hill he gert thaim set him downe,	
405	Straik off his hed or thai wald forthir go.	Struck; before
	To the herrold said syne withoutyn ho,	then without pause
	"For thow art fals till armys and maynsuorn	perjured
	Throuch thi chokkis thi tong sall be out schorn."	cheeks; tongue; cut out
	Quhen that was doyne than to the thrid said he,	
410	"Armys to juge thow sall nevir graithly se."	readily see
	He gert a smyth with his turkas rycht thar	made; smith; pair of pincers
	Pow out his eyne, syne gaiff thaim leiff to far.	Pull; eyes; leave to go
	"To your fals king thi falow sall thee leid;	your companion; lead
	With my ansuer turs him his nevois heid.	pack up for him; nephew's head
415	Thus sar I drede thi king and all his bost."	extremely; fear; threatening
	His dum falow led him onto thar ost.	His mute companion
	Quhen King Eduuard his herroldis thus has seyne	
	In propyr ire he wox ner wode for teyne,	pure rage; grew; mad with grief
	That he nocht wyst on quhat wis him to wreke;	way to avenge himself
420	For sorow almaist a word he mycht nocht spek.	speak
	A lang quhill he stud wrythand in a rage.	
	On loud he said, "This is a fell owtrage.	grievous
	This deid to Scottis full der it sall be bocht;	Scots will pay dearly for this action
	Sa dispitfull in warld was nevir wrocht.	So malicious [a deed]
425	Of this regioun I think nocht for to gang	leave
	Quhill tyme that I sall se that rybald hang."	Until [the] time; rebel
	Lat I him thus intill his sorow duell;	I leave him thus
	Of thai gud Scottis schortly I will yow tell.	
	Furth fra his men than Wallace rakit rycht;	Further; went directly
430	Till him he cald Schir Jhon Tynto the knycht,	
	And leit him witt to vesy himselff wald ga	let him know; reconnoiter; go [to]
	The Inglis ost, and bad him tell na ma,	[To]; ordered; no one else
	Quhatevir thai speryt, quhill that he come agayne.	asked, until; returned
	Wallace dysgysit thus bownyt out the playne.	set out for the plain
435	Betwix Cultir and Bygar as he past	Culter; Biggar
	He was sone war quhar a werkman come fast,	aware; laborer; approached
	Dryfande a mere and pychars had to sell.	Driving; mare; pitchers
	"Gud freynd," he said, "in treuth will thow me tell	
	With this chaffar quhar passis thow treuly?"	merchandise
440	"Till ony, schir, quha likis for to by.	To any; who; buy

Book 6

	It is my crafft and I wald sell thaim fayne."	*occupation; willingly*
	"I will thaim by, sa God me saiff fra payne.	*buy*
	Quhat price lat her. I will tak thaim ilkayne."[1]	
	"Bot half a mark, for sic prys haiff I tayne."	*Only; such; incurred*
445	"Twenty schillingis," Wallace said, "thow sall haiff.	
	I will haiff mer, pychars, and als the laiff.	*[the] mare; also the rest*
	Thi gowne and hois in haist thow put off syne	*stockings; next*
	And mak a chang, for I sall geyff thee myne,	*change; give*
	And thi ald hud becaus it is thredbar."	*old hood; threadbare*
450	The man wend weyll that he had scornyt him thar.	*thought; mocked*
	"Do tary nocht, it is suth I thee say."	*[the] truth*
	The man kest off his febill weid of gray,	*threw; meager gray garment*
	And Wallace his and payit silvir in hand.	
	"Pas on," he said, "thou art a proud merchand."	
455	The gown and hois in clay that claggit was,	*stockings; clogged*
	The hude heklyt, and maid him for to pas.	*fringed*
	The qwhipe he tuk syne furth the mar can call.	*whip; then summoned the mare*
	Atour a bray the omast pot gert fall,	*[Going] over a hill; uppermost; fell*
	Brak on the ground; the man lewch at his fair,	*laughed; way of going*
460	"Bot thow be war thow tynys of thi chaiffair."	*Unless; are careful; will lose; wares*
	The sone be than was passit out of sicht;	*sun; disappeared*
	The day our went and cummyn was the nycht.	*passed*
	Amang Sotheroun full besyly he past;	*[the] English*
	On athir side his eyne he gan to cast	*either; eyes*
465	Quhar lordis lay and had thar lugeyng maid,	*camp*
	The kingis palyone quharon the libardis baid;	*pavilion; leopards stood*
	Spyand full fast quhar his availl suld be	*advantage should*
	And couth weyll luk and wynk with the ta e.	*look; other eye*
	Sum scornyt him, sum "gleid carll" cald him thar;	*"squint-eyed fellow" called*
470	Agrevit thai war for thar herroldis mysfayr.	*Vexed; mishap*
	Sum sperd at him how he sald of the best.	*what was his best price*
	"For forty pens," he said, "quhill thai may lest."	*pence*
	Sum brak a pot, sum pyrlit at his e.	*poked at his eye*
	Wallace fled out and prevalé leit thaim be;	*let*
475	Ontill his ost agayne he past full rycht.	*host; straightaway*
	His men be than had tayne Tynto the knycht.	*by then; seized*

---

[1] *Let [me] know (hear) the price. I will take every one of them*

The Wallace

	Schyr Jhon the Grayme gert bynd him wondir fast,	*securely*
	For he wyst weill he was with Wallace last:	
	Sum bad byrn him, sum hang him in a cord;	*wished to burn; on a rope*
480	Thai swor that he had dissavit thar lord.	*deceived*
	Wallace be this was entryt thaim amang;	*by this [time]*
	Till him he yeid and wald nocht tary lang,	*To him he went*
	Syne he gart lous him of thai bandis new	*Then; had him loosed from*
	And said he was baith suffer, wys, and trew.	*both trusty*
485	To souper sone thai bound but mar abaid.	*supper soon; without further delay*
	He tald to thaim quhat merket he had maid,	*trading*
	And how at he the Sotheroun saw full weill.	*that; English*
	Schyr Jhon the Grayme displessit was sumdeill	
	And said till him, "Nocht chyftaynlik it was	*It was not chieftain-like*
490	Throw wilfulnes in sic perell to pas."	*headstrong conduct; such*
	Wallace ansuerd, "Or we wyn Scotland fre	*Before we achieve Scotland's freedom*
	Baith ye and I in mar perell mon be,	*Both; more; must*
	And mony othir the quhilk full worthi is.	*which*
	Now of a thing we do sum part amys,	*somewhat amiss*
495	A litill slepe I wald fayne that we had,	*be glad*
	With yone men syne luk how we may us glaid."	*then*
	The worthi Scottis tuk gud rest quhill ner day.	*until near*
	Than rais thai up, till ray sone ordand thai.	*to battle order quickly they were ready*
	The hill thai left and till a playne is gayne;	*went*
500	Wallace himselff the vantgard he has tayne;	*vanguard; assumed command*
	With him was Boid and Awchinlek but dreid,	*without doubt*
	With a thousand of worthi men in weid.	*men in armor*
	Als mony syne in the mydwart put he;	*As; middle force*
	Schir Jhone the Grayme he gert thar ledar be,	*made*
505	With him Adam, young lord of Ricardtoun,	
	And Somervaill, a squier of renoun.	
	The thrid thousand in the rerward he dycht,	*to the rearguard he assigned*
	Till Waltir gaiff of Newbyggyn the knycht,	*gave*
	With him Tynto that douchty wes in deid	*was bold in deed*
510	And Davi son of Schir Waltir, to leid.	*lead*
	Behynd thaim ner the fute men gert he be	*[Close] behind; foot soldiers*
	And bade thaim bid quhill thai thar tyme mycht se:	*commanded; stay until*
	"Ye want wapynnys and harnes in this tid;	*lack; armor at this time*
	The fyrst cowntir ye may nocht weill abid."	*encounter; withstand*
515	Wallace gert sone the chyftaynis till him call.	

Book 6

	This charge he gaiff, for chance that mycht befall,	*order; whatever might happen*
	Till tak no heid to ger nor of pylage,	*pay no heed; pillage*
	"For thai will fle as wod folk in a rage.	*mad*
	Wyne fyrst the men, the gud syne ye may haiff;	*Conquer; goods afterwards*
520	Than tak na tent of covatys to craiff.	*pay no attention*
	Throuch covatys sum losis gud and lyff;	*goods and life*
	I commaund yow forber sic in our stryff.	*keep away from such; struggle*
	Luk that ye saiff na lord, capteyne, nor knycht;	*spare*
	For worschipe wyrk and for our eldris rycht.	*ancestors'*
525	God blys us that we may in our viage	*bless; enterprise*
	Put thir fals folk out of our heretage."	*these*
	Than thai inclynd all with a gudly will;	*bowed*
	His playne commaund thai hecht for to fullfill.	*promised*
	On the gret ost thir partice fast can draw,	*these divisions quickly approached*
530	Cumand to thaim out of the south thai saw	*Coming*
	Thre hundreth men intill thar armour cler,	*bright*
	The gaynest way to thaim approchit ner.	*nearest; close*
	Wallace said sone thai war na Inglismen,	*soon; not*
	"For by this ost the gatis weyll thai ken."[1]	
535	Thom Haliday thai men he gydyt rycht;	*those; guided*
	Of Anaddirdaill he had thaim led that nycht,	
	His twa gud sonnis, Jhonstoun and Rudyrfurd.	
	Wallace was blyth fra he had hard thar wourd,[2]	
	So was the laiff of his gud chevalry.	*rest; band of knights*
540	Jarden thar come intill thar cumpany,	*into*
	And Kyrkpatrik, befor in Esdaill was,	
	A weyng thai war in Wallace ost to pas.	*[military] wing*
	The Inglis wach, that nycht had beyne on steir,	*scout; astir*
	Drew to thar ost rycht as the day can per.	*dawned*
545	Wallace knew weill, for he befor had seyne,	
	The kingis palyon quhar it was buskit beyne.	*pavilion; had been pitched*
	Than with rych hors the Scottis befor thaim raid;	*fine horses; rode*
	The fyrst cowntir so gret abaysing maid	*[At] the first encounter; discomfiture*
	That all the ost was stunyst of that sicht;	*dismayed at the sight [of the Scots]*
550	Full mony ane derffly to ded was dicht.	*Very many were violently killed*

---

[1] *"For by [the look of it] this army knows the roads well"*

[2] *Wallace was pleased when he had heard that call (lit., word)*

The Wallace

	Feill of thaim was as than out of aray,	Many; in disarray
	The mair haisté and awfull was the fray.	more; frightening; din
	The noyis rouschit throuch strakis that thai dang;	deafened; blows; struck
	The rewmour rais so rudly thaim amang	alarm; strongly
555	That all the ost was than in poynt to fle.	at [the] point of fleeing
	The wys lordis fra thai the perell se,	
	The fellone fray all rasyt wes about	terrible din; roused
	And how thar king stud in so mekill dout,	such great danger
	Till his palyone how mony thousand socht	
560	Him to reskew be ony way thai mocht.	any; might
	The erll of Kent that nycht walkand had beyne	watching
	With five thousand of men in armour cleyne;	bright
	About the king full sodandly thai gang,	went
	And traistis weill the sailye wes rycht strang.	[you may] well believe the assault
565	All Wallace folk in wys of wer was gud,	ways of war; experienced
	Into the stour syne lychtyt quhar thai stud.	battle then dismounted
	Quhamevir thai hyt, na harnes mycht thaim stynt	
	Fra thai on fute semblit, with suerdis dynt.[1]	
	Of manheid thai in hartis cruell was,	fierce were
570	Thai thocht to wyn or nevir thine to pas.	from there
	Feill Inglismen befor the king thai slew.	Many
	Schir Jhon the Grayme come with his power new.	
	Amang the ost with the mydwart he raid;	middle division
	Gret martyrdome on Sotheroun men thai maid.	slaughter; [the] English
575	The rerward than set on sa hardely,	rearguard then; so
	With Newbyggyn and all the chevalry.	
	Palyone rapys thai cuttyt into sowndir,	Tent ropes; to pieces
	Borne to the ground and mony smoryt owndir.	smothered under
	The fute men come the quhilk I spak of ayr,	spoke; earlier
580	On frayt folk set strakis sad and sayr.	frightened; strokes firm; sore
	Thocht thai befor wantyt bath hors and ger,	Although; lacked both; weapons
	Anewch thai gat quhat thai wald waill to wer.	Enough; obtained which; choose for war
	The Scottis power than all togyddir war;	
	The kingis palyon brymly doun thai bar.	fiercely; bore
585	The erll of Kent with a gud ax in hand	

---

[1] Lines 567–68: *Whomever they hit, with sword blows, no armor could stop them once they assembled on foot*

Book 6

	Into the stour full stoutly couth he stand	battle; boldly
	Befor the king, makand full gret debait.	offering; resistance
	Quha best did than he had the heast stait.	Whoever; then; highest place [of honor]
	The felloune stour so stalwart was and strang,	terrible fighting
590	Tharto contened mervalusly and lang.	continued
	Wallace himself full sadly couth persew	steadfastly conducted himself
	And at a straik that cheiff chyftayne he slew.	stroke; prime
	The Sotheron folk fled fast and durst nocht byd,	English; dared; stay
	Horssit thar king and off the feild couth ride,	Put their king on horseback; rode
595	Agaynis his will, for he was laith to fle;	loath
	Into that tyme he thocht nocht for to de.	did not expect to die
	Of his best men four thousand thar was dede	
	Or he couth fynd to fle and leiff that stede.	Before; was persuaded; leave; place
	Twenty thousand with him fled in a staill.	body
600	The Scottis gat hors and folowit that battaill.	got; battalion
	Throuch Cultir Hope or tyme thai wan the hycht[1]	
	Feill Sotheroun folk was merryt in thar mycht,	Many English; injured
	Slayne be the gait as thar king fled away.	by the wayside
	Bathe fair and brycht and rycht cler was the day,	Both
605	The sone ryssyn, schynand our hill and daill.	shining over; dale
	Than Wallace kest quhat was his grettest vaill.	considered; advantage
	The fleand folk that off the feild fyrst past	fleeing; first left the battlefield
	Into thar king agayne releiffit fast.	Unto; rallied
	Fra athir sid so mony semblit thar	From either side; assembled
610	That Wallace wald lat folow thaim no mar:	not allow [his men] to follow; more
	Befor he raid, gart his folk turn agayne.	In front; rode, made; back
	Of Inglismen sevyn thousand thar was slayne.	
	Than Wallace ost agayne to Beggar raid	Wallace's army; rode
	Quhar Inglismen gret purvians had maid.	provision
615	The jowalré as it was thiddir led,	valuables
	Palyonnis and all, thai leifft quhen thai fled.	left behind
	The Scottis gat gold, gud, ger, and othir wage;	goods, weapons; reward
	Relevyt thai war at partit that pilage.	Relieved; who divided those spoils
	To meit thai went with myrthis and plesance;	dinner; in good spirits
620	Thai sparyt nocht King Eduuardis purveance.	They did not skimp [with]; supplies
	With solace syne a litill sleyp thai ta;	Refreshed then; took

---

[1] *Through Culter Valley before they had time to climb the hill*

The Wallace

	A preva wach he gert amang thaim ga.	*secret scout; made; go*
	Twa kukis fell, thair lyffis for to saiff,	*fierce rascals; save*
	With dede corssys that lay unputt in graiff;	*corpses; unburied*
625	Quhen thai saw weyll the Scottis war at rest,	
	Out of the feild to steill thaim thocht it best.	*steal [away]*
	Full law thai crap quhill thai war out of sicht,	*low; crept until*
	Eftir the ost syne rane in all thar mycht.	*After; [English] host; ran*
	Quhen that the Scottis had slepyt bot a quhill,	*only a [short] while*
630	Than rais thai up, for Wallace dredyt gyll.	*rose; guile*
	He said to thaim, "The Sotherone may persewe	*English; renew the attack*
	Agayne to us for thai ar folk enew.	*On us; there are enough of them*
	Quhar Inglismen provisioune makis in wer	*provision; war*
	It is full hard to do thaim mekill der.	*much harm*
635	On this playne feild we will thaim nocht abid;	*open*
	To sum gud strenth my purpos is to ryd."	*stronghold*
	The purveance that left was in that stede	*supplies; place*
	To Ropis Bog he gert servandis it lede,	*made; lead*
	With ordinance at Sothroun brocht it thar.	*[the] provisions that [the] English*
640	He with the ost to Davis Schaw can far	*Wood went*
	And thar ramaynede a gret space of the day.	*remained; part*
	Of Inglismen yeit sumthing will I say.	
	As King Eduuart throuch Cultir Hoppis socht,	*Valley made his way*
	Quhen he persavit the Scottis folowed nocht,	*perceived*
645	In Jhonnys Greyne he gert the ost ly still.	*John's Green*
	Feill fleand folk assemblit sone him till.	*Many; soon*
	Quhen thai war met the king ner worthit mad	*nearly became*
	For his der kyn that he thar lossyt had;	*lost*
	His twa emys into the feild was slayne,	*two uncles*
650	His secund sone that mekill was of mayne,	*son; of great strength*
	His brothir Hew was kelyt thar full cald,	*killed; cold*
	The erll of Kent, that cruell berne and bald,	*fierce and bold baron*
	With gret worschip tuk ded befor the king.	*died*
	For him he murnyt als lang as he mycht ryng.	*mourned; reigned*
655	At this semlay as thai in sorow stand,	*gathering; stood*
	The twa kukis come sone in at his hand	*rascals soon approached him*
	And tald till him how thai enchapyt war:	*had escaped*
	"The Scottis all as swyne lyis dronkyn thar	*like swine lie drunk there*
	Of our wicht wyne ye gert us thidder led;	*From; strong wine; lead*
660	Full weill we may be vengit of thar ded.	*avenged; deed*

Book 6

	A payne our lyvis it is suth that we tell:	On pain [of] our lives
	Raturne agayne, ye sall fynd thaim yoursell."	Return; yourself
	He blamyt thaim and said na witt it was	reproached; it made no sense
	That he agayne for sic a taill suld pas.	such a tale
665	"Thar chyftayne is rycht mervalus in wer;	war
	Fra sic perell he can full weill thaim ber.	protect
	To sek him mar as now I will nocht ryd;	ride
	Our meit is lost, tharfor we may nocht byd."	food; stay
	The hardy duk of Longcastell and lord,	
670	"Soverane," he said, "till our consaill concord.	to; counsel agree
	Gyff this be trew ye haiff the mar availl.	If; better advantage
	We may thaim wyne and mak bot licht travaill.	defeat; effort
	War yon folk dede quha may agayne us stand?	Were those; dead
	Than neid we nocht for meit to leiff the land."	we need not leave the land for food
675	The king ansuerd, "I will nocht rid agayne,	ride back
	As at this tyme my purpos is in playne."	plain
	The duk said, "Schir, gyff ye contermyt be,	are firmly set against it
	To mowff yow mor it afferis nocht for me.	move; becomes
	Commaund power agayne with me to wend	[an] army back; go
680	And I of this sall se a finaill end."	
	Ten thousand haill he chargyt for to ryd.	in all; commanded; ride
	"Her in this strenth all nycht I sall yow bid.	Here; stronghold; await you
	We may get meit of bestiall in this land;	beasts
	Gud drynk as now we can nocht bryng to hand."	
685	Of Westmorland the lord had mett him thar;	
	On with the duk he graithit him to fair.	prepared to go on
	At the fyrst straik with thaim he had nocht beyne;	When the first blow was struck
	With him he led a thousand weill beseyne.	equipped
	A Pykart lord was with a thousand bowne;	Picard; prepared
690	Of King Edward he kepyt Calys toun.	From; held Calais
	This twelve thousand onto the feild can fair.	proceeded
	The two captans sone mett thaim at Beggair	
	With the haill stuff of Roxburch and Berweike.	whole garrisons
	Schir Rawff Gray saw at thai war Sotheron leik,	they were like [the] English
695	Out of the south approchit to thar sicht;	within sight
	He knew full weill with thaim it was nocht rycht.	
	Amer Wallange with his power come als,	
	King Eduuardis man, a tyrand knycht and fals.	
	Quhen thai war mett thai fand nocht ellis thar	found nothing else there

The Wallace

700	Bot dede corsis, and thai war spulyeit bar.	*bodies; stripped of belongings*
	Than merveld thai quhar at the Scottis suld be;	*they wondered where*
	Of thaim about perance thai couth nocht se.	*They could see no sign of them*
	Bot spyis thaim tald, that come with Schir Amar,	
	In Davis Schaw thai saw thaim mak repar.	*Wood; saw them go*
705	The fers Sotheroun sone passit to that place;	*fierce English soon*
	The wach wes war and tald it to Wallace.	*sentries; aware; told*
	He warnd the ost out of that wood to ryd;	*summoned the army*
	In Roppis Bog he purpost for to byd.	*stay*
	A litill schaw upon the ta syd was	*wood; the one side*
710	That men on fute mycht of the bog out pas.	*from*
	Thar hors thai left into that litill hauld;	*stronghold*
	On fute thai thocht the mos that thai suld hauld.	*marsh; keep*
	The Inglis ost had weill thar passage seyne	
	And folowed fast with cruell men and keyne.	*fierce; bold*
715	Thai trowit that bog mycht mak thaim litill vaill,	*believed; difficulty*
	Growyn our with reys, and all the sward was haill.¹	
	On thaim to ryd thai ordand in gret ire.	*ordered*
	Of the formest a thousand in the myre	*foremost; swamp*
	Of hors with men was plungyt in the deipe.	*deep*
720	The Scottis men tuk of thar cummyng kepe,	*heed*
	Apon thaim set with strakis sad and sar;	*firm; severe*
	Yeid nane away of all that entrit thar.	*Went*
	Lycht men on fute apon thaim derffly dang;	*Dismounted; violently attacked them*
	Feill undyr hors was smoryt in that thrang,	*Many; crushed; throng*
725	Stampyt in mos and with rud hors ourgayne.	*Trampled; [the] bog; strong; crushed*
	The worthy Scottis the dry land than has tayne,	*reached*
	Apon the laiff fechtand full wondyr fast,	*rest fighting very vigorously*
	And mony groyme thai maid full sar agast.	*men; afraid*
	Than Inglismen that besy was in wer	*fighting*
730	Assailyeit sar thaim fra the mos to ber	*Tried hard; carry*
	On athir syd, bot than it was no but.	*either side; to no avail*
	The strenth thai held rycht awfully on fut	*stronghold; awesomely; foot*
	Till men and hors gaiff mony grevous wound;	*To*
	Feyll to the dede thai stekit in that stound.	*Many; stabbed (killed); time*
735	The Pykart lord assailyeit scharply thar	*attacked eagerly*

---

¹ *Overgrown with brushwood, and all the grass was growing vigorously*

Book 6

	Upon the Grayme with strakis sad and sar.	blows
	Schir Jhone the Grayme with a staff suerd of steill	stabbing sword of steel
	His brycht byrneis he persyt evirilkdeill,	corslet; pierced completely
	Throuch all the stuff, and stekit him in that sted;	cloth; stabbed; place
740	Thus of his dynt the bauld Pykart is ded.	blow; bold
	The Inglis ost tuk playne purpos to fle;	clear
	In thar turnyng the Scottis gert mony de.	retreat
	Wallace wald fayne at the Wallang haiff beyne;	gladly
	Of Westmorland the lord was thaim betweyne.	The lord of Westmoreland
745	Wallace on him he set ane awfull dynt,	formidable blow
	Throuch basnet stuff that na steill mycht it stynt;	helmet; steel; stop
	Derffly to dede he left him in that place.	Violently
	The fals knycht thus eschapit throuch this cace.	escaped; chance
	And Robert Boid has with a captayne mett	
750	Of Berweik, than a sad straik on him set	firm
	Awkwart the crag and kervyt the pissane,	Across; neck; severed; gorget
	Throuch all his weid in sondyr straik the bane.	armor [and] shattered the bone
	Feill horssyt men fled fast and durst nocht byd;	Many; remain
	Raboytit evill onto thar king thai rid.	Badly repulsed; ride
755	The duk him tald of all thar jornay haill;	feat of arms
	His hart for ire bolnyt for bytter baill.	swelled; woe
	Haill he hecht he suld nevyr London se	Wholeheartedly; vowed
	On Wallace deid quhill he ravengit be,	Until he was revenged for Wallace's deed
	Or los his men agayne as he did ayr.	lose; before
760	Thus socht he south with gret sorou and cair;	he made his way; sorrow
	At the Byrkhill a litill tary maid,	short halt
	Syne throuch the land but rest our Sulway raid.	Then; without stopping; Solway
	The Scottis ost a nycht ramanyt still;	remained
	Apon the morn thai spulyete with gud will	plundered
765	The dede corssis, syne couth to Braidwood fayr;	Braidwood
	At a consaill four dayis sojornyt thar.	stayed there
	At Forestkyrk a metyng ordand he.	
	Thai chesd Wallace Scottis wardand to be,	chose; Guardian
	Traistand he suld thar paynfull sorow ces.	
770	He rasavyt all that wald cum till his pes.	received; peace
	Schir Wilyham come that lord of Douglas was,	
	Forsuk Eduuard, at Wallace pes can ass;	asked
	In thar thrillage he wald no langar be.	subjection to them
	Trewbut befor till Ingland payit he.	Tribute

The Wallace

775	In contrar Scottis with thaim he nevir raid,	*Against; rode*
	Far bettir cher Wallace tharfor him maid.	*welcome*
	Thus tretyt he and cheryst wondir fair	*treated; dearly*
	Trew Scottis men that fewté maid him thar,	*fealty*
	And gaiff gretly feill gudis at he wan.	*gave generously many; won*
780	He warnd it nocht till na gud Scottis man.	*refused; to*
	Quha wald rebell and gang contrar the rycht	*go against*
	He punyst sar, war he squier or knycht.	*severely, were*
	Thus mervalusly gud Wallas tuk on hand;	*undertook*
	Lykly he was, rycht fair and weill farrand,	*Well-made; good-looking*
785	Mandly and stout and tharto rycht liberall,	*Manly; strong; generous*
	Plesand and wys in all gud governall.	*Pleasant; leadership*
	To sla forsuth Sotheroun he sparyt nocht;	*slay in truth Englishmen*
	To Scottis men full gret profyt he wrocht.	
	Into the south sone efftir passit he;	*soon*
790	As him best thocht he rewllyt that contré.	*governed; region*
	Schirrais he maid that cruell was to ken	*Sheriffs; fierce; know*
	And captans als of wis trew Scottis men.	*loyal*
	Fra Gamlis Peth the land obeyt him haill,	*Gamelspath; entirely*
	Till Ur Wattir, bath strenth, forest, and daill.	*[the] Urr River; strongholds*
795	Agaynis him in Galloway hous was nayne	*castles*
	Except Wigtoun, byggyt of lyme and stayne.	*built; stone*
	That captayne hard the reullis of Wallace;	*proceedings*
	Away be sey he staw out of that place,	*by sea; stole*
	Levyt all waist and couth in Ingland wend.	*Left; went to England*
800	Bot Wallace sone a kepar till it send,	*warden*
	A gud squier and to nayme he was cald	
	Adam Gordone, as the storie me tald.	*history; told*
	A strenth thar was on the wattir of Cre,	*castle; Cree River*
	Within a roch, rycht stalwart, wrocht of tre;	*rock; made of wood*
805	A gait befor mycht no man to it wyn,	*passageway at the front; find*
	But the consent of thaim that duelt within.	*Without*
	On the bak sid a roch and wattir was;	*At the rear; river*
	A strait entré forsuth it was to pas.	*narrow*
	To wesy it Wallace himselff sone went;	*reconnoiter; soon*
810	Fra he it saw he kest in his entent	*considered how*
	To wyn that hauld; he has chosyne a gait	*conquer; way*
	That thai within suld mak litill debait.	*resistance*
	His power haill he gert bid out of sicht,	*whole company; wait*

Book 6

	Bot three with him, qwhill tyme that it was nycht.	*Except; until*
815	Than tuk he twa, quhen that the nycht was dym,	*two; dim*
	Stevyn of Irland and Kerle that couth clyme	*mount*
	The wattir undir, and clame the roch so strang.	*under; climb*
	Thus entir thai the Sothrone men amang.	*English*
	The wach befor tuk na tent to that syd;	*watch in front paid no attention*
820	Thir three in feyr sone to the port thai glid.	*These; together; gate; moved smoothly*
	Gud Wallace than straik the portar himsell;	*struck*
	Dede our the roch into the dik he fell;	*Dead over; ditch*
	Leit doun the brig and blew his horne on hycht.	*Let; bridge; loudly*
	The buschement brak and come in all thar mycht,	*ambush broke; came*
825	At thar awne will sone enterit in that place;	*own pleasure soon*
	Till Inglismen thai did full litill grace.	*To; showed little kindness*
	Sexty thai slew; in that hauld was no ma	*stronghold; more*
	Bot ane ald preist and sympill wemen twa.	*Except; harmless*
	Gret purveance was in that roch to spend;	*supplies*
830	Wallace baid still quhill it was at ane end,	*stayed; until; finished*
	Brak doune the strenth, bath bryg and bulwark all.	*bridge*
	Out our the roch thai gert the temyr fall,	*over; timber*
	Undid the gait and wald no langar bid.	*Destroyed; stay*
	In Carrik syne thai bownyt thaim to rid,	*prepared; ride*
835	Haistit thaim nocht bot sobyrly couth fair	*They did not hurry; steadily traveled*
	Till Towrnbery; that captane was of Ayr	*To; [castle's] captain went to Ayr*
	With lord Persie, to tak his consaill haill.	*sound counsel*
	Wallace purpoisit that place for to assaill.	*planned*
	Ane woman tauld quhen the capitane was gane.	*told [him]; gone*
840	Gude men of fence into the steid was nane.	*defense; place; none*
	Thay fillit the dyke with eird and tymmer haill,	*ditch; earth; timber completely*
	Syne fyrd the gett na succour mycht availl.	*Then set fire to the gate*
	A prest thar was and gentill wemen within	*priest*
	Quhilk for the fyr maid hiddewis noyis and dyn.	*hideous*
845	"Mercy," thai criit, "for Him that deit on Tre."	*who died on [the] Cross (i.e., Jesus)*
	Wallace gert slaik the fyr and leit thaim be.	*caused the fire to be put out; let*
	To mak defens na ma was levyt thar.	*more were left there*
	He thaim commaund out of the land to far,	*to go*
	Spulyeit the place and spilt all at thai mocht.	*Plundered; destroyed*
850	Apon the morn in Cumno sone thai socht,	*Cumnock; went*
	To Laynrik syne and set a tyme of ayr;	*Lanark; for [a] justice-ayre*
	Mysdoaris feill he gert be punyst thar.	*Many wrongdoers*

The Wallace

	To gud trew men he gaiff full mekill wage,	*gave very large rewards*
	His brothir sone put to his heretage.	
855	To the Blak Crag in Cumno past agayne,	
	His houshauld set with men of mekill mayn.	*appointed; great strength*
	Thre monethis thar he duellyt in gud rest;	
	Suttell Sotheroune fand weill it was the best	*Cunning Englishmen found*
	Trewis to tak for till enchew a chans;	*To have [a] truce; obtain*
860	To furthir this thai send for knycht Wallans.	
	Bothwell yeit that tratour kepyt still,	*yet; protected*
	And Ayr all haill was at the Perseis will.	*completely*
	The byschope Beik in Glaskow duellyt thar,	
	Throucht gret supplé of the captayne of Ayr.	*provision*
865	Erll of Stamffurd, was chanslar of Ingland,	*chancellor*
	With Schir Amar this travaill tuk on hand,	*task*
	To procur pes be ony maner of cace.	*by any manner possible*
	A saiff condyt thai purchest of Wallacc.	*safe conduct*
	In Ruglen Kyrk the tryst than haiff thai set,	*Church; meeting; arranged*
870	A promes maid to meit Wallace but let.	*promise; meet; straight away*
	The day of this approchit wondyr fast.	
	The gret chanslar and Amar thiddir past,	
	Syne Wallace come and his men weill beseyn,	*Then; equipped*
	With him fyfty arayt all in greyne.	*dressed; green*
875	Ilk ane of thaim a bow and arrowis bar	*Each one; carried*
	And lang suerdis, the quhilk full scharply schar.	*long [very sharp] swords; cut*
	Into the kyrk he gert a preyst rawes,	*church; priest put on his vestments*
	With humyll mind rycht mekly hard a mes.	*meekly heard a mass*
	Syn up he rais and till ane alter went	*After he rose*
880	And his gud men full cruell of entent.	*fierce in purpose*
	In ir he grew that traitour quhen he sawe;	*anger; traitor (i.e., Sir Amer)*
	The Inglismen of his face stud gret aw.	
	Witt reullyt him that he did no owtrage.	*Reason*
	The erlle beheld fast till his hye curage,	*took great heed of*
885	Forthocht sum part that he come to that place,	*Regretted somewhat*
	Gretlye abaysit for the vult of his face.	*dismayed; expression on*
	Schir Amer said, "This spech ye mon begyne.	
	He will nocht bow to na part of your kyn.	
	Sufferyt ye ar, I trow yhe may spek weill.	*Assured [by safe conduct]; believe*
890	For all Ingland he will nocht brek adeyll	*at all*
	His saiff cundyt, or quhar he makis a band."	*conduct; where; bond*

Book 6

	The chanslar than approfferit him his hand.	*proffered*
	Wallace stud still and couth na handis ta;	*did not take hands*
	Frendschipe to thaim na liknes wald he ma.	*semblance; make*
895	Schir Amar said, "Wallace, yhe undyrstand	
	This is a lord and chanslar of Ingland.	
	To salus him ye may be propyr skill."	*greet; as is right and proper*
	With schort avys he maid ansuer him till:	*Without delay; to him*
	"Sic salusyng I oys till Inglismen	*greeting; use to*
900	Sa sall he haiff, quharevir I may him ken	*know*
	At my power, that God I mak avow,	*I vow to God*
	Out of soverance gyff that I had him now!	*safe conduct if*
	Bot for thi liff and all his land so braid	*broad*
	I will nocht brek this promes that is maid.	
905	I had levir at myn awn will haiff thee	*rather*
	Without cundyt, that I mycht wrokyne be	*[safe] conduct; revenged*
	Of thi fals deid thou dois in this regioune,	*you do*
	Than of pur gold a kingis gret ransoune.	*pure; ransom*
	Bot for my band as now I will lat be.	*Because of my bond*
910	Chanslar, schaw furth quhat ye desyr of me."	*expound*
	The chanslar said, "The most caus of this thing,	*the main reason for*
	To procur pees I am send fra our king	*from*
	With the gret seill and voice of hys parliament.	*seal; voice (i.e., support)*
	Quhat I bynd her oure barnage sall consent."	*agree [to] here; barons*
915	Wallace ansuerd, "Our litill mendis we haiff	*Very little reparation*
	Syne of oure rycht ye occupy the laiff.	*Since what is rightfully ours*
	Quytcleyme our land and we sall nocht deny."	*Relinquish*
	The chanslar said, "Of na sic charge haiff I.	*I have no such orders*
	We will gyff gold or oure purpos suld faill."	*give; before*
920	Than Wallace said, "In waist is that travaill.	*That is a useless offer*
	Be favour gold we ask nayne of your kyn.	*Gold [given as] a favor; none; kin*
	In wer of you we tak that we may wyn."	*We take by conquest what we can from you*
	Abaissid he was to mak ansuer agayne.	*He was [too] abashed to reply*
	Wallace said, "Schir, we jangill nocht in vayne.	*bandy words*
925	My consell gyffis, I will na fabill mak,	*decrees; not lie*
	As for a yer a finaill pes to tak.	*year; conclusive*
	Nocht for myselff that I bynd to your seill,	*seal*
	I can nocht trow that evir yhe will be leill,	*believe; loyal*
	Bot for pur folk gretlye has beyne supprisyt,	*poor; oppressed*
930	I will tak pees quhill forthir we be avisit."	*until; advised*

The Wallace

	Than band thai thus, thar suld be no debait,	agreed formally; strife
	Castell and towne suld stand in that ilk stait	same state
	Fra that day furth quhill a yer war at end,	until; was
	Sellyt this pes and tuk thar leyff to wend.	Sealed the truce; leave; go
935	Wallace fra thine passit into the west,	from there
	Maid playne repayr quhar so him likit best.	went openly where
	Yeit sar he dred or thai suld him dissaiff.	Yet he feared greatly; deceive
	This endentour to Schir Ranald he gaiff,	indenture
	His der uncle, quhar it mycht kepit be.	dear
940	In Cumno syne till his duellyng went he.	afterwards

Incipit Septimus

Book 7

	In Feveryher befell the sammyn cace	February; same case
	That Inglismen tuk trewis with Wallace.	agreed [to a] truce
	This passyt our till Marche till end was socht.	until the end of March
	The Inglismen kest all the wayis thai mocht,	considered; might
5	With suttelté and wykkit illusione,	deceit
	The worthi Scottis to put to confusione.	
	In Aperill the king of Ingland come	
	In Cumerland of Pumfrat fro his home;[1]	
	Into Carleill till a consell he yeid,	council; went
10	Quhar of the Scottis mycht haiff full mekill dreid.	great fear
	Mony captane that was of Ingland born	Many captains
	Thiddir thai past and semblit thar king beforn.	assembled; before
	Na Scottis man to that consell thai cald	called
	Bot Schir Amer, that traytour was of ald.	Except; old
15	At hym thai sperd how thai suld tak on hand	They asked him; undertake
	The rychtwys blud to scour out of Scotland.	rightful
	Schir Amer said, "Thar chyftayne can weill do,	Their chieftain is outstanding
	Rychtwys in wer and has gret power to,	war; very powerful too
	And now this trew gyffis thaim sic hardyment	truce; such courage
20	That to your faith thai will nocht all consent.	

---

[1] *In Cumberland from his home in Pontefract*

Book 7

	Bot wald ye do rycht as I wald yow ler,	*exactly; advise*
	This pes to thaim it suld be sald full der."	*cost them dearly*
	Than demyt he the fals Sotheroun amang	*he gave his opinion; English*
	How thai best mycht the Scottis barownis hang.	*barons*
25	For gret bernys that tyme stud intill Ayr,	*Four large barns*
	Wrocht for the king quhen his lugyng wes thar,	*Made; lodging*
	Byggyt about that no man entir mycht	*Built*
	Bot ane at anys, nor haiff of othir sicht;	*Except one at a time; have; sight*
	Thar ordand thai thir lordis suld be slayne.	*these*
30	A justice maid quhilk wes of mekill mayne.	*[They] appointed a judge; great power*
	To lord Persye of this mater thai laid.	*They laid this matter before Lord Percy*
	With sad avys agayne to thaim he said:	*stern expression*
	"Thai men to me has kepit treuth so lang	*loyalty*
	Desaitfully I may nocht se thaim hang.	
35	I am thar fa and warn thaim will I nocht;	*foe*
	Sa I be quytt I rek nocht quhat yhe wrocht.[1]	
	Fra thine I will and towart Glaskow draw.	*From thence*
	With our byschope to her of his new law."	*hear*
	Than chesyt thai a justice fers and fell	*they chose; fierce; cruel*
40	Quhilk Arnulff hecht, as my auctour will tell,	*was called*
	Of South Hantoun, that huge hie her and lord;	*very powerful high magistrate*
	He undirtuk to pyne thaim with the cord.	*torment*
	Ane othir ayr in Glaskow ordand thai	*justice-ayre*
	For Cliddisdaill men to stand that sammyn day;	
45	Syne chargyt thaim in all wayis ernystfully	*Then ordered; earnestly*
	Be no kyn meyne Wallace suld nocht chaip by,	*By no kind of means; escape*
	For weill thai wyst and thai men war ourthrawin	*knew; overthrown*
	Thai mycht at will bruk Scotland as thar awin.	*possess; own*
	This band thai clois undir thar seillis fast;	*agreement; concluded; seals*
50	Syne south our mur agayn King Edward past.	*Then; over [the] moor again*
	The new justice rasavit was in Ayr;	*received*
	The lord Persye can on to Glaskow fayr.	*went on to Glasgow*
	This ayr was set in Jun the auchtand day	*justice-ayre; June; eighth*
	And playnly criyt na fre man war away.	*proclaimed; should be*
55	The Scottis merveld, and pes tane in the land,	*since peace [has been] agreed*
	Quhy Inglismen sic maistré tuk on hand.	*such [a] display of might*

---

[1] *So long as I am quit [of responsibility] I care not what you do*

The Wallace

	Schir Ranald set a day befor this ayr,	*appointed*
	At Monktoun Kyrk; his freyndis mett him thar.	
	Wilyham Wallace onto that tryst couth pas,	*meeting passed*
60	For he as than wardane of Scotland was.	*Guardian*
	This Maister Jhone, a worthi clerk, was thar;	
	He chargyt his kyne for to byd fra that ayr.	*kinsfolk; stay away from*
	Rycht weyll he wyst, fra Persey fled that land,	*He knew very well, when*
	Gret perell was till Scottis apperand.	*imminent*
65	Wallace fra thaim to the kyrk he yeid;	*went*
	Pater Noster, Ave he said and Creid,	*Our Father, Hail [Mary]; [the Apostles'] Creed*
	Syne to the grece he lenyt him sobyrly;	*Then; stair; headed resolutely*
	Apon a sleip he slaid full sodandly.	*fell into a sleep*
	Kneland folowed and saw him fallyn on sleip;	
70	He maid na noyis bot wysly couth him kepe.	*protect*
	In that slummer cummand him thocht he saw	*slumber he thought he saw coming*
	Ane agit man fast towart him couth draw.	*aged*
	Sone be the hand he hynt him haistelé.	*Soon; grabbed*
	"I am," he said, "in viage chargit with thee."	*on a journey commanded [to go]*
75	A suerd him gaiff of burly burnist steill.	*sword; strong burnished steel*
	"Gud sone," he said, "this brand thou sall bruk weill."	*sword; make good use of*
	Of topaston him thocht the plumat was,	*topaz; pommel*
	Baith hilt and hand all gliterand lik the glas.	*handle*
	"Dere sone," he said, "we tary her to lang.	*too long*
80	Thow sall go se quhar wrocht is mekill wrang."	*much wrong*
	Than he him led till a montane on hycht;	*high*
	The warld him thocht he mycht se with a sicht.	*at a glance*
	He left him thar, syne sone fra him he went.	*then afterwards*
	Tharoff Wallace studiit in his entent;	*wondered in his mind*
85	Till se him mar he had full gret desyr.	*To see; more*
	Tharwith he saw begyne a felloune fyr	*fierce*
	Quhilk braithly brynt on breid throu all the land,	*vigorously burned extensively*
	Scotland atour fra Ros to Sulway sand.	*Over Scotland from*
	Than sone till him thar descendyt a qweyne,	*soon*
90	Inlumyt lycht schynand full brycht and scheyne.	*Illumined light shining; clear*
	In hyr presens apperyt so mekill lycht	*much*
	At all the fyr scho put out of his sicht;	*That*
	Gaiff him a wand of colour reid and greyne,	*red and green*
	With a saffyr sanyt his face and eyne.	*sapphire blessed; eyes*
95	"Welcum," scho said, "I cheis thee as my luff.	*choose; beloved*

Book 7

	Thow art grantyt be the gret God abuff	*above*
	Till help pepill that sufferis mekill wrang.	*To*
	With thee as now I may nocht tary lang.	
	Thou sall return to thi awne oys agayne;	*own way of living*
100	Thi derrast kyne ar her in mekill payne.	*dearest kin; here; great*
	This rycht regioun thow mon redeme it all;	*must*
	Thi last reward in erd sall be bot small.	*on earth shall*
	Let nocht tharfor tak redres of this mys,[1]	
	To thi reward thou sall haiff lestand blys."	*shall have everlasting bliss*
105	Of hir rycht hand scho betaucht him a buk.	*From; gave to; book*
	Humylly thus hyr leyff full sone scho tuk,	*her leave*
	Onto the cloud ascendyt of his sycht.	*from*
	Wallace brak up the buk in all his mycht.	*opened*
	In three partis the buk weill wrytyn was:	
110	The fyrst writtyng was gross letter of bras,	*[in] large; brass*
	The secound gold, the thrid was silver scheyne;	*third; bright*
	Wallace merveld quhat this writyng suld meyne.	*mean*
	To rede the buk he besyet him so fast,	*busied himself*
	His spreit agayne to walkand mynd is past,	*spirit; waking*
115	And up he rays, syne sowdandly furth went.	*then suddenly*
	This clerk he fand and tald him his entent	*described in detail*
	Of this visioun at I haiff said befor,	
	Completly throuch. Quhat nedis wordis mor?	*through; more*
	"Der sone," he said, "my witt unabill is	*unable*
120	To runsik sic for dreid I say of mys.	*interpret such; fear; amiss*
	Yeit I sall deyme, thocht my cunnyng be small,	*Yet; understanding*
	God grant na charge efftir my wordis fall.	*God grant [that]; blame; befall*
	Saynct Androw was, gaiff thee that suerd in hand;	*[It] was St. Andrew; sword*
	Of sanctis he is vowar of Scotland.	*patron*
125	That montayne is, quhar he thee had on hycht,	*high*
	Knawlage to haiff of wrang that thou mon rycht.	*Knowledge; must [set] right*
	The fyr sal be fell tithingis or ye part	*disastrous news before*
	Quhilk will be tald in mony syndry art.	*many different directions*
	I can nocht witt quhat qweyn at it suld be,	*do not know what queen that*
130	Quhethir Fortoun or Our Lady so fre.	*noble*
	Lykly it is be the brychtnes scho brocht,	*It is likely by; she*

---

[1] *Do not fail therefore to redress this wrong*

99

The Wallace

	Modyr of Hym that all this warld has wrocht.	*world; made*
	The party wand I trow be myn entent,	*particolored; believe*
	Assignes rewlle and cruell jugement.	*fierce*
135	The red colour, quha graithly understud,	*readily*
	Betaknes all to gret battaill and blud;	*Betokens; blood*
	The greyn, curage that thou art now amang,[1]	
	In strowbill wer thou sall conteyne full lang.	*painful war; continue*
	The saphyr stayne scho blissit thee withall	*stone with which she blessed*
140	Is lestand grace, will God sall to thee fall.	*lasting*
	The thrynfald buk is bot this brokyn land	*threefold; simply*
	Thou mon rademe be worthines of hand.	*must redeem by*
	The bras letteris betakynnys bot to this,	*only*
	The gret oppres of wer and mekill mys	*oppression; war; wrong*
145	The quhilk thow sall bryng to the rycht agayne;	*Which*
	Bot thou tharfor mon suffer mekill payne.	*for that must endure great suffering*
	The gold takynnis honour and worthinas,	*betokens*
	Victour in armys that thou sall haiff be grace.	*Victory; through grace*
	The silvir schawis cleyne lyff and hevynnys blys,	*signifies pure life; heaven's*
150	To thi reward that myrth thou sall nocht mys.	*joy; lack*
	Dreid nocht tharfor, be out of all dispayr.	*Fear*
	Forthir as now herof I can no mair."	*about this; [say] no more*
	He thankit him and thus his leyff has tayne,	*leave; taken*
	Till Corsbé syne with his uncle raid hayme.	*To Crosbie [Castle] then; rode home*
155	With myrthis thus all nycht thai sojornyt thar.	*Merrily*
	Apon the morn thai graith thaim to the ar	*set off; justice-ayre*
	And furth thai ryd quhill thai come to Kingace.	*rode until*
	With dreidfull hart thus sperit wicht Wallace	*fearful; asked bold*
	At Schir Ranald for the charter of pes.	*peace*
160	"Nevo," he said, "thir wordis ar nocht les.	*Nephew; these; lies*
	It is levyt at Corsbé in the kyst,	*left; chest*
	Quhar thou it laid; tharoff na othir wist."	*no one else knows its whereabouts*
	Wallace ansuerd, "Had we it her to schaw,	*[If] we had; here; show*
	And thai be fals we suld nocht entir awe."	*they were; all enter*
165	"Der sone," he said, "I pray thee pas agayne.	*son; go back*
	Thocht thou wald send, that travaill war in vayne;[2]	

---

[1] *The green [signifies] the courageous effort in which you are now engaged*

[2] *Although you would send [a messenger], [going to] that trouble would be in vain*

Book 7

	Bot thou or I can nane it bryng this tid."	*Except; time*
	Gret grace it was maid him agayne to ryd.	*ride back*
	Wallace raturnd and tuk with him bot thre;	*returned*
170	Nane of thaim knew this endentour bot he.	*indenture*
	Unhap him led, for bid him couth he nocht;	*Ill-luck led him (Sir Ranald); await; could*
	Of fals dissayt this gud knycht had na thocht.	*deceit; thought*
	Schir Ranald raid but restyng to the town,	*without*
	Wittand nathing of all this fals tresown.	*Knowing nothing; treason*
175	That wykked syng so rewled the planait,	*sign; ruled; planet*
	Saturn was than intill his heast stait;	*highest state (in the ascendant)*
	Aboun Juno in his malancoly,	*Above*
	Jupiter, Mars, ay cruell of invy	*always fierce; malice*
	Saturn as than avansyt his natur.	*then displayed*
180	Of terandry he power had and cur,	*tyranny; responsibility*
	Rebell renkis in mony seir regioun,	*Rebellious men; different*
	Trubbill weddir makis schippis to droun.	*Troubled weather; ships sink*
	His drychyn is with Pluto in the se	*tarrying*
	As of the land full of iniquité.	
185	He waknys wer, waxing of pestilence,	*stirs up war*
	Fallyng of wallis with cruell violence.	*fierce violence*
	Pusoun is ryff amang thir othir thingis,	*Poison; rife; these*
	Sodeyn slauchter of emperouris and kingis.	
	Quhen Sampsone powed to grond the gret piller	*pulled*
190	Saturn was than intill the heast sper.	*sphere*
	At Thebes als of his power thai tell,	
	Quhen Phiorax sank throuch the erd till hell;	*earth*
	Of the Trojans he had full mekill cur	*great charge*
	Quhen Achilles at Troy slew gud Ectur;	
195	Burdeous schent and mony citeis mo,	*Bordeaux ruined; many; more*
	His power yeit it has na hap to ho.	*destiny to stop*
	In braid Brytane feill vengeance has beyne seyne	*Across great*
	Of this and mar, ye wait weill quhat I meyn.	*more; know; mean*
	Bot to this hous that stalwart wes and strang	
200	Schir Ranald come and mycht nocht tary lang.	
	A bauk was knyt all full of rapys keyne;[1]	
	Sic a towboth sen syne wes nevir seyne.	*Such a tolbooth (i.e., Scots jail) since then*

---

[1] *Tightly drawn ropes were fastened all along a beam*

The Wallace

	Stern men was set the entré for to hald;	*Strong; guard*
	Nayne mycht pas in bot ay as thai war cald.	*except; called*
205	Schir Ranald fyrst, to mak fewté for his land,	*pay homage (fealty)*
	The knycht went in and wald na langar stand.	
	A rynnand cord thai slewyt our his hed	*running cord (i.e., noose); swung over*
	Hard to the bauk and hangyt him to ded.	*beam; to death*
	Schyr Brys the Blayr next with his eyme in past;	*uncle*
210	Onto the ded thai haistyt him full fast.	*death*
	Be he entrit his hed was in the swar,	*As soon as; snare (noose)*
	Tytt to the bawk, hangyt to ded rycht thar.	*Pulled; beam*
	The thrid entrit, that peté was forthy,	*therefore*
	A gentill knycht, Schir Neill of Mungumry,	*Montgomery*
215	And othir feill of landit men about.	*many others; land-owning*
	Mony yeid in bot na Scottis com out.	*Many went*
	Of Wallace part thai putt to that derff deid;	*party; violent death*
	Mony Craufurd sa endyt in that steid.	*thus; place*
	Of Carrik men Kennadys slew thai als,	*also*
220	And kynd Cambellis that nevir had beyne fals.	
	Thir rabellit nocht contrar thar rychtwis croun,	*These did not rebel against*
	Sotheroun forthi thaim putt to confusioun.	*[The] Englishmen therefore; destruction*
	Berklais, Boidis, and Stuartis of gud kyn,	*kin*
	Na Scot chapyt that tyme that entrit in.	*escaped*
225	Upon the bawk thai hangit mony par;	*beam; nobles*
	Besid thaim ded in the nuk kest thaim thar.	*corner cast*
	Sen the fyrst tyme that ony wer wes wrocht,	*Since; any; was waged*
	To sic a dede so mony sic yeid nocht	*such a death; such went*
	Upon a day throuch curssit Saxons seid.	*In a [single] day; accursed*
230	Vengeance of this throughout that kynrik yeid,	*kingdom (i.e., England) went*
	Grantyt wes fra God in the gret hevyn,	*heaven*
	Sa ordand he that law suld be thar stevyn	*So decreed; doom*
	To fals Saxons for thar fell jugement;	*cruel judgement*
	Thar wykkydnes our all the land is went.	
235	Yhe nobill men that ar of Scottis kind,	*descent*
	Thar petous dede yhe kepe into your mynd	*Their wretched deaths*
	And us ravenge quhen we ar set in thrang.	*revenge; placed in danger*
	Dolour it is heron to tary lang.	*It is distressing on this*
	Thus eighteen scor to that derff dede thai dycht	*they killed in that violent way*
240	Of barronis bald and mony worthi knycht.	*bold*
	Quhen thai had slayne the worthiast that was thar,	

Book 7

	For waik peple thai wald na langar spar,	*helpless; would no longer forbear*
	Intill a garth kest thaim out of that sted	*garden; place*
	As thai war born, dispulyeit, bar, and ded.	*stripped of belongings, naked*
245	Gud Robert Boid ontill a tavern yeid	*tavern went*
	With twenty men that douchty war in deid,	*bold*
	Of Wallace hous, full cruell of entent;	*household, fiercely enterprising*
	He governyt thaim quhen Wallace was absent.	
	Kerle turnyt with his master agayne,	*turned back*
250	Kneland and Byrd that mekill war of mayn.	*strength*
	Stevyn of Irland went furth apon the streit;	
	A trew woman full sone with him couth meit.	*loyal; soon met him*
	He speryt at hir quhat hapnyt in the ayr.	*enquired of her; justice-ayre*
	"Sorou," scho said, "is nothing ellis thar."	*else*
255	Ferdly scho ast, "Allace, quhar is Wallace?"	*Full of fear; asked*
	"Fra us agayne he passit at Kingace."	*He left us again*
	"Go warn his folk and haist thaim of the toun.	*hurry; from*
	To kepe himselff I sall be reddy boun."	*protect; all prepared*
	With hir as than no mar tary he maid.	*her*
260	Till his falowis he went withoutyn baid	*delay*
	And to thaim told of all this gret mysfair.	*disaster*
	To Laglane Wood thai bownyt withoutyn mar.	*headed immediately*
	Be this Wallace was cummand wondir fast;	*By this [time]; had come speedily*
	For his freyndis he was full sar agast.	*extremely fearful*
265	Onto the bern sadly he couth persew	*barn resolutely; made his way*
	Till entir in, for he na perell knew.	
	This woman than apon him loud can call:	*then*
	"O fers Wallace, feill tempest is befall!	*fierce; great disaster*
	Our men ar slayne that peté is to se,	
270	As bestiall houndis hangit our a tre.	*bestial dogs; over*
	Our trew barrouns be twa and twa past in."	*loyal; in pairs*
	Wallace wepyt for gret los of his kyne,	*kin*
	Than with unes apon his hors he baid.	*difficulty; stayed*
	Mair for to sper to this woman he raid.	*More; ask; rode*
275	"Der nece," he said, "the treuth giff thow can tell,	*kinswoman; if*
	Is my eyme dede, or hou the cace befell?"	*uncle; how this came about?*
	"Out of yon bern," scho said, "I saw him born,	*carried*
	Nakit, laid law on cald erd me beforn.	*low; cold earth; before*
	His frosty mouth I kissit in that sted,	*place*
280	Rycht now manlik, now bar and brocht to ded;	*One moment . . . the next bare; death*

The Wallace

	And with a claith I coverit his licaym,	*cloth; dead body*
	For in his lyff he did nevir woman schayme.	*shame*
	His systir sone thou art, worthi and wicht.	*nephew (sister's son); bold*
	Ravenge thar dede for Goddis saik at thi mycht.	*Revenge their deaths*
285	Als I sall help as I am woman trew!"	*Also*
	"Der wicht," he said, "der God sen at thou knew	*creature; since that*
	Gud Robert Boid, quhar at thou can him se,	
	Wilyham Crawfurd als, giff he lyffand be,	*if; is living*
	Adam Wallace, wald help me in this striff!	
290	I pray to God send me thaim all in liff.	*alive*
	For Marys saik bid thaim sone cum to me.	*immediately come*
	The justice innys thow spy for cheryté	*love of God*
	And in quhat feir that thai thar lugyne mak.	*company; lodging*
	Son efftir that we will our purpos tak	*it is our purpose to go*
295	Into Laglane, quhilk has my succour beyne.	
	Adew merket and welcum woddis greyne!"	*Adieu worldliness; green woods*
	Herof as than till hir he spak no mair,	*About this; then to her; more*
	His brydill turnyt and fra hir can he fair;	*went*
	Sic murnyng maid for his der worthi kyn	
300	Him thocht for baill his breyst ner bryst in twyn.	*sorrow; breast; burst; two*
	As he thus raid in gret angyr and teyne,	*rode; grief*
	Of Inglismen thar folowed him fyfteyn	
	Wicht vallyt men, at towart him couth draw	*Specially picked strong; that; drew*
	With a maser to tach him to the law.[1]	
305	Wallace raturnd in greiff and matelent,	*turned back; wrath*
	With his suerd drawyn amang thaim sone he went.	*sword; right away*
	The myddyll of ane he mankit ner in twa,	*one [of them]; severed almost*
	Ane othir thar apon the hed can ta;	*struck*
	The thrid he straik and throuch the cost him claiff;	*struck; side of the body; split*
310	The ferd to ground rycht derffly ded doun he draiff;	*fourth; violently cut down*
	The fyft he hit with gret ire in that sted;	*place*
	Without reskew dreidles he left thaim ded.	*for sure*
	Than his thre men had slayne the tothir five,	
	Fra thaim the laiff eschapit into lyff,	*rest; with their lives*
315	Fled to thar lord and tald him of this cas.	
	To Laglane Wode than ridis wicht Wallas;	*bold*

---

[1] *With a law-court servant to bring him before the court*

Book 7

	The Sotheroun said quhat ane that he hit rycht	English; whichever one
	Without mercye dredles to ded wes dycht.	assuredly was killed
	Mervell thai had sic strenth in ane suld be,	such; one [man] should
320	Ane of thar men at ilk straik he gert de.	each blow; caused to die
	Than demyt thai it suld be Wallace wicht.	thought; bold
	To thar langage maid ansuer ane ald knycht:	talk
	"Forsuth," he said, "be he chapyt this ayr,	if he escaped; justice-ayre
	All your new deid is eking of our cair."	action; increasing; distress
325	The justice said, quhen thar sic murmur rais,	such [a] complaint rose
	"Yhe wald be ferd and thar come mony fais,	would be frightened if; foes
	That for a man me think yow lik to fle	one man
	And wait nocht yeit indeid gyff it be he!	know not yet indeed if
	And thocht it be I cownt him bot full lycht.	although it is
330	Quha bidis her, ilk gentill man sall be knycht.	Whoever remains here, each noble
	I think to deill thar landis haill to morn	deal [out] all their lands tomorrow
	To yow about that ar of Ingland born."	To [those of] you around
	The Sotheron drew to thar lugyng but mar;	English; lodging straightaway
	Four thousand haill that nycht was intill Ayr.	in all
335	In gret bernys biggyt without the toun	barns built outside
	The justice lay with mony bald barroun.	many bold
	Than he gert cry about thai waynys wide	had proclaimed; camps (lit. carts)
	Na Scottis born amang thaim thar suld bid.	stay
	To the castell he wald nocht pas for eys	comfort (ease)
340	Bot sojornd thar with thing that mycht him pleys.	stayed; please
	Gret purvians be se to thaim was brocht,	supplies by sea
	With Irland ayle the mychteast couth be wrocht.	Irish ale; strongest
	Na wach wes set becaus thai had na dout	watch; fear
	Of Scottis men that leiffand was without.	living; outside
345	Lawberand in mynd thai had beyne all that day,	Laboring
	Of ayle and wyne yneuch chosyne haiff thai,	enough
	As bestly folk tuk of thaimselff no keip.	care
	In thar brawnys sone slaid the sleuthfull sleip,	limbs; slid; slothful
	Throuch full gluttré in swarff swappyt lik swyn;[1]	
350	Thar chyftayne than was gret Bachus of wyn.	
	This wys woman besy amang thaim was;	
	Feill men scho warnd and gart to Laglayne pas,	Many; caused

---

[1] *Through great gluttony fell suddenly into a stupor like swine*

105

The Wallace

      Hyrselff formest quhill thai with Wallace met.   *leading the way until*
      Sum comfort than intill his mynd was set.
355 Quhen he thaim saw he thankit God of mycht.
      Tithandis he ast; the woman tald him rycht: *News; asked; told*
      "Slepand as swyn ar all yone fals menyhe.   *Sleeping as swine; company*
      Na Scottis man is in that cumpané."
      Than Wallace said, "Giff thai all dronkyn be
360 I call it best with fyr for thaim to se."   *to provide fire to see them*
      Of gud men than thre hundreth till him socht.
      The woman had tald three trew burges at brocht   *loyal burgesses that brought*
      Out of the toun with nobill aile and breid,   *ale; bread*
      And othir stuff als mekill as thai mycht leid.   *provisions as much; lead*
365 Thai eit and drank, the Scottis men at mocht.   *ate; that might*
      The noblis than Jop has to Wallace brocht.   *nobles then*
      Sadly he said, "Der freyndis, now ye se   *Resolutely*
      Our kyn ar slayn, tharoff is gret peté,
      Throuch feill murthyr, the gret dispite is mor.   *large scale murder; contempt; more*
370 Now sum rameid I wald we set tharfor.   *amends; arrange*
      Suppos that I was maid wardane to be;   *Although*
      Part ar away sic chargis put to me,   *Some; such responsibilities placed on*
      And ye ar her cummyn of als gud blud,   *as good blood (birth)*
      Als rychtwis born be aventur and als gud,   *well-born by [good] fortune; as*
375 Als forthwart, fair, and als likly of persoun,   *As promising; well-built*
      As evir was I; tharfor, till conclusioun,
      Lat us cheys five of this gud cumpanye,   *Let us choose*
      Syne caflis cast quha sall our master be."   *Then cast lots [to decide]*
      Wallace and Boid and Craufurd of renoun
380 And Adam als than lord of Ricardtoun —
      His fadir than wes wesyed with seknes;   *afflicted; sickness*
      God had him tayne intill his lestand grace —   *taken into; lasting*
      The fyft Awchinlek, in wer a nobill man,   *war*
      Caflis to cast about thir five began.   *Lots; these*
385 It wald on him for ocht thai cuth devys,[1]
      Continualy quhill thai had castyn thrys.   *until*
      Than Wallace rais and out a suerd can draw.   *rose; sword drew*
      He said, "I vow to the Makar of aw   *vow; of all*

---

[1] *It would [fall] to him (i.e., Wallace), for anything they could devise*

Book 7

	And till Mary his modyr, Virgyne cler,	to; bright
390	My unclis dede now sall be sauld full der,	dearly paid for
	With mony ma of our der worthi kyn.	more; kin
	Fyrst or I eit or drynk we sall begyn,	before
	For sleuth nor sleip sall nayne remayne in me	sloth; none
	Of this tempest till I a vengeance se."	disaster
395	Than all inclynd rycht humyll of accord	bowed; humbly in agreement
	And him resavit as chyftayne and thar lord.	received
	Wallace a lord he may be clepyt weyll	may well be called a lord
	Thocht ruryk folk tharoff haff litill feill,	Although rustic; understanding
	Na deyme na lord bot landis be thar part.[1]	
400	Had he the warld and be wrachit of hart	base
	He is no lord as to the worthines.	He is not worthy to be a lord
	It can nocht be but fredome, lordlyknes.	without magnanimity
	At the Roddis thai mak full mony ane	Rhoddes; many [a] one
	Quhilk worthy ar, thocht landis haiff thai nane.	though
405	This disscussyng I leiff herroldis till end;	discussion; leave
	On my mater now breiffly will I wend.	On my subject-matter
	Wallace commaunde a burges for to get	ordered
	Fyne cawk eneuch that his der nece mycht set	chalk enough; mark
	On ilk yeit quhar Sotheroun wer on raw.	each gate; [the] English together
410	Than twenty men he gert fast wetheis thraw,	made quickly twist withies
	Ilk man a pair, and on thar arme thaim threw.	Two for each man
	Than to the toune full fast thai cuth persew.	made their way
	The woman past befor thaim suttelly,	ahead of them inconspicuously
	Cawkit ilk gett that thai neid nocht gang by.	Chalked each gate; go
415	Than festnyt thai with wetheis duris fast	they fastened; doors
	To stapill and hesp with mony sekyr cast.	staple and clasp; secure fastenings
	Wallace gert Boid ner hand the castell ga	on the near side
	With fyfté men a jeperté to ma.	surprise attack; make
	Gyff ony ischet the fyr quhen that thai saw,	If; left; fire
420	Fast to the gett he ordand thaim to draw.	gate
	The laiff with him about the bernys yheid.	barns went
	This trew woman servit thaim weill indeid	indeed
	With lynt and fyr that haistely kendill wald.	flax; kindle
	In evirilk nuk thai festnyt blesis bald.	nook; torches bold

---

[1] *Nor consider anyone [a] lord unless he owns land*

The Wallace

425	Wallace commaund till all his men about	
	Na Sotheron man at thai suld lat brek out.	*No English*
	"Quhatevir he be reskewis of that kyn	*Whoever rescues [any] of; kin*
	Fra the rede fyr himselff sall pas tharin."	*red fire*
	The lemand low sone lanssyt apon hycht.	*gleaming flame; soon leapt high*
430	"Forsuth," he said, "this is a plessand sicht;	*Truly; pleasant*
	Till our hartis it suld be sum radres.	*redress*
	War thir away thar power war the les."	*these; less*
	Onto the justice himselff loud can caw:	*call*
	"Lat us to borch our men fra your fals law	*give surety for*
435	At leyffand ar, that chapyt fra your ayr.	*That are living; escaped*
	Deyll nocht thar land, the unlaw is our sayr.	*Deal; penalty; too severe*
	Thou had no rycht, that sall be on thee seyne."	*made clear to you*
	The rewmour rais with cairfull cry and keyne.	*alarm; painful; sharp*
	The bryme fyr brynt rycht braithly apon loft;	*fierce; burned; vigorously on high*
440	Till slepand men that walkand was nocht soft.	*To; waking; gentle*
	The sycht without was awfull for to se;	*outside*
	In all the warld na grettar payne mycht be	
	Than thai within insufferit sor to duell,	*compelled sorely*
	That evir was wrocht bot purgatory or hell:	
445	A payne of hell weill ner it mycht be cauld.	*called*
	Mad folk with fyr hampryt in mony hauld:	*trapped in many houses*
	Feill byggyns brynt that worthi war and wicht,	*Many buildings burned; noble*
	Gat nane away, knaiff, captane, nor knycht,	*None got away, knave*
	Quhen brundis fell off ruftreis thaim amang.	*burning pieces of wood; rafters*
450	Sum rudly rais in byttir paynys strang,	*rose violently; strong*
	Sum nakyt brynt bot beltles all away,	*undressed*
	Sum nevir rais bot smoryt quhar thai lay,	*[were] smothered [by smoke]*
	Sum ruschit fast tyll Ayr gyff thai mycht wyn,	
	Blyndyt in fyr thar deidis war full dym.	
455	The reik mellyt with fylth of carioune	*smoke mingled; foul carrion*
	Amang the fyr rycht foull of offensioune.	*Amidst; vile and offensive*
	The peple beryt lyk wyld bestis in that tyd,	*[were] buried; at that time*
	Within the wallis rampand on athir sid,	*raging; either side*
	Rewmyd in reuth with mony grysly grayne.	*Lamented ruefully; horrible groans*
460	Sum grymly gret quhill thar lyff dayis war gayne,[1]	

---

[1] *Some grimly wept as they departed this life*

108

Book 7

	Sum durris socht, the entré for to get,	*doors; reach*
	Bot Scottismen so wysly thaim beset,	
	Gyff ony brak be awnter of that steid	*[That] if any broke by chance out of that place*
	With suerdis sone bertnyt thai war to dede,	*swords soon put; to death*
465	Or ellys agayne be force drevyn in the fyr.	*back by force driven into*
	Thar chapyt nayne bot brynt up bayne and lyr.	*escaped; [were] burned; bone and flesh*
	The stynk scalyt of ded bodyis sa wyde	*spread; widely*
	The Scottis abhord ner hand for to byd,	*nearby; remain*
	Yeid to the wynd and leit thaim evyn allayne	*Went; windward; left; alone indeed*
470	Quhill the rede fyr had that fals blude ourgayne.	*Until; red fire; blood overwhelmed*
	A frer Drumlay was priour than of Ayr,	*friar; prior*
	Sevyn scor with him that nycht tuk herbry thar	*Seven; refuge*
	In his innys, for he mycht nocht thaim let.	*dwelling-places; stop*
	Till ner mydnycht a wach on thaim he set;	*guard*
475	Hymselff wouk weyll quhill he the fyr saw rys;	*kept good watch until*
	Sum mendis he thocht to tak of that supprys.	*amends; outrage*
	Hys brethir sevyn till harnes sone thai yeid,	*seven brethren soon armed themselves*
	Hymselff chyftayne the ramanand to leid.	*rest; lead*
	The best thai waill of armour and gud ger,	*chose*
480	Syne wapynnys tuk, rycht awfull in affer.	*Then; awesome; appearance*
	Thir eight freris in four partis thai ga,	*These; directions; go*
	With suerdis drawyn till ilk hous yeid twa;	*swords; each; went*
	Sone entrit thai quhar Sotheroune slepand war,	*[the] English; were*
	Apon thaim set with strakis sad and sar.	*Set upon them; blows firm; severe*
485	Feill frekis thar thai freris dang to dede;	*Many men; slaughtered*
	Sum nakit fled and gat out of that sted,	*got; place*
	The wattir socht, abaissit out of slepe.	*startled*
	In the furd weill that was bath wan and depe	*ford-well; dark*
	Feyll of thaim fell that brak out of that place,	*Many; broke*
490	Dowkit to grounde and deit withoutyn grace.	*Plunged to [the] bottom; died*
	Drownyt and slayne was all that herbryt thar.	*lodged*
	Men callis it yeit "the freris blyssyng of Ayr."	*yet; friar's blessing*
	Few folk of waill was levyt apon cace	*worth; left by chance*
	In the castell; lord Persye fra that place	
495	Befor the ayr fra thine to Glaskow drew,	*justice-ayre from there*
	Of men and stuff it was to purva new.	*provisions; furnish anew*
	Yeit thai within saw the fyr byrnand stout,	*Yet; strong*
	With schort awys ischet and had na dout.	*Without delay came out; hesitation*
	The buschement than, as weryouris wys and wicht,	*ambush; warriors; bold*

The Wallace

500	Leit thaim allayne and to the hous past rycht.	*Left; alone; castle; directly*
	Boyd wan the port, entryt and all his men;	*reached; gate*
	Keparis in it was left bot nine or ten.	*Defenders*
	The formast sone hymselff sesyt in hand,	*soon; seized*
	Maid quyt of hym, syne slew all at thai fand.	*Dispatched him, then; that; found*
505	Of purvyaunce in that castell was nayne;	*provisions*
	Schort tyme befor Persye was fra it gayne.	*gone*
	The erll Arnulff had rasavit that hauld	*received; castle*
	Quhilk in the toune was brynt to powder cauld.	*burnt; cold ashes*
	Boyd gert ramayn of his men twenty still;	*made twenty of his men remain*
510	Hymselff past furth to witt of Wallace will,	*learn*
	Kepand the toun quhill nocht was levyt mar	*Guarding; of which no more was left*
	Bot the wode fyr and beyldis brynt full bar.	*Except; houses burned*
	Of lykly men that born was in Ingland	*war-like*
	Be suerd and fyr that nycht deit five thousand.	*By sword; died*
515	Quhen Wallace men was weill togydder met,	
	"Gud freyndis," he said, "ye knaw that thar wes set	*know; appointed*
	Sic law as this now into Glaskow toun	*Such [a] law-court*
	Be Byschope Beik and Persye of renoun.	
	Tharfor I will in haist we thidder fair.	*go*
520	Of our gud kyn sum part ar lossyt thair."	*kin; lost*
	He gert full sone the burges till him caw	*had; soon; called to him*
	And gaiff commaund in generall to thaim aw,	*all*
	In kepyng thai suld tak the hous of Ayr,	*[That] they should defend the castle*
	"And hald it haill quhill tyme that we her mayr.	*safeguard it until; hear more*
525	To byd our king castellys I wald we had;	*await*
	Cast we doun all we mycht be demyt our rad."	*[If] we cast down; considered too rash*
	Thai gart meit cum, for thai had fastyt lang;	*had food fetched; fasted*
	Litill he tuk, syne bownyt thaim to gang.	*then they prepared to go*
	Horsis thai cheys that Sotheroun had brocht thar,	*chose; [the] English*
530	Anew at will and of the toune can fair.	*Newly; went*
	Thre hundreth haill was in his cumpany.	*in all*
	Richt wondir fast raid this gud chevalry	*band of knights*
	To Glaskow Bryg that byggyt was of tre,	*Bridge; built; wood*
	Weyll passit our or Sotheroun mycht thaim se.	*Passed safely across before*
535	Lorde Persye wyst, that besy wes in wer,	*knew; diligent; war*
	Semblyt his men fell awfull in affer.	*Assembled; very awesome; appearance*
	Than demyt thai that it was wicht Wallace;	*they believed; stalwart*
	He had befor chapyt throw mony cace.	*escaped many times by chance*

Book 7

	The byschope Beik and Persye that was wicht	*active*
540	A thousand led of men in armys brycht.	*Led a thousand men*
	Wallace saw weill quhat nowmyr semblit thar;	*numbers assembled*
	He maid his men in twa partis to fair,	*divisions to go*
	Graithit thaim weill without the townys end.	*Equipped themselves; outside*
	He callit Awchinlek for he the passage kend.	*knew*
545	"Uncle," he said, "be besy into wer.	*prepare for battle*
	Quhethir will yhe the byschoppys taill upber,	*Whether; carry*
	Or pas befor and tak his benysone?"	*in front; blessing*
	He ansuerd hym with rycht schort provision,	*little hesitation*
	"Unbyschoppyt yeit forsuth I trow ye be.[1]	
550	Yourselff sall fyrst his blyssyng tak for me,	
	For sekyrly ye servit it best the nycht.	*surely; deserved; tonight*
	To ber his taill we sall in all our mycht."	*carry; with all our might*
	Wallace ansuerd, "Sen we mon sindry gang	*must go separately*
	Perell thar is and ye bid fra us lang,	*if you stay [away] from us [for] long*
555	For yone ar men will nocht sone be agast.	*those; afraid*
	Fra tyme we meit for Goddis saik haist yow fast.	*From [the] time we meet*
	Our disseveryng I wald na Sotheroune saw;	*separation; no English*
	Behynd thaim cum and in the northast raw.	*north-east row*
	Gud men of wer ar all Northummyrland."	*war*
560	Thai partand thus tuk othir be the hand.	*parting; [each] other by*
	Awchinlek said, "We sall do at we may.	*what*
	We wald lik ill to byd oucht lang away;	*not like to stay away long at all*
	A boustous staill betwix us sone mon be,	*strong force; soon must*
	Bot to the rycht allmychty God haiff e."	*give heed*
565	Adam Wallace and Awchinlek was boune,	*were ready*
	Sevyn scor with thaim on the baksid the toune.	*Seven; back end [of]*
	Rycht fast thai yeid quhill thai war out of sycht;	*went until*
	The tothir part arrayit thaim full rycht.	*The other division arrayed; directly*
	Wallace and Boid the playne streyt up can ga;	*open street went up*
570	Sotheroun merveld becaus thai saw na ma.	*[The] English marveled; no more*
	Thar senyhe cryit upon the Persys syde,	*signal*
	With Byschop Beik that bauldly durst abide.	*boldly dared withstand*
	A sayr semlay was at that metyng seyne,	*painful encounter; seen*
	As fyr on flynt it feyrryt thaim betweyne.	*sparked*

---

[1] *Indeed, I believe you have not yet been blessed by a bishop*

The Wallace

575	The hardy Scottis rycht awfully thaim abaid,	*awesomely; withstood*
	Brocht feill to grounde throuch weid that weill was maid,	*Struck many down; armor*
	Perssyt plattis with poyntis stiff of steill,	*Pierced plate-armor; strong; steel*
	Be fors of hand gert mony cruell kneill.	*By force; made fierce men to kneel*
	The strang stour rais as reik upon thaim fast,	*dense dust rose; smoke*
580	Or myst throuch sone up to the clowdis past.	*Before; sun*
	To help thaimselff ilk ayne had mekill neid.	*each one; great need*
	The worthy Scottis stud in fellone dreid,	*stood; terrible danger*
	Yeit forthwart ay thai pressit for to be	*Yet forward ever*
	And thai on thaim gret wondir was to se.	
585	The Perseis men in wer was oysit weill,	*were experienced in war*
	Rycht fersly faucht and sonyeit nocht adeill.	*fiercely fought; hesitated not at all*
	Adam Wallace and Awchinlek com in	
	And partyt Sotheron rycht sodeynly in twyn,	*parted [the] English; two*
	Raturnd to thaim as noble men in wer.	*Rallied; war*
590	The Scottis gat rowme and mony doun thai ber.	*mastery; many*
	The new cowntir assailyeit thaim sa fast,	*encounter attacked*
	Throuch Inglismen maid sloppys at the last.	*breaches*
	Than Wallace selff into that felloune thrang	*[threw] himself; terrible press*
	With his gud swerd that hevy was and lang,	*sword; heavy*
595	At Perseis face witht a gud will he bar.	*he struck vigorously*
	Bath bayne and brayne the forgyt steill throw schair.	*bone; brain; forged steel cut*
	Four hundreth men quhen Lord Persie was dede	
	Out of the gait the byschop Beik thai lede,	*street; lead*
	For than thaim thocht it was no tyme to bid,	*stay*
600	By the frer kyrk till a wode fast besyd.	*friars' church to a forest close by*
	In that forest forsuth thai taryit nocht;	*indeed*
	On fresch horsis to Bothwell sone thai socht.	*soon; made their way*
	Wallace folowed with worthi men and wicht;	*strong*
	Forfouchtyn thai war and trawald all the nycht,	*Exhausted [from fighting]; toiled*
605	Yeit feill thai slew into the chace that day.	*many; in the pursuit*
	The byschope selff and gud men gat away;	*himself*
	Amar Wallang reskewit him in that place.	
	That knycht full oft did gret harme to Wallace.	*often*
	Wallace began of nycht ten houris in Ayr,	
610	On day be nine in Glaskow semlyt thair.	*by nine o'clock; assembled*
	Be ane our nowne at Bothwell yeit he was,	*By one o'clock; gate*
	Repreiffit Wallang or he wald forthir pas,	*Denounced; before*
	Syne turnd agayne, as weyll witnes the buk,	*Then; back, as the book well attests*

Book 7

	Till Dundaff raid, and thar restyng he tuk,	*To; rode; there*
615	Tald gud Schir Jhon of thir tithandis in Ayr.	*Told; these tidings*
	Gret mayne he maid he was nocht with him thar.	*He greatly lamented that*
	Wallace sojornd in Dundaff at his will	*stayed*
	Five dayis out, quhill tithandis come him till	*altogether, until news; to*
	Out of the hycht quhar gud men was forlorn,	*highlands; lost*
620	For Bouchane rais, Adell, Menteth, and Lorn.	*Buchan; Atholl*
	Apon Argyll a fellone wer thai mak;	*grievous war*
	For Eduuardis saik thus can thai undirtak.	*did they undertake*
	The knycht Cambell in Argyll than wes still	
	With his gud men agayne King Eduuardis will	
625	And kepyt fre Lowchow, his heretage,	*kept independent Loch Awe*
	Bot Makfadyan than did him gret owtrage.	*MacFadden; wrong*
	This Makfadyan till Inglismen was suorn;	*to; sworn*
	Eduuard gaiff him bath Argill and Lorn.	*both*
	Fals Jhon of Lorn to that gyft can concord;	*gift; agree*
630	In Ingland than he was a new-maid lord.	
	Thus falsly he gaiff our his heretage	*handed over*
	And tuk at London of Eduuard grettar wage.	*payment*
	Dunkan of Lorn yeit for the landis straiff,	*still; contended*
	Quhill Makfadyan ourset him with the laiff,	*Until; overcame; rest*
635	Put him of force to gud Cambell the knycht	*Entrusted himself of necessity*
	Quhilk into wer was wys, worthi, and wicht.	*war*
	Thus Makfadyan was entrit into Scotland	
	And mervalusly that tyrand tuk on hand	
	With his power, the quhilk I spak of ayr.	*spoke; earlier*
640	Thai four lordschippis all semlyt till him thair,	*assembled*
	Fifteen thousand of curssyt folk indeid	*accursed; indeed*
	Of all gaddryn in ost he had to leid,	*gathering; lead*
	And mony of thaim was out of Irland brocht.	*many; the Hebrides*
	Barnys nor wyff thai peple sparyt nocht,	*Children; wives; spared*
645	Waistyt the land als fer as thai mycht ga,	*Laid waste; as far; go*
	Thai bestly folk couth nocht bot byrn and sla.	*burn; slay*
	Into Louchow he entryt sodeynly;	*Loch Awe*
	The knycht Cambell maid gud defens forthi.	*therefore*
	Till Crage Unyn with thre hundir he yeid:	*To; went*
650	That strenth he held for all his cruell deid,	*stronghold; despite; fierce action*
	Syne brak the bryg that thai mycht nocht out pas	*Then broke; bridge; pass over*
	Bot throuch a furd quhar narow passage was.	*ford*

The Wallace

	Abandounly Cambell agayne thaim baid,	*Boldly; stood*
	Fast upon Avis that was bathe depe and braid.	*[Loch] Awe; both; wide*
655	Makfadyane was apon the tothir sid	
	And thar on force behuffit him for to byd,	*of necessity behooved; stay*
	For at the furde he durst nocht entir out,	
	For gud Cambell mycht set him than in dout.	*place; at risk*
	Makfadyane socht and a small passage fand;	*found*
660	Had he lasar thai mycht pas of that land	*leisure*
	Betuix a roch and the gret wattirsid,	*rock; lochside*
	Bot four in front, na ma mycht gang nor rid.	*Only; no more; go; ride*
	Intill Louchow wes bestis gret plenté;	*beasts [in] great plenty*
	A quhill he thocht thar with his ost to be	*[In] a [little] while; army*
665	And othir stuff that thai had with thaim brocht,	
	Bot all his crafft availyeit him rycht nocht.	*skill availed*
	Dunkane of Lorn has seyne the sodeyne cace.	*seen; sudden danger*
	Fra gud Cambell he went to seik Wallace,	*From; seek*
	Sum help to get of thar turment and teyne.	*anguish; trouble*
670	Togydder befor in Dundé thai had beyne,	*Dundee*
	Lerand at scule into thar tendyr age.	*Learning at school*
	He thocht to slaik Makfadyanys hie curage.	*extinguish; high*
	Gylmychell than with Dunkan furth him dycht;	*prepared*
	A gyd he was and fute man wondir wicht.	*guide; foot soldier; nimble*
675	Sone can thai witt quhar Wallace lugyt was;	*Soon; know*
	With thar complaynt till his presence thai pas.	*grievance*
	Erll Malcom als the Lennox held at es,	*also; in comfort*
	With his gud men to Wallace can he pres.	*did he press*
	Till him thar come gud Rychard of Lundy;	
680	Intill Dundaff he wald no langar ly.	*lie*
	Schir Jhon the Graym als bownyt him to ryd.	*also prepared himself; ride*
	Makfadyanis wer so grevit thaim that tid	*war; vexed; time*
	At Wallace thocht his gret power to se,	*That*
	In quhat aray he reullyt that cuntré.	*state; governed; region*
685	The Rukbé than he kepit with gret wrang	*wrong*
	Stirlyng Castell that stalwart wes and strang.	*was*
	Quhen Wallace come be sowth it in a vaill	*by [the] south [of] it (the castle); valley*
	Till Erll Malcome he said he wald assaill.	*To; attack*
	In divers partis he gert sevir thar men,	*parties; caused to divide*
690	Of thar power that Sotheroun suld nocht ken.	*[the] English should not know*
	Erll Malcome baid in buschement out of sicht.	*waited in ambush*

Book 7

	Wallace with him tuk gud Schir Jhone the knycht	
	And a hundreth of wys wermen but dout,	*fearless warriors*
	Throuch Stirlyng raid gyff ony wald ysche out.	*rode if any; sally out*
695	Towart the bryg the gaynest way thai pas;	*bridge; nearest*
	Quhen Rukbé saw quhat at thar power was	*the size of their army*
	He tuk sevyn scor of gud archaris was thar.	*seven; archers*
	Upon Wallace thai folowed wondyr sayr.	*extremely hard*
	At fell bykkyr thai did thaim mekill der.	*fierce encounters; great harm*
700	Wallace in hand gryppyt a nobill sper,	*gripped; spear*
	Agayne raturnd and has the formast slayne.	*Turned back*
	Schir Jhon the Grayme, that mekill was of mayn,	*was very powerful*
	Amang thaim raid with a gud sper in hand.	*rode*
	The fyrst he slew that he befor him fand;	*found*
705	Apon anothir his sper in sowndyr yeid;	*shattered*
	A suerd he drew quhilk helpyt him in neid.	*sword*
	Ynglis archaris apon thaim can ranew,	*English; renewed [the attack]*
	That his gud hors with arrowis sone thai slew.	*soon*
	On fute he was; quhen Wallace has it seyne	*foot*
710	He lychtyt sone with men of armys keyne,	*dismounted right away; fierce*
	Amang the rout fechtand full wondyr fast.	*throng fighting*
	The Inglismen raturnyt at the last.	*turned back*
	At the castell thai wald haiff beyne full fayne,	*have liked to be*
	Bot Erll Malcome with men of mekill mayne	*great strength*
715	Betuix the Sotheroun and the gettis yeid.	*English; gates went*
	Mony thai slew that douchty wes in deid.	*Many; valiant; deeds*
	In the gret pres Wallace and Rukbé met,	
	With his gud suerd a straik apon him set;	*sword; stroke*
	Derffly to dede the ald Rukbé he draiff.	*Violently to death; old; dashed [him]*
720	His twa sonnys chapyt amang the laiff.	*escaped; rest*
	In the castell be aventur thai yeid	*by [good] luck; went*
	With twenty men; na ma chapyt that dreid.	*more escaped; peril*
	The Lennox men with thar gud lord at was,	*that was*
	Fra the castell thai said thai wald nocht pas,	
725	For weill thai wyst it mycht nocht haldyn be	*knew; be held [against attack]*
	On na lang tyme; forthi thus ordand he.	*For a long time; therefore; ordered*
	Erll Malcom tuk the hous and kepyt that tyd.	*castle; held [it at] that time*
	Wallace wald nocht fra his fyrst purpos bid.	*stray*
	Instance he maid to this gud lord and wys,	*He entreated*
730	Fra thine to pas he suld on na kyn wys	*From there; no kind of way*

The Wallace

	Quhill he had tayne Stirlyng the castell strang;	*Until; captured; strong*
	Trew men him tald he mycht nocht hald it lang.	*told; hold*
	Than Wallace thocht was maist on Makfadyane;	*mostly*
	Of Scottis men he had slayne mony ane.	*many [a] one*
735	Wallace avowide that he suld wrokyn be	*vowed; avenged*
	On that rebald or ellis tharfor to de.	*rebel; else die in the attempt*
	Of tyrandry King Eduuard thocht him gud;	*For oppression; good*
	Law-born he was and of law, simpill blud.	*Low-born; low; blood*
	Thus Wallace was sar grevyt in his entent;	*extremely vexed; mind*
740	To this jornay rycht ernystfully he went.	*feat of arms; earnestly*
	At Stirlyng Bryg assemlyt till him rycht	*Bridge; directly*
	Twa thowsand men that worthi war and wycht.	*were; strong*
	Towart Argyll he bownyt him to ryd;	*prepared; ride*
	Dunkan of Lorn was thar trew sekyr gid.	*reliable guide*
745	Of ald Rukbé the quhilk we spak of ayr,	*old; earlier*
	Twa sonnys on lyff in Stirlyng levit thair.	*alive; lived there*
	Quhen thai brethir consavit weill the rycht	*those brothers understood*
	This hous to hald that thai na langar mycht,	*castle; keep*
	For caus quhi thai wantyt men and meit,	*Because; lacked; food*
750	With Erll Malcome thai kest thaim for to treit	*prepared; negotiate*
	Grace of thar lyff and thai that with thaim was;	*Saving their lives; those; were*
	Gaiff our the hous, syne couth in Ingland pas	*Handed over the castle, then did*
	On the thrid day that Wallace fra thaim raid.	*rode*
	With King Eduuard full mony yer thai baid,	*very many years; remained*
755	In Brucis wer agayne come in Scotland.	*Bruce's war*
	Stirlyng to kepe the toune of thaim tuk on hand.	*keep*
	Mencione of Bruce is oft in Wallace buk;	
	To fend his rycht full mekill payne he tuk.	*defend; great trouble*
	Quharto suld I her of tary ma?	*should; here; make*
760	To Wallace furth now schortlye will I ga.	*shortly; go*
	Dunkan of Lorne Gilmychall fra thaim send	*sent*
	A spy to be, for he the contré kend.	*region knew*
	Be our party was passit Straith Fulan,	
	The small fute folk began to irk ilk ane,[1]	
765	And hors of fors behuffyt for to faill.	*horses of necessity behooved*

---

[1] Lines 763–64: *By [the time] our party was past Strath Fillan, / Every one [of] the small band of outlaws began to tire*

Book 7

	Than Wallace thocht that cumpany to vaill.	*help*
	"Gud men," he said, "this is nocht meit for us;	*fitting*
	In brokyn ray and we cum on thaim thus	*array if*
	We may tak scaith and harme our fayis bot small.	*receive injury; foes only a little*
770	To thaim in lik we may nocht semble all.	*in the same way; gather*
	Tary we lang a playne feild thai will get;	*[If] we tarry long; open battlefield*
	Apon thaim sone sa weill we may nocht set.	*Soon we may not set upon them so well*
	Part we mon leiff us folowand for to be;	*Part [of our company]; leave*
	With me sall pas our power into thre."	
775	Five hundyr fyrst till himselff he has tayne	*hundred; taken*
	Of westland men, was worthi knawin ilk ane.	*known each one*
	To Schir Jhon Grayme als mony ordand he,	*as many he decreed*
	And five hundreth to Rychard of Lundye.	
	In that part was Wallace of Ricardtoun;	*division*
780	In all gud deid he was ay redy boun.	*deeds; always ready and willing*
	Five hundreth left that mycht nocht with thaim ga,	*go*
	Suppos at thai to byd was wondyr wa.	*Even though; remain behind; very loath*
	Thus Wallace ost began to tak the hicht,	*army; highlands*
	Our a montayne sone passit of thar sicht.	*Over; soon; [out] of their sight*
785	In Glendowchar thair spy mett thaim agayn,	*Glen Dochart*
	With Lord Cambell; than was our folk rycht fayn.	*very glad*
	At that metyng gret blithnes mycht be seyn;	*joy*
	Thre hundreth he led that cruell was and keyn.	*fierce; bold*
	He comford thaim and bad thaim haiff no dreid:	*comforted them; commanded; fear*
790	"Yon bestly folk wantis wapynnys and weid.	*Those; lack; armor*
	Sune thai will fle, scharply and we persew."	*Soon; and we [will] pursue keenly*
	Be Louchdouchyr full sodeynly thaim drew.	*By Loch Dochart; came*
	Than Wallace said, "A lyff all sall we ta,	*take*
	For her is nayne will fra his falow ga."	*here; no one; fellow go*
795	The spy he send the entré for to se;	
	Apon the mos a scurrour sone fand he.	*moor; scout soon found*
	To scour the land Makfadyane had him send;	*search; sent*
	Out of Cragmor that day he thocht to wend.	*go*
	Gylmychall fast apon him folowed thar;	
800	With a gud suerd that weill and scharply schar	*sword; pierced*
	Maid quyt of him; at tithandis tald he nayne;[1]	

---

[1] *Made an end of him; [so] that he told no news*

The Wallace

	The out spy thus was lost fra Makfadyhane.	*spy sent out*
	Than Wallace ost apon thar fute thai lycht;	*on foot; alighted*
	Thar hors thai left thocht thai war nevir so wicht;	*strong*
805	For mos and crag thai mycht no langar dre.	*bog; rock; endure*
	Than Wallace said, "Quha gangis best lat se."	*Let's see who makes his way best*
	Throuchout the mos delyverly thai yeid,	*nimbly; went*
	Syne tuk the hals, quharof thai had most dreid.	*Then entered the pass; fear*
	Endlang the schoir ay four in frownt thai past	*Along; shore [of the loch] always; front*
810	Quhill thai within assemblit at the last.	*Until*
	Lord Cambell said, "We haiff chewyst this hauld.	*chosen; stronghold*
	I trow to God thar wakyning sall be cauld.	*trust; awakening shall; cold*
	Her is na gait to fle yone peple can	*Here; way; those*
	Bot rochis heich and wattir depe and wan."	*Except [by] high rocks; dark*
815	Eighteen hundreth of douchty men in deid	*valiant; action*
	On the gret ost but mar process thai yeid,	*without further delay; advanced*
	Fechtand in frownt and mekill maistry maid.	*Fighting; front; deeds of arms achieved*
	On the frayt folk buskyt withoutyn baid.	*scared; set on; hesitation*
	Rudly till ray thai ruschit thaim agayne;	*Strongly; array*
820	Gret part of thaim wes men of mekill mayne.	*great strength*
	Gud Wallace men sa stowtly can thaim ster	*boldly bestirred themselves*
	The battaill on bak five akyr breid thai ber.	*breadth of five acres; conducted*
	Into the stour feill tyrandis gert thai kneill.	*fighting many oppressors made*
	Wallace in hand had a gud staff of steyll;	*sword of steel*
825	Quhomevir he hyt to ground brymly thaim bar;	*Whomever; hit; fiercely; dashed*
	Romde him about a large rude and mar.[1]	
	Schir Jhon the Grayme in deid was rycht worthy,	*action*
	Gud Cambell als, and Rychard of Lundy,	*also*
	Adam Wallace and Robert Boid in feyr	*together*
830	Amang thar fais quhar deidis was sald full der.	*Among; foes; were paid very dearly*
	The felloun stour was awfull for to se.	*cruel fighting*
	Makfadyane than so gret debait maid he	*resistance*
	With Yrage men hardy and curageous;	*Highlanders*
	The stalwart stryff rycht hard and peralous,	*struggle*
835	Boundance of blud fra woundis wid and wan,	*Abundance of blood; wide and deep*
	Stekit to deid on ground lay mony man.	*Stabbed to death; many men*
	The fersast thar ynewch of fechtyn fand;	*fiercest; enough; fighting found*

---

[1] *Cleared a space around him as large as a rood (a measure) or more*

Book 7

	Twa houris large into the stour thai stand,	long; battle; stood their ground
	At Jop himselff weill wyst nocht quha suld wyn.[1]	
840	Bot Wallace men wald nocht in sowndyr twyn;	asunder break
	Till help thaimselff thai war of hardy will.	To
	Of Yrage blud full hardely thai spill,	Highlander blood
	With feyll fechtyn maid sloppys throuch the thrang.	fierce fighting; gaps; throng
	On the fals part our wicht wermen sa dang	party; strong warriors; struck
845	That thai to byd mycht haiff no langar mycht.	stay
	The Irland folk than maid thaim for the flycht,	Highland; prepared for flight
	In craggis clam and sum in wattir flett,	crags climbed; floated
	Twa thousand thar drownyt withoutyn lett.	at once
	Born Scottis men baid still into the feild,	remained
850	Kest wapynnys thaim fra and on thar kneis kneild.	Threw; knees kneeled
	With petous voice thai criyt apon Wallace,	piteous
	For Goddis saik to tak thaim in his grace.	
	Grevyt he was bot rewth of thaim he had,	Vexed; pity
	Rasavit thaim fair with contenance full sad.	Received; stern
855	"Of our awne blud we suld haiff gret peté.	[On those]; own
	Luk yhe sla nane of Scottis will yoldyn be.	who will surrender
	Of outland men lat nane chaip with the liff."	foreign
	Makfadyane fled for all his felloun stryff	fierce opposition
	Ontill a cave within a clyfft of stayne,	stone cliff
860	Undyr Cragmor with fifteen is he gayne.	
	Dunkan of Lorn his leyff at Wallace ast;	asked Wallace's permission to leave
	On Makfadyane with worthi men he past;	followed
	He grantyt him to put thaim all to ded.	granted him [permission]; death
	Thai left nane quyk, syne brocht Wallace his hed,	none alive; head
865	Apon a sper throuchout the feild it bar.	spear; carried
	The lord Cambell syne hynt it by the har;	then seized; hair
	Heich in Cragmor he maid it for to stand,	High
	Steild on a stayne for honour of Irland.	Placed; stone; clansmen
	The blessit men that was of Scotland born,	fortunate
870	Funde at his faith Wallace gert thaim be sworn,	Found in his allegiance
	Restorit thaim to thar landis but les.	indeed
	He leit sla nayne that wald cum till his pes.	let [them] kill no one who; peace
	Efftir this deid in Lorn syne couth he fayr;	After; feat; afterwards; go

---

[1] That Jop himself did not know for sure who would win

The Wallace

	Reullyt the land had beyne in mekill cayr.	*Governed; much suffering*
875	In Archatan a consell he gert cry,	*Ardchattan; council; had proclaimed*
	Quhar mony man socht till his senyory.	*flocked to; leadership*
	All Lorn he gaiff till Duncan at was wicht	*strong*
	And bad him: "Hald in Scotland with the rycht,	*commanded*
	And thow sall weill bruk this in heretage.	*enjoy possession*
880	Thi brothir sone at London has grettar wage,	*(i.e., nephew); reward*
	Yeit will he cum he sall his landis haiff.	*If he will come [into Wallace's grace]*
	I wald tyne nayne that rychtwisnes mycht saiff."	*lose none; protect*
	Mony trew Scot to Wallace couth persew;	*Many; flocked to Wallace*
	At Archatan fra feill strenthis thai drew.	*many strongholds*
885	A gud knycht come and with him men sexté;	
	He had beyne oft in mony strang jeperté	*dangerous exploits*
	With Inglismen and sonyeid nocht a deill.	*hesitated*
	Ay fra thar faith he fendyt him full weill,	*Ever; allegiance; defended*
	Kepyt him fre, thocht King Eduuard had sworn;[1]	
890	Schir Jhon Ramsay, that rychtwys ayr was born,	*rightful heir*
	Of Ouchterhous and othir landis was lord,	
	And schirreff als, as my buk will record,	*also*
	Of nobill blud and als haill ancrasé	*sound ancestry*
	Contenyt weill with worthi chevalré.	*continued*
895	Intill Straithern that lang tyme he had beyne	
	At gret debait agaynys his enemys keyne;	*Offering great resistance; cruel*
	Rycht wichtly wan his leving into wer.	*vigorously; livelihood in war*
	Till him and his Sotheroun did mekill der;	*To; [the] English; great injury*
	Weill he eschewit and sufferyt gret distress.	*He accomplished much*
900	His sone was cald the flour of courtlyness,	*son; called; flower*
	As witnes weill into the schort tretty	*account*
	Eftir the Bruce, quha redis in that story.	
	He rewllit weill bathe into wer and pes;	*governed; war; peace*
	Alexander Ramsay to nayme he hecht but les.	*name; called indeed*
905	Quhen it wes wer till armes he him kest;	*war; he devoted himself*
	Under the croun he wes ane of the best.	
	In tyme of pees till courtlynes he yeid,	*peace; courtly pursuits; turned*
	Bot to gentrice he tuk nayne othir heid.	*noble birth; heed*
	Quhat gentill man had nocht with Ramsay beyne	*noble*

---

[1] *Kept himself independent, though sworn to King Edward*

Book 7

910	Of courtlynes thai cownt him nocht a preyne.	*[worth] a pin*
	Fredome and treuth he had as men wald as;[1]	
	Sen he begane na bettir squier was,	*Since*
	Roxburch Hauld he wan full manfully,	*Roxburgh Castle; conquered*
	Syne held it lang quhill tratouris tresonably	*Then; until traitors*
915	Causit his dede, I can nocht tell yow how;	*death*
	Of sic thingis I will ga by as now.	*such; pass over for now*
	I haiff had blayme, to say the suthfastnes,	*been reproached; truth*
	Tharfor I will bot lychtly ryn that cace,	*lightly touch on that case*
	Bot it be thing that playnly sclanderit is.	*Unless; something censured*
920	For sic I trow thai suld deyme me no mys;	*such; not find fault with me*
	Of gud Alexander as now I spek no mar.	*more*
	His fadir come as I told of befor.	
	Wallace of hym rycht full gud comford hais	*comfort has*
	For weill he coud do harmyng till his fais.	*certainly; harm; foes*
925	In wer he was rycht mekill for to prys,	*war; greatly to prize*
	Besy and trew, bath sobyr, wicht, and wys.	*Diligent; both steadfast, strong*
	A gud prelat als to Archatan socht;	*prelate; made his way*
	Of his lordschip as than he brukyt nocht.	*possessed*
	This worthi clerk cummyn of hie lynage,	*high lineage*
930	Of Synclar blude, nocht forty yer of age,	*Sinclair blood*
	Chosyne he was be the papis consent,	*by the pope's*
	Of Dunkell lord him maid with gud entent.	*Dunkeld bishop; purpose*
	Bot Inglismen that Scotland gryppit all	*seized*
	Of benyfice thai leit him bruk bot small.	*benefice; allowed him [to] possess*
935	Quhen he saw weill tharfor he mycht nocht mute,	*treat*
	To saiff his lyff thre yer he duelt in But;	*save; Bute*
	Leifyde as he mycht and kepyt ay gud part[2]	
	Under saifté of Jamys than Lord Stewart,	*protection*
	Till gud Wallace, quhilk Scotland wan with payne,	*Until; won; difficulty*
940	Restord this lord till his leyffing agayne.	*land*
	And mony ma that lang had beyne ourthrawin,	*many more; overthrown*
	Wallace thaim put rychtwisly to thar awn.	*restored rightfully; own*
	The small ost als the quhilk I spak of ayr,	*also; earlier*
	Into the hycht that Wallace lewyt thar,	*In the highlands; left there*

---

[1] *Generosity and loyalty he had as [much as] any one could ask*

[2] *Lived as he could and always kept good faith [with the Scottish rebels]*

The Wallace

945	Come to the feild quhar Makfadyane had beyne,	Came
	Tuk at was left, baithe weid and wapynnys scheyne;	what; both armor; bright
	Throw Lorn syne past als gudly as thai can.	then; well
	Of thar nowmir thai had nocht lost a man.	number
	On the fyft day thai wan till Archatan	reached
950	Quhar Wallace baid with gud men mony ane.	camped; many [a] one
	He welcummyt thaim apon a gudly wys	warmly
	And said thai war rycht mekill for to prys.	greatly to prize
	All trew Scottis he honourit into wer,	war
	Gaiff that he wan, hymselff kepyt no ger.	Gave [away] what; won; gear
955	Quhen Wallace wald no langar sojorn thar,	stay
	Fra Archatan throuout the land thai far	From; traveled
	Towart Dunkell, with gud men of renoun.	
	His maist thocht than was haill on Sanct Jhonstoun.	His mind was set then wholly
	He cald Ramsai, that gud knycht of gret vaill,	summoned; worth
960	Sadly avysyt besocht him of consaill.	Firmly resolved beseeched; advice
	"Of Saynct Jhonstoun now haiff I in remembrance;	memory
	Thar I haiff beyne and lost men apon chance,	by misfortune
	Bot ay for ane we gert ten of thaim de,	always for one [of ours]; caused
	And yeit me think that is no mendis to me.	amends
965	I wald assay of this land or we gang	attack; before; go
	And lat thaim witt thai occupy her with wrang."	let them know; here wrongly
	Than Ramsay said, "That toune thai may nocht kep.	keep
	The wallis ar laych suppos the dyk be depe.	low; ditch
	Ye haiff enewch that sall thaim cummyr sa;	enough; harass
970	Fyll up the dyk that we may playnly ga	Fill; go
	In haill battaill, a thowsand our at anys;	full battle order; across at once
	Fra this power thai sall nocht hald yon wanys."	force; these buildings
	Wallace was glaid that he sic comfort maid;	such
	Furth talkand thus on to Dunkell thai raid.	Forth talking; rode
975	Four dayis thar thai lugyt with plesance,	lodged comfortably
	Quhill tyme thai had forseyne thar ordinance.	Until; made ready their preparations
	Ramsay gert byg strang bestials of tre	had built; siege machines; wood
	Be gud wrychtis, the best in that cuntré;	wrights; region
	Quhen thai war wrocht betaucht thaim men to leid	made assigned men to lead them
980	The wattir doun quhill thai come to that steid.	Down the river until; came; place
	Schir Jhon Ramsay rycht gudly was thar gid,	was their excellent guide
	Rewillyt thaim weill at his will for to bid.	Directed; to follow his will
	The gret ost than about the village past;	army; around

Book 7

	With erd and stayne thai fillit dykis fast.	*earth; stones; ditches*
985	Flaikis thai laid on temir lang and wicht;	*Hurdles; timber long; strong*
	A rowme passage to the wallis thaim dycht.	*clear path; prepared*
	Feill bestials rycht starkly up thai rais;	*Many siege engines; strongly; raised*
	Gud men of armys sone till assailye gais.	*soon; attack went*
	Schir Jhon the Grayme and Ramsay that was wicht	*powerful*
990	The Turat Bryg segyt with all thar mycht,	*besieged*
	And Wallace selff at mydsid of the toun	*middle way*
	With men of armys that was to bargane bown.	*were ready to fight*
	The Sotheron men maid gret defence that tid	*English; time*
	With artailye that felloune was to bid,	*artillery; grievous; endure*
995	With awblaster, gaynye, and stanys fast	*crossbow, crossbow bolts; stones*
	And hand gunnys, rycht brymly out thai cast;	*guns; fiercely; shot*
	Punyeid with speris men of armys scheyn.	*Pierced; bright*
	The worthi Scottis that cruell war and keyne,	*fierce; bold*
	At hand strakis, fra thai togidder met,	*In close combat, from [when]*
1000	With Sotheroun blud thar wapynnys sone thai wet.	*English*
	Yeit Inglismen that worthi war in wer	*Yet; war*
	Into the stour rycht bauldly can thaim ber,	*fighting; boldly conducted themselves*
	Bot all for nocht availyeid thaim thar deid;	*availed; actions*
	The Scottis throw force apon thaim in thai yeid.	*forced their way in*
1005	A thousand men our wallis yeid hastely;	*hurried over walls*
	Into the toun rais hidwis noyis and cry.	*rose hideous noise*
	Ramsay and Graym the turat yet has wown	*turret; reached*
	And entrit in quhar gret striff has begown.	*battle; begun*
	A trew squier quhilk Rwan hecht be nayme	*was called; name*
1010	Come to the salt with gud Schir Jhon the Grayme;	*assault*
	Thirty with him of men that previt weill	*proved [their mettle]*
	Amang thar fais with wapynnys stiff of steill.	*Among; foes; strong of steel*
	Quhen at the Scottis semblit on athir sid	*that; assembled; either*
	Na Sotheroun was that mycht thar dynt abid.	*[There] was no Englishman; blows endure*
1015	Twa thousand sone was fulyeid under feit	*soon; trampled; foot*
	Of Sotheroun blud, lay stekit in the streit.	*Englishmen; stabbed; street*
	Schir Jhon Sewart saw weill the toun was tynt,	*lost*
	Tuk him to flycht and wald no langar stynt;	*fled away; stay*
	In a lycht barge and with him men sexté	*light*
1020	The water doun socht succour at Dundé.	*Down the river; help; Dundee*
	Wallace baid still quhill the ferd day at morn	*stayed until; fourth*
	And left nane thar that war of Ingland born.	

The Wallace

	Riches thai gat of gold and othir gud,	*got; goods*
	Plenyst the toun agayne with Scottis blud.	*Settled; Scottish people*
1025	Rwan he left thar capteyn for to be,	
	In heretage gaiff him office to fee	*As heritable office*
	Of all Straithern, and schirreiff of the toun;	*[to be] sheriff*
	Syne in the north gud Wallace maid him boune.	*Then; set off*
	In Abyrdeyn he gert a consaill cry	*council*
1030	Trew Scottis men suld semble hastely.	*[To which] loyal Scottish; assemble*
	Till Cowper he raid to wesy that abbay;	*To Coupar; inspect*
	The Inglis abbot fra thine was fled away.	*from there*
	Bischop Synclar without langar abaid	*delay*
	Met thaim at Glammys, syne furth with thaim he raid.	*then forth; rode*
1035	Intill Breichyn thai lugyt all that nycht;	*In Brechin; lodged*
	Syne on the morn Wallace gert graith thaim rycht,	*Then; prepare [equip]*
	Displayed on breid the baner of Scotland	*abroad; banner*
	In gud aray with noble men at hand;	*battle order*
	Gert playnly cry that sawfté suld be nayne[1]	
1040	Of Sotheroun blud quhar thai mycht be ourtayn.	*English; overtaken*
	In playne battaill throuch out the Mernys thai rid.	*open; Mearns; rode*
	The Inglismen, at durst thaim nocht abid,	*that dared*
	Befor the ost full ferdly furth thai fle	*fled in terror*
	Till Dwnottar, a snuk within the se;	*Dunnottar [Castle]; promontory*
1045	Na ferrar thai mycht wyn out of the land.	*No farther; escape*
	Thai semblit thar quhill thai war four thousand;	*assembled; until*
	To the kyrk rane, wend gyrth for till haiff tayne.	*church ran, thought sanctuary*
	The laiff ramaynd apon the roch of stayne.	*rest remained; stone rock*
	The byschope than began tretty to ma,	*negotiations; make*
1050	Thar lyffis to get out of the land to ga,	*lives; save; go*
	Bot thai war rad and durst nocht weill affy.	*afraid; dared; trust*
	Wallace in fyr gert set all haistely,	*on fire*
	Brynt up the kyrk and all that was tharin.	*Burnt; church*
	Atour the roch the laiff ran with gret dyn:	*Over; rock (castle); rest; din*
1055	Sum hang on craggis rycht dulfully to de,	*hung onto rocks; painfully; die*
	Sum lap, sum fell, sum floteryt in the se.	*leapt; floundered*
	Na Sotheroun on lyff was levyt in that hauld	*Englishman was left alive; stronghold*
	And thaim within thai brynt in powder cauld.	*burnt; cold ashes*

---

[1] *Had [it] openly proclaimed that there would be no sparing*

Book 7

	Quhen this was done feill fell on kneis doun,	*many fell down on [their] knees*
1060	At the byschop askit absolucioun.	
	Than Wallace lewch, said, "I forgiff yow all.	*laughed*
	Ar ye wermen, rapentis for sa small?	*warriors, [that] repent; little*
	Thai rewid nocht us into the toun of Ayr,	*had no pity on us*
	Our trew barrowns quhen that thai hangit thar."	*hanged there*
1065	Till Abyrdeyn than haistely thai pas,	*To Aberdeen*
	Quhar Inglismen besyly flittand was.	*busily were removing*
	A hundreth schippys that ruthyr bur and ayr,	*hundred ships; rudder carried; oar*
	To turs thair gud, in havyn was lyand thar.	*pack; goods; haven*
	Bot Wallace ost come on thaim sodeynlye;	*Wallace's army*
1070	Thar chapyt nane of all that gret menyhe,	*None escaped there; company*
	Bot feill servandis in thaim levyt nane.	*Except many servants; left*
	At ane eb se the Scottis is on thaim gayn,	*an ebb tide; went on them*
	Tuk out the ger, syne set the schippys in fyr.	*goods, then; on fire*
	The men on land thai bertynyt bayne and lyr;	*battered bone; flesh*
1075	Yeid nane away bot preistis, wyffis, and barnys;	
	Maid thai debait thai chapyt nocht but harmys.[1]	
	Into Bowchane Wallace maid him to ryd,	*Buchan; went on horseback*
	Quhar Lord Bewmound was ordand for to bid.	*commanded; stay*
	Erll he was maid bot of schort tyme befor;[2]	
1080	He brukit nocht for all his bustous schor.	*did not enjoy possession; rude threatening*
	Quhen he wyst weill that Wallace cummand was,	*knew*
	He left the land and couth to Slanys pas	*traveled to Slains*
	And syne be schip in Ingland fled agayne.	*then by ship*
	Wallace raid throw the northland into playne.	*rode; openly*
1085	At Crummade feill Inglismen thai slew.	*Cromarty many*
	The worthi Scottis till him thus couth persew;	*flocked*
	Raturnd agayne and come till Abirdeyn	*Returned; came*
	With his blith ost apon the Lammes Evyn;	*pleased army; July 31*
	Stablyt the land as him thocht best suld be,	*Settled; should*
1090	Syne with ane ost he passit to Dundé,	*Then; army*
	Gert set a sege about the castell strang.	*Caused a siege to be laid*
	I leyff thaim thar and forthir we will gang.	*leave; go*

---

[1] Lines 1075–76: *None went away except priests, women, and children; / [If] they resisted they did not escape without harm*

[2] *He was made an earl only a short time before*

The Wallace

	Schir Amar Wallang haistit him full fast,	*hurried very quietly*
	Intill Ingland with his haill houshald past.	*entire retinue*
1095	Bothwell he left, was Murrays heretage,	*[which] was*
	And tuk him than bot till King Eduuardis wage.	*only to; hire*
	Thus his awne land forsuk for evirmar;	*own; forsook*
	Of Wallace deid gret tithandis tald he thar.	*Wallace's deeds; news told*
	Als Inglismen sair murnyt in thar mude,	*profoundly lamented; minds*
1100	Had lossyt her bathe lyff, landis, and gud.	*[For they] had lost here both*
	Eduuard as than couth nocht in Scotland fair,	*go*
	Bot Kercyingame that was his tresorair,	*treasurer*
	With him a lord than erll was of Waran,	
	He chargyt thaim with nowmeris mony ane	*ordered; large numbers [of troops]*
1105	Rycht weill beseyn in Scotland for to ryd.	*well equipped; ride*
	At Stirlyng still he ordand thaim to bid	*commanded; wait*
	Quhill he mycht cum with ordinance of Ingland.	*Until; supplies from*
	Scotland agayne he thocht to tak in hand.	*subdue*
	This ost past furth and had bot litill dreid;	*fear*
1110	The erle Patrik rasavit thaim at Tweid.	*received; [the River] Tweed*
	Malice he had at gud Wallace befor,	*Ill will; towards*
	Lang tyme by past and than incressit mor,	*then [it] increased more*
	Bot throuch a cas that hapnyt of his wyff:	*circumstance; [on account] of*
	Dunbar scho held fra him into thar striff	*struggle*
1115	Throuch the supplé of Wallace into playne;	*assistance; indeed*
	Bot he be meyne gat his castell agayne	*means*
	Lang tyme or than, and yeit he couth nocht ces.	*before then; desist*
	Agayne Wallace he previt in mony pres,	*Against; proved [his mettle]; combats*
	With Inglismen suppleit thaim at his mycht.	*supported*
1120	Contrar Scotland thai wrocht full gret unrycht.	*Against; wrought; injustice*
	Thar mustir than was awfull for to se,	*muster; awesome*
	Of fechtand men thousandis thai war sexté,	*fighting; there were sixty thousand*
	To Stirlyng past or thai likit to bid.	*before; chose to stop [stay]*
	To Erll Malcome a sege thai laid that tid	*siege; time*
1125	And thocht to kep the commaund of thar king;	*keep*
	Bot gud Wallace wrocht for ane othir thing.	*planned*
	Dundé he left and maid a gud chyftane	
	With twa thousand to kepe that hous of stayne,	*stone*
	Of Angwis men and duellaris of Dundé;	*Angus; inhabitants*
1130	The sammyn nycht till Sanct Jhonstoun went he.	*same*
	Apon the morn till Schirreff Mur he raid	*rode*

Book 7

	And thar a quhill in gud aray thai baid.	*while; order; stayed*
	Schir Jhon the Grayme and Ramsay that was wicht,	*strong*
	He said to thaim, "This is my purpos rycht.	
1135	Our mekill it is to proffer thaim battaill	*It is too ambitious*
	Apon a playne feild bot we haiff sum availl."	*a battlefield unless; advantage*
	Schir Jhon the Grayme said, "We haiff undirtayn	*undertaken*
	With les power sic thing that weill is gayn."	*less; such; has gone well*
	Than Wallace said, "Quhar sic thing cummys of neid,	*such; of necessity*
1140	We suld thank God that makis us for to speid.	*succeed*
	Bot ner the bryg my purpos is to be	*near; bridge*
	And wyrk for thaim sum suttell jeperté."	*plan; a surprise attack*
	Ramsay ansuerd, "The brig we may kepe weill.	
	Of way about Sotheroun has litill feill."	*knowledge*
1145	Wallace sent Jop the battaill for to set,	*[time of] the battle; appoint*
	The Tuysday next to fecht withoutyn let.	*fight; delay*
	On Setterday onto the bryg thai raid,	*bridge; rode*
	Of gud playne burd was weill and junctly maid;	*board; firmly*
	Gert wachis wait that nane suld fra thaim pas.	*sentries; knew; none should from*
1150	A wricht he tuk, the suttellast at thar was,	*carpenter; most skilled*
	And ordand him to saw the burd in twa,	*ordered; board*
	Be the myd trest that nayne mycht our it ga;	*By; middle beam; over*
	On charnaill bandis nald it full fast and sone,	*hinges nailed*
	Syne fyld with clay as nathing had beyne done.	*Then filled; as [if] nothing*
1155	The tothir end he ordand for to be,	
	How it suld stand on thre rowaris of tre,	*wooden rollers*
	Quhen ane war out that the laiff doun suld fall.	*rest*
	Himselff undir he ordand thar withall,	*underneath; ordered*
	Bownd on the trest in a creddill to sit,	*beam; wooden support*
1160	To lous the pyne quhen Wallace leit him witt;	*loosen; pin; let him know*
	Bot with a horn quhen it was tyme to be,	
	In all the ost suld no man blaw bot he.	*blow*
	The day approchit of the gret battaill;	
	The Inglismen for power wald nocht faill.	
1165	Ay sex thai war agayne ane of Wallace;	*six; were against one*
	Fyfty thousand maid thaim to battaill place.	*went*
	The ramaynand baid at the castell still;	*remainder stayed*
	Baithe feild and hous thai thocht to tak at will.	*Both; castle; capture*
	The worthi Scottis apon the tothir side	*other side*
1170	The playne feild tuk, on fute maid thaim to bid.	*field of battle entered; foot; stand*

The Wallace

	Hew Kercyngayme the vantgard ledis he	*vanguard; led*
	With twenty thousand of likly men to se.	*war-like*
	Thirty thousand the erll of Waran had,	
	Bot he did than as the wys man him bad;	*wise man (see note)*
1175	All the fyrst ost befor him our was send.	*army; across*
	Sum Scottis men that weill the maner kend	*thought they knew better*
	Bade Wallace blaw and said thai war enew.	*Told; blow [his horn]; enough*
	He haistyt nocht bot sadly couth persew	*did not rush; resolutely came on*
	Quhill Warans ost thik on the bryg he saw.	*Until; bridge*
1180	Fra Jop the horn he hyntyt and couth blaw	*seized*
	Sa asprely and warned gud Jhon wricht.	*sharply; John [the] carpenter*
	The rowar out he straik with gret slycht;	*roller; knocked; cunning*
	The laiff yeid doun quhen the pynnys out gais.	*rest went down; went out*
	A hidwys cry amang the peple rais;	*hideous; rose*
1185	Bathe hors and men into the wattir fell.	*Both*
	The hardy Scottis that wald na langar duell	
	Set on the laiff with strakis sad and sar,	*rest; blows firm; sore*
	Of thaim thar our as than soverit thai war.	*over; secured [from attack]*
	At the forbreist thai previt hardely,	*van of the army; proved [themselves]*
1190	Wallace and Grayme, Boid, Ramsay, and Lundy,	
	All in the stour fast fechtand face to face.	*battle; fighting*
	The Sotheron ost bak rerit of that place	*English; drew back from*
	As thai fyrst tuk five akyr breid and mar.	*breadth of an acre; more*
	Wallace on fute a gret scharp sper he bar;	*spear; carried*
1195	Amang the thikest of the pres he gais.	*press; goes*
	On Kercyngaym a strak chosyn he hais	*stroke delivered; has*
	In the byrnes that polyst was full brycht.	*corslet; polished*
	The punyeand hed the plattis persyt rycht,	*piercing head; penetrated right through*
	Throuch the body stekit him but reskew.	*stabbed him fatally*
1200	Derffly to dede that chyftane was adew;	*That chieftain was violently killed*
	Baithe man and hors at that strak he bar doun.	*Both; dashed*
	The Inglis ost, quhilk war in battaill boun,	*English army, which; ready*
	Comfort thai lost quhen thar chyftayne was slayn,	*They lost courage*
	And mony ane to fle began in playne.	*many [a] one openly began to flee*
1205	Yeit worthi men baid still into the sted	*Yet; remained; place*
	Quhill ten thousand was brocht onto thar dede.	*brought to their deaths*
	Than fled the laiff and mycht no langar bid.	*rest; stay*
	Succour thai socht on mony divers sid,	*Help; many diverse sides*
	Sum est, sum west, and sum fled to the north.	

Book 7

1210	Sevyn thousand large at anys flottryt in Forth,[1]	
	Plungyt the depe and drownd without mercye,	depths
	Nayne left on lyff of all that feill menyhe.	were left alive; large company
	Of Wallace ost na man was slayne of vaill	no man of worth was slain
	Bot Andrew Murray into that strang battaill.	Except; hard
1215	The south part than saw at thar men was tynt,	were lost
	Als fersly fled as fyr dois of the flynt.	As fiercely
	The place thai left, castell and Stirlyng toun,	
	Towart Dunbar in gret haist maid thaim boun.	made their way
	Quhen Wallace ost had won that feild throuch mycht,	
1220	Tuk up the bryg and loussit gud Jhon wricht,	Raised the bridge; released
	On the flearis syne folowed wondir fast.	those fleeing then
	Erll Malcom als out of the castell past	also
	With Lennox men to stuff the chace gud speid.	provide pursuit speedily
	Ay be the way thai gert feill Sotheroun bleid;	Ever by; caused many; [to] bleed
1225	In the Torwod thai gert full mony de.	caused a great many [to] die
	The erll of Waran that can full fersly fle,	fiercely flee
	With Corspatrik that graithly was his gyd,	readily; guide
	On changit hors throuchout the land thai rid	harnessed
	Strawcht to Dunbar, bot few with thaim thai led;	Straight
1230	Mony was slayne our sleuthfully at fled.	Many; that fled too slowly
	The Scottis hors that had rown wondir lang,	galloped (run) a very long time
	Mony gaiff our that mycht no forthyr gang.	Many collapsed; go
	Wallace and Grayme evir togidder baid;	stayed
	At Hathyntoun full gret slauchter thai maid	
1235	Of Inglismen quhen thair hors tyryt had.	tired
	Quhen Ramsay come gud Wallace was full glad;	
	With him was Boid and Richard of Lundy,	
	Thre thousand haill was of gud chevalry;	in all; horsemen
	And Adam als Wallace of Ricardtoun	also Adam Wallace
1240	With Erll Malcome thai fand at Hathyntoun.	found
	The Scottis men on slauchtir taryt was,	were occupied with slaughter
	Quhill to Dunbar the twa chyftanys coud pas	Until; passed
	Full sitfully for thar gret contrar cas.	Very sadly; adverse fortune
	Wallace folowed till thai gat in that place.	got
1245	Of thar best men and Karcyngaym of renoun,	

---

[1] *Seven thousand in all floundered at once in [the River] Forth*

The Wallace

	Twenty thousand was dede but redempcioun.	*without ransoming*
	Besyd Beltoun Wallace raturnd agayn;	*Beside; returned*
	To folow mar as than was bot in vayn.	*[any] more; then*
	In Hathyntoun lugyng thai maid that nycht,	*lodging*
1250	Apon the morn to Stirling passit rycht.	*directly*
	Assumpcioun day of Marye fell this cas;	*On Assumption Day (August 15); happened*
	Ay lowyt be Our Lady of hir grace.	*Ever praised; her*
	Convoyar offt scho was to gud Wallace	*Protector often she*
	And helpyt him in mony syndry place.	*many diverse places*
1255	Wallace in haist sone efftir this battaill	*soon after*
	A gret haith tuk of all the barrons haill	*oath; every single baron*
	That with gud will wald cum till his presens;	*into his presence*
	He hecht thaim als to bid at thar defens.	*also gave them an undertaking; work for*
	Schir Jhon Menteth, was than of Aran lord,	
1260	Till Wallace come and maid a playne record;	*To; plain statement*
	With witnes thar be his ayth he him band	*Before witnesses there by his oath; bound*
	Lauta to kep to Wallace and to Scotland.	*Loyalty*
	Quha with fre will till rycht wald nocht apply	*Who; agree*
	Wallace with force punyst rygorusly,	*punished rigorously*
1265	Part put to dede, part set in prysone strang.	*Some . . . some*
	Gret word of him throuch bathe thir regions rang.	*news; both these*
	Dundé thai gat sone be a schort treté,	*Dundee; got soon; negotiation*
	Bot for thar lyves and fled away be se.	*Escaped with their lives*
	Inglis capdans that hous had into hand	*castle; occupied*
1270	Left castellis fre and fled out of the land.	
	Within ten dayis efftir this tyme was gayne	*past*
	Inglis captanys in Scotland left was nane,	*none*
	Except Berweik and Roxburch Castell wicht;	*strong*
	Yeit Wallace thocht to bryng thai to the rycht.	
1275	That tyme thar was a worthi trew barroun,	
	To nayme he hecht gud Cristall of Cetoun.	*name; was called*
	In Jedwort Wod for saiffgard he had beyne,	*refuge*
	Agayne Sotheroun full weill he couth opteyn.	*Against [the] English; win*
	In utlaw oys he levit thar but let;[1]	
1280	Eduuard couth nocht fra Scottis faith him get.	*get him [to leave] his Scottish faith*
	Herbottell fled fra Jadwort Castell wycht	*strong*

---

[1] *He lived there freely as an outlaw*

Book 8

	Towart Ingland, thar Cetoun met him rycht.	*where*
	With forty men Cristall in bargane baid	*battle stood*
	Agayne eight scor and mekill mastré maid,	*Against; bold actions*
1285	Slew that captane and mony cruell man.	*many fierce men*
	Full gret ryches in that jornay he wan,	*enterprise (day's work); won*
	Houshald and gold as thai suld pas away,	*General provisions*
	The quhilk befor thai kepit mony day.	*which; kept many a*
	Jedwort thai tuk; ane Ruwan levit he,	*captured; left*
1290	At Wallace will captane of it to be.	*Wallace's will*
	Bauld Cetoun syne to Lothiane maid repair;	*Bold; then; went*
	In this storye ye ma her of him mair,	*narrative; may hear; more*
	And into Bruce, quha likis for to rede;	*in The Bruce, whoever likes to read*
	He was with him in mony cruell deid.	*fierce deeds*
1295	Gud Wallace than full sadly can devys	*firmly arranged*
	To rewill the land with worthi men and wys.	*rule*
	Captans he maid and schirreffis that was gud,	*sheriffs*
	Part of his kyn and of trew othir blud.	*Some; kin; other true blood*
	His der cusyng in Edynburgh ordand he,	*cousin; decreed*
1300	The trew Crawfurd that ay was full worthé,	*always*
	Kepar of it with noble men at wage;	*Keeper; in his pay*
	In Mannuell than he had gud heretage.	
	Scotland was fre that lang in baill had beyn,	*free; woe*
	Throw Wallace won fra our fals enemys keyn.	*won from; fierce*
1305	Gret governour in Scotland he couth ryng,	*ruled*
	Wayttand a tyme to get his rychtwis king	*Awaiting; rightful*
	Fra Inglismen, that held him in bandoun,	*From; subjection*
	Lang wrangwysly fra his awn rychtwis croun.	*wrongfully; own*

Explicit liber septimus
and Incipit ottamus

Book 8

	Fyve monethis thus Scotland stud in gud rest.	*enjoyed peace*
	A consell cryit, thaim thocht it wes the best	*council proclaimed*
	In Sanct Jhonston at it suld haldyn be.	*that it should be held*
	Assemblit thar clerk, barown, and bowrugie;	*clerks, barons; burgesses*
5	Bot Corspatrik wald nocht cum at thar call,	*summons*

The Wallace

	Baid in Dunbar and maid scorn at thaim all.	*Stayed*
	Thai spak of him feill wordis in that parlyment.	*many*
	Than Wallace said, "Will ye her to consent,	*here*
	Forgyff him fre all thing that is bypast	*fully*
10	Sa he will cum and grant he has trespast,	*If; admit*
	Fra this tyme furth kepe lawta till our croun?"	*maintain loyalty to*
	Thai grant tharto, clerk, burges, and barroun,	*granted*
	With haill consent thar writyng till him send.	*full; petition to*
	Richt lawly thus till him thai thaim commend,	*humbly*
15	Besocht him fair as a peyr of the land	*Beseeched; peer*
	To cum and tak sum governaill on hand.	*government*
	Lychtly he lowch in scorn as it had beyn,	*Contemptuously; laughed*
	And said he had sic message seyldyn seyne:	*such [an] embassy seldom seen*
	"That Wallace now as governowr sall ryng,	*rule*
20	Her is gret faute of a gud prince or kyng.	*Here; lack*
	That king of Kyll I can nocht undirstand:	
	Of him I held nevir a fur of land.	*furrow*
	That bachiller trowis, for Fortoun schawis hyr quhell,	*believes; displays her wheel*
	Tharwith to lest it sall nocht lang be weill.	*last*
25	Bot to yow lordis, and ye will undirstand,	*if you will*
	I mak yow wys I aw to mak na band.	*let you know; ought*
	Als fre I am in this regioun to ryng	*As I am free to rule in this region*
	Lord of myn awne, as evir was prince or king.	*own*
	In Ingland als gret part of land I haiff;	*also; quantity*
30	Manrent tharoff thar will no man me craiff.	*Homage thereof*
	Quhat will ye mar? I warne yow I am fre.	*independent*
	For your somoundis ye get no mar of me."	*summons; more*
	Till Saynct Jhonstone this wryt he send agayne,	*To; writ*
	Befor the lordis was manifest in playne.	*plainly declared*
35	Quhen Wallace herd the erll sic ansuer mais,	*such; make*
	A gret hate ire throu curage than he tais;	*hot anger*
	For weyll he wyst thar suld be bot a king	*knew; only one king*
	Of this regioun at anys for to ryng;	
	A "king of Kyll" for that he callyt Wallace.	
40	"Lordis," he said, "this is ane uncouth cace.	*strange*
	Be he sufferyt we haiff war than it was."	*[If] he is allowed; worse*
	Thus rais he up and maid him for to pas:	*rose*
	"God has us tholyt to do so for the laiff;	*permitted; rest*
	In lyff or dede in faith him sall we haiff,	*Alive or dead*

Book 8

45	Or ger him grant quhom he haldis for his lord,	make; admit; regards as
	Or ellis war schaym in story to racord.	[it] were [a] shame; history; record
	I vow to God with eys he sall nocht be	ease
	Into this realme bot ane of us sall de,	die
	Les than he cum and knaw his rychtwis king.	Unless; acknowledges; rightful
50	In this regioun weill bathe we sall nocht ryng.	we shall not both reign
	His lychtly scorn he sall rapent full sor,	contemptuous; repent; extremely
	Bot power faill or I sall end tharfor,	Unless [my] power fails or I die in the attempt
	Sen in this erd is ordand me no rest.	Since; earth; decreed
	Now God be juge, the rycht he kennys best."	[the] judge; knows
55	At that consaill langar he taryit nocht,	council
	With two hundreth fra Sanct Jhonston he socht.	left Perth
	To the consaill maid instans or he yeid,	Entreated the council before he left
	Thai suld conteyn and of him haiff no dreid.[1]	
	"I am bot ane and for gud caus I ga."	only one; go
60	Towart Kyngorn the gaynest way thai ta;	Kinghorn; shortest; take
	Apon the morn atour Forth south thai past;	over [the River] Forth
	On his vyage thai haistit wondir fast.	expedition
	Robert Lauder at Mussilburgh met Wallace,	
	Fra Inglismen he kepyt weill his place.	defended
65	Couth nayne him trete, knycht, squier, nor lord,	None could persuade him
	With King Eduuard to be at ane accord.	in agreement
	On Erll Patrik to pas he was full glaid;	advance
	Sum said befor the Bas he wald haiff haid.	had
	Gude men come als with Crystell of Cetoun;	also
70	Than Wallace was four hundreth of renoun.	Wallace's [army]
	A Squier Lyll, that weill that cuntré knew,	region
	With twenty men to Wallace couth persew	did come on
	Besyd Lyntoun, and to thaim tald he than	told; then
	The erll Patrik, with mony likly man,	many warlike men
75	At Coburns Peth he had his gaderyng maid,	Trail (Path); mustered his men
	And to Dunbar wald cum withoutyn baid.	delay
	Than Lawder said, "It war the best, think me,	
	Faster to pas, in Dunbar or he be."	go; before
	Wallace ansuerd, "We may at laysar ryd.	leisure ride
80	With yon power he thinkis bargane to bid;	that force; battle

---

[1] *They should continue and have no fear of him (i.e., Earl Patrick)*

133

The Wallace

	And of a thing ye sall weill understand,	*one thing*
	A hardyar lord is nocht into Scotland.	
	Mycht he be maid trew, stedfast till a king,	*loyal; to*
	Be wit and force he can do mekill thing,	*great things*
85	Bot willfully he likis to tyne himsell."	*ruin himself*
	Thus raid thai furth, and wald na langar duell,	
	Be est Dunbar, quhar men him tald on cas	*men happened forth to tell him*
	How Erll Patrik was warnyt of Wallace,	*warned about*
	Ner Enerweik chesyt a feild at vaill	*Innerwick chose; to advantage*
90	With nine hundreth of likly men to waill.	*warriors to choose*
	Four hundreth was with Wallace in the rycht	*(i.e., on the side of) right*
	And sone onon approchit to thar sicht.	*forthwith*
	Gret fawte thar was of gud trety betweyn	*want; good negotiation*
	To mak concord and that full sone was seyne.	
95	Without rahers of accioun in that tid	
	On athir part togydder fast thai rid.	*either*
	The stour was strang and wondir peralous,	*fighting*
	Contenyt lang with dedis chevalrous;	*Continued*
	Mony thar deit of cruell Scottis blud.	*Many; died; fierce*
100	Of this trety the mater is nocht gud,	*account; subject*
	Tharfor I ces to tell the destruccioun.	
	Peté it was, and all of a nacioun.	*Pity; of one*
	Bot Erll Patrik the feild left at the last,	
	Rycht few with him to Coburns Peth thai past,	
105	Agrevit sar that his men thus war tynt.	*Grief-stricken; lost*
	Wallace raturnd and wald no langar stynt	
	Towart Dunbar, quhar suthfast men him tald[1]	
	Na purveance was left into that hald,	*No provisions; castle*
	Nor men of fens, all had beyne with thar lord.	*defense*
110	Quhen Wallace hard the sekyr trew record,	*reliable; report*
	Dunbar he tuk all haill at his bandown,	*completely; will*
	Gaiff it to kepe to Crystell of Cetoun,	*into the keeping of*
	Quhilk stuffit it weill with men and gud victall.	*furnished; good*
	Apon the morn Wallace that wald nocht faill,	
115	With three hundreth to Coburns Peth he socht;	*made his way*

---

[1] Lines 106–07: *Wallace would stop there no longer and turned back / Towards Dunbar, where reliable men told him*

Book 8

	Erll Patrik uschyt, for bid him wald he nocht.	*sallied forth; await*
	Sone to the park Wallace a range has set;	*pursuit*
	Till Bonkill Wood Corspatrik fled but let	*without delay*
	And out of it till Noram passit he.	
120	Quhen Wallace saw it mycht na bettir be	
	Till Caudstreym went and lugit him on Tweid.	*Coldstream; lodged*
	Erll Patrik than in all haist can him speid.	*speed*
	And passit by or Wallace power rais,	*before; awakened*
	Without restyng in Atrik Forrest gais.	*went*
125	Wallace folowed bot he wald nocht assaill;	*attack*
	A rang to mak as than it mycht nocht vaill;	*chase; avail*
	Our few he had, the strenth was thik and strang,	*Too; stronghold*
	Sevyn myill on breid and tharto twys so lang.	*miles wide; twice as long*
	Intill Gorkhelm Erll Patrk leiffit at rest.	*In; lived in peace*
130	For mar power Wallace past in the west.	*more forces; went into*
	Erll Patrik than him graithit hastelye,	*prepared*
	In Ingland past to get him thar supplye;	*supplies*
	Out throuch the land rycht ernystfully couth pas	*earnestly passed*
	To Anton Beik that lord of Durame was.	
135	Wallace him put out of Glaskow befor,	*had put him out*
	And slew Persye, thar malice was the mor.	*[so] their; more*
	The byschope Beik gert sone gret power rys,	*caused; army*
	Northummyrland apon ane awfull wys.[1]	
	Than ordand Bruce in Scotland for to pas	*Bruce prepared*
140	To wyn his awne, bot ill dissavit he was;	*own; deceived*
	Thai gert him trow that Wallace was rabell	*made him believe; [a] rebel*
	And thocht to tak the kynryk to hymsel.	*kingdom; himself*
	Full fals thai war and evir yeit has beyn.	*They were*
	Lawta and trouth was ay in Wallace seyn;	*Loyalty; trustworthiness; always*
145	To fend the rycht all that he tuk on hand,	*defend*
	And thocht to bryng the Bruce fre till his land.	*freely*
	Of this mater as now I tary nocht.	*will not linger*
	With strang power Sotheroun togidder socht,	*[the] English came together*
	Fra Owys Watter assemblit haill to Tweid.	*[the] Ouse River; [the River] Tweed*
150	Thar land ost was thirty thousand indeid;	*army; indeed*
	Of Tynnys mouth send schippis be the se	*Tynemouth; ships*

---

[1] *Northumberland [men presenting] an awesome sight*

135

The Wallace

	To kep Dunbar at nayne suld thaim supplé.	*guard [entry to]; [so] that; supply*
	Erll Patrik with twenty thousand but lett	*straightaway*
	Befor Dunbar a stalwart sege he sett.	
155	The bischope Beik and Robert Bruce baid still	*stayed*
	With ten thousand at Noram at thar will.	
	Wallace be this that fast was lauborand,	*by this [time]*
	In Lothyane com witht gud men five thowsand,	*Lothian*
	Rycht weill-beseyn, all into armys brycht,	*well-equipped*
160	Thocht to reskew the Cetoun bauld and wicht.	*bold and valiant*
	Under Yhester that fyrst nycht lugit he.	*Yester [Castle]; camped*
	Hay com till him with a gud chevalré:	*company of knights*
	In Duns Forest all that tyme he had beyne;	
	The cummyng thar of Sotheroun he had seyne.	*[the] English*
165	Fifty he had of besy men in wer;	*active; war*
	Thai tald Wallace of Patrikis gret affer.	*array*
	Hay said, "Forsuth and ye mycht him ourset	*overthrow*
	Power agayne rycht sone he mycht nocht get.	*[An] army*
	My consaill is that we gyff him battaill."	*counsel*
170	He thankit him of comfort and consaill	*for his comforting words and advice*
	And said, "Freynd Hay, in this caus that I wend,	*go*
	Sa that we wyn I rek nocht for till end.	*So long as; care not to die*
	Rycht suth it is that anys we mon de.	*we must die once*
	Into the rycht quha suld in terrour be?"	*On the [side of] right*
175	Erll Patrik than a messynger gert pas,	*sent a messenger*
	Tald Anton Beik that Wallace cummand was.	*[Who] told*
	Of this tithingis the byschope was full glaid,	*this news; very pleased*
	Amendis of him full fayne he wald haiff haid.	*Amends; he was very keen to have*
	Bot mar prolong throuch Lammermur thai raid,	*Without further delay*
180	Ner the Spot Mur in buschement still he baid,	*ambush quietly; waited*
	As Erll Patrik thaim ordand for to be.	*ordered*
	Wallace of Beik unwarnyt than was he.	*was not warned then*
	Yeit he befor was nocht haisty in deid;	*Yet; before [then]*
	Bot than he put bathe him and his in dreid.	*both; danger*
185	Apon swyft horsis scurrouris past betweyn;	*scouts*
	The cummyng than of Erll Patrik was seyn.	*coming*
	The hous he left and to the mur is gayn,	*castle (i.e., Dunbar); moor; gone*
	A playne feild thar with his ost he has tayn.	*An open*
	Gud Cetoun syne uschet with few menyhe;	*then sallied forth; [a] small company*
190	Part of his men intill Dunbar left he;	

Book 8

	To Wallace raid, was on the rychtwys sid.	*rode; rightful*
	In gud aray to the Spot Mur thai ryd.	*array; rode*
	Sum Scottis dred the erll sa mony was,	*feared; had so many*
	Twenty thousand agayn sa few to pas.	*against; advance*
195	Quhen Jop persavit, he bad Wallace suld bid:	*saw [this]; begged; wait*
	"Tyne nocht thir men, bot to sum strenth ye ryd,	*Lose; these; strong positions; ride*
	And I sall pas to get yow power mar.	*go; more forces*
	Thir ar our gud thus lychtly for to war."	*These are too great; lightly; fight*
	Than Wallace said, "In trewth I will nocht fle	
200	For four of his ay ane quhill I may be.[1]	
	We ar our ner sic purpos for to tak;	*too close such; take [up]*
	A danger chace thai mycht upon us mak.	*dangerous chase*
	Her is twenty with this power today	*Here*
	Wald him assay suppos I war away.	*[Who] would attack him*
205	Mony thai ar; for Goddis luff be we strang,	*staunch*
	Yon Sotheron folk in stour will nocht bid lang."	*Those English; battle; endure*
	The brym battaill braithly on athir sid,	*fierce; violently; either*
	Gret rerd thar rais all sammyn quhar thai ryd.	*Great din rose there all together*
	The sayr semblé quhen thai togidder met,	*painful encounter*
210	Feyll strakis thar sadly on athir set.	*Many blows; firmly*
	Punyeand speris throuch plattis persit fast;	*Piercing spears; armor penetrated*
	Mony of hors to the ground doun thai cast;	*Many*
	Saidlys thai teym of hors but maistris thar;	*Saddles; empty*
	Of the south sid five thousand doun thai bar.	*they overthrew*
215	Gud Wallace ost the formast kumraid sa	*foremost overthrew in this way*
	Quhill the laiff was in will away to ga.	*While; rest wished to go away*
	Erll Patrik baid sa cruell of entent	*remained so fiercely determined*
	At all his ost tuk of him hardiment.	*That; courage*
	Agayne Wallace in mony stour was he.	*Against; battles*
220	Wallace knew weill that his men wald nocht fle	
	For na power that leiffand was in lyff,	*no power alive*
	Quhill thai in heill mycht ay be ane for fyfe.	*strength; one against five*
	In that gret stryff mony was handlyt hate;	*were dealt with violently*
	The feill dyntis, the cruell hard debait,	*many blows; fierce strife*
225	The fers steking, maid mony grevous wound,	*ferocious stabbing; painful*
	Apon the erd the blud did till abound.	*ground; flowed*

---

[1] Lines 199–200: *In truth I will not flee / As long as I have one against four of his [men]*

The Wallace

	All Wallace ost intill a cumpais baid;	*ring formed*
	Quharsa thai turnd full gret slauchtir thai maid.	*Wherever*
	Wallace and Grayme and Ramsay full worthi,	
230	The bauld Cetoun and Richard of Lundy,	*bold*
	And Adam als Wallace of Ricardtoun,	*also Adam Wallace*
	Bathe Hay and Lyll with gud men of renoun,	
	Boyde, Bercla, Byrd, and Lauder that was wicht,	*valiant*
	Feill Inglismen derffly to ded thai dycht.	*Many; they violently killed*
235	Bot Erll Patrik full fersly faucht agayn;	*fiercely fought back*
	Throuch his awn hand he put mony to payn.	*own; distress*
	Our men on him thrang forthwart into thra,	*pressed forward boldly*
	Maide throuch his ost feill sloppis to and fra.	*many breaches*
	The Inglismen began playnly to fle;	
240	Than Byschope Beik full sodeynly thai se,	
	And Robert Bruce contrar his natiff men.	*against; compatriots*
	Wallace was wa fra tyme he couth him ken:	*grieved; knew*
	Of Brucis deid he was agrevit far mar	*distressed; more*
	Than all the laiff that day at semblit thar.	*Than all the rest; that*
245	The gret buschement at anys brak on breid,	*ambush; once burst out*
	Ten thousand haill that douchty war in deid.	*in all; valiant; deeds*
	The flearis than with Erll Patrik relefd	*Those fleeing; rallied*
	To fecht agayn, quhar mony war myscheifd.	*many; destroyed*
	Quhen Wallace knew the buschement brokyn was,	*ambush had broken*
250	Out of the feild on hors thai thocht to pas,	*battlefield*
	Bot he saw weill his ost sownd in thar weid;	*swooned; armor*
	He thocht to fray the formast or thai yeid.	*scare; before; went*
	The new cummyn ost befor thaim semblit thar	*newly arrived army; assembled*
	On athir sid with strakis sad and sar.	*either side; grave and sore*
255	The worthi Scottis sa fersly faucht agayne	*fiercely fought back*
	Of Antonys men rycht mony haiff thai slayne;	*many*
	Bot that terand so usit was in wer	*tyrant; practiced; war*
	On Wallace ost thai did full mekill der;	*a great deal of harm*
	And the bauld Bruce sa cruelly wrocht he	*bold; fiercely*
260	Throuch strenth of hand feill Scottis he gert de.	*many Scots he caused to die*
	To resist Bruce Wallace him pressit fast,	
	Bot Inglismen so thik betuixt thaim past;	
	And Erll Patrik in all the haist he moucht	*might*
	Throucout the stour to Wallace sone he socht,	*battle; soon*
265	On the the-pes a felloun strak him gaiff,	*thigh-piece; grievous blow*

138

Book 8

	Kervit the plait with his scharp groundyn glaiff	Cleft; armor; sharply ground sword
	Throuch all the stuff and woundyt him sumdeill.	cloth; somewhat
	Bot Wallace thocht he suld be vengit weill,	revenged
	Folowed on him and a straik etlyt fast.	stroke aimed deftly
270	Than ane Mawthland rakles betwix thaim past:	Maitland recklessly
	Apon the heid gud Wallace has him tane,	head; struck
	Throuch hat and brawn in sondyr bryst the bane,	helmet; brain; shattered; bone
	Dede at that straik doun to the ground him drave.	stroke
	Thus Wallace was dissevirit fra the lave	separated; rest
275	Of his gud men, amang thaim him allane.	them (i.e., the English); alone
	About him socht feill enemys mony ane,	drew; many
	Stekit his hors; to ground behufid him lycht	stabbed; [he was] compelled to dismount
	To fend himselff als wysly as he mycht.	defend; prudently
	The worthy Scottis that mycht no langar bid	withstand
280	With sair hartis out of the feild thai ryd.	heavy; rode
	With thaim in feyr thai wend Wallace had beyn;	in company; thought
	On fute he was amang his enemys keyn.	cruel
	Gud rowme he maid about him into breid	space; all around him
	With his gud suerd that helpyt him in neid.	sword; need
285	Was nayne sa strang that gat of him a strak	
	Eftir agayne maid nevir a Scot to waik.[1]	
	Erll Patrik than that had gret crafft in wer	knowledge of war
	With speris ordand gud Wallace doun to ber.	to bear down [on] good Wallace
	Anew thai tuk was haill into the feild,	Enough; unhurt
290	Till him thai yeid thocht he suld haiff no beild,	went; escape (refuge)
	On athir sid fast poyntand at his ger.	either side; stabbing; armor
	He hewid off hedys and wysly coud him wer.	hacked; defend himself prudently
	The worthy Scottis of this full litill wyst,	knew very little
	Socht to gud Graym quhen thai thar chyftane myst.	Sought out; missed
295	Lauder and Lyle and Hay, that was full wicht,	extremely vigorous
	And bauld Ramsay, quhilk was a worthy knycht,	bold
	Lundy and Boid and Crystell of Cetoun	
	With five hundreth that war in bargan boun,	ready for fighting
	Him to reskew full rudly in thai raid,	vigorously rode
300	About Wallace a large rowme thai maid.	space
	The byschop Beik was braithly born till erd;	violently knocked down to the ground

---

[1] Lines 285–86: *None was so strong that, [once] injured by Wallace, / Ever again troubled a Scot*

The Wallace

	At the reskew thar was a glamrous rerd.	*noisy uproar*
	Or he gat up feill Sotheroun thai slew.	*Before; many*
	Out of the pres Wallace thai couth raskew,	*press [of battle]; rescued*
305	Sone horssit him apon a coursour wicht,	*Soon; bold steed*
	Towart a strenth ridis in all thar mycht,	*stronghold rode*
	Rycht wysly fled, reskewand mony man.	*wisely; rescuing many men*
	The Erll Patrik to stuff the chace began;	*prepare; pursuit*
	On the flearis litill harm than he wrocht.	*On those withdrawing*
310	Gud Wallace folk away togiddyr socht.	*slipped away together*
	Thir five hundreth the quhilk I spak of ayr	*These; earlier*
	Sa awfully abawndownd thaim sa sar	*So well defended themselves; fiercely*
	Na folowar durst out fra his falow ga,	*dared go ahead of his fellows*
	The gud flearis sic raturnyng thai ma.	*such counter-attacking; make*
315	Four thousand haill had tane the strenth befor	*in all; reached the stronghold*
	Of Wallace ost, his comfort was the mor;	*more*
	Of Glaskadane that forrest thocht till hauld.	*hold*
	Erll Patrik turnd, thocht he was nevir sa bauld,	*returned; bold*
	Agayne to Beik quhen chapyt was Wallace,	*escaped*
320	Curssand Fortoun of his myschansit cace.	*unlucky circumstances*
	The feild he wan and sevyn thowsand thai lost,	*won*
	Dede on that day for all the byschoppis bost.	*Died; boast*
	Of Wallace men five hundreth war slayne I ges,	*estimate*
	Bot na chyftayne his murnyng was the les.	*mourning; less*
325	Ner evyn it was bot Beik wald nocht abid;	*It was nearly evening; remain*
	In Lammermur thai tranuntyt that tid,	*moved camp; time*
	Thar lugyng tuk quhar him thocht maist availl,	*lodging; most advantage*
	For weyll he trowit the Scottis wald assaill	*believed; attack*
	Apon the feild quhar thai gaiff battaill last.	*gave*
330	The contré men to Wallace gaderyt fast.	*men of the region*
	Of Edynburch wyth Crawfurd that was wicht	*From; strong*
	Thre hundreth come intill thar armour brycht,	*came*
	Till Wallace raid be his lugeyng was tayne.	*To; rode by [the time]; chosen*
	Fra Tavydaill come gud men mony ane	*From Teviotdale; many [a] one*
335	Out of Jedwart with Ruwane at that tyd,	*Jedburgh; time*
	Togidder socht fra mony divers sid.	*approached; many different directions*
	Schir Wilyham Lang that lord was of Douglas,	
	With him four scor that nycht come to Wallace.	
	Twenty hundreth of new men met that nycht	
340	Apon thair fais to veng thaim at thair mycht.	*their foes; avenge; with their*

Book 8

	At the fyrst feild thire gud men had nocht beyn.	*field [of battle] these; been*
	Wallace wachis thair adversouris had seyn,	*Wallace's sentries*
	Into quhat wis thai had thar lugeyng maid.	*In what manner; camp*
	Wallace bownyt eftir soupper but baid,	*set out; without delay*
345	In Lammermur thai passit hastely.	
	Sone till aray yheid this gud chevalry.	*Soon; battle order went*
	Wallace thaim maid in twa partis to be:	*two*
	Schir Jhon the Graym and Cetoun ordand he,	*commanded*
	Lawder and Hay with thre thousand to ryd;	
350	Hymselff the layff tuk wysly for to gid,	*rest; guide*
	With him Lundy, bathe Ramsay and Douglace,	*both*
	Berkla and Boid and Adam gud Wallace.	
	Be this the day approchit wondir neir	*By this [time]; close*
	And brycht Titan in presens can apper.	*(i.e., the sun); appeared*
355	The Scottis ostis sone semblit into sycht	*soon assembled within sight*
	Of thar enemys, that was nocht redy dycht;	*ready [for them]*
	Owt of aray feill of the Sotheroun was.	*array many*
	Rycht aufully Wallace can on thaim pas.	*Relentlessly; did*
	At this entray the Scottis so weill thaim bar	*onset; conducted*
360	Feill of thar fais to ded was bertnyt thar.	*Many; foes were put to death there*
	Redles thai rais and mony fled away;	*In confusion; many*
	Sum on the ground war smoryt quhar thai lay.	*crushed where*
	Gret noyis and cry was raissit thaim amang.	
	Gud Grayme come in, that stalwart was and strang.	*powerful*
365	For Wallace men was weill togydder met,	*Because*
	On the south part sa aufully thai set	*awesomely*
	In contrar thaim the frayt folk mycht nocht stand;	*Against them; frightened*
	At anys thar fled of Sotheroun five thousand.	*once*
	The worthi Scottis wrocht apon sic wys	*performed in such [a] way*
370	Jop said hymselff thai war mekill to prys.	*greatly to be praised*
	Yeit Byschope Beik, that felloun tyrand strang,	*Yet; fierce; powerful*
	Baid in the stour rycht awfully and lang.	*Remained; battle; starkly*
	A knycht Skelton that cruell was and keyn	*ferocious; bold*
	Befor him stud intill his armour scheyn,	*bright*
375	To fend his lord full worthely he wrocht.	*defend*
	Lundy him saw and sadly on him socht,	*resolutely approached him*
	With his gud suerd ane aukwart straik him gaiff,	*sword; cross-wise blow*
	Throuch pesan stuff his crag in sondir draiff,	*Right through the gorget; neck; dashed*
	Quharof the layff astunyt in that sted.	*Whereof; remainder were dismayed; place*

The Wallace

380	The bauld Skelton of Lundyis hand is dede.	*bold; dead*
	Than fled thai all and mycht no langar bid.	*stay*
	Patrik and Beik away with Bruce thai ryd.	
	Five thousand held intill a slop away	*gap*
	Till Noram Hous in all the haist thai may.	*Castle*
385	Our men folowed, that worthi war and wicht;	*valiant*
	Mony flear derffly to dede thai dycht.	*Many; violently they killed*
	The three lordis on to the castell socht;	*went*
	Full feyll thai left that was of Ingland brocht.	*Very many; brought*
	At this jornay twenty thousand thai tynt,	*clash; lost*
390	Drownyt and slayn be sper and suerdis dynt.	*spear; sword blows*

[*After wasting and plundering Earl Patrick's lands in Merse and Lothian, Wallace attends a council of barons in Perth (lines 405–07), while Patrick goes to Edward in England, in pursuit of lands there. Wallace becomes governor, the barons pay homage to him, and he rewards the faithful, taking care not to give lands, only office, to his own family members. The Scots start to feel optimism for the first time in a long while. (Lines 391–434)*]

435	Tithandis than come King Eduuard grevit was,	*News; vexed*
	With his power in Scotland thocht to pas,	*army*
	For Erll Patrik had gyffyn him sic consaill.	*given; such counsel*
	Wallace gat wit and semblit power haill,	*got [to] know; assembled [his] whole army*
	Forty thousand on Roslyn Mur thar met.	*Roslin Moor*
440	"Lordis," he said, "thus is King Eduuard set	
	In contrar rycht to sek us in our land.	*Against [the] right; seek*
	I hecht to God and to yow be my hand,	*vow; by*
	I sall him meit for all his gret barnage	*meet; great baronage*
	Within Ingland to fend our heretage.	*defend*
445	His fals desyr sall on himselff be seyn;	*be paid back*
	He sall us fynd in contrar of his eyn.	
	Sen he with wrang has ryddyn this regioun	*ridden [over]*
	We sall pas now in contrar of his crown.	*in opposition to*
	I will nocht bid gret lordis with us fayr,	*command; [to] go*
450	For myn entent I will playnly declar.	*intention*
	Our purpos is othir to wyn or de.	*die*
	Quha yeildis him sall nevir ransownd be."	*Whoever surrenders; ransomed*
	The barrons than him ansuerd worthely	
	And said thai wald pas with thar chevalry.	*followers*
455	Himselff and Jop providyt that menyhe.	*made that company ready*

142

Book 8

	Twenty thousand of vaillit men tuk he;	*distinguished*
	Harnes and hors he gert amang thaim waill,	
	Wapynnys enew at mycht thaim weill availl,[1]	
	Grathyt thar men that cruell wes and keyn.	*Equipped; fierce; bold*
460	Bettir in wer in warld coud nocht be seyn.	*war; world*
	He bad the laiff on laubour for to bid.	*commanded; rest*
	In gud aray fra Roslyn Mur thai ryd.	*array from*
	At thar muster gud Wallace couth thaim as.	*asked them [to be]*
	Quhat mysteryt ma in a power to pas?[2]	
465	"All of a will, as I trow set ar we,	*believe determined*
	In playne battaill can nocht weill scumfit be.	*defeated*
	Our rewme is pur, waistit be Sotheroun blud.	*realm is poor, laid waste; English*
	Go wyn on thaim tresour and othir gud."	*win from*

[*Wallace's leading supporters are named, and Earl Malcom in particular is praised. Wallace takes a small force to Roxburgh and demands that the constable hand over the keys; a similar demand is sent to Berwick. (Lines 469–511)*]

	The ost but mar full awfully he dycht,	*army without delay; awesomely; readied*
	Began at Tweid and spard nocht at thai fand,	*spared none that; found*
	Bot brynt befor throuch all Northummyrland.	*burned [all] before them*
515	All Duram toun thai brynt up in a gleid.	*burnt to an ember*
	Abbays thai spard and kyrkis quhar thai yeid.	*spared; churches; went*
	To York thai went but baid or thai wald blyn;	*without delay before; stop*
	To byrn and sla of thaim he had na syne.	
	Na syn thai thocht the sammyn thai leit us feill,[3]	
520	Bot Wilyam Wallace quyt our quarell weill.	*settled; dispute*
	Fortrace thai wan and small castellis kest doun,	*Fortresses; captured; cast down*
	With aspre wapynnys payit thar ransoune.	*sharp; ransom (see note)*
	Of presonaris thai likit nocht to kep;	*keep*
	Quhom thai ourtuk thai maid thar freyndis to wepe.	*overtook; weep*
525	Thai sawft na Sotheroun for thar gret riches;	*saved; Englishmen*

---

[1] Lines 457–58: *He arranged for them to choose the best armor and horse / And enough weapons to serve them well*

[2] *What need was there of a greater force to go [to battle]?*

[3] Lines 518–19: *He did not sin by burning and slaying them (the English). / They thought it no sin when they let us feel the same*

The Wallace

	Of sic koffre he callit bot wrechitnes.	*such bargaining*
	On to the gettis and faboris of the toun	*gates; suburbs*
	Braithly thai brynt and brak thar byggyngis doun;	*Fiercely; burned; broke; buildings*
	At the wallys assayed fifteen dayis,	*Assailed the walls*
530	Till King Eduuard send to thaim in this wayis	*Until*
	A knycht, a clerk, and a squier of pes,	*in peace*
	And prayit him fayr of byrnyng to ces,	*courteously; to cease burning*
	And hecht battaill or forty dayis war past,	*called for; before; were*
	Soverance so lang gyff him likit till ast;[1]	
535	And als he sperd quhy Wallace tuk on hand	*also; inquired*
	The felloun stryff in defens of Scotland,	*fierce struggle*
	And said he merveld on his wyt forthy	*in his mind therefore*
	Agayn Inglande was of so gret party:	*Against; [which] was so huge*
	"Sen ye haiff maid mekill of Scotland fre	*Since; much*
540	It war gret tym for to lat malice be."	
	Wallace had herd the message say thar will;	*heard; messengers*
	With manly wytt rycht thus he said thaim till:	
	"Yhe may knaw weill that rycht ynewch we haiff.	*enough*
	Of his soverance I kepe nocht for to craiff.	*safe conducts I care not to crave*
545	Becaus I am a natyff Scottis man	
	It is my dett to do all that I can	*duty*
	To fend our kynrik out of dangeryng.	*defend; kingdom from all harm*
	Till his desyr we will grant to sumthing;	
	Our ost sall ces, for chans that may betid,	*cease, whatever happens*
550	Thir forty dayis bargane for till bid.	*battle; await*
	We sall do nocht les than it move in yow;	*nothing unless; you begin it*
	In his respyt myselff couth never trow."	*reprieve; trust*
	King Eduuardis wrytt undir his seill thai gaiff,	*writ; seal*
	Be fourty dayis that thai suld battaill haiff.	*In forty days*
555	Wallace thaim gaiff his credence of this thing.	
	Thair leyff thai tuk syne passit to the king	*leave; then*
	And tauld him haill how Wallace leit thaim feill:	*told; completely; know*
	"Of your soverance he rekis nocht adeill.	*safe conduct; cares not at all*
	Sic rewllyt men, sa awfull of affer,	*Such well-led; terrifying in appearance*
560	Ar nocht crystynyt than he ledis in wer."	*christened (baptized); leads; war*
	The king ansuerd and said, "It suld be kend	*known*

---

[1] *And assurance of safety for as long as he wished to ask [it]*

Book 8

	It cummys of witt enemys to commend.	*It is wise; praise*
	Thai ar to dreid rycht gretly in certane.	*to be feared; greatly for certain*
	Sadly thai think of harmys thai haiff tane."	*Gravely; suffered*

[*Wallace marches from York to Northallerton, observing the forty days peace. He successfully ambushes an English force planning to attack his army, killing the leader, Richard Rymunt. Malton is plundered, and carriage-loads of supplies removed and sent to his host. At a parliament at Pomfrey the English debate whether to battle with Wallace or not: they fear the consequences of defeat.* (Lines 565–629)]

630	And this decret thar wit amang thaim fand,[1]	
	Gyff Wallace wald apon him tak the croun	*If; (i.e., crown of Scotland)*
	To gyff battaill thai suld be redy boun.	*all ready*
	The sammyn message till him thai send agayn	*same messengers to*
	And thar entent thai tald him into playn.	*intention; told; plainly*
635	Wallace thaim chargyt his presens till absent,	*ordered them to leave his presence*
	His consaill callyt and schawit thaim his entent.	*council; revealed*
	He and his men desyrit battaill till haiff	
	Be ony wayis of Ingland our the laiff.	*By any means; above all else*
	He said, "Fyrst it war a our hie thing	*were an overly ambitious*
640	Agayne the faith to reyff my rychtwis king.	*Against good faith; deprive; rightful*
	I am his man, born natiff of Scotland;	
	To wer the croun I will nocht tak on hand.	*wear; undertake*
	To fend the rewm it is my dett be skill;	*defend; realm; duty by reason*
	Lat God above reward me as He will."	*Let; above*
645	Sum bad Wallace apon him tak the croun.	*beseeched; [to] take*
	Wys men said, "Nay, it war bot derysioun	*would be only*
	To croun him king but voice of the parlyment,"	*without approval*
	For thai wyst nocht gyff Scotland wald consent.	*knew not if*
	Othir sum said it was the wrangwis place.	*Some others; wrong*
650	Thus demyt thai on mony divers cace.	*they offered diverse opinions*
	This knycht Cambell, of witt a worthi man,[2]	
	As I said ayr was present with thaim than,	*earlier; then*
	Herd and ansuerd quhen mony said thar will:	*many expressed their wishes*
	"This war the best, wald Wallace grant thartill,	*were; [if] Wallace will agree to it*

---

[1] *And this they decided among themselves*

[2] *This knight Cambell, a man distinguished for his wisdom*

The Wallace

655	To croun him king solemply for a day,	*solemnly*
	To get ane end of all our lang delay."	*bring to an end*
	The gud Erll Malcome said that Wallace mycht	
	As for a day, in fens of Scotlandis rycht,	*Only for a day; defense*
	Thocht he refusyt it lestandly to ber,	*Although; to bear it lastingly*
660	Resawe the croun as in a fer of wer.	*Accept; circumstance of war*
	The pepill all till him gaiff thar consent:	
	Malcome of auld was lord of the parlyment.	*old*
	Yeit Wallace tholyt, and leit thaim say thar will.	*Yet; was patient; let*
	Quhen thai had demyt be mony divers skill,	*considered by many; arguments*
665	In his awn mynd he abhorryt with this thing.	*own; abhorred*
	The comouns cryit, "Mak Wallace crownyt king."	*common people*
	Than smylyt he and said, "It suld nocht be.	
	At termys schort, ye get no mar for me.	*In a few words; more from*
	Undyr colour we mon our ansuer mak,	*Using pretense; must*
670	Bot sic a thing I will nocht on me tak.	*such; take on me*
	I suffer yow to say that it is sa.	*so*
	It war a scorn the croun on me to ta."	*mockery; place*
	Thai wald nocht lat the message of Ingland	*let; English messengers*
	Cum thaim amang or thai suld understand.	*before they reached an understanding*
675	Twa knychtis passit to the message agayn,	*messengers*
	Maid thaim to trow Wallace was crownyt in playn,	*Made them believe; openly*
	Gart thaim traist weill that this was suthfast thing.	*Gave them to understand*

[*On Woodstock's advice, the English decide to avoid open battle with the Scots and to seek some way of picking off Wallace. In retaliation, the Scots ravage Northallerton and Yorkshire, besieging York itself. When the Scots retire to rest, the English plan a surprise skirmish, but Wallace and his night watch spy them, sound the alarm and the Scots, still in battle dress, rally and trounce them. (Lines 678–855)*]

	The layff raturnyt into the toun agayn	*rest returned*
	And ruyt full sar that evyr thai furth coud found;	*profoundly regretted; forth had gone*
	Amang thaim was full mony werkand wound.	*many painful*
	The ost agayn ilk ane to thar ward raid,	*each one; section rode*
860	Comaundyt wachis and no mayr noyis maid,	*sentries; more noise*
	Bot restyt still quhill that the brycht day dew,	*until; dawned*
	Agayne began the toun to sailye new.	*attack anew*
	All thus thai wrocht with full gud worthines,	
	Assailyeit sayr with witt and hardines.	*Attacked hard; prudence*

Book 8

865	The ostis victaill worth scant and failyeit fast;	*army's provisions grew*
	Thus lay thai thair quhill divers dayis war past.	*until; were*
	The land waistyt and meit was fer for to wyn,	*land wasted; [too] far away to obtain*
	Bot that wyst nocht the stuff that was within;	*knew not; garrison*
	Thai drede full sar for thar awn warnysoun.[1]	
870	For soverance prayed the power of the toun;	*assurance of safety entreated; forces*
	To spek with Wallace thai desyryt fast	
	And he aperyt and speryt quhat thai ast.	*appeared; inquired; asked*
	The mayr ansuerd, said, "We wald gyff ransoun	*mayor; would give ransoms*
	To pas your way and der no mayr the toun.	*[If you would]; harm; more*
875	Gret schaym it war that we suld yoldyn be	*were; surrender*
	And townys haldyn of les power than we.	*[have] held; less*
	Yhe may nocht wyn us, suthlie, thocht ye bid.	*conquer; though; wait*
	We sall gyff gold and yhe will fra us rid.	*give; if you will ride [away] from us*
	We may gyff battaill, durst we for our king;	*[if] we dared*
880	Sen he has left, it war ane our hie thing	*too ambitious a thing*
	Till us to do without his ordinance.	*For us; orders*
	This toun of him we hald in governance."	*hold and govern on his behalf*
	Wallace ansuerd, "Of your gold rek we nocht;	*We care nothing for your gold*
	It is for battaill that we hydder socht.	*came here*
885	We had levir haiff battaill of Ingland	*rather*
	Than all the gold that gud King Arthour fand	*found*
	On the Mont Mychell, quhar he the gyand slew.	*Mont St. Michel; giant*
	Gold may be gayn, bot worschip is ay new.	*gone, but honor; always*
	Your king promyst that we suld battaill haiff;	
890	His wrytt tharto undyr his seyll he gaiff.	*writ; seal*
	Letter nor band ye se may nocht availl.	*agreement*
	Us for this toun he hecht to gyff battaill.	*He promised to give us battle for this town*
	Me think we suld on his men vengit be;	*be revenged*
	Apon our kyn mony gret wrang wrocht he.	*kin; many great wrongs*
895	His devyllyk deid he did into Scotland."	*devilish deed*
	The mayr said, "Schir, rycht thus we understand;	*mayor*
	We haiff no charge quhat our king gerris us do,[2]	
	Bot in this kynd we sall be bundyn yow to,	*manner; bound to you*
	Sum part of gold to gyff you with gud will	

---

[1] *They were extremely fearful about their own troops*

[2] *We have no responsibility for what our king makes us do*

The Wallace

900	And nocht efftyr to wait yow with na ill,	*afterwards to lie in wait for; ill-will*
	Be no kyn meyn, the power of this toun,	*manner of means; garrison*
	Bot gyff our king mak him to battaill boun."	*Unless; prepares for battle*
	Into the ost was mony worthi man	*Within; many valiant men*
	With Wallace, ma than I now rekyn can.	*more; reckon (calculate)*
905	Bettir it was for at his will thai wrocht,	*performed*
	Thocht he wes best, no nothir lak we nocht.[1]	
	All servit thank to Scotland evir mar	*deserved; more*
	For manheid, wit, the quhilk thai schawit thar.	*prudence; demonstrated there*
	The haill consaill thus demyt thaim amang,	*whole council; considered*
910	The toun to sege thaim thocht it was to lang,	*besiege; would take too long*
	And nocht apayn to wyn it be no slycht.	*practicable; by stratagem*
	The consaill fand it was the best thai mycht	
	Sum gold to tak gyff that thai get no mar,	*if they could get; more*
	Syne furth thar way in thar viage thai far.	*Then; journey; went*
915	Than Wallace said, "Myselff will nocht consent	
	Bot gyff this toun mak us this playne content:	*satisfaction*
	Tak our baner and set it on the wall	*Take*
	(For thar power our rewme has ridyn all),	*army; realm; ridden all [over]*
	Yoldyn to be quhen we lik thaim to tak,	*Prepared to surrender*
920	Intill Ingland residence gyff we mak."	*If we stay in England*
	This ansuer sone thai send into the mair.	*mayor*
	Than thai consent, the remanent that was thar,	*consented; rest*
	The baner up and set it in the toun,	
	To Scotland was hie honour and renoun.	*high*
925	That baner thar was fra eight houris to none.	*from eight o'clock to noon*
	Thar finance maid, delyverit gold full sone.	*payment; soon*
	Ten thousand pund all gud gold of Ingland	*pounds*
	The ost rasavit with victaill haboundand.	*received; abundant food*
	Baith breid and wyne rycht gladly furth thai gaiff	*Both bread; wine*
930	And othir stuff at thai likit to haiff.	*that*
	Twenty dais owt the ost remaynit thar,	*altogether*
	Bot want of victaill gert thaim fra it far;	*lack; provisions; go*
	Yeit still of pees the ost lugyt all nicht	*Yet; [in time] of peace; lodged*
	Quhill on the morn the sone was ryssyn on hycht.	*sun; high*
935	In Aperill amang the schawis scheyn,	*fair woods*

---

[1] *Although he was the best, we do not find fault with any other*

Book 8

	Quhen the paithment was cled in tendir greyn,	*path; clad; green*
	Plesand war it till ony creatur	*to any*
	In lusty lyff that tym for till endur.	*vigorous life*
	Thir gud wermen had fredome largely,	*These; warriors*
940	Bot fude was scant, thai mycht get nayn to by,	*none; buy*
	Tursyt tentis and in the contré raid.	*Packed up; country rode*
	On Inglismen full gret herschipe thai maid,	*destruction*
	Brynt and brak doun, byggyngis sparyt thai nocht;	*Burned; buildings spared*
	Rycht worthi wallis full law to ground thai brocht.	*sturdy; low*
945	All Mydlam land thai brynt up in a fyr,	*Middleham; burned*
	Brak parkis doun, distroyit all the schyr.	*woodlands; shire*
	Wyld der thai slew for othir bestis was nayn,	*deer; none*
	Thir wermen tuk of venysoune gud wayn.	*These warriors; quantity*
	Towart the south thai turnyt at the last,	
950	Maid byggyngis bar als fer as evir thai past.	*Stripped buildings everywhere*
	The commons all to London ar thai went	
	Befor the king and tald him thar entent,	*told; intention*
	And said thai suld, bot he gert Wallace ces,	*should, unless; made; cease*
	Forsaik thair faith and tak thaim till his pes.	*to his peace*
955	Na herrald thar durst than to Wallace pas,	*No; dared*
	Quharoff the king gretly agrevit was.	*annoyed*
	Thus Eduuard left his pepill into baill.	*people; woe*
	Contrar Wallace he wald nocht giff battaill,	*Against; give*
	Nor byd in feild, for nocht at thai mycht say,	*stay in battlefield*
960	Gayff our the caus, to London past his way.	*Gave up*
	At men of wit this questioun her I as,	*knowledge; here; ask*
	Amang noblis gyff evir ony that was,	*Among nobles if; any*
	So lang throw force in Ingland lay on cas	*[Who] so long; happened to lie*
	Sen Brudus deit, but battaill, bot Wallace.[1]	
965	Gret Julius, the empyr had in hand,	
	Twys of force he was put of Ingland.	*Twice through force; [out] of*
	Wytht Arthour als, of wer quhen that he previt,	*With; also; war; attempted*
	Twys thai fawcht, suppos thai war myschevit.	*Twice; fought; undone*
	Awfull Eduuard durst nocht Wallace abid	*Formidable; dared*
970	In playn battaill, for all Ingland so wid.	*open; wide*
	In London he lay and tuk him till his rest,	

---

[1] *Since the death of Brutus, without battle, except Wallace*

The Wallace

And brak his vow. Quhilk hald ye for the best?	*broke; Which hold*
Rycht clayr it is to ransik this questioun.	*clear; examine*
Deyme as ye lest, gud men of discrecioun.	*Judge; wish*

[*Short of food, the Scots head for Richmond where they not only find plentiful supplies, but reinforcements. (Lines 975–1002)*]

	In Richmunt schyr thai fand a gret boundans,	*In [the] shire [of] Richmond; abundance*
	Breid, ayll, and wyn, with othir purveans;	*Bread, ale, and wine; provisions*
1005	Brak parkis doun, slew bestis mony ane,	*woods; many [a] one*
	Of wild and tayme forsuth thai sparyt nane.	*truly; spared none*
	Throuchowt the land thai past in gud aray.	*order*
	A semely place so fand thai in thar way	*handsome; found*
	Quhilk Ramswaith hecht, as Jop himselff thaim tald.	*Which was called Ravensworth*
1010	Fehew was lord and captayne in that hald.	*stronghold*
	Five hundreth men was semblit in that place	*were assembled*
	To save thaimselff and thar gud fra Wallace.	*save; goods from*
	A ryoll sted fast by a forest sid,	*royal dwelling*
	With turrettis fayr and garrettis of gret prid	
1015	Beildyt about, rycht lykly to be wicht,	*Built; strong*
	Awfull it was till ony mannis sicht.	*Awesome; to any*
	Feill men abown on the wallis buskyt beyn	*Many; above; were prepared*
	In gud armour that burnyst was full scheyn.	*burnished; fair*
	The ost past by and bot vesyt that place,	*only inspected*
1020	Yeit thai within on lowd defyit Wallace	*Yet; aloud*
	And trumpattis blew with mony werlik soun.	*many war-like sounds*
	Than Wallace said, "Had we yon gallandis doun	*those gallants*
	On the playn ground thai wald mor sobyr be."	*temperate*
	Than Jop said, "Schir, ye gart his brodyr de	*caused the death of his brother*
1025	In harrold weid, ye wait, on Tynto Hill."	*herald's clothing, you know*
	Wallace ansuerd, "So wald I with gud will	*would I [deal with him]*
	Had I hymselff; bot we may nocht thaim der.	*injure*
	Gud men mon thoill of harlottis scorn in wer."[1]	
	Schir Jhon the Graym wald at a bykkyr beyn,	*would [have] been at an encounter*
1030	Bot Wallace sone that gret perell has seyn,	*soon*
	Commaundit him to lat his service be.	*let*

---

[1] *Good men must endure [the] scorn of worthless fellows in war*

Book 8

	"We haiff no men to waist in sic degré.	*in such [a] way*
	Wald ye thaim harm I knaw ane othir gait	*way*
	How we throuch fyr within sall mak thaim hait.	*hot*
1035	Fyr has beyn ay full felloun into wer:	*ever; harmful in war*
	On sic a place it ma do mekill der.	*may; great damage*
	Thar auld bulwerk I se of wydderyt ayk;	*old; dried oak*
	War it in fyr thai mycht nocht stand a straik.	*on fire; withstand an attack*
	Housis and wod is her enewch plenté.	*here enough*
1040	Quha hewis best of this forest lat se.	*hews; let's see*
	Pow housis doun we sall nocht want adeill;	*Pull; at all*
	The auld temyr will ger the greyn byrn weill."	*old timber; make; green [wood] burn*
	At his commaund full besyly thai wrocht;	*worked*
	Gret wod in haist about the hous thai brocht.	*castle*
1045	The bulwerk wan thir men of armys brycht,[1]	
	To the barmkyn laid temyr apon hycht.	*rampart piled up timber; high*
	Than bowmen schot to kep thaim fra the cast;	*Then; protect; discharge [of missiles]*
	The wall about had festnyt firis fast.	*[they] had fastened torches*
	Women and barnys on Wallace fast thai cry;	*children; cry [out]*
1050	On kneis thai fell and askit him mercy.	
	At a quartar quhar fyr had nocht ourtayn,	*place where; overtaken*
	Thai tuk thaim out fra that castell of stayn,	*took; stone*
	Syn bet the fyr with brundys brym and bauld.	*Then beat; brands fierce; bold*
	The rude low rais full heych abown that hauld.	*strong flame rose; high above; castle*
1055	Barrellis of pyk for the defens was hungyn thar,	*pitch*
	All strak in fyr, the myscheiff was the mar.	*burst into flames; damage; more*
	Quhen the brym fyr atour the place was past	*flaming; through*
	Than thai within mycht nothir schut no cast.	*neither shoot nor throw [missiles]*
	Als bestiall as hors and nowt within	*Also; [such] as horses and cattle*
1060	Amang the fyr thai maid a hidduys dyn.	*hideous din*
	The armyt men in harnes was so hait,	*armor; hot*
	Sum doun to ground duschit but mar debait;	*fell without further resistance*
	Sum lap, sum fell into the felloun fyr,	*leapt; terrible fire*
	Smoryt to dede and brynt bathe bayn and lyr.	*Crushed; burnt both bone; flesh*
1065	The fyr brak in at all opynnys about;	*openings*
	Nayn baid on loft, so felloun was the dout.	*None stayed above; grave; risk*
	Fehew himself lap rudly fra the hycht,	*leapt swiftly; top*

---

[1] *These men in shining armor reached the bulwark*

The Wallace

	Throuch all the fyr can on the barmkyn lycht.	ramparts alight
	With a gud suerd Wallace strak off his hed;	sword; struck; head
1070	Jop hynt it up and turst it fra that sted.	grabbed; threw; place
	Five hundreth men that war into that place,	
	Gat nayne away bot dede withoutyn grace.	None got away; died
	Wallace baid still with his power that nycht;	remained quietly
	Apon the morn the fyr had failyeit mycht.	diminished in strength
1075	Beffor the gett quhar it was brynt on breid	In front of; gate; burned widely
	A red thai maid and to the castell yeid,	clearing; went
	Strak doun the gett and tuk that thai mycht wyn,	Struck; gate; pillage
	Jowellys and gold, gret riches war tharin;	
	Spulyeit the place and left nocht ellis thar	Plundered
1080	Bot bestis brynt, bodyis, and wallis bar.	charred beasts, corpses, and bare walls
	Than tuk thai hyr that wyff was to Fehew,	her
	Gaiff this commaund, as scho was woman trew,	she
	To turs that hed to London to King Eduuard.	carry that head in a pack
	Scho it rasavyt with gret sorow in hart.	She received it; heart
1085	Wallace himselff thir chargis till hyr gaiff:	these orders gave to her
	"Say to your king, bot gyff I battaill haiff,	unless
	At London gettis we sall assailye sayr.	gates; attack strenuously
	In this moneth we think for to be thair.	month; there
	Trastis in treuth, will God, we sall nocht faill,	Believe [that] in truth
1090	Bot I rasyst throw chargis of our consaill.	Unless; stop; orders; council
	The southmaist part of Ingland we sall se	southern-most
	Bot he sek pes or ellis bargan with me.	Unless; sues for peace; else fights
	Apon a tym he chargyt me on this wys,	commanded; manner
	Rycht boustously, to mak till him service:	menacingly; subjection
1095	Sic sall he haiff as he us caus has maid."	Such shall
	Than movit thai without langer abaid.	moved [on]; longer delay
	Deliverit scho was fra this gud chevalry.	Released; from
	Towart London scho socht rycht ernystfully,	went; earnestly
	On to the tour but mar proces scho went,	tower [of London] without further delay
1100	Quhar Eduuard lay sayr murnand in his entent.	deeply lamenting; mind
	His nevois hede quhen he saw it was brocht,	nephew's head
	So gret sorow sadly apon him socht,	gravely welled in him
	With gret unes apon his feit he stud,	difficulty
	Wepand for wo for his der tendyr blud.	relation
1105	The consaill rais and prayit him for to ces:	
	"We los Ingland bot gyff ye purches pes."	[will] lose; unless; solicit peace

Book 8

	Than Wodstok said, "This is my best consaill:	*counsel*
	Tak pees in tyme as for our awn availl,	*[a] truce; own advantage*
	Or we tyne mar yeit slaik of our curage.	*Before; lose; lessen; spirit*
1110	Erest ye may get help to your barnage."	*Soonest; baronage*
	The king grantyt and bad thaim message send;	*ordered them a messenger*
	Na man was thar that durst to Wallace wend.	*go*
	The queyn apperyt and saw this gret distance.	*queen; reluctance*
	Weill born scho was, of the rycht blud of France;	*true*
1115	Scho trowit weill tharfor to speid the erar.	*trusted; succeed sooner*
	Hyrselff purpost in that message to far.	*proposed; embassy; go*
	Als scho forthocht at the king tuk on hand	*Also; regretted that; undertook*
	Agayn the rycht so oft to reyff Scotland.	*Against; take Scotland by force*
	And feill men said the vengeance hapnyt thar,	*many; had come*
1120	Of gret murthyr his men maid intill Ayr.	*For; murder*
	Thus demyt thai the consaill thaim amang.	*deliberated*
	To this effect the queyn bownyt to gang.	*With this object; prepared; go*
	Quhen scho has seyn ilk man forsak this thing	*each; refuse*
	On kneis scho fell and askyt at the king:	*knees*
1125	"Soverane," scho said, "gyff it your willis be,	*Sovereign*
	At I desyr yon chyftayn for to se.	*That; that chieftain*
	For he is knawin bath hardy, wys, and trew,	*known as*
	Perchance he will erar on wemen rew	*Perhaps; sooner; have pity*
	Than on your men; yhe haiff don him sic der,	*done; such injury*
1130	Quhen he thaim seis it movis him ay to wer.	*moves; always; war*
	To help this land I wald mak my travaill;	*labor hard*
	It ma nocht scaith suppos it do na vaill."	*may do no harm; good (avail)*
	The lordis all of hir desir was fayn;	*were glad*
	Onto the king thai maid instans in playn	*entreated openly*
1135	That scho mycht pas. The king with aukwart will,	
	Halff into yr, has giffyn consent thartill.	*Half in anger*
	Sum of thaim said the queyn luffyt Wallace	
	For the gret voice of his hie nobilnas.	*reputation; high*
	A hardy man that is lykly withall	*well-made besides*
1140	Gret favour will of fortoun till him fall	*favor*
	Anent wemen, is seyne in mony place.	*With respect to women*
	Sa hapnyt it in his tyme with Wallace.	
	In his rysing he was a luffar trew	*true lover*
	And chesit ane, quhill Inglismen hir slew.	*chose one, until; her*
1145	Yeit I say nocht the queyn wald on hir tak	*take*

153

The Wallace

	All for his luff sic travaill for to mak.	*such [an] undertaking*
	Now luff or leiff, or for help of thar land,	
	I mak rahers as I in scriptour fand.	*recite; writing found*
	Scho graithit hir apon a gudlye wis	*furnished herself; handsome fashion*
1150	With gold and ger and folk at hir devis;	*equipment; according to her plan*
	Ladyis with hir, nane othir wald thai send,	*no others*
	And ald preystis that weill the cuntré kend.	*old priests; knew*
	Lat I the queyn to message redy dycht	*Leave; preparing for her embassy*
	And spek furth mar of Wallace travaill rycht.	*more; Wallace's right actions*
1155	The worthy Scottis amang thar enemys raid;	*rode*
	Full gret distruccioun amang the Sotheron thai maid;	
	Waistit about the land on athir sid.	*Laid waste [to]; either*
	Na wermen than durst in thar way abid.	*No warriors; dared*
	Thai ransoun nane bot to the dede thaim dycht,	*ransomed none; death; consigned*
1160	In mony steid maid fyris braid and brycht.	*many places; broad*
	The ost was blith and in a gud estate,	*condition*
	Na power was at wald mak thaim debate;	*[There] was no army; offer them resistance*
	Gret ryches wan of gold and gud thaim till,	
	Leyffyng enewch to tak at thar awn will.	*Provisions enough; own*
1165	In awfull fer thai travaill throuch the land,	*awesome state; journeyed*
	Maid byggynis bar that thai befor thaim fand,	*Stripped buildings*
	Gret barmkynnys brak of stedis stark and strang,	*defense walls broke; places; powerful*
	Thir wicht wermen of travaill thocht nocht lang.	*These bold; labor did not weary*
	South in the land rycht ernystfully thai socht	*earnestly; went*
1170	To Sanct Tawbawnys, bot harm thar did thai nocht.	*St. Albans*
	The priour send thaim wyne and venesoun,	*wine*
	Refreshyt the ost with gud in gret fusioun.	*good [things]; plenty*
	The nycht apperyt quhen thai war at the place:	
	Thai herbreyt thaim fra thine a litill space,	*sheltered; thence; while*
1175	Chesyt a sted quhar thai suld bid all nycht;	*Chose a place; stay*
	Tentis on ground and palyonis proudly pycht	*pavilions; pitched*
	Intill a vaill be a small ryver fayr,	*valley by; fair river*
	On athir sid quhar wild der maid repayr;	*either side where*
	Set wachis owt that wysly couth thaim kepe,	*sentries; guard*
1180	To souppar went and tymysly thai slepe.	*supper; duly*
	Of meit and sleip thai ces with suffisiance.	*refrained [when they had] plenty*
	The nycht was myrk, our drayff the dyrkfull chance;	*murky, passed over; dark*
	The mery day sprang fra the oryent,	*merry; rose; east*
	With bemys brycht enlumynyt the occident.	*illuminated the west*

154

Book 8

1185	Eftir Titan Phebus up rysyt fayr,	*(i.e., the sun)*
	Heich in the sper the signes maid declayr.	*High; sphere; planets decreed*
	Zepherus began his morow cours,	*(i.e., the west wind); morning course*
	The swete vapour thus fra the ground resours,	*rose*
	The humyll breyth doun fra the hevyn availl,	*mild breath; heaven descended*
1190	In every meide, bathe fyrth, forrest, and daill,	*meadow, both stream; dale*
	The cler rede amang the rochis rang,	*clear voice; rocks*
	Throuch greyn branchis quhar byrdis blythly sang,	
	With joyus voice in hevynly armony.	*voice*
	Than Wallace thocht it was no tyme to ly.	*lie [in bed]*
1195	He croyssit him, syne sodeynli up rais;	*made the sign of the cross; arose*
	To tak the ayr out of his palyon gais.	*take; air; tent went*
	Maister John Blar was redy to rawes,	*ready to put on priestly vestments*
	In gud entent syne bownyt to the mes.	*With good intent then prepared for the mass*
	Quhen it was done Wallace can him aray	*dressed himself*
1200	In his armour, quhilk gudly was and gay.	*fine; handsome*
	His schenand schoys that burnyst was full beyn,	*shining shoes; burnished; well*
	His leg harnes he clappyt on so clene;	*leg harness*
	Pullane greis he braissit on full fast,	*Knee-armor greaves; clasped*
	A clos byrny with mony sekyr cast	*tight corslet; many firm clasps*
1205	Breyst plait, brasaris, that worthy was in wer.	*Breast; armor for the arms; war*
	Besid him furth Jop couth his basnet ber;	*helmet carry*
	His glytterand glovis gravin on athir sid,	*gloves engraved; either*
	He semyt weill in battaill till abid.	*seemed well; withstand*
	His gud gyrdyll and syne his burly brand,	*belt; then; strong sword*
1210	A staff of steyll he gryppyt in his hand.	*steel*
	The ost him blyst and prayit God of his grace	*blessed*
	Him to convoy fra all mystymyt cace.	*preserve; unlucky circumstances*
	Adam Wallace and Boid furth with him yeid	*went*
	By a revir throwout a floryst meid.	*river; flowery meadow*
1215	And as thai walk atour the feyldis greyn	*across; green fields*
	Out of the south thai saw quhar at the queyn	*where*
	Towart the ost come ridand sobyrly,	*demurely*
	And fyfty ladyis was in hyr cumpany,	*her*
	Vaillyt of wit and demyt of renoun;	*Distinguished; held in*
1220	Sum wedowis war and sum of religioun,	*Some were widows; nuns*
	And sevyn preistis that entrit war in age.	*were advanced in age*
	Wallace to sic did nevir gret owtrage	*such; violence*
	Bot gyff till him thai maid a gret offens.	*Unless; wrongdoing*

155

The Wallace

	Thus prochyt thai on towart thar presens.	*they approached; presence*
1225	At the palyoun quhar thai the lyoun saw	*pavilion*
	To ground thai lycht and syne on kneis can faw;	*alight; fell*
	Prayand for pece thai cry with petous cher.	*peace; piteous countenance*
	Erll Malcom said, "Our chyftayn is nocht her."	*here*
	He bad hyr rys and said it was nocht rycht,	*asked her [to] rise*
1230	A queyn on kneis till ony lauar wycht.	*any lower person*
	Up by the hand the gud erll has hyr tayn,	*taken*
	Atour the bent to Wallace ar thai gayn.	*Around the field; gone*
	Quhen scho him saw scho wald haiff knelyt doun.	
	In armys sone he caucht this queyn with croun	*soon; caught*
1235	And kyssyt hyr withoutyn wordis mor;	
	So dyd he nevir to na Sotheron befor.	*Englishmen*
	"Madem," he said, "Rycht welcum mot ye be.	*You are very welcome*
	How plesis yow our ostyng for to se?"	*pleases; muster*
	"Rycht weyll," scho said, "of frendschip haiff we neid.	*need*
1240	God grant ye wald of our nesis to speid.	*help us in our hour of need*
	Suffer we mon suppos it lik us ill,	*Endure; must*
	Bot trastis weyll it is contrar our will."	*trust; against*
	"Ye sall remayn. With this lord I mon gang.	*must go*
	Fra your presens we sall nocht tary lang."	*From; tarry*
1245	The erll and he on to the palyon yeid	*pavilion went*
	With gud avys to deym mar of this deid.	*consideration; ponder more; action*
	Till consell son Wallace gart call thaim to.	*council soon; had them summoned*
	"Lordys," he said, "ye wait quhat is ado.	*know*
	Of thar cummyng myselff has na plesance;	*pleasure*
1250	Herfor mon we wyrk with ordinance.	*Therefore must; proceed with caution*
	Wemen may be contempnyng into wer	*Women; cause of shame; war*
	Amang fullis that can thaim nocht forber.	*Among fools; cannot keep away from them*
	I say nocht this be thir, nor yeit the queyn;	*these [women]; yet*
	I trow it be bot gud that scho will meyn.	*believe it is only good; mean*
1255	Bot sampyll tak of lang tym passit by.	*example take*
	At Rownsyvaill the tresoun was playnly	
	Be wemen maid, that Ganyelon with him brocht,	*By women devised*
	And Turke wyn; forber thaim couth thai nocht.	*[the] Turks conquered; resist*
	Lang us in wer gert thaim desyr thar will,	*war made*
1260	Quhilk brocht Charlis to fellon los and ill.	*Charlemagne; grievous loss; evil*
	The flour of France withoutyn redempcioun	
	Throuch that foull deid was brocht to confusioun.	*destruction*

Book 8

	Commaund your men tharfor in prevay wys	*secret wise*
	Apayn of lyff thai wyrk nocht on sic wys;	*On penalty of [losing their] lives*
1265	Nane spek with thaim bot wys men of gret waill,	*No one; worth*
	At lordis ar and sworn to this consaill."	*That*
	Thir chargis thai did als wysly as thai mocht;	*These commands; carried out as; might*
	This ordynance throw all the ost was wrocht.	*decree; conveyed*
	He and the erll bathe to the queyn thai went,	
1270	Rasavyt hyr fayr and brocht hyr till a tent;	*Greeted her*
	To dyner bownyt als gudly as thai can	*made their way as well*
	And servit was with mony likly man.	*fitting*
	Gud purvyance the queyn had with hyr wrocht;	*supplies; carried*
	A say scho tuk of all thyng at thai brocht.	*sample; that*
1275	Wallace persavyt and said, "We haiff no dreid.	*observed; fear*
	I can nocht trow ladyis wald do sic deid	*believe; such [a] deed*
	To poysoun men, for all Ingland to wyn."	
	The queyn ansuerd, "Gyff poysoun be tharin	*If*
	Of ony thyng quhilk is brocht her with me,	*any*
1280	Apon myselff fyrst sorow sall ye se."	*grief (ill-effects) shall*
	Sone eftir meit a marchell gart absent	*[the] meal; steward dismissed all*
	Bot lordis and thai at suld to consaill went.	*Except; that should go to council*
	Ladyis apperyt in presens with the queyn.	
	Wallace askyt quhat hir cummyng mycht meyn.	*her coming; mean*
1285	"For pes," scho said, "at we haiff to yow socht.	*that; sought*
	This byrnand wer in baill has mony brocht.	*burning campaign; sorrow; many*
	Ye grant us pees for Him that deit on Tre."	*Grant us peace; died; Tree (i.e., Cross)*
	Wallace ansuerd, "Madeym that may nocht be.	
	Ingland has doyne sa gret harmys till us	*done so; injuries to us*
1290	We may nocht pas and lychtly leiff it thus."	*go away; leave*
	"Yeis," said the queyne, "for Crystyn folk we ar.	
	For Goddis saik, sen we desyr no mar,	*since*
	We awcht haiff pes." "Madeym, that I deny.	*ought [to] have*
	The perfyt caus I sall yow schaw forquhy;	*show why*
1295	Ye seke na pes bot for your awn availl.	*seek; own advantage*
	Quhen your fals king had Scotland gryppyt haill,	*seized entirely*
	For na kyn thing that he befor him fand	*no kind of thing; found*
	He wald nocht thoill the rycht blud in our land,	*permit; blood (lineage)*
	Bot reft thar rent, syne put thaimselff to ded.	*took by force; property, then; death*
1300	Ransoun of gold mycht mak us na remed.	*[A] ransom; reparation*
	His fell fals wer sall on himselff be seyn."	*disastrous; war he shall pay for dearly*

The Wallace

	Than sobyrly till him ansuerd the queyn,	*gravely*
	"Of thir wrangis amendis war most fair."	*For these wrongs; were*
	"Madeym," he said, "of him we ask no mar	*more*
1305	Bot at he wald byd us into battaill,	*that he would stand against*
	And God be juge, he kennys the maist haill."	*knows; most righteous*
	"Sic mendis," scho said, "war nocht rycht gud, think me.	*Such amends*
	Pes now war best, and it mycht purchest be.	*Peace; were; obtained*
	Wald yhe grant pes and trwys with us tak,	*truce; agree*
1310	Throuch all Ingland we suld gar prayeris mak	*have prayers offered*
	For yow and thaim at in the wer war lost."	*those who; war were*
	Than Wallace said, "Quhar sic thing cummys throuch bost,[1]	
	Prayer of fors, quharso at it be wrocht,	*of necessity, where; offered*
	Till us helpys litill or ellis nocht."	*To; else not [at all]*
1315	Warly scho said, "Thus wys men has us kend,	*Carefully; taught*
	Ay efftir wer pees is the finall end,	*Always after war peace*
	Quharfor ye suld of your gret malice ces;	*cease*
	The end of wer is cheryté and pes.	*war; charity; peace*
	Pees is in hevyn with blys and lestandnas.	*bliss; lastingness*
1320	We sall beseke the pape of his hie grace	*beseech; pope; high*
	Till commaund pes sen we may do na mar."	*To; since; more*
	"Madeym," he said, "or your purches cum thar	*before; soliciting comes there*
	Mendys we think of Ingland for to haiff."	*Amends*
	"Quhat set yow thus," scho said, "so God yow saiff,	*determined; save*
1325	Fra violent wer at ye lik nocht to duell?"	*From; war that; stay away*
	"Madem," he said, "the suth I sall yow tell.	*truth*
	Eftir the dayt of Alexanderis ryng	*After; time; reign*
	Our land stud thre yer desolate but king,	*stood three years; without [a] king*
	Kepyt full weyll at concord in gud stait.	*Maintained; in harmony; state*
1330	Throuch two clemyt thar hapnyt gret debait,	*[who] claimed [the throne]; happened*
	So ernystfully, accord thaim nocht thai can.	*earnestly, they could not agree*
	Your king thai ast for to be thar ourman.	*asked; arbiter*
	Slely he slayd throuch strenthis of Scotland;	*Slyly; passed; strongholds*
	The kynryk syne he tuk in his awn hand.	*kingdom then; own*
1335	He maid a king agayn our rychtwys law	*contrary to; righteous*
	For he of him suld hald the regioun aw.	*from him should hold [in fealty]; all*
	Contrar this band was all the haill barnage	*Against; bond; entire baronage*

---

[1] Then Wallace said, "Where such things come through menacing["]

Book 8

	For Scotland was yeit nevir into thrillage.	*subjection*
	Gret Julius that tribut gat of aw,	*got from everyone*
1340	His wynnyng was in Scotland bot full smaw.	*conquest; only very small*
	Than your fals king, under colour but mar,	*Then; under pretense forthwith*
	Throuch band he maid till Bruce that is our ayr,	*bond; heir*
	Throuch all Scotland with gret power thai raid,	
	Undid that king quhilk he befor had maid.	*Undid; (i.e., Balliol) which*
1345	To Bruce sen syne he kepit na connand.	*afterwards; no covenant*
	He said he wald nocht ga and conques land	*go and conquer*
	Till othir men, and thus the cas befell.	*For other; case*
	Than Scotland throuch he demayned himsell,	*throughout; ruled himself*
	Slew our elderis, gret peté was to se.	*ancestors; pity*
1350	In presone syne lang tyme thai pynit me	*afterwards; tormented*
	Quhill I fra thaim was castyn out for ded.	*Until; from; dead*
	Thankit be God he send me sum remed!	*remedy (cure)*
	Vengyt to be I prevyt all my mycht;	*Avenged; tried with*
	Feyll of thar kyn to dede syn I haiff dycht.	*Many; kin I have since killed*
1355	The rage of youth gert me desyr a wyff;	*passion; made; desire*
	That rewit I sayr and will do all my liff.	*sorely regretted; life*
	A tratour knycht but mercy gert hyr de,	*traitor; without; caused her*
	Ane Hessilryg, bot for dispit of me.	*One; only; malice towards*
	Than rang I furth in cruell wer and payn	*prevailed; fierce war*
1360	Quhill we redemyt part of our land agayn.	*Until; redeemed*
	Than your curst king desyryt of us a trew,	*accursed; truce*
	Quhilk maid Scotland full rathly for to rew.	*Which; quickly; repent*
	Into that pes thai set a suttell ayr,	*During; arranged; perfidious justice-ayre*
	Than eighteen scor to dede thai hangyt thair	*death; hanged there*
1365	At noblis war and worthi of renoun,	*That were nobles*
	Of cot armys eldest in that regioun;[1]	
	Thar dede we think to veng in all our mycht.	*Their deaths; avenge*
	The woman als that dulfully was dycht,	*also; painfully was killed*
	Out of my mind that dede will nevir bid	*stay*
1370	Quhill God me tak fra this fals warld so wid!	*Until; takes; world; wide*
	Of Sotheroun syn I can no peté haiff.	*On Englishmen's sins; pity*
	Your men in wer I think nevirmor to saiff."	*war; spare*
	The breith teris, was gret payn to behald,	*vehement tears; pain*

---

[1] *[Bearers] of [the] oldest coats [of] arms in that region*

The Wallace

	Bryst fra his eyn be he his taill had tald.	*Burst; when; account; told*
1375	The queyn wepyt for peté of Wallace.	
	"Allace," scho said, "wa worth the curssyt cace!	*woe betide; accursed case*
	In waryit tym that Hesilryg was born!	*[a] blighted time*
	Mony worthi throuch his deid ar forlorn.	*Many worthy [men]; action; lost*
	He suld haiff payn that saikles sic ane slewch.[1]	
1380	Ingland sen syn has bocht it der enewch,	*afterwards; paid dearly enough for it*
	Thocht scho had beyn a queyn or a prynsace."	*[As] though; princess*
	"Madem," he said, "as God giff me gud grace,	*so God grant*
	Intill hir tym scho was als der to me,	*While she lived; as dear . . . [as]*
	Prynsace or queyn, in quhat stait so thai be."	*estate*
1385	"Wallace," scho said, "of this talk we will ces;	*cease*
	The mendis heroff is gud prayer and pes."	*amends hereof*
	"I grant," he said, "of me as now na mayr.	*no more*
	This is rycht nocht bot ekyng of our cayr."	*increasing; distress*
	The queyn fand weyll langage nothing hyr bet.[2]	
1390	Scho trowit with gold that he mycht be ourset.	*trusted; won over (overcome)*
	Thre thousand pound of fynest gold so red	
	Scho gert be brocht to Wallace in that sted.	*caused to be brought; place*
	"Madeym," he said, "na sic tribut we craiff.	*no such tribute we crave*
	Anothir mendis we wald of Ingland haiff	*Other amends; would*
1395	Or we raturn fra this regioun agayn,	*Before; remove*
	Of your fals blud that has our elderis slayn.	*forebears*
	For all the gold and ryches ye in ryng.	*you possess*
	Ye get no pes but desir of your king."	*without*
	Quhen scho saw weill gold mycht hyr nocht releiff,	*help*
1400	Sum part in sport scho thocht him for to preiff.	*Some; play; test*
	"Wallace," scho said, "yhe war clepyt my luff;	*you were called; love*
	Mor baundounly I maid me for to pruff,[3]	
	Traistand tharfor your rancour for to slak.	*Trusting; assuage*
	Me think ye suld do sumthing for my saik."	*sake*
1405	Rycht wysly he maid ansuer to the queyn:	*wisely*
	"Madem," he said, "and verité war seyn	*if it were truly so*
	That ye me luffyt, I awcht yow luff agayn.	*ought to love you in return*

---

[1] *He should be punished for slaying such an innocent creature*

[2] *The queen discovered words did not help her [case]*

[3] *This emboldened me all the more to try you*

Book 8

	Thir wordis all ar nothing bot in vayn.	*These*
	Sic luff as that is nothing till avance,	*Such love; not praiseworthy*
1410	To tak a lak and syne get no plesance.	*suffer censure; then; pleasure*
	In spech of luff suttell ye Sotheroun ar;	*wily; English are*
	Ye can us mok, suppos ye se no mar."	*mock*
	"In London," scho said, "for yow I sufferyt blaym;	
	Our consall als will lauch quhen we cum haym.	*council also; laugh; come home*
1415	So may thai say, wemen ar fers of thocht	*boldly think*
	To seke frendschip and syne can get rycht nocht."	*seek; then*
	"Madem," he said, "we wait how ye ar send.	*know; you are sent*
	Yhe trow we haiff bot litill for to spend.	*You believe*
	Fyrst with your gold, for ye ar rych and wys,	*rich; wise*
1420	Yhe wald us blynd, sen Scottis ar so nys;	*You would; since; foolish*
	Syn plesand wordis of yow and ladyis fair,	*Then pleasing; from*
	As quha suld dryff the byrdis till a swar	*drive; to; snare*
	With the small pype, for it most fresche will call.	*the whistle; vigorously*
	Madeym, as yit ye ma nocht tempt us all.	*yet; may*
1425	Gret part of gud is left amang our kyn;	*kinsfolk*
	In Ingland als we fynd enewch to wyn."	*also; enough; capture*
	Abayssyt scho was to mak ansuer him till.	*Afraid; make him an answer*
	"Der schir," scho said, "sen this is at your will,	*since; pleasure*
	Wer or pes, quhatso yow likis best,	*War or peace, whatever*
1430	Lat your hye witt and gud consaill degest."	*Let; noble mind; counsel settle*
	"Madem," he said, "now sall ye understand	*shall you*
	The resone quhy that I will mak na band.	*why; no bond*
	With yow ladyis I can na trewis bynd	*agree no truce*
	For your fals king hereftir sone wald fynd,	*hereafter soon would find*
1435	Quhen he saw tyme, to brek it at his will	*pleasure*
	And playnly say he grantyt nocht thartill.	*thereto*
	Than had we nayn bot ladyis to repruff.	*none except; reprove*
	That sall he nocht, be God that is abuff!	*by; above*
	Apon wemen I will no wer begyn;	*war*
1440	On you, in faith, no worschip is to wyn.	*honor; win*
	All the haill pas apon himselff he sall tak	*the whole responsibility upon; take*
	Of pees or wer, quhat hapnyt we to mak."	*war, whatever we decide*
	The qweyn grantyt his ansuer sufficient;	
	So dyd the layff in place that was present.	*others that were present in [the] place*
1445	His delyverance thai held of gret availl	*decision; advantage*
	And stark enewch to schaw to thar consaill.	*powerful enough; reveal; council*

The Wallace

	Wa was the qweyn hyr travaill helpyt nocht.	*Dejected; effort*
	The gold scho tuk that thai had with hyr brocht;	*she took; her*
	Into the ost rycht frely scho it gayff	*Unto; army; generously; gave*
1450	Till evirylk man that likyt for till haiff.	*To every; have [it]*
	Till menstraillis, harroldis, scho delt haboundanlé,[1]	
	Besekand thaim hyr frend at thai wald be.	*Beseeching; her friend that*
	Quhen Wallace saw the fredom of the queyn	*generosity*
	Sadly he said, "The suth weyll has beyn seyn,	*Sternly; truth*
1455	Wemen may tempt the wysest at is wrocht.	*wisest [creature]*
	Your gret gentrice it sall nevir be for nocht.	*noble conduct*
	We yow assuuer our ost sall muff nathing	*assure; not move at all*
	Quhyll tym ye may send message fra your king.	*Until [such] time as*
	Gyff it be sa at he accord and we,	*If; he and we agree*
1460	Than for your saik it sall the better be.	
	Your harroldys als sall saiffly cum and ga;	*also shall safely come; go*
	For your fredom we sall trowbill na ma."[2]	
	Scho thankit him of his grant mony sys	*concession many times*
	And all the ladyis apon a gudly wys.	*goodly manner*
1465	Glaidly thai drank, the queyn and gud Wallace,	
	Thir ladyis als and lordis in that place.	*These; also*
	Hyr leyff scho tuk without langar abaid,	*Her leave; took; delay*
	Five myile that nycht south till a nonry raid.	*miles; to a nunnery rode*
	Apon the morn till London passit thai.	
1470	In Westmenster quhar at the consaill lay	*parliament*
	Wallace ansuer scho gart schaw to the king.	*caused to be shown*
	It nedis nocht her rahers mar of this thing.	*It is not necessary to repeat here more*
	The gret commend that scho to Wallace gaiff	*praise; gave*
	Befor the king in presens of the laiff,	*others*
1475	Till trew Scottis it suld gretly apples,	*To; please*
	Thocht Inglismen tharoff had litill es.	*comfort*
	Of worschip, wyt, manheid, and governans,	*honor, intelligence; leadership*
	Of fredom, trewth, key of remembrans,	
	Scho callyt him thar into thar hye presens,	*in their august presence*
1480	Thocht contrar thaim he stud at his defens.	*Though against; stood in his resistance*
	"So chyftaynlik," scho said, "as he is seyn,	*chieftain-like*

---

[1] *To minstrels, heralds, she gave abundantly*

[2] *Because of your generosity we shall cause no more trouble*

Book 8

	Intill Inglande I trow has nevir beyn.	*believe*
	Wald ye of gold gyff him this rewmys rent	*realm's revenue*
	Fra honour he will nocht turn his entent.	*From; mind*
1485	Sufferyt we ar quhill ye may message mak.	*We are assured of safety until; send*
	Of wys lordis sum part I reid yow tak	*some; advise; take*
	To purches pees withoutyn wordis mar;	*solicit peace; more*
	For all Ingland may rew his raid full sayr.	*repent; extremely*
	Your harroldys als to pas to him has leyff,	*also; permission*
1490	In all his ost thar sall no man thaim greiff."	*harm*
	Than thankit thai the queyn for hir travaill,	*endeavor*
	The king and lordis that was of his consaill.	*council*
	Of hyr ansuer the king applessit was.	*was pleased*
	Than thre gret lordys thai ordand for to pas.	
1495	Thar consaill haill has fownd it was the best	*found*
	Trewis to tak, or ellis thai get no rest.	*To take [a] truce; else*
	A harrold went in all the haist he may	
	Till Tawbane waill quhar at the Scottis lay,	*St. Albans bulwark where*
	Condeyt till haiff quhill thai haiff said thar will.	*[Safe] conduct*
1500	The consaill sone a condeyt gaiff him till.	*soon*
	Agayn he past with soverance till his king.	*assurance of safety to*
	Than chesyt thai thre lordis for this thing.	*chose*
	The keyn Clyffurd was than thar warden haill,	*bold; wholly*
	Bewmont, Wodstok, all men of mekill waill;	*great worth*
1505	Quhat thir thre wrocht the layff suld stand thartill.	*these three; others; stand by it*
	The kingis seyll was gyffyn thaim at thar will.	*king's seal; given; pleasure*
	Sone thai war brocht to spekyng to Wallace.	*Soon; speak with*
	Wodstok him schawit mony suttell cace.	*presented many cunning arguments*
	Wallace he herd the sophammis evire deill.	*every one of the sophisms*
1510	"As yeit," he said, "me think ye meyn bot weill.	*mean only*
	In wrang ye hald, and dois us gret owtrage,	*Wrongfully you occupy; do us great injury*
	Of housis part that is our heretage.	*some castles*
	Owt of this pees in playn I mak thaim knawin,	*Out; clearly; known*
	Thaim for to wyn, sen that thai ar our awin,	*win [back]; since; own*
1515	Roxburch, Berweik, at ouris lang tym has beyn,	*that ours long time*
	Into the handis of you fals Sotherone keyn.	*fierce English*
	We ask her als be vertu of this band	*here also by virtue; agreement*
	Our ayris, our king, be wrang led of Scotland.	*justice-ayres; wrong led [out] of*
	We sall thaim haiff withoutyn wordis mar."	*have [back]; more*
1520	Till his desyr the lordis grantis thair,	*To; granted there*

163

The Wallace

	Rycht at his will thai haiff consentit haill,	*according to; all*
	For na kyn thing the pees thai wald nocht faill.	*no kind of thing*
	The yong Randell at than in London was,	*who then*
	The lord of Lorn, in this band he can as,	*under this agreement did ask [to be released]*
1525	Erll of Bowchane bot than in tendyr age —	*but then; youthful*
	Eftir he grew a man of hycht, wys and large.	*After; tall; generous*
	Cumyn and Soullis he gart deliver als,	*had freed also*
	Quhilk eftir was till King Robert full fals.	*Who afterwards; to*
	Wallang fled our, and durst nocht bid that mute,	*overseas; stay in that court*
1530	In Pykardté; to ask him was na bute,	*futile*
	Bot Wallace wald erar haff had that fals knycht	*would sooner have*
	Than ten thousand of fynest gold so brycht.	
	The Bruce he askit, bot he was had away	*asked [for]; taken*
	Befor that tym till Calys mony day.	*Calais many [a]*
1535	King Eduuard prevyt that thai mycht nocht him get;	*proved*
	Of Glosister his uncle had him set,	*placed [there]*
	At Calys than had haly in kepyng.	*That; wholly; keeping*
	Wallace that tym gat nocht his rychtwys king.	*got*
	The erll Patrik fra London alsua send	*also*
1540	Wyth Wallace to mak, as weill befor was kend,	*known*
	Of his mater a fynaill governance;	*affairs; settlement*
	Till King Eduuard gaiff up his legeance	*gave up; allegiance*
	And tuk till hald of Scotland evirmar.	*undertook to remain true to*
	With full glaid hart Wallace resavit him thar.	*received; there*
1545	Thai honowryt him rycht reverendly as lord;	*honored; respectfully*
	The Scottis was all rejosyt of that conford.	*gladdened; comfort*
	A hundreth hors with yong lordis of renoune	*hundred horses*
	Till Wallace com, fred out of that presoune.	*freed*
	Undyr his seill King Eduuard thaim gert send	*seal; had sent*
1550	For till gyff our and mak a fynaill end	*hand over; final settlement*
	Roxburch, Berweik, quhilk is of mekill vaill,	*worth*
	To Scottis men and all the boundis haill.	*bounds entirely*
	To fyve yer trew thai promyst be thar hand.	*A five-year truce; their signatures*
	Than Wallace said, "We will pas ner Scotland	
1555	Or ocht be seld, and tharfor mak us boun.	*Before anything is sealed; ready*
	Agayn we will besid Northallyrtoun	*We will return*
	Quhar King Eduuard fyrst battaill hecht to me;	*promised*
	As it began thar sall it endyt be.	
	Gret weyll your queyn," he chargyt the message,	*Greet well; charged; messengers*

164

Book 8

1560	"It is for hyr at we leyff our viage."	*that; leave [off]; campaign*
	A day he set quhen he suld meit him thar	*meet; there*
	And seill this pees withoutyn wordis mar.	*seal; peace; more*
	Apon the morn the ost but mar avys	*without further delay*
	Tranountyt north apon a gudly wys	*Marched; in good order*
1565	To the set tryst that Wallace had thaim maid.	*appointed meeting*
	The Inglis message com but mar abaid;	*messengers; straightaway*
	Thai seyllyt the pes without langar delay.	*sealed the peace immediately*
	The message than apon the secund day	*messengers then*
	Till London went in all the haist thai can.	
1570	The worthi Scottis with mony gudly man	*many good men*
	Till Bambwrch com with all the power haill,	*Bamburgh; complete*
	Sexté thousand, all Scottis of gret waill.	*Sixty; great worth*
	Ten dayis befor All Halow Evyn thai fur;	*Halloween; went*
	On Lammes Day thai lycht on Caram Mur.	*dismounted; Carham Moor*
1575	Thar lugyt thai with plesance as thai mocht,	*lodged; gladly; might*
	Quhill on the morn at preistis to thaim socht	*that priests sought them*
	In Caram Kyrk, and sessyt in his hand	*delivered into*
	Roxburch keyis as thai had maid connand,	*agreement*
	And Berweik als, quhilk Sotheroun had so lang.	*[the] English; held so long*
1580	Thai frede the folk in Ingland for to gang,	*freed; go*
	For thar lyffis uschet of athir place;	*lives sallied forth from other places*
	Thai durst nocht weill bid rekynnyng of Wallace.	*dared; wait for Wallace's reckoning*
	Capdane he maid in Berweik of renoun	
	That worthy was, gud Crystell of Cetoun.	
1585	Kepar he left till Roxburch Castell wicht	*Keeper; strong*
	Schir Jhon Ramsay, a wys and worthi knycht.	
	Syn Wallace selff with Erll Patrik in playn	*Then; himself; openly*
	To Dunbar raid and restoryt him agayn	*rode; restored*
	In his castell and all that heretage,	
1590	With the consent of all that haill barnage.	*the entire baronage*
	Quhen Wallace was agreit and this lord,	*agreed*
	To rewll the rewm he maid him gudly ford.	*rule the realm; ready*
	Scotlande atour fra Ros till Soloway Sand	
	He raid it thrys and statut all the land.	*rode it thrice and ruled*
1595	In the Leynhous a quhyll he maid repayr;	*Lennox he went frequently*
	Schyr Jhon Menteth that tym was captane thar.	
	Twys befor he had his gossep beyn,	
	Bot na frendschip betwix thaim syn was seyn.	*then was seen*

The Wallace

	Twa monethis still he duelt in Dunbertane;	
1600	A hous he foundyt apon the Roch of stayne.	*castle*
	Men left he thar till byg it to the hycht,	*build it high*
	Syn to the March agayn he rydis rycht.	*Then*
	Into Roxburch thai chesyt him a place,	*chose*
	A gud tour thar he gert byg in schort space.	*tower; had built; short time*
1605	The kynrik stud in gud worschip and es;	*kingdom stood; prosperity*
	Was nayn so gret durst his nychtbour disples.	
	The abill ground gert laubour thryftely,	*fertile*
	Victaill and froyte thar grew aboundandly.	*Food*
	Was nevir befor, syn this was callyt Scotland,	*since*
1610	Sic welth and pes at anys in the land.	*at once*
	He send Jop twys to Bruce in Huntyntoun,	
	Besekand him to cum and tak his croun.	*Asking*
	Conseill he tuk at fals Saxionis, allace!	*English*
	He had nevir hap in lyff to get Wallace.	*[the good] fortune*
1615	Thre yer as thus the rewm stud in gud pes.	
	Of this sayn my wordis for to ces,	
	And forthyr furth of Wallace I will tell	
	Intill his lyff quhat aventur yeit fell.	

Book 9

[*Impressed by his fame, the king of France invites Wallace to come to his realm. Wallace sets sail with a few companions and a small armed force. On the voyage he defeats the pirate, the Red Reiver, who reveals to him that he is the exiled French knight Thomas of Longueville and one of Wallace's greatest admirers. As a favor to Wallace, the French king is reconciled with Longueville. Wallace, with Longueville, attacks the English settlement in Guyenne. When Edward learns of this he resolves to take advantage of Wallace's absence to invade Scotland and occupy the major strongholds. Wallace hurries back to Scotland as soon as he is told that the truce has been so blatantly broken.*]

Book 10

[*Wallace seizes three passing English hay carts and, disguised, he, Bisset, and Guthrie, with fifteen men concealed in the carts, gain entry to Perth, kill the English occupants, and install*

Book 10

Sir John Ramsay as captain with other Scottish officers. Wallace makes his way to Fife, followed by Sir John Siward. (Lines 1–92)]

	Thar Wallace was and mycht no message send	
	Till Sanct Jhonstoun to mak this jornay kend,	*military action known*
95	For Inglismen that full sutell has beyn	*cunning*
	Gart wachis walk that nayn mycht pas betweyn.	*Made sentries watch; no one*
	Than Wallace said, "This mater payis nocht me."	*pleases not*
	He cald till him the squier gud Guthré,	
	And Besat als, that knew full weyll the land,	*also*
100	And ast at thaim quhat deid was best on hand,	*asked; action*
	"Message to mak our pouer for to get;	*Messengers to bring our forces*
	With Sotheroun sone we sall be unbeset;	*[the] English soon; beset*
	And wykked Scottis that knawis this forest best,	*(i.e., collaborators)*
	Thai ar the caus that we may haiff no rest.	
105	I dreid fer mar Wallang that is thar gyd,	*fear far more; guide*
	Than all the layff that cummys on that syd."	*others; come*
	Than Guthré said, "Mycht we get ane or tway	*one or two*
	To Saynct Jhonstoun, it war the gaynest way,	*shortest*
	And warn Ramsay, we wald get succour sone.	*inform; help soon*
110	Our suth it is it can nocht now be don.	*Too true; done*
	Rycht weyll I wait veschell is levyt nayn	*know no boats are left*
	Fra the Woodhavyn to the ferry cald Aran."	
	Than Wallace said, "The water cald it is.	*cold*
	Myselff can swym, I trow, and fall na mys,	*suffer no harm*
115	Bot currours oys that gaynis nocht for me;	
	And leyff yow her yet had I levir de.[1]	
	Throw Goddis grace we sall better eschew;	*achieve better [than that]*
	The strenth is stark, als we haiff men inew.	*stronghold; stalwart; enough*
	In Elchoch Park bot fourty thar war we	*only*
120	For sevyn hundreth and gert feill Sothron de,	*caused many English to die*
	And chapyt weill in mony unlikly place;	*escaped*
	So sall we her throw help of Goddis grace.	*here*
	Quhill men may fast thir woddis we may hauld still;	*As long as; these; keep*
	Forthi ilk man be of trew hardy will,	*Therefore each; steadfast*
125	And at we do so nobill into deid	

---

[1] Lines 115–16: *But I am not cut out to be a courtier; / And I would rather die than leave you here*

167

The Wallace

	Of us be found no lak efter to reid.	*no fault be found; read*
	The rycht is ouris, we suld mor ardent be.	
	I think to freith this land or ellis de."	*liberate; die*
	His waillyt spech, with wit and hardyment,	*well-chosen words*
130	Maid all the layff so cruell of entent	*rest; fierce; purpose*
	Sum bad tak feyld and gyff battaill in playn.¹	
	Wallace said, "Nay, thai wordys ar in vayn.	
	We will nocht leyff that may be our vantage.	*leave; advantage*
	The wod till us is worth a yeris wage."	*wood; payment*
135	Of hewyn temir in haist he gert thaim tak,	*hewn timber*
	Syllys of ayk and a stark barres mak	*Beams; oak; strong barrier*
	At a foyr frount, fast in the forest syd,	*forward position, close to*
	A full gret strenth quhar thai purpost to bid;	*place of defense*
	Stellyt thaim fast till treis that growand was	*Fixed; to trees that were growing*
140	That thai mycht weyll in fra the barres pas,	*barrier*
	And so weill graithit on athir sid about	*arranged; either*
	Syn com agayn quhen thai saw thaim in dout.	*Then; danger*
	Be that the strenth arayit was at rycht,	*By [the time] the barrier; all ready*
	The Inglis ost approchyt to thair sycht.	
145	Than Sewart com that way for till haiff wend	*gone*
	As thai war wount, so his gydis thaim kend.	*accustomed; knew*
	At that entré thai thocht till haiff passage,	*entrance*
	Bot sone thai fand that maid thaim gret stoppage.	*soon; found*
	A thousand he led of men in armes strang;	
150	With five hundreth he gert Jhon Wallang gang	*ordered; go*
	Without the wod that nayn suld pas thaim fra.	*outside; from*
	Wallace with him had fourty archarys thra;	*bold*
	The layff was speris, full nobill in a neid.	*others were spear-carriers; necessity*
	On thar enemys thai bykkyr with gud speid.	*attack quickly*
155	A cruell cuntyr was at the barres seyn.	*fierce encounter; barrier*
	The Scottis defens so sykkyr was and keyn	*sure; strong*
	Sotheroun stud aw to enter thaim amang.	*stood [in] awe*
	Feill to the ground thai ourthrew in that thrang.	*Many; press*
	A rowm was left quhar part in frount mycht fayr;	*clearing; go*
160	Quha entrit in agayn yeid nevirmar.	*never left again*
	Fourty thai slew that formast wald haiff past.	*would have entered first*

---

¹ *[That] some advocated taking to the battlefield to offer open battle*

Book 10

	All dysarayit the ost was and agast,	*disarrayed; afraid*
	And part of hors throw schot to dede was brocht,	*some horses; shot; death*
	Brak to a playn, the Sotheroun fra thaim socht.[1]	
165	The Sewart said, "Allace, how may this be	
	And do no harm? Our gret rabut haiff we."[2]	
	He cald Wallang and askyt his consaill.	
	"Schyrreff thow art. Quhat may be our availl?	*advantage*
	Bot few thai ar that makis this gret debait."	*They are only [a] few; resistance*
170	Jhon Wallang said, "This is the best I wait:	*know*
	To ces herof and remayn her besyd,	*cease hereof; here*
	For thai may nocht lang in this forest byd;	
	For fawt of fud thai mon in the cuntré.	*lack; must [go] into*
	Than war mar tym to mak on thaim mellé.	*more time to do battle*
175	Or thai be won be fors into this stryff	*Before; conquered by force*
	Feyll at ye leid sall erar los the lyff."	*Many that you lead; sooner*
	Than Sewart said, "This reid I will nocht tak;	*counsel*
	And Scottis be warnyt reskew sone will thai mak.	*If; informed; soon*
	Of this dispyt amendys I think to haiff,	*defiance*
180	Or de tharfor in nowmer with the laiff.	*die; company; rest*
	Intill a rang myselff on fut will fayr."	*In a column; foot; go*
	Eight hundreth he tuk of liklyest that was thair,	
	Syn bad the layff bid at the barres still	*Then ordered; remain; barrier*
	With Jhon Wallang to rewyll thaim at his will.	*rule*
185	"Wallang," he said, "be forthwart in this cace.	*active*
	In sic a swar we couth nocht get Wallace.	*such a snare*
	Tak hym or sla, I promes thee be my lyff	*Take him [alive] or dead*
	That King Edwart sall mak thee erll of Fyff.	
	At yon est part we think to enter in.	*that eastern part*
190	I bid no mar. Mycht ye this barres wyn,	*I stay no longer; capture*
	Fra thai be closyt graithly amang us sa,	*quickly*
	Bot mervell be, thai sall na ferrer ga.	*Saving a miracle; further go*
	Assailye sayr quhen ye wit we cum ner;	*Attack forcefully; know*
	On athir sid we sall hald thaim on ster."	*either; a stir*
195	Thus semlyt thai apon ane awfull wys	*assembled; formidable way*
	Wallace has seyn quhat was thair haill devys.	*entire plan*

---

[1] *Fled to a plain, the English sought [to escape] from them*

[2] *And [yet we] do not injure [them]? We have too great a repulse*

The Wallace

	"Gud men," he said, "understud ye this deid?	action
	Forsuth thai ar rycht mekill for to dreid.	many to fear
	Yon Sewart is a nobill, worthy knycht,	That
200	Forthwart in wer, rycht worthy, wys, and wicht.	Active; war; bold
	His assailye he ordannys wondir sayr	attack; marvelously
	Us for to harm, no mannys wyt can do mar.	more
	Plesand it is to se a chyftane ga	
	So chyftanlyk; it suld recomfort ma	encourage more
205	Till his awn men, and thai of worschip be,	if; honor
	Than for to se ten thousand cowartis fle.	cowards
	Sen we ar stud with enemys on ilk sid	are placed; each side
	And her on fors mon in this forest bid,	here of necessity must
	Than fray the fyrst for Goddis saik cruellye,	scare the first [of them]
210	That all the layff of us abayssyt be."	[So] that; are terrified of us
	Crawfurd he left and Longaweill the knycht,	
	Fourty with thaim to kepe the barres wicht.	defend; boldly
	With him saxté of worthy men in weid	sixty; armor
	To meit Sewart with hardy will thai yeid.	went
215	A maner dyk into that wod wes maid	A kind of ditch
	Of thuortour rys, quhar bauldly thai abaid.	brushwood placed crosswise; waited
	Adoun with vaill the Sothroun to thaim had.	Downward; advantage
	Son semblyt thai with strakis sar and sad.	Soon they gathered; blows
	Scharp sperys fast duschand on athir sid	striking; either
220	Throw byrnys brycht maid woundis deip and wid.	corslets
	This vantage was, the Scottis thaim dantyt swa,	daunted so
	Nayn Inglisman durst fra his feris ga	No; dared; companions
	To brek aray or formast enter in.	
	Of Crystin blud to se it was gret syn	
225	For wrangwis caus, and has beyn mony day.	wrongful
	Feyll Inglismen in the dyk deid thai lay.	Many; ditch dead
	Speris full sone all into splendrys sprang;	splinters broke
	With scharp suerdys thai hew on in that thrang.	swords; hacked; press of battle
	Blud byrstyt out throw fyn harnes of maill.	Blood gushed; fine mail armor
230	Jhon Wallang als full scharply can assaill	
	Apon Crawfurd and the knycht Longaweill,	
	At thar power kepyt the barres weill,	That; defended
	Maid gud defens be wyt, manheid, and mycht,	manliness
	At the entré feyll men to dede thai dycht.	many; killed
235	Thus all at anys assailyeit in that place,	once assailed

Book 10

	Nayn that was thar durst turn fra the barrace	None; dared; barrier
	To help Wallace, nor none of his durst pas	
	To reskew thaim, so feyll the fechtyng was.	terrible; fighting
	At athir ward thai handelyt thaim full hayt;	In either group; hotly
240	Bot do or de na succour ellis thai wayt.	die no other help; sought
	Wallace wes stad into that stalwart stour,	beset; battle
	Guthré, Besat with men of gret valour,	valor
	Rychard Wallace that worthi was of hand.	
	Sewart merveillyt that contrar thaim mycht stand,	marveled
245	That evir so few mycht byd in battaill place	withstand
	Agaynys thaim metyng face for face.	face to face (i.e., in close combat)
	He thocht hymselff to end that mater weill,	
	Fast pressyt in with a gud suerd of steill;	sword; steel
	Into the dyk a Scottis man gert he de.	ditch; made; die
250	Wallace tharoff in hart had gret pyté;	
	Amendis till haiff he folowit on him fast,	To get retribution
	Bot Inglismen so thik betwex thaim past	
	That apon him a strak get mycht he nocht;	blow
	Uthyr worthy derffly to dede he brocht.	Other; violently
255	Sloppys thai maid throu all that chevalry,	Breaches
	The worthy Scottis thai wrocht so worthely.	
	Than Sothron saw of thar gud men so drest,	[the] Englishmen; roughly handled
	Langar to bid thai thocht it nocht the best.	Longer
	Four scor was slayn or thai wald leyff that steid	before; leave; place
260	And fyfty als was at the barrace deid.	barrier dead
	A trumpet blew and fra the wod thai draw;	from the wood; withdraw
	Wallang left off, that sycht fra that he saw,	
	To sailye mar thaim thocht it was no speid.	attack; no use
	Wythowt the wod to consaill son thai yeid.	Outside; soon; went
265	The worthy Scottis to rest thaim was full fayn;	content
	Feyll hurtis had, bot few of thaim was slayn.	Many had injuries
	Wallace thaim bad of all gud comfort be:	told to be of good heart
	"Thankit be God, the fayrer part haiff we.	
	Yon knycht Sewart has at gret jornay beyn;	exerted himself today
270	So sair assay I haiff bot seildyn seyn.	severe attack; seldom
	I had levir of Wallang wrokyn be	rather; revenged
	Than ony man that is of yon menyhe."	company
	The Scottis all on to the barres yeid,	barrier went
	Stanchit woundis that couth full braithly bleid.	Stanched; profusely bled

The Wallace

275	Part Scottis men had bled full mekill blud.	*Some; a great deal of blood*
	For faut of drynk and als wantyng of fud	*want; also*
	Sum feblyt fast that had feill hurtis thar.	*weakened; great*
	Wallace tharfor sichit with hart full sar.	*sighed with [a] very heavy heart*
	A hat he hynt, to get water is gayn;	*helmet; seized*
280	Othir refut as than he wyst of nayn.	*help; knew; none*
	A litill strand he fand that ran hym by;	*stream; found*
	Of cler watter he brocht haboundandly,	*plentifully*
	And drank himselff, syn said with sobyr mud,	*then; seriously*
	"The wyn of Frans me thocht nocht halff so gud."	
285	Than of the day thre quartaris was went.	
	Schir Jhon Sewart has castyn in his entent:	*considered in his mind*
	To sailye mar as than he couth nocht preiff,	*attack again; try*
	Quhill on the morn that mar men couth raleiff	*Until; more; relieve*
	And kep thaim in, quhill thai for hungyr sor	*until; acute hunger*
290	Cum in his will or ellis de tharfor.	*die*
	"Wallange," he said, "I charge thee for to bid	*stay*
	And kep thaim in. I will to Coupar rid.	
	Thow sall remayn with five hundreth at thi will	*command*
	And I the morn sall cum with power thee till."	*[in] the morning; reinforcements*
295	Jhon Wallange said, "This charg her I forsaik.	*commission here; refuse*
	Eftir this day all nycht I may nocht waik,	*watch*
	For trastis weill, thai will ische to the playn	*sally forth*
	Thocht ye bid als, or ellis de in the payn."	*Although; wait also; attempt*
	Sewart bad him byd undyr the blaym:	*charged him to stay; reproach*
300	"I thee commaund on gud King Eduuardis naym,	*name*
	Or thar to God a vow I mak beforn,	
	And thai brek out, to hyng thee heych tomorn!"	*If; escape; hang thee high*
	Of that commaund Jhon Wallang had gret dreid.	*dread*
	Sewart went fra thaim with nine scor into deid	
305	Next hand the wod and his gud men of Fyff,	*Nearby*
	That with him baid in all term of thar lyff.	*remained for the entire term*
	Wallace drew ner, his tym quhen that he saw,	
	To the wod syd and couth on Wallang caw:	*call*
	"Yon knycht to morn has hecht to hyng thee hie.	*promised; hang*
310	Cum intill us. I sall thi warrand be	*protection*
	In contrar him and all King Eduuardis mycht.	
	Tak we hym quyk I sall him hyng on hycht,	*alive; high*
	And gud lordschip I sall gyff thee hereft	*hereafter*

Book 10

	In this ilk land, that thi brothir has left."	*same*
315	Wallange was wys, full sone couth understand	
	Be lyklynes Wallace suld wyn the land,	*likelihood*
	And better him war into the rycht to bid	
	Than be in wer apon the Sotheroun sid.	*war*
	Wytht schort vysment to Wallace in thai socht.	*With; consideration*
320	Than Sewart criyt and said, "That beis for nocht,	
	And fals of kynd thow art in heretage.	*nature*
	Eduuard on thee has waryt evill gret wage.	*wasted his expense*
	Her I sall bid my purpos to fullfill,	*Here; stay*
	Othir to de or haiff thee at my will."	
325	For all his spech to pas he wald nocht spar;	*refrain*
	Wyth full glaid hart Wallace resavyt thaim thar.	*received*
	Be that Ruwan and Ramsay of renown,	*By then*
	Be a trew Scot that past to Sanct Jhonstoun,	*By*
	Thaim warnyng maid that Sewart folowit fast	
330	Apon Wallace, than war thai sayr agast.	*greatly aghast*
	Owt of the toun thai uschit with all thar mycht,	*sallied forth*
	With thre hundreth that worthi war and wicht,	*bold*
	Till Blak Irnsid assemblyt in that place	
	As Wallang was gayn into gud Wallace.	
335	The knycht Sewart has weill thar cummyng seyn;	
	A fayr playn feild he chesyt thaim betweyn.	

[*Joined by Ruthven and Ramsay, Wallace prepares to battle Siward's much larger army. Siward kills Bisset and in turn is killed by Wallace. The Scottish leaders disperse to different parts of Fife, ejecting the English and destroying strongholds. With his army camped near Scotlandwell, Wallace swims across Loch Leven and steals a boat in which he and a small band of men cross to an island for a night attack on the English. Having stormed the stronghold, Wallace summons his army to a celebratory feast. Wallace then goes to the west where he rescues his uncle from one Thomlyn of Ware's prisons. He then attacks and wins Dumbarton. (Lines 337–830)*]

	At Cristinmes thar Wallace sojornyt still.	
	Of his modyr tithandis was brocht him till	*news; to*
	That tym befor scho had left Elrisle;	*[some] time before; Elderslie*
	For Inglismen in it scho durst nocht be.	*dared*
835	Fra thine dysgysyt scho past in pilgrame weid,	*From there disguised*
	Sum gyrth to sek to Dunfermlyn scho yeid.	*refuge; Dunfermline; went*

The Wallace

	Seknes hyr had so socht into that sted	*affected her; place*
	Decest scho was, God tuk hir spreit to leid.	*Deceased; spirit; lead*
	Quhen Wallace hard at that tithandis was trew,	*heard; news*
840	How sadnes so in ilka sid can persew,	*each side*
	In thank he tuk becaus it was naturaill.	*thanks; took [it]*
	He lowyt God with sekyr hart and haill.	*praised; sure; whole*
	Better him thocht that it was hapnyt sa;	
	Na Sotheroun suld hyr put till othir wa.	*No Englishman; cause; suffering*
845	He ordand Jop and als the maister Blayr	*commanded; also*
	Thiddyr to pas and for no costis spayr,	*Thither; spare no expense*
	Bot honour do the corp till sepultur.	*corpse; burial*
	At his commaund thai servit ilka hour,	
	Doand tharto as dede askis till hav.	*as befits the dead*
850	With worschip was the corp graithit in grave.	*placed in the grave*
	Agayn thai turnyt and schawit him of hir end.	*They returned; made known to*
	He thankit God quhat grace that evir he send;	
	He seis the warld so full of fantasie.	*sees; illusion*
	Confort he tuk and leit all murnyng be.	*let; mourning*
855	His most desyr was for to freith Scotland.	*free*
	Now will I tell quhat new cas com on hand.	*event*
	Schyr Wilyam Lang, of Douglace Daill was lord,	
	Of his fyrst wyff, as rycht was to record,	
	Decest or than out of this warldly cair,	*Deceased before then; care*
860	Twa sonnys he had with hyr that leyffyt thair	*her; left there*
	Quhilk likly war and abill in curage,	*well-made*
	To sculle was send into thar tendre age.	*school*
	James and Hew, so hecht thir brethyr twa;	*these two brothers were called*
	And eftir sone thar uncle couth thaim ta,	*soon after*
865	Gud Robert Keth had thaim fra Glaskow toun,	
	Atour the se in Frans he maid thaim boun.	*Across the sea; go*
	At study syn he left thaim into Parys	*then*
	With a maister that worthy was and wys.	
	The king Eduuard tuk thar fadir that knycht	
870	And held him thar thocht he was nevir so wicht,	*strong*
	Till him, he said, assentit till his will.	*Until he; assented to*
	A mariage als thai gert ordand him till	*commanded*
	The lady Fers, of power and hye blud,	
	Bot tharoff com till his lyff litill gud.	
875	Twa sonnys he gat on this lady but mar.	*forthwith*

174

Book 10

	With Eduuardis will he tuk his leiff to far,	approval; go
	In Scotland com and brocht hys wyff on pes,	in peace
	In Douglas duelt, forsuth this is no les.	these are no lies
	Kyng Eduuard trowyt that he had stedfast beyn,	believed
880	Fast to thar faith, bot the contrar was seyn.	Firmly; opposite
	Ay Scottis blud remaynyt into Douglace;	Ever; blood
	Agayn Ingland he prevyt in mony place.	proved himself
	The Sawchar was a castell fayr and strang;	Sanquhar Castle
	Ane Inglis capdane that dyd feyll Scottis wrang	wronged many Scots
885	Intill it duelt, and Bewffurd he was cauld,	called
	That held all waist fra thine to Douglace Hauld.	[as] wasteland from thence; Castle
	Rycht ner of kyn was Douglace wiff and he,	near of kin
	Tharfor he trowyt in pes of hym to be.	believed
	Schyr Wylyham saw at Wallace rais agayn	that; had risen
890	And rycht likly to freyth Scotland of payn.	[was] very likely to free; suffering
	Till help him part intill his mynd he kest,	some way; cast
	For in that lyff rycht lang he coud nocht lest.	life; last
	He thocht na charge to brek apon Ingland;	[there was] no blame; break [his bond]
	It was throuch force that evir he maid thaim band.	homage
895	A yong man than that hardy was and bauld,	bold
	Born till himselff and Thom Dycson was cauld,	Born on his land
	"Der freynd," he said, "I wald preyff at my mycht	attempt what I can
	And mak a fray to fals Bewfurd the knycht,	make a surprise attack on
	In Sawchar duellys and dois full gret owtrage."	violence
900	Than Dycson said, "Myselff in that viage	enterprise
	Sall for yow pas with Anderson to spek;	
	Cusyng to me, frendschip he will nocht brek.	My cousin
	For that ilk man thar wod ledys thaim till,	same; leads them to
	Throuch help of him purpos ye may fullfill."	
905	Schyr Wilyham than in all the haist he mycht	
	Thirty trew men in this viage he dycht,	expedition; readied
	And tauld his wyff till Drumfres he wald fayr.	told; go
	A tryst, he said, of Ingland he had thair.	meeting; with
	Thus passyt he quhar that na Sotheroun wyst	no Englishman knew
910	With thir thirty throw waistland at his lyst.	these; pleasure
	Quhill nycht was cummyn he buschit thaim full law	
	Intyll a clewch ner the wattyr of Craw.	ravine near the River Craw
	To the Sauchar Dykson allayn he send	
	And he son maid with Anderson this end,	arrangement

175

The Wallace

915	Dicson suld tak bathe his hors and his weid	*both; clothes*
	Be it was day a drawcht of wod to leid.	*By [the time]; load; lead*
	Agayn he past and tauld the gud Dowglace,	*told*
	Quhilk drew him sone intill a prevay place.	*secret*
	Anderson tauld quhat stuff that was tharin	*garrison*
920	Till Thom Dicson, that was ner of his kyn:	
	"Forty thai ar of men of mekill vaill;	*great power*
	Be thai on fute thai will yow sayr assayll.	*severely assail*
	Gyff thow hapnys the entré for to get	*If you happen*
	On thi rycht hand a stalwart ax is set,	
925	Tharwith thow may defend thee in a thrang.	
	Be Douglace wys he bydis nocht fra thee lang."	*If Douglas is wise; stays*
	Anderson yeid to the buschement in hy;	*went; haste*
	Ner the castell he drew thaim prevaly	*Near*
	Intill a schaw Sotheroun mystraistyt nocht.	*thicket; did not suspect*
930	To the next wode wyth Dycson syn he socht,	*then; went*
	Graithyt him a drawcht on a braid slyp and law,	*Prepared; load; broad and low sledge*
	Changyt a hors and to the hous can caw.	*called*
	Arayit he was in Andersonnis weid	*Dressed; Anderson's clothes*
	And bad haiff in. The portar com gud speid.	*quickly*
935	"This hour," he said, "thow mycht haiff beyn away.	
	Untymys thow art, for it is scantly day."	*Untimely; hardly*
	The yet yeid up, Dicson gat in but mar.	*gate went up; forthwith*
	A thourtour bande that all the drawcht upbar,	*cross-wise band; load*
	He cuttyt it; to ground the slyp can ga,	*sledge went*
940	Cumryt the yet, stekyng thai mycht nocht ma.	*Blocked; shutting; more*
	The portar son he hynt into that stryff,	*soon; pulled; fighting*
	Twys throuch the hede he stekit him with a knyff.	*stabbed*
	The ax he gat that Anderson of spak,	
	A bekyn maid; tharwith the buschement brak.	*signal; ambush broke*
945	Dowglace himselff was formest in that pres,	*foremost; press (melee)*
	In our the wod enteryt or thai wald ces.	*across; before; cease*
	Fifty-two wachmen sa, of wallis was cummyn new,	*guards saw*
	Within the clos the Scottis son thaim slew.	*courtyard; soon*
	Or ony scry was raissyt in that stour	*Before any cry*
950	Douglace had tane the yet of the gret tour,	*gate; tower*
	Rane up a grece quhar at the capdane lay,	*Ran; flight of stairs*
	On fut he gat and wald haiff beyn away.	*[his] feet he got*
	Our lait it was; Dowglace strak up the dur,	*Too late; struck down*

176

Book 10

	Bewfurd he fand into the chawmir flour;	*found on; chamber floor*
955	With a styff suerd to dede he has him dycht.	*sword; death; delivered*
	His men folowit that worthy was and wycht.	*strong*
	The men thai slew that was into thai wanys,	*those dwellings*
	Syn in the clos thai semblit all at anys.	*Then; courtyard; assembled; once*
	The hous thai tuk and Sotheroun put to ded,	*castle; captured; death*
960	Gat nane bot ane with lyff out of that sted,	*Got none but one; place*
	For that the get so lang unstekit was.	*Because; gate; unshut*
	This spy he fled, till Dursder can pas,	*Durisdeer [Castle] went*
	Tauld that captane that thai had hapnyt sa.	*Told; what had happened to them*
	Ane othir he gert into the Enoch ga;	*Enoch [Castle] go*
965	In Tybris Mur was warnyt of this cas,	*Tibbers Moor; warned*
	And Louchmaban all semblyt to that place.	*Lochmaben; gathered*
	The cuntré rais quhen thai herd of sic thing	*such [a] thing*
	To sege Dowglace, and hecht thai suld him hyng.	*besiege; vowed; hang*
	Quhen Douglace wyst na wayis fra thaim chaip,	*knew; to escape*
970	To sailye him he trowyt thai wald thaim schaip.	*attack; proceed*
	Dicson he send apon a cursour wycht	*strong courser*
	To warn Wallace in all the haist he mycht.	
	Of Lewyhous Wallace had tayn in playn	*Lennox; taken to the open*
	Witht thre hundreth gud men of mekill mayn.	*With; great strength*
975	Kynsith, a castell, he thocht to vesy it;	*inspect*
	Ane Ravynsdaill held, bot trew men leit him wyt	*One Ravensworth held [it]; let*
	That he was out that tym of Cummyrnauld.	*Cumbernauld*
	Lord Cumyn duelt on tribut in that hauld.	*stronghold*
	Quhen Wallace wyst, he gert Erll Malcom ly	*knew; lie*
980	With two hundreth in a buschement ner by,	*an ambush nearby*
	To kep the hous that nane till it suld fayr.	*guard; none; go*
	He tuk the layff and in the wod ner thar	*rest; near there*
	A scurrour he set, to warn quhen he saw ocht	*spy; anything*
	Son Ravynsdaill com; of thaim he had na thocht.	*Soon*
985	Quhen he was cummyn the twa buschementis betweyn,	
	The scurrour warnd the cruell men and keyn.	*spy alerted; fierce*
	Than Wallace brak and folowit on thaim fast;	*Wallace['s ambush] broke*
	The Sotheroun fled for thai war sar agast.	*English; greatly afraid*
	Ravynsdaill had than bot fifty men;	
990	Amang the Scottis thar deidis was litill to ken.	*mentioned*
	Quhen Erll Malcom had bard thaim fra the place,	*barred*
	Na Sotheroun yeid with lyff that thai did grace.	*No Englishmen went (escaped)*

The Wallace

	Part Lennox men thai left the hors to ta;	*Some; take*
	On spulyeyng than thai wald na tary ma.	*plundering; make*
995	To sege the hous than Wallace coud nocht bid;	*besiege; castle, stay*
	Throuout the land in awfull feyr thai ryd.	*frightening array; rode*
	Than Lithquow toun thai brynt into thar gayt;	*Linlithgow; burned; way*
	Quhar Sotheroun duelt thai maid thar byggyngis hayt.	*set fire to their buildings*
	The peyll thai tuk and slew that was tharin;	*peel (stockade); captured*
1000	Of Sotheroun blud thai Scottis thocht na syn.	*[Spilling] of; sin*
	Syn on the morn brynt Dawketh in a gleid,	*Then; burned Dalketh to an ember*
	Than till a strenth in Newbottyll Wod thai yeid.	*stronghold; Newbattle; went*
	Be that Lawder and Crystall of Cetoun	*By then*
	Com fra the Bas and brynt North Berwik toun,	*Bass; burned*
1005	For Inglismen suld thar na succour get;	*help*
	Quham thai ourtuk thai slew withoutyn let.	*Whoever; overtook; immediately*
	To meit Wallace thai past with all thar mycht,	*meet*
	A hundreth with thaim of men in armes brycht.	
	A blyth metyng that tym was thaim betweyn.	*happy meeting*
1010	Quhen Erll Malcom and Wallace has thaim seyn,	
	Thom Dycson than was met with gud Wallace,	
	Quhilk grantyt sone for to reskew Douglace.	*agreed soon; rescue*
	"Dicson," he said, "wait thow thar multiple?"	*know; number*
	"Three thowsand men thar power mycht nocht be."	
1015	Erll Malcom said, "Thocht thai war thousandys five	*Although*
	For this accioun me think that we suld stryff."	*strive*
	Than Hew the Hay, that duelt undyr trewage,	*tribute*
	Of Inglismen son he gaiff our the wage;	*soon; gave up; payment*
	Mar for to pay as than he likyt nocht.	*More; liked not*
1020	With fyfté men with Wallace furth he socht,	*forth he went*
	To Peblis past, bot no Sotheroun thar baid.	*Peebles; remained*
	Thar at the croice a playn crya thai maid.	*[market] cross; proclamation*
	Wallace commaund quha wald cum to his pes	*peace*
	And byd tharat reward suld haiff but les.	*without a lie*
1025	Gud Ruthirfurd that evir trew has beyn,	
	In Atryk Wode agayn the Sotheroun keyn	*Ettrick Forest; cruel*
	Bydyn he had and done thaim mekill der;	*Waited; great harm*
	Saxté he led of nobill men in wer.	*Sixty; war*
	Wallace welcummyt quha com in his supplé	*to support him*
1030	With lordly feyr, and chyftaynlik was he.	*manners*
	Thaim till aray thai yeid without the toun;	*went outside*

Book 10

	Thar nowmir was six hundreth of renoun,	
	In byrneis brycht, all men of mekill vaill.	*corslets; great worth*
	With glaid hartis thai past in Clyddisdaill.	
1035	The sege be than was to the Sauchar set.	*siege by then*
	Sic tithingis com quhilk maid tharin a let:	*Such tidings; delay*
	Quhen Sotheroun hard that Wallace was so ner,	*close*
	Throw haisty fray the ost was all on ster.	*confusion; astir*
	Na man was thar wald for ane othir byd;	*No; there; stay*
1040	Purpos thai tuk in Ingland for to ryd.	
	The chyftane said, sen thar king had befor	*since*
	Fra Wallace fled, the causis was the mor.	*reasons were all the more*
	Fast south thai went; to bid it was gret waith.	*stay; peril*
	Douglace as than was thus quyt of thar scaith.	*repaid for the damage they did*

[*Wallace and three hundred Scots follow and attack the English army as it moves south. The English withdraw from all the Scottish castles except Dundee, which Wallace proceeds to besiege. Edward prepares to return from France to mount a third invasion of Scotland; meanwhile the French king requests Wallace's assistance in Guyenne. (Lines 1045–1214)*]

1215	The wyt of Frans thocht Wallace to commend.	*best minds*
	Into Scotland with this harrold thai send	
	Part of his deid, and als the discriptioune	*An account of his deeds; also*
	Of him tane thar be men of discrecioun,	*taken there by*
	Clerkis, knychtis, and harroldys that him saw,	
1220	Bot I herof can nocht rehers thaim aw.	*repeat; all*
	Wallace statur, of gretnes and of hycht,	*figure; size; height*
	Was jugyt thus be dyscrecioun of rycht,	*by right judgement [of those]*
	That saw him bath dischevill and in weid.	*both unarmed and in armor*
	Nine quartaris large he was in lenth indeid;	*quarters [of an ell] (i.e., about 8'5" tall)*
1225	Thryd part that lenth in schuldrys braid was he,	*[A] third part [of]; broad*
	Rycht sembly strang and lusty for to se;	*seemly; pleasing*
	Hys lymmys gret, with stalwart pais and sound,	*limbs large; step*
	Hys browys hard, his armes gret and round;	
	His handis maid rycht lik till a pawmer,	*palm tree leaf*
1230	Of manlik mak, with nales gret and cler;	*make*
	Proporcionyt lang and fair was his vesage,	*face*
	Rycht sad of spech and abill in curage;	*serious*
	Braid breyst and heych with sturdy crag and gret,	*Broad chest; high; neck*
	His lyppys round, his noys was squar and tret;	*well-shaped*

The Wallace

1235	Bowand bron haryt on browis and breis lycht,[1]	
	Cler aspre eyn lik dyamondis brycht.	*sharp eyes*
	Undir the chyn on the left sid was seyn	
	Be hurt a vain; his colour was sangweyn.	*Through injury a scar; sanguine*
	Woundis he had in mony divers place,	*many different places*
1240	Bot fair and weill kepyt was his face.	
	Of ryches he kepyt no propyr thing,	*things of his own*
	Gaiff as he wan, lik Alexander the king.	*[He] gave; won*
	In tym of pes mek as a maid was he;	*peace; meek*
	Quhar wer approchyt the rycht Ector was he.	*war; Hector*
1245	To Scottis men a gret credens he gaiff,	*credence; gave*
	Bot knawin enemys thai couth him nocht dissayff.	*known; deceive*
	Thir properteys was knawin into Frans	*These attributes*
	Of him to be ane gud remembrans.	
	Maister Jhon Blayr that patron couth rasaiff,	*description; receive*
1250	In Wallace buk brevyt it with the layff.	*wrote; rest*
	Bot he herof as than tuk litill heid,	*hereof; then took little heed*
	His lauborous mynd was all on othir deid.	*busy; deeds*
	At Dundé sege thus ernystfully thai lay.	
	Tithandis to him Jop brocht on a day,	
1255	How Eduuard king with likly men to waill,	*in [his] command*
	A hundyr thowsand com for to assaill.	
	Than Scotland ground thai had tane apon cace.	*Scottish territory; taken*
	Into sum part it grevyt gud Wallace.	*grieved*
	He maid Scrymiour still at the hous to ly	*to remain*
1260	With two thousand, and chargyt him forthi	
	That nayn suld chaip with lyff out of that sted	*none; escape alive; place*
	At Sotheroun war, bot do thaim all to ded.	*That English were; put them; death*
	Scrymgeour grantyt rycht faithfully to bid.	*stay*
	With eight thousand Wallace couth fra him ryd	
1265	To Sanct Jhonstoun; four dayis he graithit him thar,	*prepared*
	With sad avys towart the south can fayr;	*serious deliberation; went*
	For King Eduuard that tym ordand had	
	Ten thousand haill to pas at was full glaid,	*together*
	With yong Wodstok, a lord of mekill mycht.	*great might*
1270	At Sterlyng Bryg he ordand thaim full rycht	*Stirling Bridge*

---

[1] *Curling brown hair on [his] forehead and light eyebrows*

Book 11

	And thar to bid the entré for to wer;	*wait; signal for war*
	Of Wallace than he trowit to haiff no der.	*expected; injury*
	Thar leyff thai laucht and past but delay,	*took their leave; without*
	Rycht saraly and in a gud aray,	*closely*
1275	To Sterlyng com and wald nocht thar abid;	*wait*
	To se the north furth than can he ryd,	*see*
	Sic new curage so fell in his entent,	*Such; mind*
	Quhilk maid Sotheroun full sar for to rapent.	*repent full dearly*

& Incipit decimus

Book 11

[*While English ships arrive in the Tay, Woodstock rides to Dundee and is killed in a battle with the Scots. Then Wallace meets various Scottish forces at Stirling Bridge before moving to Falkirk.* (Lines 1–72)]

	The Scottis chyftane than owt of Stirlyng past;	
	To the Fawkyrk he sped his ost full fast.	*hurried; army*
75	Wallace and his than till aray he yeid	*[battle] array; went*
	With ten thousand of douchty men in deid.	*valiant; action*
	Quha couth behald thar awfull lordly vult,	*awesome; bearing (face)*
	So weill beseyn, so forthwart, stern, and stult,	*well turned-out; active; valiant*
	So gud chyftanys as with sa few thar beyn,	
80	Without a king was nevir in Scotland seyn.	
	Wallace himselff and Erll Malcom that lord,	
	Schir Jhon the Graym and Ramsay at accord,	
	Cetoun, Lawder, and Lundy that was wicht,	*strong*
	Adam Wallace to that jornay him dycht,	*undertaking; rallied*
85	And mony gud quhilk prevyt weill in pres.	*good [men]; proved; battle*
	Thar namys all I may nocht her rehres.	*names; recite*
	Sotheroun or than out of Torfychan fur,	*[The] English before; Torphichen went*
	Thar passage maid into Slamanan Mur;	*Slamannan Moor*
	Intill a playn set tentis and palyon,	*On a plain set [up]; pavilions*
90	South hald Fawkyrk, a litill abon the ton.	*towards; above the town*
	Gud Jop himselff jugit thaim be his sycht	*judged them [to be] by*
	In haill nowmir a hundyr thousand rycht.	*In total*
	Of Wallace com the Scottis sic comfort tuk,	*Of Wallace's coming; such*

The Wallace

	Quhen thai him saw all raddour thai forsuk,	*fear*
95	For of invy was few thar at it wyst.	*envy; knew*
	Tresonable folk thar mater wyrkis throu lyst,	*Treacherous; cunning*
	Poyson sen syn "at the Fawkyrk" is cald,	*since then; called*
	Throu treson and corrupcion of ald.	*old*
	Lord Cumyn had invy at gud Wallace,	
100	For Erll Patrik that hapnyt upon cace;	*On account of; happened once*
	Cunttas of Merch was Cumyns sister der.	*Countess; dear*
	Undyr colour he wrocht in this maner,	*pretense*
	Into the ost had ordand Wallace dede	*Wallace's death*
	And maid Stewart with him to fall in pled.	*argument*
105	He said that lord at Wallace had no rycht	
	Power to leid and he present in sycht.	
	He bad him tak the vantgard for to gy;	*vanguard; guide*
	So wyst he weyll at thai suld stryff forthi.	*knew; that; argue therefore*
	Lord Stewart ast at Wallace his consaill,	*asked*
110	Said, "Schir, ye knaw quhat may us maist availl.	*most help*
	Yon felloun king is awfull for to bid."	*That cruel; formidable; withstand*
	Rycht unabasyt Wallace ansuerd that tyd:	*undismayed; time*
	"And I haiff seyn may twys into Scotland	*more than twice*
	Wytht yon ilk king, quhen Scottis men tuk on hand	*With that same king; undertook*
115	Wytht fewar men than now ar hydder socht	
	This realm agayn to full gud purpos brocht.	
	Schyr, we will fecht, for we haiff men inew	*fight; enough*
	As for a day, sa that we be all trew."	*so long as; steadfast*
	The Stewart said he wald the vantgard haiff.	
120	Wallace ansuerd and said, "Sa God me saiff,	
	That sall ye nocht als lang as I may ryng,	*govern*
	Nor no man ellis quhill I se my rycht king.	*until; rightful*
	Gyff he will cum and tak on him the croun	*If*
	At his commaund I sall be reddy boun.	*ready [and] prepared*
125	Throw Goddis grace I reskewed Scotland twys.	
	I war to mad to leyff it on sic wys,	*too; leave; such [a] way*
	To tyn for bost that I haiff governd lang."	*lose for [a] threat; governed*
	Thus halff in wraith frawart him can he gang.	*anger away from*
	Stewart tharwith all bolnyt into baill.	*swelled with anger*
130	"Wallace," he said, "be thee I tell a taill."	*by*
	"Say furth," quod he, "of the fairest ye can."	
	Unhappyly his taill thus he began.	

182

Book 11

	"Wallace," he said, "thow takis thee mekill cur.	take [on]; great responsibility
	So feryt it, be wyrkyng of natur,	It happened, in the course of nature
135	How a howlat complend of his fethrame,	an owl complained; feathers
	Quhill Deym Natur tuk of ilk byrd but blame	Until; without reproach
	A fayr fethyr and to the howlat gaiff.	gave
	Than he throuch pryd reboytyt all the layff.	repulsed; others
	Quharoff suld thow thi senye schaw so he?	ensign display so high
140	Thow thinkis nan her at suld thi falow be;	none; that; fellow
	This makis it thow art cled with our men.	clad
	Had we our awn thin war bot few to ken."	own your; indeed
	At thir wordis gud Wallace brynt as fyr.	these; flared; fire
	Our haistely he ansuerd him in ire.	Too
145	"Thow leid," he said. "The suth full oft has ben,	lied; truth; been
	Thair I have biddin quhar thow durst nocht be seyn,	There I stood firm where
	Contrar enemys, na mar for Scotlandis rycht	more
	Than dar the howlat quhen that the day is brycht.	dares; owl
	That taill full meit thow has tauld be thisell;	fittingly; illustrated; yourself
150	To thi desyr thow sall me nocht compell.	
	Cumyn it is has gyffyn this consaill;	given; counsel
	Will God, ye sall of your fyrst purpos faill.	God willing
	That fals traytour that I of danger brocht	from
	Is wondyrlik till bryng this realm till nocht.	very likely to
155	For thi ogart othir thow sall de,	pride either
	Or in presoun byd, or cowart lik to fle.	stay; like a coward
	Reskew of me thow sall get nane this day."	
	Tharwith he turnd and fra thaim raid his way.	rode
	Ten thousand haill fra thaim with Wallace raid.	
160	Nan was bettir in all this warld so braid	None; wide
	As of sic men at leiffand was in lyff.	such; that living were
	Allace, gret harm fell Scotland throuch that stryff!	
	Past till a wod fra the Fawkyrk be est,	to a wood; to the east
	He wald nocht byd for commaund na request,	stay; command
165	For charge of nan bot it had ben his king,	On the orders; no one unless
	At mycht that tym bryng him fra his etlyng.	That; intention
	The tothir Scottis that saw this discensioun	other
	For dysconford to leiff the feild was boun,	Through discouragement; leave; ready
	Bot at thai men was natyff till Stuart,	Except that these
170	Principaill of But, tuk hardement in hart.	Lord Superior; courage
	Lord Stuart was at Cumyn grevyt thar,	vexed

The Wallace

	Hecht and he leiffd, he suld repent full sar	*Vowed if he lived; exceedingly*
	The gret trespace that he throw raklesnace	*wrong; recklessness*
	Had gert him mak to Wallace in that place.	*made him*
175	For thair debait it was a gret peté;	*dispute*
	For Inglismen than mycht na treté be,	*reconciliation*
	Haistyt sa fast a battaill to the feild,	
	Thirty thowsand that weill coud wapynnys weild.	*weapons wield*
	Erll of Harfurd was chosyn thar chyftane.	
180	The gud Stewart than till aray is gane;	*[battle] order; gone*
	The feild he tuk as trew and worthy knycht.	
	The Inglismen come on wytht full gret mycht.	
	Thar fell metyng was awfull for to se;	*terrible; awesome*
	At that countour thai gert feill Sotheroun de.	*encounter; many; die*
185	Quhen speris was spilt hynt owt with suerdis son;	*destroyed drew; swords soon*
	On athir sid full douchty deid was don.	*either; valiant*
	Feill on the ground was fellyt in that place.	*Many; felled*
	Stewart and his can on his enemys race;	*did; press*
	Blud byrstyt out throuch maile and byrneis brycht.	*mail-armor; corslet*
190	Twenty thowsand with dredfull wapynnys dycht	*equipped*
	Of Sotheroun men derffly to dede thai dyng;	*English; violently; dashed*
	The ramanand agayn fled to thar king.	*remainder*
	Ten thousand thar that fra the dede eschewyt	*death escaped*
	With thar chyftane into the ost relevyt.	*rallied*
195	Agayn to ray the hardy Stuart yeid.	*[battle] order; went*
	Quhen Wallace saw this nobill, worthi deid,	
	Held up his handys with humyll prayer prest.	*humble; joined*
	To God he said, "Gyff yon lord grace to lest	*Give that*
	And power haiff his worschip till attend,	*honor*
200	To wyn thar folk and tak the haill commend.	*defeat; whole praise*
	Gret harm it war at he suld be ourset	*that; overthrown*
	With new power thai will on him rebet."	*forces; renew the attack*
	Be that the Bruce ane awfull battaill baid,	*By that time; battalion commanded*
	And Byschop Beik, quhilk oft had beyn assayd,	*who often; attacked*
205	Forty thowsand apon the Scottis to fair.	*advance*
	With fell affer thai raissit up rycht thair	*fierce array; rose*
	The Bruce baner, in gold of gowlis cler.	*gules (heraldic red)*
	Quhen Wallace saw battallis approchyt ner,	*battalions*
	The rycht lyon agayn his awn kynryk,	*upright lion against; own kingdom*
210	"Allace," he said, "the warld is contrar lik!	*upside-down*

Book 11

	This land suld be yon tyrandis heretage,	*that oppressor's*
	That cummys thus to stroy his awn barnage.	*destroy; own lords*
	Sa I war fre of it that I said ayr,	*If I were; earlier*
	I wald forswer Scotland for evirmar.	*renounce*
215	Contrar the Bruce I suld reskew thaim now,	*In opposition to*
	Or de tharfor, to God I mak a vow."	*die*
	The gret debait in Wallace wit can waid	*Wallace's mind raged*
	Betwix kyndnes and wyllfull vow he maid.	*[the] willful vow*
	Kyndnes him bad reskew thaim fra thar fa,	*charged; from their foe*
220	Than Wyll said, "Nay, quhy, fuyll, wald thow do sa?	*Will; why, fool, would; so*
	Thow has na wyt wyth rycht thiselff to leid	*no mind (inclination)*
	Suld thow help thaim that wald put thee to deid?"	*death*
	Kyndnes said, "Yha, thai ar gud Scottis men."	
	Than Will said, "Nay, veryté thow may ken,	*[the] truth; know*
225	Had thai bene gud all anys we had ben;	*united; been*
	Be reson heyr the contrar now is seyn,	*here; opposite; seen*
	For thai me hayt mar na Sotheroun leid."	*more than English people*
	Kyndnes said, "Nay, that schaw thai nocht in deid.	*show; their deeds*
	Thocht ane of thaim be fals intill his saw,	*in his word*
230	For caus of him thow suld nocht los thaim aw.	*Because; lose; all*
	Thai haiff done weill into yon felloun stour;	*that cruel battle*
	Reskew thaim now and tak a hye honour."	*high*
	Wyll said, "Thai wald haiff reft fra me my lyff.	*deprived me of my life*
	I baid for thaim in mony stalwart stryff."	*stood; severe combats*
235	Kyndnes said, "Help, thar power is at nocht;	*very small*
	Syn wreik on him that all the malice wrocht."	*Then take revenge*
	Wyll said, "This day thai sall nocht helpyt be.	
	That I haiff said sall ay be said for me.	*always*
	Thai ar bot dede; God grant thaim of his blys!	*[all] but dead*
240	Invy lang syn has done gret harme bot this."	*Envy long since; apart from*
	Wallace tharwith turnyt for ire in teyn,	*from anger to grief*
	Braith teris for baill byrst out fra bathe his eyn.	*Profuse tears; sorrow burst*
	Schyr Jhon the Graym and mony worthi wicht	*many; people*
	Wepyt in wo for sorow of that sycht.	
245	Quhen Bruce his battaill apon the Scottis straik,	*Bruce's battalion; struck*
	Thar cruell com maid cowardis for to quaik:	*ferocious coming; quake*
	Lord Cumyn fled to Cummyrnauld away.	
	About the Scottis the Sotheroun lappyt thay.	*drew close*
	The men of But befor thar lord thai stud,	*stood*

The Wallace

250	Defendand him quhen fell stremys of blud	*many streams of blood*
	All thaim about in flothis quhar thai yeid.	*floods; went*
	Bathid in blud was Bruce suerd and his weid	*sword; armor*
	Throw fell slauchtir of trew men of his awn.	*cruel; own (i.e., his countrymen)*
	Son to the dede the Scottis was ourthrawn;	*Soon; overpowered*
255	Syn slew the lord, for hc wald nocht be tayn.	*(i.e., Stewart); taken [prisoner]*
	Quhen Wallace saw that thir gud men was gayn,	*these; gone*
	"Lordis," he said, "quhat now is your consaill?"	*advice*
	Twa choys thar is, the best I rede us waill:	*advise us to choose*
	Yonder the king his ost abandonand,	*army*
260	Heyr Bruce and Beyk in yon battaill to stand.	*there; that battalion*
	Yon king in wer has wys and felloun beyn;	*war; wise; cruel*
	Thar capdans als full cruell ar and keyn.	*their; fierce; bold*
	Bettir of hand is nocht leiffand, iwys,	*living, certainly*
	In tyrandry, ye trow me weill of this,	*domination; believe me*
265	Than Bruce and Beik, to quhat part thai be set.	*whatever they are set to do*
	We haiff a chois quhilk is full hard but let.	*without doubt*
	And we turn est for strenth in Lowtheane land	*If; a stronghold*
	Thai stuff a chas rycht scharp, I dar warrand.	*will mount a chase; keenly*
	Tak we the mur, yon king is us befor.	*If we take to the moor, that*
270	Thar is bot this, withoutyn wordis mor,	*only; more*
	To the Tor Wod, for our succour is thar.	*salvation*
	Throuch Brucis ost forsuth fyrst mon we far;	*must we go*
	Amang us now thar nedis no debayt.	*there is no need*
	Yon men ar dede. We will nocht stryff for stayt."	*Those; stand on ceremony*
275	Thai consent haill to wyrk rycht as he will;	*consented completely; work*
	Quhat him thocht best thai grantyt to fullfill.	
	Gud Wallace than, that stoutly couth thaim ster,	*boldly; lead*
	Befor thaim raid intill his armour cler,	*rode; bright*
	Rewellyt speris all in a nowmir round:	*Directed spears*
280	"And we have grace for to pas throw thaim sound	*whole (safely)*
	And few be lost, till our strenth we will ryd.	*stronghold*
	Want we mony, in faith we sall all byd."	*If we lose many [men]; stay*
	Thai hardnyt hors fast on the gret ost raid.	*Those emboldened horsemen; rode*
	The rerd at rays quhen sperys in sondyr glaid.	*noise that rose; went easily*
285	Duschyt in glos, devyt with speris dynt.	*Struck with dizziness, deafened; din of spears*
	Fra forgyt steyll the fyr flew out but stynt.	*From forged steel; sparks; endlessly*
	The felloun thrang quhen hors and men removyt	*grievous press of battle; moved away*
	Up drayff the dust quhar thai thar pithtis provyt.	*Drove up; strength proved*

Book 11

	The tothir ost mycht no deidis se	action
290	For stour at rais quhill thai disseverit be.	dust that rose; were separated
	The worthy Scottis eight thousand doun thai bar;	struck
	Few war at erd at gud Wallace brocht thar.	(i.e., Scots) were on the ground
	The king criyt hors apon thaim for to ryd,	commanded [his] horsemen
	Bot this wys lord gaiff him consaill to bid:	wait
295	The erll of York said, "Schir, ye wyrk amys	
	To brek aray. Yon men quyt throuch thaim is.	break [battle] array. Those; quite
	Thai ken the land and will to strenthis draw;	know; strongholds
	Tak we the playn we ar in perell aw."	[If] we take to the plain; all
	The king consavyt at his consaill was rycht,	realized that; advice
300	Rewllyt his ost and baid still in thar sycht.	Directed; remained
	Or Bruce and Beik mycht retorn thar battaill	Before; rally; battalion
	The Scottis was throuch and had a gret availl.	advantage
	Wallace commaund the ost suld pas thar way	ordered
	To the Tor Wod in all the haist thai may.	
305	Hymselff and Graym and Lawder turnyt in	returned
	Betwex battaillys prys prowys for to wyn;	Between battles worthy reputation; win
	And with thaim baid in that place hundrethis thre	stayed
	Of westland men, was oysyt in jeperté,	experienced; feats of arms
	Apon wycht hors that weselé coud ryd.	strong; skillfully
310	A slop thai maid quhar thai set on a syd;	breach; attached
	Na speris thai had bot suerdys of gud steyll;	No spears; swords; steel
	Tharwith in stour thai leit thar enemys feill	With those in the fighting; let; feel
	How thai full oft had prevyt beyn in pres.	proved; battle
	Of Inglismen thai maid feill to deces.	many
315	Or Bruce tharoff mycht weill persavyng haiff	Before; perceiving have
	Thre hundreth thar was graithit to thar graiff.	sent to their graves
	The hardy Bruce ane ost abandownyt;	allowed to charge
	Twenty thowsand he rewllyt be force and wit	commanded by
	Upon the Scottis his men for to reskew.	
320	Servyt thai war with gud speris enew,	spears enough
	And Byschop Beik a stuff till him to be.	support
	Quhen gud Wallace thar ordinans coud se	strategy
	"Allace," he said, "yon man has mekill mycht	that; great power
	And our gud will till undo his awn rycht."	overly great; to undo; own
325	He bad his men towart his ost in rid;	ordered
	Thaim for to sayff he wald behynd thaim byd.	save; stay
	Mekill he trowys in God and his awn weid;	Much; trusts; armor

187

The Wallace

	Till sayff his men he did full douchty deid.	*protect; brave deeds*
	Upon himselff mekill travaill he tais;	*a great deal of labor; takes*
330	The gret battaill compleit apon him gais.	*entire battalion; approaches*
	In the forbreyst he retornyt full oft;	*van of the army*
	Quhamevir he hyt thar sawchnyng was unsoft.	*Whomever; peace-making; rough*
	That day in warld knawin was nocht his maik;	*his match was not known*
	A Sotheroun man he slew ay at a straik.	*at every stroke*
335	Bot his a strenth mycht nocht agayn thaim be;	*single; against*
	Towart his ost behuffyd for to fle.	*it was necessary*
	The Bruce him hurt at the returnyng thair,	*as he returned there*
	Undyr the hals a deip wound and a sayr.	*neck; grievous [one]*
	Blude byrstyt owt braithly at speris lenth;	*burst; profusely; spear's*
340	Fra the gret ost he fled towart his strenth.	*forces*
	Sic a flear befor was nevir seyn!	*fugitive*
	Nocht at Gadderis of Gawdyfer the keyn,	*bold*
	Quhen Alexander reskewed the foryouris,	*forayers*
	Mycht tyll him be comperd in tha houris,	*at that time*
345	The fell turnyng on folowaris that he maid,	*many*
	How bandounly befor the ost he raid;	*boldly; rode*
	Nor how gud Graym wyth cruell hardement,	*fierce courage*
	Na how Lawder, amang thar fayis went;	*Nor; foes*
	How thaim allayn into that stour thai stud	*they singly; fighting; withstood*
350	Quhill Wallace was in stanchyng of his blud.	
	Be than he had stemmyt full weill his wound,	*By the time; stanched*
	With thre hundreth into the feild can found	*go*
	To reskew Graym and Lawder that was wicht;	*bold*
	Bot Byschop Beik com with sic force and slycht	*such; cunning*
355	The worthy Scottis weryt fer on bak,	*wearied far back*
	Sevyn akyrbreid in turnyng of thar bak.	*breadths of an acre*
	Yeit Wallace has thir twa delyveryt weill	*these two rescued*
	Be his awn strenth and his gud suerd of steill.	*By; own; sword*
	The awfull Bruce amang thaim with gret mayn	*formidable force*
360	At the reskew three Scottis men he has slayn;	
	Quham he hyt rycht ay at a straik was ded.	*Whomever; hit; always; stroke*
	Wallace preyst in tharfor to set rameid;	*remedy the situation*
	With a gud sper the Bruce was servyt but baid.	*without delay*
	With gret invy to Wallace fast he raid	*malice*
365	And he till him assonyeit nocht forthi.	*did not refuse the challenge therefore*
	The Bruce him myssyt as Wallace passyt by.	

188

Book 11

	Awkwart he straik with his scharp groundyn glave;	Cross-wise; struck; sword
	Sper and horscrag intill sondyr he drave.	horse's neck he dashed to pieces
	Bruce was at erd or Wallace turned about.	on the ground before
370	The gret battaill of thousandis, stern and stout,	battalion; strong; bold
	Thai horssyt Bruce with men of gret valour.	put Bruce back on a horse
	Wallace allayn was in that stalwart stour.	alone; vigorous fighting
	Graym pressyt in and straik ane Inglis knycht	struck
	Befor the Bruce apon the basnet brycht.	In front of; helmet
375	That servall stuff and all his othir weid,	inferior equipment; armor
	Bathe bayn and brayn, the nobill suerd throuch yeid.	brawn; sword; went
	The knycht was dede; gud Graym retornet tyte.	quickly
	A suttell knycht tharat had gret despyt,	cunning; spite
	Folowyt at wait and has persavyt weill	Followed watching his opportunity
380	Gramys byrny was to narow sumdeill	Graham's corslet; too
	Beneth the waist, that clos it mycht nocht be.	closed
	On the fyllat full sternly straik that sle,	loin; forcefully; rogue
	Persyt the bak, in the bowalys him bar	hit
	Wyth a scharp sper, that he mycht leiff no mar.	live no more
385	Graym turnd tharwith and smate that knycht in teyn	struck; anger
	Towart the vesar, a litill beneth the eyn.	visor
	Dede of that dynt to ground he duschyt doun.	blow; fell
	Schyr Jhon the Graym that swonyt on his arsoun	swooned; saddle-bow
	Or he ourcom till pas till his party,	Before; overcame to pass towards
390	Feill Sotheroun men that was on fute him by	Many English; foot
	Stekit his hors, that he no forthir yeid;	Stabbed; went
	Graym yauld to God his gud speryt and his deid.	yielded; spirit; deeds
	Quhen Wallace saw this knycht to dede was wrocht,	death
	The pytouous payn so sor thyrllyt his thocht	piteous; pierced
395	All out of kynd it alteryt his curage.	nature; spirit
	His wyt in wer was than bot a wod rage.	skill; war; mad
	Hys hors him bur in feild quharso him lyst,	carried; wished
	For of himselff as than litill he wyst.	knew little
	Lik a wyld best that war fra reson rent,	beast; was; reason torn
400	As wytlace wy into the ost he went	Behaving like a madman; host
	Dingand on hard; quhat Sotheroun he rycht hyt	Striking hard; English; directly
	Straucht apon hors agayn mycht nevir syt.	Upright
	Into that rage full feill folk he dang doun;	many; struck
	All hym about was reddyt a gret rowm.	cleared; space
405	Quhen Bruce persavyt with Wallace it stud sa,	perceived; stood so

189

The Wallace

	He chargyt men lang sperys for to ta	*long spears; take*
	And sla hys hors, sa he suld nocht eschaip.	*escape*
	Feyll Sotheroun than to Wallace fast can schaip,	*Many English; made their way*
	Persyt hys hors wyth sperys on athir syd;	*pierced; spears; either*
410	Woundys thai maid that was bathe deip and wyd.	
	Of schafftis part Wallace in sondyr schayr,	*shafts [of spears]; cut*
	Bot fell hedys intill his hors left thair.	*many spear heads in their*
	Sum wytt agayn to Wallace can radoun,	*sense; returned*
	In hys awn mynd so rewllyt him resoun;	*own*
415	Sa for to de him thocht it no vaslage.	*So to die in such a way; honor*
	Than for to fle he tuk no taryage,	*made no delay*
	Spuryt the hors, quhilk ran in a gud randoun	*Spurred; swift course*
	Till his awn folk was bydand on Carroun.	*[who] were waiting; at [the River] Carron*
	The sey was in, at thai stoppyt and stud.	*sea; that*
420	On loud he criyt and bad thaim tak the flud,	*Aloud; enter the river*
	"Togyddyr byd, ye may nocht los a man."	*Stay together*
	At his commaund the watter thai tuk than;	*took to the water*
	Hym returned the entré for to kepe,	*entrance; guard*
	Quhill all his ost was passyt our the depe;	*across the deep water*
425	Syn passyt our and dred his hors suld faill,	*Then crossed over; feared*
	Hymselff hevy, cled into plait of maill.	*heavy, clad; plate*
	Set he couth swom he trowit he mycht nocht weill.	*Although; swim; believed*
	The cler watter culyt the hors sumdeill.	*cooled*
	Atour the flud he bur him to the land,	*Over; he (the horse) carried him (Wallace)*
430	Syn fell doun dede and mycht no langar stand.	*Then*
	Kerle full son a cursour till him brocht;	*soon; courser to*
	Than up he lap, amange the ost he socht.	*leapt*
	Graym was away and fifteen othir wicht.	*people*
	On Magdaleyn Day thir folk to ded was dycht:	*(i.e., July 22) these; death; done*
435	Thirty thousand of Inglismen for trew	*truly*
	The worthy Scottis apon that day thai slew,	
	Quhat be Stuart, and syn be wicht Wallace.	*by; then by bold*
	For all his prys King Eduuard rewyt that race.	*reputation; regretted; encounter*
	To the Tor Wod he bad the ost suld ryd;	*commanded*
440	Kerle and he past upon Caroun syd,	
	Behaldand our apon the south party.	*Looking across*
	Bruce formast com and can on Wallace cry:	
	"Quhat art thow thar?" "A man," Wallace can say.	*said*
	The Bruce ansuerd, "That has thow prevyt today.	*proved*

Book 11

445	Abyd," he said, "thow nedis nocht now to fle."	*Wait*
	Wallace ansuerd, "I eschew nocht for thee,	*flee*
	Bot that power has thi awn ner fordon.	*own [countrymen]; destroyed*
	Amendis of this, will God, we sall haiff son."	*soon*
	"Langage of thee," the Bruce said, "I desyr."	*Speech*
450	"Say furth," quod he; "thow may for litill hyr.	*cost*
	Ryd fra that ost and gar thaim bid with Beik.	*make them wait*
	I wald fayn heir quhat thow likis to speik."	*gladly hear; say*
	The ost baid styll, the Bruce passyt thaim fra;	*stayed*
	He tuk wyth him bot a Scot that hecht Ra.	*was called*
455	Quhen that the Bruce out of thar heryng wer,	*their hearing was*
	He turned in and this question can sper:	*asked*
	"Quhy wyrkis thow thus and mycht in gud pes be?"	*do you work thus*
	Than Wallace said, "Bot in defawt of thee,	*Only in your absence*
	Throuch thi falsheid thin awn wyt has myskend.	*your own; deceived*
460	I cleym no rycht bot wald this land defend,	*claim*
	At thow undoys throu thi fals cruell deid.	*That; undoes; fierce*
	Thow has tynt twa had beyn worth fer mair meid	*lost two; reward*
	On this ilk day with a gud king to found,	*same; go*
	Na five mylyon of fynest gold so round	*Than*
465	That evir was wrocht in werk or ymage brycht!	*in deed*
	I trow in warld was nocht a bettir knycht	*believe*
	Than was the gud Graym of trewth and hardement."	*loyalty; courage*
	Teris tharwith fra Wallace eyn doun went.	*Tears thereupon; eyes*
	Bruce said, "Fer ma on this day we haiff losyt."	*Far more*
470	Wallace ansuerd, "Allace, thai war evill cosyt	*evilly exchanged*
	Throuch thi tresson, that suld be our rycht king,	*treason*
	That willfully dystroyis thin awn offspryng."	*own*
	The Bruce askyt, "Will thow do my devys?"	*follow my advice*
	Wallace said, "Nay, thow leyffis in sic wys	*you live; such [a] way*
475	Thow wald me mak at Eduuardis will to be;	*would*
	Yeit had I levir tomorn be hyngyt hye."	*Yet I would rather; hanged high*
	"Yeit sall I say as I wald consaill geyff,	*give*
	Than as a lord thow mycht at liking leiff	*in comfort live*
	At thin awn will in Scotland for to ryng	*own liking; live*
480	And be in pece and hald of Eduuard king."	*hold [land]*
	"Of that fals king I think nevir wagis to tak	*payment*
	Bot contrar him with my power to mak.	*against*
	I cleym nothing as be titill of rycht,	*claim; title*

The Wallace

	Thocht I mycht reiff, sen God has lent me mycht,	*take by force, since*
485	Fra thee thi crowne of this regioun to wer,	*From; wear*
	Bot I will nocht sic a charge on me ber.	*such a responsibility; bear*
	Gret God wait best quhat wer I tak on hand	*knows; war; undertake*
	For till kep fre that thow art gaynstandand.	*standing against*
	It mycht beyn said of lang gone herof forn,	*long ago formerly*
490	In cursyt tym thow was for Scotland born.	
	Schamys thow nocht that thow nevir yeit did gud,	*Are you not ashamed*
	Thow renygat devorar of thi blud?	*renegade devourer*
	I vow to God, ma I thi maister be	*may I overpower you*
	In ony feild, thow sall fer werthar de	*any; more deservedly die*
495	Than sall a Turk, for thi fals cruell wer.	*war*
	Pagans till us dois nocht so mekill der."	*much injury*
	Than lewch the Bruce at Wallace ernystfulnas	*laughed; earnestness*
	And said, "Thow seis at thus standis the cas.	*You see that*
	This day thow art with our power ourset,	*overwhelmed*
500	Agayn yon king warrand thow may nocht get."	*Against that; protection*
	Than Wallace said, "We ar be mekill thing	*by a great deal*
	Starkar this day in contrar of yon king	*Stronger; against that*
	Than at Beggar, quhar he left mony of his,	
	And als the feild; sa sall he do with this	*also*
505	Or de tharfor, for all his mekill mycht.	*die*
	We haiff nocht losyt in this feild bot a knycht,	
	And Scotland now in sic perell is stad	*such peril; placed*
	To leyff it thus myselff mycht be full mad."	*leave*
	"Wallace," he said, "it prochys ner the nycht.	*approaches near*
510	Wald thow to morn quhen at the day is lycht	*that*
	Or nyn of bell, meit me at this chapell	*Before nine o'clock*
	Be Dunypas? I wald haiff your consell."	*By*
	Wallace said, "Nay, or that ilk tyme be went,	*before; same; passed*
	War all the men hyn till the orient	*from here to*
515	Intill a will with Eduuard, quha had suorn,	*in submission to; sworn [to the contrary]*
	We sall bargane be nine houris to morn;	*fight by nine o'clock tomorrow*
	And for his wrang reyff othir he sall think scham,	*wrongful plunder either; shame*
	Or de tharfor, or fle in Ingland haym.	*home*
	Bot and thow will, son be the hour of thre	*if; soon by*
520	At that ilk tryst, will God, thow sall se me.	*same meeting*
	Quhill I may lest this realme sall nocht forfar."	*last; perish*
	Bruce promest him with twelve Scottis to be thar,	

Book 11

	And Wallace said, "Stud thow rychtwys to me,	*correctly*
	Cownter palys I suld nocht be to thee.	*[An] opponent*
525	I sall bryng ten, and for thi nowmer ma,	*more*
	I gyff no force thocht thow be freynd or fa."	*do not care*
	Thus thai departyt. The Bruce past his way,	*parted*
	Till Lythqwo raid quhar that King Eduuard lay,	*To Linlithgow rode*
	The feild had left and lugyt a south the toun,	*to [the] south [of] the town*
530	To souper set as Bruce at the palyoun	*pavilion*
	So entryt in and saw vacand his seit.	*vacant; seat*
	No watter he tuk bot maid him to the meit.	*made his way*
	Fastand he was and had beyn in gret dreid;	*Fasting; danger*
	Bludyt was all his wapynnys and his weid.	*Bloodied; armor*
535	Sotheroun lordys scornyt him in termys rud.	*rough*
	Ane said, "Behald, yon Scot ettis his awn blud."	*that; eats; own blood*
	The king thocht ill thai maid sic derisioun.	*thought [it] wrong; such*
	He bad haiff watter to Bruce of Huntyntoun.	*ordered water be brought to*
	Thai bad hym wesche. He said that wald he nocht.	*wash*
540	"This blud is myn, that hurtis most my thocht."	
	Sadly the Bruce than in his mynd remordyt.	*regretted*
	Thai wordis suth that Wallace had him recordyt.	*These; true; said*
	Than rewyt he sar, fra resoun had him knawin	*repented; deeply; he understood*
	At blud and land suld all lik beyn his awin.	*That; all alike*
545	With thaim he was lang or he couth get away,	*before*
	Bot contrar Scottis he faucht nocht fra that day.	*against; fought; from*

[*The Scots bury their dead, and Wallace delivers a eulogy over the body of Sir John Graham, before he is interred at Falkirk. At a meeting with Bruce, Wallace, upset by Graham's death in particular, accuses him of killing his own people. When Bruce expresses his remorse and vows never to fight against his countrymen again, they are reconciled. When battle resumes, Bruce refuses to attack Scots, and eventually the English flee and Edward is forced to retreat, pursued by the Scots. Edward realizes that Bruce's support for him is shaky and so keeps a close eye on him. The Scots eventually turn back, Wallace makes for Edinburgh, and peace is restored in Scotland. Morton is executed and Dundee razed. Wallace resigns as Guardian and sets sail for France, with his close companions, on a merchant ship, which is attacked near the Humber by pirates led by a notorious Scot-hater, John of Lyn. Thomas Gray, one of Wallace's companions, is said to be the authority for this account. He kills John of Lyn. Wallace arrives in Paris, and is welcomed by the French king who offers him Guyenne, which is occupied by the English. All Scots in the area flock to his support and go to war on the English. Wallace finds an ally in the duke of Orleans. Meanwhile John of Menteith makes a*

The Wallace

pact with Amer of Valence, and Edward marches into Scotland again, meeting little opposition, and installs English officers in key towns and strongholds. Boyd, Sinclair, and others write to Wallace, seeking his aid. (Lines 547–1076)]

	Of King Eduuard yeit mar furth will I meill,	*tell*
	Into quhat wys that he couth Scotland deill.	*way; he divided Scotland*
	In Sanct Jhonstoun the erll of York he maid	
1080	Capdane to be of all thai landis braid	*Captain; wide*
	Fra Tay to Dee, and undyr him Butlar.	*From*
	His grantschyr had at Kynclevin endyt thar,	*grandfather; Kinclaven*
	His fadyr als; Wallace thaim bathe had slayn;	*also; both*
	Eduuard tharfor maid him a man of mayn.	*power*
1085	The lord Bewmound into the north he send.	
	Thai lordschippys all thai gaiff him in commend.	*Those; assigned to him*
	To Sterlyn syn fra Sanct Jhonstoun he went,	*Stirling then from*
	Thair to fulfill the layff of his entent.	*rest of his purpose*
	The lord Clyffurd he gaiff than Douglace Daill,	
1090	Rewllar to be of the South Marchis haill.	*Warden; entirely*
	All Galloway than he gaiff Cumyn in hand:	*Comyn*
	Wyst nayn bot God how lang that stait suld stand.	*Knew none but; condition*
	The gentill lord, gud Byschop Lammyrtoun	*noble*
	Of Sanct Androws, had Douglace of renoun.	
1095	Befor that tyme Jamys, wicht and wys,	*strong*
	Till him was cummyn fra scullis of Parys.	*[the] schools*
	A preva favour the bischop till him bar;	*secret; carried*
	Bot Inglismen was so gret maisteris thar	
	He durst nocht weill in playn schaw him kindnes,	*openly show*
1100	Quhill on a day he tuk sum hardines.	*Until one day; courage*
	Douglace he cald and couth to Stirlyng fayr,	*called; went*
	Quhar King Eduuard was deland landis thair.	*dividing*
	He proferd him into the kingis service	
	To bruk his awin; fra he wist in this wys	*possess as; when he knew*
1105	Douglace he was, than he forsuk planlé,	
	Swor, "Be Sanct George, he brukis na landis of me!	*By; possesses*
	His fadir was in contrar of my crown,	*opposition to*
	Tharfor as now he bidis in our presoun."	*stays*
	To the byschop nane othir grant he maid,	*no*
1110	Bot as he plesd delt furth thai landis braid.	*dealt out there*
	To the lord Soullis all haill the Mers gaiff he	*all of the Merse*

Book 11

	And captane als of Berweik for to be.	*also*
	Olyfant than, that he in Stirlyng fand,	*found*
	Quhen he him had he wald nocht kep his band,	
1115	The quhilk he maid or he him Stirlyng gaiff.	*which; before; gave*
	Desaitfully thus couth he him dissayff:	*Deceitfully; he deceived him*
	Intill Ingland send him till presoun strang;	
	In gret distres he levyt thar full lang.	*lived there*
	Quhen Eduuard king had delt all this regioun,	
1120	His leyff he tuk, in Ingland maid him boun.	*leave; bound*
	Out of Stirlyng southward as thai couth ryd	*they rode*
	Cumyn hapnyt ner hand the Bruce to bid.	*happened nearby; stay*
	Thus said he, "Schir, and yhe couth keip consaill	*counsel*
	I can schaw her quhilk may be your availl."	*show here; advantage*
1125	The Bruce ansuerd, "Quhatevir yhe say to me	
	As for my part sall weill conseillyt be."	*advised*
	Lord Cumyn said, "Schir, knaw ye nocht this thing,	
	That of this realm ye suld be rychtwys king?"	*rightful*
	Than said the Bruce, "Suppos I rychtwys be	
1130	I se no tym to tak sic thing on me.	*such [a] thing*
	I am haldin into my enemys hand	
	Undyr gret ayth, quhen I com in Scotland	*oath*
	Nocht part fra him for profyt nor request,	*Not [to]*
	Na for na strenth bot gyff ded me arest.	*Nor; unless death; stop*
1135	He hecht agayn to gyff this land to me.	*promised*
	Now fynd I weill it is bot suteltè,	*deception*
	For thus thow seis he delys myn heretage	*apportions*
	To Sotheroun part, and sum to traytouris wage."	*[the] English some; [as] reward*
	Than Cumyn said, "Will ye herto accord,	*hereto agree*
1140	Of my landys and ye lik to be lord,	
	Ye sall thaim have for your rycht of the croun;	*in exchange; claim*
	Or, and ye lik, schir, for my warisoun	*if; reward*
	I sall yow help with power at my mycht."	
	The Bruce ansuerd, "I will nocht sell my rycht.	
1145	Bot on this wys, quhat lordschip thou will craiff	
	For thi supplé I hecht thou sall it haiff."	*your assistance I promise*
	"Cum fra yon king, schir, with sum jeperté.	*stratagem*
	Now Eduuard has all Galloway geyffyn to me.	*given*
	My nevo Soullis, that kepis Berweik toun,	*nephew*
1150	At your commaund this power sall be boun.	*ready*

The Wallace

	My nevo als, a man of mekill mycht,	*nephew also; great*
	The lord of Lorn has rowme into the hycht.	*space; the highlands*
	My thrid nevo, a lord of gret renoun,	*third nephew*
	Will rys with us, of Breichin the barroun."	
1155	Than said the Bruce, "Fell thar sa far a chance	*fair*
	That we micht get agane Wallace of France;	
	Be witt and force he couth this kynryk wyn.	*By wisdom; kingdom*
	Allace we haiff our lang beyn haldyn in twyn!"	*too long; separated*
	To that langage Cumyn maid na record,	*speech; reply*
1160	Of ald deidis intill his mynd remord.	*old deeds; remorse*
	The Bruce and he completyt furth thar bande,	*bond*
	Syn that sammyn nycht thai sellyt with thar hande.	*Then; same; sealed*
	This ragment left the Bruce with Cumyn thar;	*bond*
	With King Eduuard haym in Ingland can far	*home; went*
1165	And thar remaynyt quhill this ragment war knawin,	*remained until; bond; disclosed*
	Thre yer and mar or Bruce persewyt his awin.	*before; sought; own [claim]*
	Sum men demys that Cumyn that ragment send;	*judge*
	Sum men tharfor agaynys makis defend.	
	Nayn may say weill Cumyn was saklasing	*guiltless*
1170	Becaus his wiff was Eduuardis ner cusing.	*cousin*
	He servyt dede be rycht law of his king,	*deserved death*
	So raklesly myskepyt sic a thing.	*recklessly failed to keep*
	Had Bruce past by but baid to Sanct Jhonstoun	*without delay*
	Be haill assent he had rasavyt the croune.	*By total; received*
1175	On Cumyn syn he mycht haiff done the law.	*applied*
	He couth nocht thoill fra tym that he him saw,	*endure*
	Thus Scotland left in hard perplexité.	
	Of Wallace mar in sum part spek will we.	

Explicit decimus passus
et Incipit undecimus passus

Book 12

[*Wallace overcomes the English in Guyenne and then deals with various disaffected Frenchmen, including a knight, two champions at court, and two squires, who all use trickery to trap him. The final insult for Wallace is when he is led to believe that the French king wishes him to fight a captured lion. Having dispatched the animal, Wallace demands: "Is thar*

Book 12

ma doggis at ye wald yeit haiff slayne?" (line 256) and resolves to return to Scotland. He and his men leave, against the French king's wishes.

He arrives at Elcho, on the shores of the Earn and, keeping under cover, stays with his cousin Crawford. When Crawford goes to St. Johnston (Perth) for more meat than usual, the suspicions of the English are roused and they imprison and interrogate him. When they release him he is followed by Butler and a large armed force. Forewarned of the danger in a dream, Wallace and his men leave the house to avoid open battle because they are heavily outnumbered, and hide in Elcho Park. But when the English threaten to burn Crawford's wife unless she reveals his whereabouts, Wallace comes out to accuse Butler of shameful behavior. Incensed and desperate to avenge the deaths of his father and grandfather, Butler pursues Wallace to the park where, through strategic deployment of his twenty men and with the help of a misty night, Wallace manages to kill Butler and make his way to Methven where he can supply his hungry men with food and reinforcements. Finding food continues to be a problem so Wallace and his men move from Birnam to Lorne. Wallace separates from his men to seek food for them, but as he sleeps under an oak five traitors who have been bought by the earl of York try unsuccessfully to capture him and are killed. After feasting, Wallace and his men make their way to Rannock where they are looked after by friends and acquire more support. Wallace then decides to stop skulking in mountains and woods and to seek open battle. He goes to Dunkeld and then north to be united with Scottish supporters there. (Lines 1–729)]

730	Fra he com haym, to fle thai mak thaim boun	*When; ready*
	And Scottis men semblyt to Wallace fast.	*flocked*
	In awfull feyr throuchowt the land thai past;	*awesome array*
	Strenthis was left, witt ye, all desolate;	*Castles*
	Agayn thir folk thai durst mak no debate.	*Against these; dared; resistance*
735	In raid battaill thai raid till Abyrdeyn;	*In battle order; rode to*
	The haill nowmyr, sevyn thousand, than was seyn;	*entire number*
	Bot Inglismen had left that toun all waist,	
	On ilka syd away thai can thaim haist,	*every; did; hasten*
	In all that land left nothir mar nor les.	*neither more*
740	Lord Bewmound tuk the sey at Bowchan Nes,	*took to sea*
	Throu Scotland than was manifest in playn;	*openly*
	The lordis that past in hart was wondir fayn.	*were very glad*
	The knycht Climes of Ross com sodeynly	
	In Murray land with thar gud chevalry.	*company of knights*
745	The hous of Narn that gud knycht weill has tane,	*castle; taken*
	Slew the capdane and strang men mony ane.	*many [a] one*
	Out of Murray in Bowchane land com thai	
	To sek Bewmound be he was past away.	*seek; but; gone*

The Wallace

	Than thir gud men to Wallace passyt rycht.	these
750	Quhen Wallace saw Schir Jhon Ramsay the knycht	
	And othir gud at had bene fra him lang,	good [men] that had been from
	Gret curag than was rasyt thaim amang.	evoked among them
	The land he reullyt as at him likit best,	ruled; that
	To Sanct Jhonstoun syn raid or thai wald rest.	then rode before
755	At everilk part a stalwart wach he maid,	every place; watch
	Fermyt a sege and stedfastly abaid.	Established; waited
	Byschop Synclar intill all haist him dycht,	prepared
	Com out of Bute with symly men to sycht;	good
	Owt of the ilys of Rauchlé and Aran	isles; Rathlin
760	Lyndsay and Boid with gud men mony ane.	many [a] one
	Adam Wallace, barroun of Ricardtoun,	
	Full sadly socht till Wallace of renoun,	resolutely
	At Sanct Jhonstoun baid at the sailye still.	remained; siege
	For Sotheroun men thai mycht weill pas at will,	English
765	For in thar way thar durst na enemys be	dared
	Bot fled away be land and als be se.	also by sea
	About that toun thus semblyt thai but mor,	gathered; immediately
	For thai had beyn with gud Wallace befor.	
	Cetoun, Lauder, and Richard of Lundé,	
770	In a gud barge thai past about be se.	by sea
	Sanct Jhonstoun havyn thar ankyr haiff thai set.	haven; anchor
	Twa Inglys schippys thai tuk withoutyn let:	hindrance
	The tane thai brynt, syn stuffyt the tothir weill	one; burned, then supplied
	With artailye and stalwart men in steyll,	artillery
775	To kep the port; thar suld cum na victaill	defend; gate
	Into that toun, nor men at mycht thaim vaill	help
	Fra south and north mony of Scotland fled,	From; many from
	Left castellys waist; feill lost thar lyff to wed.	wasted; many; pledge
	The south byschop, befor at left Dunkell,	English-appointed
780	Tyll London past and tald Eduuard himsell	told; himself
	In Scotland thar had fallyn a gret myschance.	disaster
	Than send he son for Amar the Wallance	soon
	And askyt him than quhat war best to do.	
	He hecht to pas and tak gret gold tharto,	vowed; go
785	Into Scotland sic menys for to mak	such means; use
	Agane Wallace, on hand this can he tak.	Against; undertake
	Thai said he wald undo King Eduuardis croun	rule

198

Book 12

	Bot gyff thai mycht throu tresoun put him doun.	Unless
	King Eduuard hecht quhat thing at Wallang band	promised; contracted
790	He suld it kep, war it bathe gold and land.	keep (honor)
	Wallange tuk leyff and is in Scotland went;	leave
	To Bothwell com, syn kest in his entent	then considered
	Quhat man thar was mycht best Wallace begyll;	beguile
	And sone he fand within a litill quhill	while
795	Schyr Jhon Menteth. Wallace his gossop was.	[children's] godfather
	A messynger Schir Amar has gert pas	made
	Onto Schir Jhon and sone a tryst has set;	soon; meeting
	At Ruglyn Kyrk thir twa togydder met.	Rutherglen Church these two
	Than Wallang said, "Schir Jhon, thow knawis this thing.	you know
800	Wallace agayn rysis contrar the king,	
	And thow may haiff quhat lordschip thow will	choose
	And thow wald wyrk as I can gyff consaill.	If; advise
	Yon tyrand haldys the rewmys at trowbill bathe;	That; both realms
	Till thryfty men it dois full mekill scaith.	To thriving; harm
805	He traistis thee. Rycht weyll thow may him tak.	trusts; take
	Of this mater ane end I think to mak.	matter
	War he away, we mycht at liking ryng	Were; pleasure reign
	As lordys all and leiff undyr a king."	live
	Than Menteth said, "He is our governour.	
810	For us he baid in mony felloun stour,	stood; grievous battle
	Nocht for himselff bot for our heretage.	
	To sell him thus, it war a foull owtrage."	betray
	Than Wallang said, "And thow weill undyrstud,	
	Gret neid it war; he spillis so mekill blud	much blood
815	Of Crystin men, puttis saullis in peraill.	souls; peril
	I bynd me als he sall be haldyn haill	pledge; also; kept safe
	As for his lyff and kepyt in presoune;	
	King Eduuard wald haiff him in subjeccioun."	
	Than Menteth thocht sa thai wald kepe connand,	so [long as]; the agreement
820	He wald full fayn haiff had him of Scotland.	gladly; [out] of
	Wallange saw him intill a study be,	deep in thought
	Thre thowsand pundys of fyn gold leit him se	
	And hecht he suld the Lewynhous haiff at will.	promised; Lennox
	Thus tresonably Menteth grantyt thartill;	agreed to that
825	Obligacioun with his awn hand he maid.	A compact
	Syn tuk the gold and Eduuardis seill so braid	Then took; broad

199

The Wallace

     And gaiff thaim his, quhen he his tym mycht se   *over; freely*
     To tak Wallace our Sulway, giff him fre   *To; By; agreement*
     Till Inglismen. Be this tresonabill concord
830 Schyr Jhon suld be of all the Lennox lord.
     Thus Wallace suld in Ingland kepyt be,
     So Eduuard mycht mak Scotland till him fre.   *subject to his sole authority*
     Thar covatys was our gret maister seyn;   *covetousness (covetise)*
     Nane sampill takis how ane othir has beyn   *No one example*
835 For covatice put in gret paynys fell,   *extreme*
     For covatice the serpent is of hell.
     Throuch covatice gud Ector tuk the ded,   *Hector died*
     For covatice thar can be no ramed;   *remedy*
     Throuch covatice gud Alexander was lost,
840 And Julius als, for all his reiff and bost;   *plundering*
     Throuch covatice deit Arthour of Bretan,   *died*
     For covatice thar had deit mony ane;
     For covatice the traytour Ganyelon
     The flour of France he put till confusion;   *death*
845 For covatice thai poysound gud Godfra   *betrayed*
     In Antioche, as the autor will sa;   *author; say*
     For covatice Menteth apon fals wys   *in a false manner*
     Betraysyt Wallace at was his gossop twys.   *Betrayed; that; twice*
     Wallang in haist with blyth will and glaid hart
850 Till London past and schawit till King Eduuart.   *To; showed [the agreement] to*
     Of this contrak he had a mar plesance   *contract; more joy*
     Than of fyn gold had geyffyn in balance.   *given*
     A grettar wecht na his ransoun mycht be.   *weight than; ransom*
     Of Wallace furth yit sumthing spek will we,
855 At Sanct Jhonstoun was at the sogeyng still.   *siege*
     In a mornyng Sotheroun with egyr will,   *[the] English; eager*
     Five hundreth men in harnas rycht juntly,   *armor in close order*
     Thai uschet furth to mak a jeperty   *issued; surprise attack*
     At the south port apon Scot and Dundas,   *gate*
860 Quhilk in that tym rycht wys and worthy was   *Who*
     Agayn thar fayis rycht scharply socht and sayr.   *Against; foes; fiercely; intensely*
     In that cownter sevyn scor to ded thai bayr.   *encounter; bore down*
     Yeit Inglismen at cruell war and keyn   *that fierce; bold*
     Full ferely faucht quhar douchty deid was seyn.   *actively fought; brave*
865 Fra the west gett drew all the Scottis haill   *From; gate; completely*

Book 12

	To the fechtaris. Quhen Sotheroun saw na vaill	*fighters; avail*
	Bot in agayn, full fast thai can thaim sped.	*[to go] in again; speed*
	The knycht Dundas prevyt so douchty deid;	*proved so bold indeed*
	Our neyr the gett full bandounly he baid,	*Too near; gate; boldly; stayed*
870	Wyth a gud suerd full gret maistré he maid,	*sword; deeds of arms*
	Nocht wittandly his falowis was him fra.	*Not realizing; were away from him*
	In at the gett the Sotheroun can him ta;	*gate; brought him*
	Onto the erll thai led him haistelé.	
	Quhen he him saw he said he suld nocht de:	*die*
875	"To slay this ane it may us litill rameid."	*one; help*
	He send him furth to Wallace in that steid.	*place*
	On the north syd his bestials had he wrocht.	*siege engines; set up*
	Quhill he him saw of this he wyst rycht nocht;	*Until; knew*
	Send to the erll and thankit him largelé,	*Sent; generously*
880	Hecht for to quyt quhen he sic cace mycht se.	*Promised; repay; such [an] opportunity*
	Bot all her for soverance he wald nocht grant,	*here; safe conducts*
	Thocht thai yoldin wald cum as recreant;	*surrendered; admitting defeat*
	For gold na gud he wald no trewbut tak.	*nor goods; tribute*
	A full strang salt than he begouth to mak.	*assault; began*
885	The erll of Fyf duelt under trewage lang	*tribute a long time*
	Of King Eduuard, and than him thocht it wrang	
	At Wallace sa was segeand Sanct Jhonstoun,	*That; so; laying siege to*
	Bot gyff he com in rycht help of the croun.	*Unless; properly to help*
	Till Inglismen he wald nocht kep that band.	*To; keep; bond*
890	Than he come sone with gud men of the land,	
	And Jhon Wallang, was than schirreff of Fyff,	*then*
	Till Wallace past, starkyt him in that stryff.	*supported; struggle*
	That erll was cummyn of trew, haill nobill blud,	*true, completely*
	Fra the ald thane, quhilk in his tym was gud.	*old thane*
895	Than all about to Sanct Jhonstoun thai gang	*went*
	With felloun salt, was hydwys, scharp, and strang.	*fierce attack; hideous*
	Full feill fagaldys into the dyk thai cast,	*many faggots; ditch*
	Hadyr and hay bond apon flakys fast.	*Heather; bound; bundles*
	Wyth treis and erd a gret passage thai maid;	*trees; earth*
900	Atour the wallis thai yeid with battaill braid.	*Across; went*
	The Sotheroun men maid gret defens agayn,	*English*
	Quhill on the wallys thar was a thousand slayn.	*Until*
	Wallace yeid in and his rayit battaill rycht;	*went; ordered battalion*
	All Sotheroun men derffly to ded thai dycht.	*English; violently killed*

The Wallace

905	To sayff the erll Wallace the harrald send,	save; herald sent
	Gud Jop himselff, the quhilk befor him kend.	knew
	For Dundas saik thai said he suld nocht de;	sake
	Wallace himselff this ordand for to be.	ordered
	A small haknay he gert till him be tak,	hackney; caused; taken
910	Silver and gold his costis for to mak;	to meet his expenses
	Set on his clok a takyn for to se,	Placed; cloak; token
	The lyoun in wax that suld his condet be;	[safe] conduct
	Convoyit him furth and na man him with all.	Escorted
	Wemen and barnys Wallace gert freith thaim all,	children; made free
915	And syn gart cry trew Scottis men to thar awn;	then caused to be called; own
	Plenyst the land quhilk lang had beyn ourthrawn,	Stocked; overthrown
	Than Wallace past the south land for to se.	
	Eduuard the Bruce, in his tym rycht worthé,	
	That yer befor he had in Irland ben	year
920	And purchest thar of cruell men and keyn.	obtained; bold; fierce
	Fyfty in feyr, was of his moderys kyn,	company; mother's kin
	At Kyrkubré on Galloway entryt in.	Kirkcudbright in
	With thai fyfté he had vencust nine scor.	vanquished
	And syn he past withoutyn tary mor	after; more delay
925	Till Wygtoun sone and that castell has tane.	Wigton soon; taken
	Sotheroun was fled and left it all allane.	[The] English
	Wallace him met with trew men reverently;	respectfully
	To Lowmabane went all that chevalry.	Lochmaben; army
	Thai maid Eduuard bath lord and ledar thar.	leader there
930	This condicioun Wallace him hecht but mar,	promised immediately
	Bot a schort tym to bid Robert the king;	Only; await
	Gyff he come nocht in this regioun to ryng,	reign
	At Eduuard suld resaiff the croun but faill.	without fail
	Thus hecht Wallace and all the barnage haill.	promised; whole
935	In Louchmabane Prynce Eduuard levyt still	lived
	And Wallace past in Cumno with blith will.	Cumnock; happily
	At the Blak Rok, quhar he was wont to be,	
	Apon that sted a ryall hous held he.	place; royal castle
	Inglis wardans till London past but mar	wardens; straightaway
940	And tauld the king of all thar gret mysfar,	told; disaster
	How Wallace had Scotland fra thaim reduce	recovered
	And how he had rasavyt Eduuard the Bruce.	welcomed
	The commouns suor thai suld cum nevermar	swore; nevermore

Book 12

	Apon Scotland and Wallace leiffand war.	while; living was
945	Than Eduuard wrayt till Menteth prevali,	wrote; privately
	Prayit him till haist; the tym was past by	hurry
	Of the promes the quhilk at he was bund.	to which he was bound
	Schyr Jhon Menteth intill his wit has fund	wisdom; found
	How he suld best his purpos to fullfill.	
950	His systir son in haist he cald him till	called to
	And ordand him in duellyng with Wallace.	ordered; to dwell
	Ane ayth agayn he gert him mak on cace,	An oath; in the event
	Quhat tym he wyst Wallace in quiet draw	knew; withdrew
	He suld him warnd, for aventur mycht befaw.	alert, whatever might befall
955	This man grantyt at sic thing suld be done;	that such
	With Wallace thus he was in service sone.	soon
	As of tresoun Wallace had litill thocht;	
	His lauborous mynd on othir materis wrocht.	busy; worked
	Thus Wallace thrys has maid all Scotland fre.	thrice
960	Than he desyryt in lestand pees to be,	lasting
	For as of wer he was in sum part yrk.	war; weary
	He purpost than to serve God and the kyrk,	church
	And for to leyff undyr hys rychtwys king;	live; rightful
	That he desyryt atour all erdly thing.	above; earthly
965	The harrold Jop in Ingland sone he send	herald; soon; sent
	And wrayt to Bruce rycht hartlie this commend,	wrote; commendation
	Besekand him to cum and tak his croun;	Beseeching
	Nane suld gaynstand, clerk, burges, no barroun.	None; oppose
	The harrald past. Quhen Bruce saw his credans,	credentials
970	Tharoff he tuk a perfyt gret plesans.	pleasure
	With hys awn hand agayn wrayt to Wallace	own; wrote
	And thankyt him of lauta and kyndnas,	loyalty
	Besekand him this mater to conseill,	Praying; conceal
	For he behuffyd owt of Ingland to steill;	needed; steal
975	For lang befor was kepyt the ragment	bond
	Quhilk Cumyn had, to byd the gret parlement	Which; await
	Into London; and gyff thai him accus,	if; accused
	To cum fra thaim he suld mak sum excus.	come away
	He prayit Wallace in Glaskow Mur to walk	keep watch
980	The fyrst nycht of Juli, for his salk,	sake
	And bad he suld bot into quiet be,	ordered
	For he with him mycht bryng few chevalré.	companions

The Wallace

      Wallace was blyth quhen he this writyng saw;
      His houshauld sone he gert to Glaskow draw. — *carried*
985 That moneth thar he ordand thaim to byd. — *month; ordered; remain*
      Kerle he tuk ilk nycht with him to ryd, — *each*
      And this yong man that Menteth till him send — — *to; sent*
      Wyst nane bot thir quhat way at Wallace wend — — *Knew none; these; went*
      The quhilk gart warn his eym the auchtand nycht. — *Who caused; uncle; eighth*
990 Sexté full sone schyr Jhone Menteth gert dycht — *caused to be ready*
      Of hys awn kyn and of alya born. — *kin; allies*
      To this tresoun he gert thaim all be suorn. — *sworn*
      Fra Dunbertane he sped thaim haistely, — *From*
      Ner Glaskow Kyrk thai bownyt thaim prevaly. — *prepared; secretly*
995 Wallace past furth quhar at the tryst was set; — *forth; meeting*
      A spy thai maid and folowed him but let — *immediately*
      Till Robrastoun, was ner be the way syd — *Robroyston (near Glasgow) by*
      And bot a hows quhar Wallace oysyt to byd. — *only one; used to stay*
      He wouk on fut quhill passyt was mydnycht; — *stood watch until*
1000 Kerle and he than for a sleip thaim dycht. — *got ready*
      Thai bad this cuk that he suld wache his part — *traitor; take his turn on watch*
      And walkyn Wallace, com men fra ony art. — *waken; any direction*
      Quhen thai slepyt this traytour tuk graith heid. — *prompt heed*
      He met his eym and bad him haiff no dreid: — *uncle; fear*
1005 "On sleip he is and with him bot a man. — *only one*
      Ye may him haiff for ony craft he can; — *skill; knows*
      Without the hous thar wapynnys laid thaim fra." — *Outside; are laid*
      For weill thai wyst, gat Wallace ane of tha — *one of them*
      And on his feyt, hys ransoun suld be sauld. — *dearly paid for*
1010 Thus semblyt thai about that febill hauld. — *abode*
      This traytour wach fra Wallace than he stall — *guard; stole*
      Bathe knyff and suerd, his bow and arowis all. — *Both; sword*
      Eftir mydnycht in handis thai haiff him tane, — *laid hands on him*
      Dyschovyll on sleipe, wyth him na man bot ane. — *Unarmed in sleep; one*
1015 Kerle thai tuk and led him of that place, — *out of*
      Dyd him to ded withoutyn langar space. — *Put him to death; time*
      Thai thocht to bynd Wallace throu strenthis strang.
      On fute he gat the feill traytouris amang, — *foot; many*
      Grippyt about, bot na wapyn he fand. — *Felt; weapon; found*
1020 Apon a syll he saw besyd him stand — *beam*
      The bak of ane he byrstyt in that thrang — *back; one; broke; crowd*

Book 12

	And of ane othir the harnes out he dang.	*brains dashed*
	Than als mony as handis mycht on him lay,	*as many as might hands*
	Be force hym hynt for till haiff him away,	*By; seized*
1025	Bot that power mycht nocht a fute him leid	*foot; lead*
	Owt of that hous quhill thai or he war deid.	*until*
	Schir Jhon saw weill be force it coud nocht be,	*by*
	Or he war tayne he thocht erar to de.	*Before; taken; sooner; die*
	Menteth bad ces and thus spak to Wallace,	*ordered [them to] stop*
1030	Syn schawyt him furth a rycht sutell fals cace:	*Then displayed*
	"Yhe haiff so lang her oysyt yow allane	*here been accustomed; alone*
	Quhill witt tharoff is intill Ingland gane.	*While word*
	Tharfor her me and sobyr your curage.	*listen to me; moderate*
	The Inglismen with a full gret barnage	
1035	Ar semblyt her and set this hous about	*gathered; surround this house*
	That ye be force on na wayis may wyn out.	*by; escape*
	Suppos ye had the strenth of gud Ectour	*Even if; Hector*
	Amang this ost ye may nocht lang endour.	
	And thai yow tak, in haist your ded is dycht.	*If they take you; death; certain*
1040	I haiff spokyn with Lord Clyffurd that knycht,	
	Wyth thar chyftanys weill menyt for your lyff.	*well disposed*
	Thai ask no mar bot be quyt of your stryff.	*leave off your struggle*
	To Dunbertane ye sall furth pas with me;	
	At your awn hous ye ma in saifté be."	*own castle; safety*
1045	Sotheroun sic oys with Menteth lang had thai	*[The] English; practice*
	That Wallace trowyt sum part at he wald say.	*believed; that*
	Menteth said, "Schir, lo, wappynnys nane we haiff;	
	We com in trayst your lyff gyff we mycht saiff."	*good faith; if; save*
	Wallace trowyt weill, and he his gossep twys,	*believed; godfather separated from*
1050	That he wald nocht be no maner of wys	*[So] that*
	Him to betrays for all Scotland so wyd.	
	Ane ayth of him he askit in that tid.	*oath; at that time*
	Thar wantit wit. Quhat suld his aythis mor?	*lacked wisdom; should [he want with]*
	Forsuorn till him he was lang tym befor.	*Perjured*
1055	The ayth he maid. Wallace com in his will;	*oath; submitted to him*
	Rycht frawdfully all thus schawyt him till.	*appeared to him*
	"Gossep," he said, "as presoner thai mon yow se,	*Godfather*
	Or thai throu force wyll ellis tak yow fra me."	*will otherwise take*
	A courch with slycht apon his handys thai laid,	*kerchief; cunning*
1060	And undyr syn with sevir cordys thai braid,	*then; strong ropes; bound*

The Wallace

	Bath scharp and tewch, and fast togydder drew.	*tough*
	Allace, the Bruce mycht sayr that byndyng rew,	*sorely; rue*
	Quhilk maid Scotland sone brokyn apon cace,	*soon*
	For Comyns ded and los of gud Wallace!	*death*
1065	Thai led him furth in feyr amang thaim awe.	*company; all*
	Kerle he myst; of na Sotheroun he saw.	*missed; no English*
	Than wyst he weyll that he betraysyt was.	*knew; betrayed*
	Towart the south with him quhen thai can pas,	
	Yeit thai him said in trewth he suld nocht de,	*die*
1070	King Eduuard wald kep him in gud saufté	*safety*
	For hie honour in wer at he had wrocht.	*high; war that*
	The sayr bandys so strowblyt all his thocht,	*severe bindings; troubled*
	Credence tharto forsuth he coud nocht geyff.	*give*
	He wyst full weyll thai wald nocht lat him leiff.	*knew; let; live*
1075	A fals foull caus thai Menteth for him tauld,	*told*
	Quhen on this wys gud Wallace he had sauld.	*way; betrayed*
	Sum of thaim said it was to saiff thar lord;	
	Thai leid all owt that maid that fals record.	*lead*
	At the Fawkyrk the gud Stewart was slayn,	
1080	Our corniclis rehersis that in playn,	*chronicles recount; plainly*
	On Madelan Day, that eighteen yer befor.	*(i.e., July 22)*
	Comyns ded tharoff it wytnesis mor.	*testified further*
	At Robrastoun Wallas was tresonabilly,	
	Thus falsly, stollyn fra his gud chevalry,	*stolen; host*
1085	In Glaskow lay and wyst nocht of this thing.	
	Thus he was lost in byding of his king.	*waiting for*
	South thai him led, ay haldand the west land,	*always keeping to*
	Delyverit him in haist our Sullway Sand.	*over Solway*
	The lord Clyffurd and Wallang tuk him thar;	
1090	To Carleyll toun full fast with him thai fayr,	*Carlisle; went*
	In presoun him stad. That was a gret dolour.	*placed; distress*
	That hous efter was callyt Wallace tour.	*building; tower*
	Sum men syn said, that knew nocht weill the cas,	*afterwards; case*
	In Berweik thai to ded put gud Wallace.	*Berwick; death*
1095	Contrar is knawin fyrst be this opinioun;	*[The] contrary; known; by*
	For Scottis men than had haly Berweik toun	*held wholly*
	And Scotland fre, quhill that Soullis it gaiff,	*until; gave [up]*
	For Lord Cumyn till Ingland with the layff.	*others*
	Ane othir poynt is, the traytouris durst nocht pas	*dared*

Book 12

1100	At sauld him sa quhar Scottis men maisteris was.	*That betrayed; so; masters*
	The thrid poynt is, the commouns of Ingland,	
	Quhat thai desyr, thai will nocht understand	
	That thing be done, for wytnes at may be,	*is done; that*
	Na credence geyff forthyr than thai may se.	*No; give further*
1105	To se him de Eduuard had mar desyr	*more desire*
	Than to be lord of all the gret empyr.	
	For thir causis thai kepyt him sa lang,	*these reasons*
	Quhill the commouns mycht on to London gang.	*Until; go*
	Allace, Scotland, to quhom sall thow compleyn?	
1110	Allace, fra payn quha sall thee now restreyn?	*who; keep away*
	Allace, thi help is fastlie brocht to ground:	*savior; quickly*
	Thi best chyftane in braith bandis is bound.	*strong*
	Allace, thow has now lost thi gyd of lycht.	*guiding light*
	Allace, quha sall defend thee in thi rycht?	
1115	Allace, thi payn approchis wondyr ner,	*suffering*
	With sorow sone thow mon bene set in feyr.	*soon; must; fear*
	Thi gracious gyd, thi grettast governour,	*guide*
	Allace, our neir is cumyn his fatell hour.	*too near; destined*
	Allace, quha sall thee beit now of thi baill?	*relieve; woe*
1120	Allace, quhen sall of harmys thow be haill?	*whole*
	Quha sall thee defend? Quha sall thee now mak fre?	
	Allace, in wer quha sall thi helpar be?	*war*
	Quha sall thee help? Quha sall thee now radem?	*redeem*
	Allace, quha sall the Saxons fra thee flem?	*expel*
1125	I can no mar bot besek God of grace	*[do] no more; beseech*
	Thee to restor in haist to rychtwysnace,	*[your] rightful place*
	Sen gud Wallace may succour thee no mar.	*Since; help; more*
	The los of him encressit mekill cair.	*increased great suffering*
	Now of his men, in Glaskow still at lay,	*who still lay in Glasgow*
1130	Quhat sorow rais quhen thai him myst away.	*rose; missed*
	The cruell payn, the wofull complenyng,	*fierce suffering*
	Tharoff to tell it war our hevy thing.	*too heavy [a]*
	I will lat be and spek of it no mar.	*let; more*
	Litill rehers is our mekill of cair	*reciting; too much; sorrow*
1135	And principaly quhar redempcioun is nayn.	
	It helpys nocht to tell thar petous mayn;	*wretched lament*
	The deid tharoff is yeit in remembrance.	

The Wallace

      I will lat slaik of sorow the ballance.[1]
      Bot Longawell to Louchmabane coud pas   *past*
1140 And thar he hecht, quhar gud Prince Eduuard was   *vowed*
      Out of Scotland he suld pas nevermor.
      Los of Wallace socht till his hart so sor   *troubled his heart so much*
      The rewlm of France he vowit he suld never se,   *vowed*
      Bot veng Wallace or ellis tharfor to de.   *avenge; else*
1145 Thar he remaynd quhill cummyn of the king;   *until [the] arrival of the king (Bruce)*
      With Bruce in wer this gud knycht furth can ryng.   *did rule*
      Remembrance syn was in the Brucys buk: *afterwards*
      Secound he was quhen thai Saynct Jhonstoun tuk,
      Folowed the king at wynnyng of the toun.
1150 The Bruce tharfor gaiff him full gret gardoun;   *gave; reward*
      All Charterys land the gud king till him gaiff;
      Charterys sen syn of his kyn is the laiff.   *afterwards; descendant*
      Quharto suld I fer in that story wend?   *go*
      Bot of my buk to mak a fynaill end:
1155 Robert the Bruce com hame on the ferd day   *came home; fourth*
      In Scotland, eft Wallace was had away,   *after; taken away*
      Till Louchmabane, quhar that he fand Eduuard,   *found Edward (his brother)*
      Quharoff he was gretlie rejossyt in hart;   *Whereof; rejoiced*
      Bot fra he wyst Wallace away was led,   *when; knew*
1160 So mekill baill within his breyst thar bred   *much grief; breast*
      Ner out of wytt he worthit for to weyd.   *nearly went mad*
      Eduuard full sone than till hys brothir yeid.   *went*
      A sodane chance this was in wo fra weill.   *change of fortune*
      Gud Eduuard said, "This helpys nocht a dell.   *at all*
1165 Lat murnyng be; it may mak na remeid.   *Let mourning*
      Ye haiff him tynt. Ye suld ravenge his deid.   *lost; should revenge; death*
      Bot for your caus he tuk the wer on hand,   *Only; war*
      In your defens, and thrys has fred Scotland,   *freed*
      The quhilk was tynt fra us and all our kyn;   *taken from; kin*
1170 War nocht Wallace we had never entryt in.   *Were [it] not [for]*
      Merour he was of lauta and manheid,   *Mirror; loyalty*
      In wer the best that ever sall power leid.   *war; army lead*
      Had he likyt for till haiff tane your croun   *taken*

---

[1] *I will let the balance of the sorrow be assuaged*

Book 12

	Wald nane him let that was in this regioun.	*None would have stopped him*
1175	Had nocht beyne he, ye suld had na entres	*entrance*
	Into this rewlm, for tresoun and falsnes.	*on account of*
	That sall ye se. The traytour that him sauld,	*betrayed*
	Fra yow he thinkys Dunbertane for till hauld.	*possess*
	Sum comfort tak and lat slaik of this sorou."	*let this sorrow be assuaged*
1180	The king chargyt Eduuard apon the morou	*the next morning*
	Radres to tak of wrang that wrocht him was.	*Redress; had been done to him*
	Till Dallswyntoun he ordand him to pas,	*ordered*
	And men of armys; gyff thai fand Cumyn thar,	*if they found*
	Put him to ded; for na dreid thai suld spar.	*death; danger; spare*
1185	Thai fand him nocht. The king himselff him slew	*found*
	Intill Drumfres, quhar witnes was inew.	*there were enough witnesses*
	That hapnys wrang, our gret haist in a king;	*too great haste*
	Till wyrk by law it may scaith mekill thing.	*harm*
	Me nedis heroff na forthyr for till schaw;	*demonstrate*
1190	How that was done is knawin to yow aw.	*known; all*
	Bot yong Douglace fyrst to the king can pas,	*went*
	In all hys wer bath wicht and worthi was;	*(i.e., Bruce's war); strong*
	Nor how the king has tane on him the croun;	*taken*
	Of all that her I mak bot schort mencioun;	*here*
1195	Nor how lord Soullis gaiff Berweik toun away,	*gave*
	How eftir syn sone tynt was Galloway;	*soon afterwards; lost*
	How Jhon of Lorn agayn his rycht king rais,	*against; rose*
	On athir sid how Bruce had mony fais;	*either side; foes*
	How bauld Breichin contrar his king coud ryd;	*bold; against; rode*
1200	Rycht few was than in wer with him to byd;	*war; withstand*
	Nor how the north was gyffyn fra the gud king,	*given away*
	Quhilk maid him lang in paynfull wer to ryng.	*war; reign*
	Ay trew till him was Jamys the gud Douglace,	*Ever true to*
	For Brucis rycht baid weill in mony place.	*remained*
1205	Undyr the king he was the best chyftayn,	
	Bot Wallace rais as chyftane him allayn;	*rose; alone*
	Tharfor till him is no comparisoun	
	As of a man, sauff reverence of the croun.	*with the exception respectfully*
	Bot sa mony as of Douglace has beyn	
1210	Gud of a kyn was never in Scotland seyn.	*kind*
	Comparisoun that can I nocht weill declar.	*state*
	Of Brucis buk as now I spek no mar.	*more*

The Wallace

	Master Barbour, quhilk was a worthi clerk,	*who*
	He said the Bruce amang his othir werk.	*composed; work*
1215	In this mater prolixit I am almaist;	*prolix; almost*
	To my purpos breiffly I will me haist,	
	How gud Wallace was set amang his fayis.	*placed; enemies*
	To London with him Clyffurd and Wallang gais,	*went*
	Quhar King Eduuard was rycht fayn of that fang.	*glad; capture*
1220	Thai haiff him stad intill a presone strang.	*confined; strong*
	Of Wallace end myselff wald leiff for dredis	*would leave [out details]; fear*
	To say the werst, bot rychtwysnes me ledis.	*worst; [a] sense of right; leads*
	We fynd his lyff was all swa verray trew,	*so*
	His fatell hour I will nocht fenye new.	*fated; falsify*
1225	Menteth was fals and that our weill was knawin;	*too; known*
	Feill of that kyn in Scotland than was sawyn,	*Many; were scattered*
	Chargyt to byd undir the gret jugement	*Commanded; decree*
	At King Robert ackyt in his parlement.	*That; enacted*
	Tharoff I mak no langar contenuans.	*continuance*
1230	Bot Wallace end in warld was displesans,	*distress*
	Tharfor I ces and puttis it nocht in rym.	*rhyme*
	Scotland may thank the blyssyt, happy tym	*blessed*
	At he was born, be prynsuall poyntis two.	*That; two principal points*
	This is the fyrst, or that we forthyr go,	*before*
1235	Scotland he fred and brocht it of thrillage;	*freed; [out] of thraldom*
	And now in hevin he has his heretage,	*heaven; inheritance*
	As it prevyt be gud experians.	*proved*
	Wys clerkys yeit it kepis in remembrans,	*still*
	How that a monk of Bery abbay than,	*then*
1240	Into that tym a rycht religious man;	*At that time*
	A yong monk als with him in ordour stud,	*also; holy orders*
	Quhilk knew his lyff was clene, perfyt, and gud.	*Who*
	This fader monk was wesyd with seknace,	*afflicted; illness*
	Out of the warld as he suld pas on cace.	*From this world; passed in time*
1245	His brothir saw the spret lykly to pas.	*brother [monk]; spirit*
	A band of him rycht ernystly he coud as,	*promise; asked*
	To cum agayn and schaw him of the meid	*reveal to; reward*
	At he suld haiff at God for his gud deid.	*That; good deeds*
	He grantyt him, at his prayer, to preiff	*try*
1250	To cum agayn gyff God wald geiff him leiff.	*if; give him leave*
	The spreyt changyt out of this warldly payn,	*translated*

Book 12

	In that sammyn hour com to the monk agayn.	*same*
	Sic thing has beyn and is be voice and sycht.	*Such*
	Quhar he apperyt thar schawyt sa mekill lycht,	*shone so much*
1255	Lyk till lawntryns it illumynyt so cler	*lanterns*
	At warldly lycht tharto mycht be no peyr.	*That; equal*
	A voice said thus, "God has me grantyt grace	
	That I sall kep my promes in this place."	
	The monk was blyth of this cler fygur fayr;	*bright*
1260	Bot a fyr brund in his forheid he bayr	*brand; forehead; bore*
	And than him thocht it myslikyt all the lave.	*made all the rest displeasing*
	"Quhar art thow spreyt? Ansuer, sa God thee save."	*spirit*
	"In purgatory." "How lang sall thow be thair?"	
	"Bot halff ane hour to cum and litill mair.	*more*
1265	Purgatory is, I do thee weill to wit,	*know*
	In ony place quhar God will it admyt.	
	Ane hour of space I was demed thar to be	*time; judged*
	And that passis, suppos I spek with thee."	
	"Quhy has thow that and all the layff so haill?"	*rest so sound*
1270	"For of science I thocht me maist availl.	*knowledge; avail*
	Quha pridys tharin that laubour is in waist,	*Whoever takes pride*
	For science cummys bot of the Haly Gaist."	*only; Holy Ghost*
	"Eftir thi hour quhar is thi passage evyn?"	*proper*
	"Quhen tym cummys," he said, "to lestand hevin."	*everlasting heaven*
1275	"Quhat tym is that, I pray thee now declar?"	
	"Twa ar on lyff mon be befor me thar."	*are alive must*
	"Quhilk two ar thai? The verité thow me ken."	*tell*
	"The fyrst has bene a gret slaar of men.	*slayer*
	Now thai him kep to martyr in London toun	
1280	On Wednysday, befor king and commoun.	*commons*
	Is nayn on lyff at has sa mony slayn."	*that*
	"Brodyr," he said, "that taill is bot in vayn,	
	For slaughter is to God abhominabill."	
	"Than," said the spreyt, "forsuth this is no fabill.	*truly; lie*
1285	He is Wallace, defendour of Scotland,	
	For rychtwys wer that he tuk apon hand.	*righteous war*
	Thar rychtwysnes is lovyt our the lave;	*praised above the rest*
	Tharfor in hevyn he sall that honour have.	
	Syn, a pure preist, is mekill to commend.	*Then; poor; greatly to be commended*
1290	He tuk in thank quhat thing that God him send.	*gratefully*

211

The Wallace

	For dayly mes and heryng of confessioun	
	Hevin he sall haiff to lestand warysoun.	*Heaven; everlasting reward*
	I am the thrid grantyt throw Goddis grace."	
	"Brothir," he said, "tell I this in our place,	
1295	Thai wyll bot deym I othir dreym or rave."	*only believe*
	"Than," said the spreyt, "this wytnes thow sall have.	
	Your bellys sall ryng, for ocht at ye do may,	*anything*
	Quhen thai him sla, halff ane hour of that day."	*for half an hour*
	And so thai did. The monk wyst quhat thaim alyt.	*knew; them ailed*
1300	Throuch braid Bretane the voice tharoff was scalyt.	*Throughout; fame; spread*
	The spreyt tuk leyff at Goddis will to be.	*spirit; leave*
	Of Wallace end to her it is peté,	*hear*
	And I wald nocht put men in gret dolour,	*sadness*
	Bot lychtly pas atour his fatell hour.	*over; fateful*
1305	On Wednysday the fals Sotheroun furth brocht	*English*
	Till martyr him, as thai befor had wrocht.	*To*
	Rycht suth it is a martyr was Wallace,	*true*
	As Osuuald, Edmunt, Eduuard, and Thomas.	
	Of men in armes led him a full gret rout.[1]	
1310	Wyth a bauld spreit gud Wallace blent about.	*bold; looked*
	A preyst he askyt, for God at deit on Tre.	*asked [for]; who died on [the] Cross*
	King Eduuard than commaundyt his clergé	*clergy*
	And said, "I charge, apayn of los of lyve,	*on pain; life*
	Nane be sa bauld yon tyrand for to schryve.	*bold; confess*
1315	He has rong lang in contrar my hienace."	*prevailed; against; highness (i.e., royal rule)*
	A blyst byschop sone present in that place,	*holy*
	Of Canterbery he than was rychtwys lord,	*Canterbury; (i.e., bishop)*
	Agayn the king he maid this rycht record	*Against; statement*
	And said, "Myself sall her his confessioun.	*hear*
1320	Gyff I haiff mycht, in contrar of thi croun.	*If; power; opposition*
	And thou throu force will stop me of this thing,	*If you; prevent*
	I vow to God, quhilk is my rychtwys king,	
	That all Ingland I sall her enterdyt	*here interdict*
	And mak it knawin thou art ane herretyk.	*known; heretic*
1325	The sacrament of kyrk I sall him geiff.	*church; give*
	Syn tak thi chos, to sterve or lat him leiff.	*Then; choice; let him live or die*

---

[1] *A very large company of armed men guarded him*

Book 12

	It war mar vaill in worschip of thi croun	*more advantage; honor*
	To kepe sic ane in lyff in thi bandoun,	*such [a] one; subjection to you*
	Than all the land and gud at thow has refyd,	*that; plundered*
1330	Bot covatice thee ay fra honour drefyd.	*covetousness; always; drove*
	Thow has thy lyff rongyn in wrangwis deid:	*ruled; wrongful deeds*
	That sall be seyn on thee or on thi seid."	*offspring*
	The king gert charge thai suld the byschop ta,	*ordered; take*
	Bot sad lordys consellyt to lat him ga.	*grave; counseled; let; go*
1335	All Inglismen said at his desyr was rycht.	*that*
	To Wallace than he rakyt in thar sicht	*went*
	And sadly hard his confessioun till ane end.	*gravely heard*
	Humbly to God his spreyt he thar comend,	*commended*
	Lawly him servyt with hartlye devocioun	*Meekly; heartfelt*
1340	Apon his kneis and said ane orysoun.	*prayer*
	His leyff he tuk and to Westmonaster raid.	*leave; Westminster rode*
	The lokmen than thai bur Wallace but baid	*executioners; brought; without delay*
	Ontill a place his martyrdom to tak;	
	For till his ded he wald no forthyr mak.	*until; go*
1345	Fra the fyrst nycht he was tane in Scotland	*taken*
	Thai kepyt him into that sammyn band.	*those same bindings*
	Nathing he had at suld haiff doyn him gud	*that; done*
	Bot Inglismen him servit of carnaill fud.	*fleshly*
	Hys warldly lyff desyrd the sustenance,	
1350	Thocht he it gat in contrar of plesance.	*against pleasure*
	Thai thirty dayis his band thai durst nocht slaik,	*loosen*
	Quhill he was bundyn on a skamyll of ayk	*fastened; oak bench*
	With irn chenyeis that was bath stark and keyn.	*iron chains; strong; cruel*
	A clerk thai set to her quhat he wald meyn.	*hear*
1355	"Thow Scot," he said, "that gret wrangis has don,	
	Thi fatell hour thou seis approchis son.	*destined; soon*
	Thow suld in mynd remembyr thi mysdeid	*wrongdoing*
	At clerkys may quhen thai thar psalmis reid	*[So] that priests; read*
	For Crystyn saullis that makis thaim to pray,	
1360	In thar nowmyr thow may be ane of thai,	
	For now thow seis on force thou mon deces."	*of necessity; die*
	Than Wallace said, "For all thi roid rahres	*severe recital*
	Thou has na charge, suppos at I did mys.	*commission, even if I did wrong*
	Yon blyst byschop has hecht I sall haiff blis	*That; promised; bliss*
1365	And I trow weill at God sall it admyt.	*believe; that; grant*

The Wallace

	Thi febyll wordis sall nocht my conscience smyt.	stir
	Conford I haiff of way at I suld gang;	Comfort; that; go
	Maist payn I feill at I bid her our lang."	[is] that; too long
	Than said this clerk, "Our king oft send thee till.	
1370	Thow mycht haiff had all Scotland at thi will	
	To hald of him and cessyt of thi stryff,	struggle
	So as a lord rongyn furth all thi lyff."	held sway
	Than Wallace said, "Thou spekis of mychty thing.	
	Had I lestyt and gottyn my rychtwys king,	
1375	Fra worthi Bruce had rasavit his croun	received
	I thocht haiff maid Ingland at his bandoun;	subject to him
	So uttraly it suld beyn at his will,	entirely
	Quhat plessyt him to sauff thi king or spill."	save; destroy
	"Weill," said this clerk, "than thow repentis nocht;	nothing
1380	Of wykkydnes thow has a felloun thocht.	grievous
	Is nayn in warld at has sa mony slane,	that; many slain
	Tharfor till ask, me think thow sald be bane,	ready
	Grace of our king and syn at his barnage."	afterwards of
	Than Wallace smyld a litill at his langage.	speech
1385	"I grant," he said, "part Inglismen I slew	some
	In my quarell, me thocht nocht halff enew.	enough
	I movyt na wer bot for to wyn our awin;	began no war; what is ours
	To God and man the rycht full weill is knawin.	known
	Thi fruster wordis dois nocht bot taris me.	useless; delay
1390	I thee commaund, on Goddis halff lat me be."	for God's sake let
	A schyrray gart this clerk son fra him pas;	sheriff caused; soon
	Rycht as thai durst thai grant quhat he wald as.	dared; ask
	A psalter buk Wallace had on him ever,	psalm
	Fra his childeid fra it wald nocht desever.	From; childhood; be separated
1395	Better he trowit in viagis for to speid,	believed; expeditions
	Bot than he was dispolyeid of his weid.	stripped; clothing
	This grace he ast at Lord Clyffurd that knycht,	asked
	To lat him haiff his Psalter buk in sycht.	let
	He gert a preyst it oppyn befor him hauld	hold
1400	Quhill thai till him had done all at thai wauld.	that they would
	Stedfast he red for ocht thai did him thar.	
	Feyll Sotheroun said at Wallace feld na sayr.	Many English; felt; pain
	Gud devocioun so was his begynnyng	
	Conteynd tharwith, and fair was his endyng,	Continued

Book 12

1405	Quhill spech and spreyt at anys all can fayr	*Until; once; did go*
	To lestand blys, we trow forevermayr.	*lasting bliss; forevermore*
	I will nocht tell how he devydyt was	*divided*
	In five partis and ordand for to pas;	
	Bot thus his spreyt be liklynes was weill.	*in all likelihood*
1410	Of Wallace lyff quha has a forthar feill	*greater knowledge*
	May schaw furth mair with wit and eloquence;	*show forth more*
	For I to this has done my diligence,	
	Efter the pruff geyffyn fra the Latyn buk	*evidence given*
	Quhilk Maister Blair in his tym undyrtuk,	*undertook*
1415	In fayr Latyn compild it till ane end;	*compiled*
	With thir witnes the mair is to commend.	*testimonies; more*
	Byschop Synclar, than lord was of Dunkell,	*Dunkeld*
	He gat this buk and confermd it himsell	*himself*
	For verray trew; tharof he had no dreid,	*very truth; doubt*
1420	Himselff had seyn gret part of Wallace deid.	*deeds*
	His purpos was till have send it to Rom,	
	Our fader of kyrk tharon to gyff his dom.	*(i.e., the pope); judgment*
	Bot Maister Blayr and als Schir Thomas Gray,	*also*
	Efter Wallace thai lestit mony day,	*survived*
1425	Thir twa knew best of gud Schir Wilyhamys deid	*These; deeds*
	Fra sixteen yer quhill twenty-nine yeid.	*had passed*
	Forty and five of age Wallace was cauld	*called*
	That tym that he was to the Sotheroun sauld.	*betrayed*
	Thocht this mater be nocht till all plesance,	*to all [a] pleasure*
1430	His suthfast deid was worthi till avance.	*true deeds; to praise*
	All worthi men at redys this rurall dyt,	*who read; unpolished composition*
	Blaym nocht the buk, set I be unperfyt.	*[although] my writing be imperfect*
	I suld have thank, sen I nocht travaill spard.	*have thanks, since; labor spared*
	For my laubour na man hecht me reward;	*work; promised*
1435	Na charge I had of king nor othir lord;	*command*
	Gret harm I thocht his gud deid suld be smord.	*lost sight of*
	I haiff said her ner as the proces gais	*narrative*
	And fenyeid nocht for frendschip nor for fais.	*not falsified; foes*
	Costis herfor was no man bond to me.	*Payment; bound*
1440	In this sentence I had na will to le;	*narrative; lie*
	Bot in als mekill as I rahersit nocht	*related*
	Sa worthely as nobill Wallace wrocht,	
	Bot in a poynt I grant I said amys.	*one*

The Wallace

	Thir twa knychtis suld blamyt be for this,	*These*
1445	The knycht Wallas, of Cragge rychtwys lord,	
	And Liddaill als, gert me mak wrang record.	*wrongful*
	On Allyrtoun Mur the croun he tuk a day	
	To get battaill, as myn autour will say.	
	Thir twa gert me say that ane othir wys;	*These*
1450	Till mayster Blayr we did sum part of dispys.	*To; disdain*
	Go nobill buk, fulfillyt of gud sentens,	*filled with; subject-matter*
	Suppos thow be baran of eloquens.	*Even if; barren*
	Go worthi buk, fullfillit of suthfast deid,	*true deeds*
	Bot in langage of help thow has gret neid.	*need*
1455	Quhen gud makaris rang weill into Scotland	*poets flourished*
	Gret harm was it that nane of thaim thee fand.	*found you*
	Yeit thar is part that can thee weill avance;	*some; recommend you [to readers]*
	Now byd thi tym and be a remembrance.	*bide your time*
	I yow besek of your banevolence,	*pray; benevolence*
1460	Quha will nocht low lak nocht my eloquence:	*praise do not find wanting*
	It is weill knawin I am a burel man.	*rustic*
	For her is said als gudly as I can;	*here; as well*
	My spreyt felis na termys of Pernase.	*spirit; knows*
	Now besek God that gyffar is of grace,	*pray; giver*
1465	Maide hell and erd and set the hevyn abuff,	*heavens above*
	That He us grant of His der lestand luff.	*lasting love*

Explicit vita nobilisum . . . .

Explanatory Notes

Abbreviations: see Textual Notes.

Book 1

1–4   The scribe indents the first four lines here and at the beginning of other books, and he indents the first two lines at the beginning of some stanzas (e.g., 2.171ff.). I have maintained the practice.

1–19   These lines provide a short prologue in which Hary highlights the commemorative function of his narrative. Although similar to Barbour's prologue in *The Bruce*, Hary's denigration of the English, the first of many such disparagements in his poem, is not characteristic of Barbour. Note the references to reading in line 1 of the Prologue, and then in the first line introducing the hero (line 17), and then later in the direct advice to readers in line 34. McDiarmid regards them as addresses to readers of histories (2.124n1–4).

21   Through the convention of providing his hero's genealogy, Hary traces Wallace's lineage back to the "gud Wallace" (line 30) who was a companion of Walter Warayn of Wales, or Walter Fitz Alan, the first Scottish Stewart. The Stewart dynasty succeeded the Bruces to the throne of Scotland.

23   Sir Reginald (Ranald) Crawford, brother of Wallace's mother, became sheriff of Ayr in May 1296.

28   *Elrisle*. Elderslie, specifically Renfrewshire land held first by the father, later by the brother of the same name, Sir Malcolm Wallace, as vassals to the Stewarts. It was part of the lordship of Paisley and Renfrew and, as Barrow (1973) points out, is right at the heart of the Stewart fief (pp. 339–40).

34   *the rycht lyne of the fyrst Stewart*. This appears to be a reference to Barbour's long lost genealogy of the Stewarts, a work whose existence is also attested by the fifteenth-century Scottish chronicler Andrew Wyntoun.

The Wallace

36   Sir Malcolm Wallace is the only brother mentioned, although other sources suggest William Wallace had at least one other brother, John, who was executed in 1307 after being captured fighting for Bruce.

41   *Alexander.* I.e., Alexander III (1249–86), whose accidental death when he was thrown from his horse near the royal manor of Kinghorn in Fife left the kingdom without a king. His three children had died before him, his two sons without offspring, so that the heir to the throne was his daughter's child, Margaret, the "Maid of Norway." Margaret died in Orkney on her way to Scotland to ascend her throne in 1290. A number of rival claimants to the throne then presented themselves, the strongest two being Robert Bruce, lord of Annandale (grandfather of the future king, Robert I), and John Balliol, who did succeed in 1292.

44   *a full grevous debate.* Hary provides a very brief and over-simplified account of the succession crisis in the following lines. In line 47, he identifies the chief competitors as "Bruce" (that is Robert Bruce, lord of Annandale), "Balyoune" (John Balliol), and "Hastyng" (John Hastings), the descendants of the three daughters of "Our Prynce Davy" (line 45), David, earl of Huntingdon and grandson of David I (1124–53). Balliol claimed the throne as the grandson of the eldest daughter, Dervoguilla, "of first gre lynialy" (line 49), and Bruce as the son of the second daughter, Isabel, and the first male descendant "of the secund gre" (line 50); Hastings was the grandson of Ada, the youngest daughter. King Edward I (Longshanks) was approached as arbiter and used the opportunity to declare his overlordship of Scotland. Bruce and Balliol emerged as the main claimants, although by the end of 1292, Bruce had resigned his claim in favour of his son and heirs, and Edward had decided in favor of Balliol (crowned at Scone on 30 November). By the rule of primogeniture, Balliol had the stronger claim but after the succession of Robert Bruce in 1306 history was re-written to make Bruce appear the divine and popular choice. See Barbour (*Bruce* 1.37–178), Wyntoun (*Cronykil* 8.i, ii, v–viii, x), and Bower (*Scotichronicon* 11.1–14), whose accounts clearly influenced Hary.

53–54   These lines may have been influenced by Barbour's passionate reproach:

> A blynd folk full off all foly,
> Haid 3e wmbethocht 3ow enkrely
> Quhat perell to 3ow mycht apper
> 3e had nocht wrocht on þat maner.
> Haid 3e tane keip how at þat king
> Alwayis for-owtyn soiournyng

Explanatory Notes to Book 1

> Trawayllyt for to wyn sen3hory
> And throw his mycht till occupy
> Landis þat war till him marcheand
> . . . .
> 3e mycht se he suld occupy
> Throw slycht þat he ne mycht throw maistri. (*Bruce* 1.91–112)

56   *Gaskone*. The war with Philip the Fair of France over Gascony did not break out until June 1294, whereas Hary is clearly referring here to events in 1291–92. Bower's mention of the envoys who journeyed to Gascony in 1286 to seek Edward's arbitration in the succession crisis (11.3) may well account for Hary's mistake, as McDiarmid suggests (2.130n56).

61   *Noram*. Norham, in Northumberland. It was here in May 1291 that Edward met the Scots and declared his right to overlordship of Scotland.

65   *Byschope Robert*. Robert Wishart, bishop of Glasgow (1261–1316), a staunch defender of Scottish independence.

70   Edward decided in Balliol's favor and the latter was crowned king in November 1292.

77   *Ane abbot*. Identified as Henry of Arbroath by McDiarmid, who cites Wyntoun and Bower as Hary's sources here (2.131n75–77).

79   *Werk on Twede*. Up river from Berwick on Tweed.

81   *Corspatryk*. Earl Patrick of Dunbar and March, one of the great magnates of Scotland who supported Edward I. His role in the sack of Berwick is also attested by the *Scalacronica*, a chronicle of English history begun in 1355 by Sir Thomas Gray when he was imprisoned in Edinburgh Castle. He was later appointed keeper of Berwick town (1298). Hary describes him as a traitor, and blames him for the defeat of the Scots at the Battle of Dunbar the following month.

85–96   Several accounts of Edward's sack of Berwick in March 1296 survive. Medieval Scottish chroniclers represent it as one of the greatest atrocities perpetrated by Edward's forces, because of the slaughter of civilians, including women and children. Wyntoun (8.11) and Bower (11.20) describe the devastating attack in detail and both reckon the toll at 7,500, as Hary does.

The Wallace

94–95   In contrast to Edward's indiscriminate slaughter, Wallace persistently refuses to slay women and children in Hary's narrative.

98–114 The Battle of Dunbar took place on 27 April 1296. Hary seems to have used a different source here from Wyntoun and Bower, who mention the presence of only one earl, Ross. The English Lanercost chronicle agrees with Hary about the four present. Modern historians tend to agree that three were present, Atholl, Ross, and Menteith. (Barrow [1988], p. 74, Watson, p. 25)

102   *Mar, Menteith, Adell, Ros*. The high-ranking earls of Mar, Menteith, Atholl, and Ross.

115–21 *Scune*. Edward's recorded itinerary after Dunbar places him in the borders during May and early June and then further north from 6 June, staying in Perth 21–24 June, in Forfar 3 July, and arriving in Montrose on 8 July, to which he summoned Balliol. If he included Scone on his route, then he must have been there in the last week of June. Both Bower and Wyntoun state that Balliol was summoned to Montrose and, stripped of the royal regalia, was there forced to resign the kingdom on 8 July 1296. Whether Edward was ever crowned at Scone is a matter for speculation. He certainly removed the Stone of Destiny, traditionally used for Scottish coronations, to London in 1296.

122   *Gadalos*. Legendary history records that Gaythelos was the husband of Scota, the eponymous mother of the Scottish people and daughter of an Egyptian pharaoh whose descendants brought to Scotland the Stone of Destiny that later became the coronation seat of Scottish monarchs and a symbol of Scottish independence. Taken by Edward to London in 1296, it was finally returned to Scotland with the Scottish royal regalia in 1996. See Fordun, *Chronica* 1.8–19, and the expanded version of this origin myth in Bower, *Scotichronicon* 1.9–18.

123   *Iber Scot*. Hiber, the son of Gaytheles, who established the Scots in Ireland.

124   *Canmor syne King Fergus*. Malcolm Canmore, king of Scots (1058–93) and the successor of Macbeth. According to legend, Fergus was the first Scottish king.

132   *Margretis ayr*. The descendants of St. Margaret, the English wife of Malcom Canmore, became the rulers of England and Scotland. Hary may be drawing on Bower, who inserts a list of their descendants in the midst of his account of the Scottish succession dispute (11.12).

Explanatory Notes to Book 1

133	After his triumphant tour through much of central and eastern Scotland, accepting homage as he went, Edward set up an English administration, with headquarters in Berwick, in August 1296. Important barons and knights, many captured at Dunbar, were taken as prisoners to England.
134	*Bruce*. I.e., Robert Bruce, the future king.
137	*Blacok Mur . . . Huntyntoun*. McDiarmid believes this should be *Blacow mur*, as it refers to Blakemore in Yorkshire where the Bruces held lands (2.136n137). *Huntyntoun* is the vast English Honour of Huntingdon, a third of which had come into the Bruce family through Isabel, one of the three daughters of Earl David.
140	*Protector*. McDiarmid (2.136n140) suggests one possible corroboration of this claim that Edward entrusted the government of all Scotland to the earl of Warenne and Earl Patrick of March (Joseph Stevenson and Robert Rodger, eds., *The Wallace Papers* [Edinburgh: Maitland Club, 1841], p. 5).
144	Hary returns to Wallace and resumes his account of the outbreak of war in early 1296. Later (line 192) Wallace is said to be eighteen years of age when he has his first violent encounter with the English in Dundee. Hary's account of his career does not add up. If Wallace is eighteen in 1296 he cannot have been forty-five at the time of his death in 1305, as Hary says he was (12.1427). It may be that Hary thought of eighteen as the age at which a youth could take up arms. In Book 3 Adam, the eldest son of Wallace's uncle Sir Richard Wallace, at the same age is the only one of the three who rides off with William Wallace to pursue a campaign against the English.
147–48	I.e., Malcolm, Wallace's father, alongside his eldest brother, also called Malcolm (line 321). The Lennox, in the west of Central Scotland, was one of the oldest earldoms of Scotland. It incorporated Dumbartonshire, much of Stirlingshire, and parts of Renfrewshire and Perthshire.
150	Kilspindie in the Gowrie district of Perthshire, where a relative on his maternal side offers refuge. Even though this relative is said to be an "agyt man" (line 154), it seems unlikely that Hary was referring to the uncle of Wallace's maternal grandfather, as line 152 seems to suggest, but rather to Wallace's uncle.
155	That part of Wallace's education included going to school in Dundee, ten miles from his uncle's home in Kilspindie, is repeated by Hary in 7.670–71.

159	*Saxons blud*. Hary quite frequently refers to the English occupiers in this racist manner. Another example is the metonym, "Sothroun" (e.g., line 188). (See Goldstein [1993], pp. 222–23.)
160–70	These sentiments are reminiscent of *Bruce* 1.179–204.
165	The English occupation is compared to Herod's slaughter of the innocents.
171–72	Although no other known source claims Glasgow diocese was handed over to the bishop of Durham, McDiarmid suggests that Hary's conviction about this may be based on a tradition (2.138n171–72).
175–76	The hanging of Scottish leaders and Wallace's revenge on the English as they slept in barns at Ayr are entirely fictitious events described in Book 7.
194	Specific examples of the strife Wallace encounters are recounted at lines 205–32 and in Book 2.
201–02	The description of Wallace's appearance and manner is quite conventional. His reticence to speak much is mentioned again at line 294. A more detailed portrait of Wallace is deferred until 10.1221–44.
205	The name of the constable of Dundee Castle in 1296 is not known, but the name Selby (line 207) is that of a Northumberland knight who was active in the wars of independence.
215	McDiarmid suggests a "geste" may be Hary's source here (2.140–41n205–07).
219	*Rouch rewlyngis*. That is, roughshod rawhide boots. In his poem on the Battle of Bannockburn, the English poet Laurence Minot used much the same term, "Rughfute riveling" (line 19), as a mocking metonym for the Scots (*The Poems of Laurence Minot*, ed. Richard Osberg [Kalamazoo: Medieval Institute Publications, 1996], p. 36).
275	*lawdayis . . . set ane ayr*. Lawdays were the days appointed for holding courts of law, and justice-ayres were the circuit courts of the sovereign's justice.
282	St. Margaret was Queen Margaret of Scotland (d. 1093), wife of Malcolm Canmore (1057–93). Originally a member of the Saxon royal family, she became

Explanatory Notes to Book 1

renowned for her piety and was canonized in 1249. Her shrine in Dunfermline Abbey (line 287) was a favorite destination for pilgrims.

285   *Landoris*. Lindores, Fife. This suggests they took the ferry across the Tay at the confluence with the River Earn, rather than the Dundee-Tayport ferry near the firth. Lindores was on a major pilgrim route, and shelter could be obtained at the Grange, the home farm of the nearby abbey.

287   Dunfermline, another early Scottish burgh, was also a major trade and communication center because of its proximity to the River Forth.

290   *Lithquhow*. Linlithgow, in what is now West Lothian, was one of the earliest royal Scottish burghs.

294   Note the qualities admired in the young Wallace, especially reticence. See explanatory note to lines 200–01.

296–97   One of the main ferry routes for pilgrims and other travelers in medieval Scotland linked Dunfermline and Queensferry (named after Queen Margaret, see explanatory note to line 282).

299–300   *his eyme . . . persone*. Bower also refers to one of Wallace's uncles as a priest.

304   *sone*. Used throughout the poem in addresses by older to younger male relatives generally.

317   *Corsby*. In Ayrshire, sometimes anglicized on maps as Crosby.

319–21   Hary claims that Wallace's father and his eldest brother Malcolm were killed at the Battle of Loudoun Hill, but Malcolm Wallace was alive in 1299 and history only testifies to a battle there in 1307. See explanatory note to 3.78.

330   *lord Persye*. Henry Percy, a Northumberland knight, was appointed warden of Ayr and Galloway by Edward I in 1296. He played a major part in the Scottish wars. He also appears in *Bruce* 4.598–603. Hary describes him as "captane than of Ayr" at line 379.

355   *uncle Wallas*. Another uncle, Sir Richard Wallace of Riccarton in Kyle, Ayrshire, conjecturally one of the Wallace fees (Barrow [1973], p. 350). It was, perhaps,

one of his three sons mentioned first in 3.43–44 (here paraphrased) who married the widow of the earl of Carrick (the father of the future king, Robert Bruce) in 1306.

363–68   Hary becomes specific about the months Wallace spends in Ayrshire, but the year is still unclear.

368–433 The source for this story of Wallace's violent encounter with Percy's men is probably a traditional tale.

383   *Scot, Martyns fysche*. McDiarmid cites an old Scottish proverb which conveys the sense of "every man for himself" (2.144n383).

399   The Englishman objects to Wallace's use of the familiar "thou" instead of the more appropriate "ye" or "yhe" (lines 385 and 391) that he adopted earlier in the exchange.

Book 2

11   *Auchincruff*. Auchincruive Castle, Ayrshire, was the fee of Richard Wallace (line 13).

16   *Laglyne Wode*. Presumably a nearby forest, later part of the Auchincruive estate. Wallace uses it as a natural stronghold and refuge a number of times in the narrative (2.66; 3.421; 7.262).

27–65   One of three episodes in this book in which Wallace flexes his muscles against the English as he limbers up for organized resistance to the occupation regime Hary has described. Opportunities to display his hero's individual feats of combat are created just as they were for Bruce in Barbour's "romanys." The motif is repeated at lines 78–136, although this time Wallace does not escape his pursuers, and at lines 384–411.

93   A similarly familiar, therefore rude, form of address is found at line 391.

171–359 Note the change of stanza form for Wallace's lament in prison from couplets to a 9-line stanza rhyming *aabaabbab*, except for the first, which rhymes *aabaababb*.

Explanatory Notes to Book 2

234   *Celinus*. Another name for Mercury. McDiarmid reads *Celinius* and relates the allusion to Chaucer's *Compleynt of Mars* where Venus flees "unto Cilenios tour" (line 113) to avoid exposure by Phebus, who catches her with Mars (2.146–47n234).

258   *His fyrst norys*. Wallace's former wet nurse (also referred to as his "foster modyr" at line 270) retrieves his "body" from the castle walls and arranges for him to be carried across the river to Newtown on the north bank of the Ayr river. This may suggest that Wallace's birthplace was in Ayrshire. On the other hand, tradition associates Wallace's birth with Elderslie in Renfrewshire, and it may be that the wet nurse came from Ayrshire to nurse the young Wallace. He later sends her, with her daughter and grand-daughter, to join his own mother in safety there (lines 366–69).

274   A. A. MacDonald notes this motif was probably taken from Valerius Maximus ("The Sense of Place in Early Scottish Verse: Rhetoric and Reality," *English Studies* 72.1 [Feb. 1991], 12–27: 18).

280   To aid the ruse that Wallace is dead the good woman, "[h]is foster modyr" (line 270), places a board covered with woolens and surrounded by lights, as if it were a place of honor for mourning the deceased.

288   Thomas of Ercildoune, otherwise known as Thomas the Rhymer, is mentioned with other soothsayers in the *Scalacronica*. A ballad dating from the fifteenth century recounts some of Thomas the Rhymer's adventures in Elfland. See *The Romance and Prophecies of Thomas of Erceldoune*, ed. James Murray, EETS o.s. 61 (London: N. Trübner, 1875). Hary attributes to Thomas the prophecy that Wallace will three times oust the English from Scotland (lines 346–50).

359   Wallace's raids in England are described in 8.512–620.

416   Sir Richard Wallace of Riccarton. See explanatory note to 1.355. He is said to have three sons (line 418).

436   Robert Boyd is presented by Hary as one of Wallace's loyal companions, along with Adam Wallace, one Kneland, whose first name is never provided, and Edward Litill. Probably he is Robert Boyd of Noddsdale, Cunningham, and coroner of Ayr and Lanark, and possibly the same Sir Robert Boyd whom Barbour identifies as one of Bruce's staunchest supporters (*Bruce* 4.342, 352–63, 505).

The Wallace

Book 3

1–14   Compare to the opening lines of Henryson's fable *The Preiching of the Swallow*.

11–20   Historically, the English did not occupy many castles in 1296. Hary establishes another contrast between the suffering and deprivation of the Scots and the well-provisioned English occupying forces. The irony is that harvest time is approaching. Hary is using a literary device, as the opening lines make apparent, and creating a motive for Wallace's revenge (lines 40–41).

17   *wyn and gud wernage*. The first suggests *vin ordinaire*, red or white, while *wernage* is a malmsey or muscadine, a strong, sweet-flavored white wine.

67   Loudoun Hill, just north of the River Irvine, Ayrshire.

72   *as myn autor me teld*. Like other medieval writers, Hary uses the authority *topos* to create the impression of authenticity.

78   Avondale, not far from Loudoun. McDiarmid suggests that Hary ingeniously created this detour from the usual route from Carlisle to Ayr, via Corsancone, so that he could invent a Battle at Loudoun Hill, drawing details from Barbour's account of Bruce's victory there in 1307 (2.153–54n81). See explanatory note to line 100.

100   There is no evidence to support Hary's account of this battle, although McDiarmid (2.153–54n81) is probably correct in saying that Hary "borrowed" it from Barbour's account of the battle Bruce fought there in 1307 (*Bruce* 8.207–358). The use of "dykes" and the flight of the English are common to both battles.

111–12   Compare to 1.319–20. Hary has mentioned only one brother, Malcolm. He was alive in 1299.

117–18   *knycht Fenweik*. No specific individual has been identified, but McDiarmid points out that a number of persons with this name are mentioned in contemporary records (2.153n62). The expeditions against the Scots may allude to cross-border raids in which Fenwicks (from Northumberland or Cumberland) are known to have been involved.

Explanatory Notes to Book 4

124	*and be*. A medial placement of an introductory conjunction is somewhat common. The sense is: "And he shall again be dragged through the town."
129–32	The polished armor of the English contrasts with the utility of the Scots' armor. The few against the many is a common romance motif, employed by Barbour too.
133–34	*A maner dyk*. This may well refer to a ditch and wall combination of the kind Barbour describes in *Bruce* 8.172–83.
188	*Bewmound*. Beaumont, a squire, is not to be confused with Beaumont, earl of Buchan (according to Hary), who appears from Book 7 on.
193	*hors repende rouschede frekis undir feit. Repende*: "kicking, plunging"; *rouschede*: "rushed," i.e., "charged." The alliterative surge of violence almost overwhelms the syntax as the horses crush men underfoot.
207	Kyle and Cunningham were two districts of Ayrshire. Boyd held land in Cunningham. See explanatory note to 2.436.
214	Clyde Forest was on the north side of the River Clyde.

Book 4

1–10	Hary's literary pretensions are most evident in rhetorical set pieces of this kind in which the month (September) and the season (autumn) are described.
3	Victuals in this sense include all harvestable foods, such as grain, berries, vegetables, and so on.
9	The mutability of worldly things is a medieval commonplace.
15–16	A sheriff was "the principal royal officer in local districts into which the kingdom was divided for the purposes of royal government" (Barrow [1988], p. 8). Sir Ranald inherited the position *throw rycht* (line 16), reflecting the tendency for a sheriff's office to become heritable.

The Wallace

18	*as witnes beris the buk.* Another invocation of his written source, or authority. The book cited here is presumably the fictitious one by Blair, which Hary claims as his main authority on Wallace.
22–54	Another instance of aggression between Wallace's and Percy's baggage men. See explanatory note to 1.368–433.
26	*Hesilden.* Hazelden, Renfrewshire, south of Glasgow.
71	*the Mernys.* Newton Mearns.
325–44	This passage, like set pieces in chronicles magnifying the qualities of the land, for better or worse, celebrates Scotland's plenty (and depravity). Compare with Barbour's account of food resources in Aberdeenshire (*Bruce* 2.577–84) after his defeat at Methven. Methven Park later became a favorite royal hunting reserve.
335–40	The device of anaphora (now . . . now) is employed to effect the full range of Scotland's character.
341	Hary points out that Wallace will fight for Scotland's independence (*Scotlandis rycht*) for 6 years and 7 months, and predicts what is to come, but of course the chronology is Hary's own.
359	*mar.* The chief magistrate of a town. According to the *DOST*, *mar* normally referred to the mayor or magistrate of an English town, but is used here of Perth, a town occupied by the English. There is also an old Scottish Gaelic term, *maor*, meaning steward or bailiff.
395–96	Sir James Butler's son, Sir John, is said to be deputy captain, and Sir Garaid (Gerard) Heroun to be the captain of Kinclaven Castle (line 396). A Robert Heron was appointed chamberlain comptroller in Scotland in 1305, but no Sir Gerard Heron has been identified as active in Scotland during this period.
441	Ninety English soldiers arrive, led by Butler, as becomes clear at line 457.
718 ff.	Hary makes clear the precariousness of the woman's actions. Death by burning was the usual punishment for high treason decreed for women.
723	Wallace is referred to as a *rebell.* He later denies this vociferously.

Explanatory Notes to Book 5

740   *Rycht unperfyt I am of Venus play*. Compare to Chaucer, whose narrators in the dream vision poems often profess inexperience in the ways of Venus.

787   *South Inche*. McDiarmid notes the town had a North and South Inch, or lawn (2.166n787).

Book 5

95   Gask Wood, like Gask Hall (line 175), is on the left bank of the River Earn.

180–214   No specific source for this ghost story is known. Hary refers to Wallace's experience as a *fantasé* (line 212), which McDiarmid notes conforms to what Chaucer calls "infernals illusions" in medieval dream lore, i.e., fantasies that lured men to their destruction (2.169n180–224). On possible Celtic sources for the Fawdoun episode, see Balaban, p. 248.

211 ff.   Hary ponders on the *fantasé* (line 212) and compares the *myscheiff* (line 217) to Lucifer's fall. Note the echo of Barbour (1.259–60) about leaving discussion of such matters to clerks (lines 223–25).

219–24   *Or quhat it was in liknes . . . .* McDiarmid refers to Dante's *Inferno* in which it is disclosed that fiends take over the bodies of traitors once the soul has departed (2.170n221–22). In his *Daemonologie* (1597), King James VI discusses possession of dead bodies by devils, calling such specters *umbrae mortuorum* (ch. 6.23–25; 7.16–18).

389–94   Note the use of the appropriately familiar form of address by the parson. But when the English adopt the familiar form the intention is to insult Wallace.

465–66   *In Bothwell . . . / With ane Craufurd*. The *Crawford* is presumably a kinsman of Wallace. After a night in Bothwell, Lanarkshire, Wallace moves on to Gilbank (line 467), not far from Lanark, where another uncle, Auchinleck, Sir Reginald Crawford's brother, shelters him (line 469).

467   Gilbank was identified by Jamieson as a property in Lanarkshire, held in tribute by Auchinleck, as noted by McDiarmid (2.174n467).

The Wallace

470–80 Presumably family tradition provided Hary with the details of these relationships; for example, that Auchinleck married Sir Reginald's widow, the daughter of the laird of Lesmahago (line 474), and fathered three children, one of whom was the son mentioned at line 477. The Crawfords, as noted before (line 466), were hereditary sheriffs of Ayr. Percy would have received homage from Sir Reginald when he was installed as part of Edward's administration in 1296.

474 *Lesmahago*. In Lanarkshire.

487 *Loran*. William Loran, Butler's nephew.

506 Percy is thinking about the need to appoint a new garrison at Perth, and he makes arrangements for this at lines 519–20. No arrangements are made for Kinclaven, which has been reduced to ruins (line 521).

508 *clerkys sayis*. Another reference to prophecies that haunt Wallace.

514 *nacioune*. One of the earliest uses of this term to refer to an identifiable nation. Wyntoun also uses it in this sense (7.408).

519 The Siwards of Tibbers and Aberdour in Fife were one of the chief Scottish baronial families. Sir Richard Siward was son-in-law to Sir John Comyn and after his capture at the Battle of Dunbar he became a prominent member of Edward I's administration in Scotland. He is known to have been sheriff of Fife and also of Dumfries, as well as warden of Nithsdale, but surviving records do not indicate whether he was ever sheriff of Perth. See also explanatory note to 7.1017.

533–45 Hary's putative sources, John Blair and Thomas Gray, are depicted as scholars and eye-witnesses. As Hary had a friend by the name of Blair, a compliment may be intended.

569–71 William Hesilrig was a Northumberland knight appointed as sheriff of Lanark in 1296 as part of the new administration. He is mentioned in the *Scalacronica*, p. 123.

579–710 Hary cites a *buk* (line 580) as authority for the story of Wallace's sweetheart. Wallace's courtship of a maiden in Lanark is also told by Wyntoun, who briefly relates how Wallace's "lemman" in Lanark dies at the hands of the town's sheriff for assisting the hero's escape from the town (8.13.2075 ff.). Unlike the

Explanatory Notes to Book 5

"lemman" in Perth, this maiden is the daughter of a late, respectable Lanarkshire landowner. She later declares that she *wyll no lemman be* (line 693). Her noble parentage, beauty, manners, and virtues are all noticed. Hary names her father as Hew Braidfute of Lammington (line 584), which is in Lanarkshire, but the family has not been identified. He stresses her vulnerability, as she lacks the protection of parents and her brother has been killed. Among her qualities is piety: Wallace falls in love when he first sees her in church. That Hary's model is Criseyde from Chaucer's *Troilus and Criseyde* is clear in lines 605–06. See Harward, pp. 48–50.

606   *The prent of luff*. Derived from Aristotelian philosophy, this conception of love as a deep impression made on, and retained in, the heart is also found in Robert Henryson's *Testament of Cresseid* (lines 505–11).

609   *hyr kynrent and hyr blud*. These are credentials that make her attractive to him.

631–32   Compare Troilus's attitude in *Troilus and Criseyde* (1.191–203).

685 ff.   See Chaucer's The Franklin's Tale (*CT* V[F]741–50) for a similar "accord" (V[F]741), especially concerning service in love.

719–61   Wallace moves into Annandale, traveling from Corehead, in Moffatdale, to Lochmaben Castle, where he kills the captain.

720   This familial relationship between Thom Haliday and Wallace is not otherwise attested. The purported relationship gives Wallace an extended family and support network. See 6.535–37 and explanatory note to 6.537, below.

721   *Litill*. Edward Litill from Annandale. See explanatory note to 2.436.

737   Sir Robert Clifford, a Westmoreland knight, was active in Scotland from 1296. He has known associations with Caerlaverock and Carlisle castles, so may well have had a cousin who was captain of Lochmaben. He was warden of Galloway from 1298 and appointed captain of the southwest garrisons, which were regularly under attack from the Scots. He defended Lochmaben from Bruce in 1307 and was killed at Bannockburn. Hary is inclined to make family vengeance a motivating force. Compare his treatment of the Butlers.

755   A marshal was originally one who tended horses. Later it was the title of a high-ranking officer in a royal court.

The Wallace

757–65 Another instance of Hary's grim humor. As well as shaving, barbers also let blood.

766–970 Wallace and his small company are pursued by soldiers from Lochmaben. Running combat ensues as the English give chase through the Knockwood (line 777) and Wallace tries to return to Corehead, avoiding open battle. Reinforcements are provided when needed most by Sir John Graham and one Kirkpatrick, whereupon the pursuit is reversed.

804–09 This is the "few against many" motif again.

815–18 Hugh of Morland, another Westmoreland knight, and a veteran according to Hary, was probably involved in border warfare long before the war with Scotland broke out. Although many of the specific persons mentioned by Hary cannot be identified precisely, their names are often authentic in that they can be linked to geographical places.

841 ff. Wallace is presented as an exemplary chieftain.

Book 6

1–104 This preamble links Wallace's fortunes to love, and anticipates the loss of his beloved. The meter adopted here is appropriate for tragedy, as in Chaucer's The Monk's Tale, and incorporates Wallace's complaint, lines 29–40. Hary appropriates the conventional spring *topos* for the opening of Book 6, associating April, the last month of spring (line 3), with Wallace's sufferings on account of love. The opening lines are not easy to follow though. Hary begins with what seems to be a reference to Christian liturgical use, with his allusion to the *utas of Feviryher* (line 1). *Utas* or "octave" was the eighth day after a feast day, counting the day itself. The term was also used of the whole period of eight days, so McDiarmid's suggestion that Hary may simply mean the weeks of February may be correct. The reference to the appearance of April when only part of March has passed (line 2), may be explained, as McDiarmid suggests, as an allusion to the Roman calends of April, which began on March 16 (2.181n1–2).

25 *feyr of wer*. Here and at line 40 but with different, though connected, meanings.

Explanatory Notes to Book 6

44–56   *concord.* The influence of the "accord" (*CT* V[F]791) between Arveragus and Dorigen in Chaucer's The Franklin's Tale (V[F]791–99) is unmistakable, especially the echoes in the next stanza. A further debt to Chaucer's *Complaint of Mars* (2.76–77) is detected by McDiarmid in lines 54–56 (2.183n54–56). An idealized relationship, based on literary models, is certainly indicated.

57   *doubill face.* The duplicitous face of Fortune is frequently used to convey the arbitrary nature of her power. See, for example, Chaucer's *The Book of the Duchess*, lines 626–34.

60–61   The rhetorical figures of antithesis and anaphora combine in the *now . . . now* construction, and again at lines 81–85.

71   *A Squier Schaw.* McDiarmid implies that Hary may have been influenced by the fact that around the time he was writing his poem one of James IV's squires was a John Shaw (2.183n71).

88   McDiarmid (2.184n88) finds an echo of *Troilus and Criseyde* 4.296: "On lyve in torment and in cruwel peyne."

94   *na hap to ho.* Literally "no destiny to stop," i.e., destined not to stop.

97–101   The role of Fortune and the contrast between this corrupt, changeable world and perfect heaven are conventional and undoubtedly influenced by Boethian philosophy. An extended treatment of the theme can be found in *The Kingis Quair* by James I of Scotland (1394–1437).

107–271   The date is very precise and alerts us to his source, Wyntoun's *Cronykil*, Book 8, ch. 13. Hary lifts the ensuing dialogue straight from Wyntoun (8.13.2038–48) but he elaborates on Wyntoun in his account of the lead-up to the confrontation (8.13.2029–37).

113   Robert Thorn, supposedly an English officer too, has not been identified.

114–18   "Has found the best way / To act against Wallace / By picking a quarrel with him as he happened to come / From the church in town, / While their company would be armed." Note the assumption that Wallace would be unarmed (i.e., without armor) and so vulnerable. See line 125 where he and his company are dressed in seasonal green.

The Wallace

124–264 Hary may have had another source for his account of the death of Wallace's sweetheart and the revenge killing of Heselrig than Wyntoun's Book 8, ch. 8. The killing of the sheriff and the burning of the town are attested in other sources.

132 *Dewgar . . . bone senyhour*. Hesilrig attempts to insult Wallace with French idioms, implying that he is an effete foreigner newly come from France (line 134) or a mock-courtier. Wallace replies to the scornful address by contemptuous use of single pronouns in his response (line 133).

136 McDiarmid suggests a contemporary reference to Princess Margaret, who was brought from Denmark to Scotland in 1469 (see 2.183n71 and 2.185n134–36).

140 Here the English mock Scots idioms of salutation. McDiarmid (2.185n140) points out that this is a series of sarcastic greetings, initially in dialect, then in pidgin-Gaelic, meaning something like: "Good evening, [give me] drink Lord, furious champion, God's blessing [on you]."

182 *The woman*. This is a reference to Wallace's wife, as the following lines indicate.

190 Cartland Crags, two miles northwest of Lanark.

193–94 Hary employs the rhetorical strategy of the "inability" *topos* and, as Goldstein (1993) observes, "The episode is no less powerful for its calculated understatement" (p. 228).

265–66 Wyntoun: "Fra he thus the Schirrawe slew, / Scottis men fast till hym drew" (8.8.2117–18).

268 *that gret barnage*. That is, the English occupying forces.

271–72 The debt to Wyntoun is apparent:

> And this Willame thai made thare
> Our thame chefftane and leddare. (8.8.2121–22)

The idea of Wallace as the people's choice is common to both.

275 Murray of Bothwell, said to be the rightful owner of Bothwell Castle, a vital stronghold which commanded the direct route from northern Scotland to the southwest (Barrow [1988], p. 121). This must be a reference to the father of

Explanatory Notes to Book 6

Andrew Murray, later Guardian of Scotland. At this time Bothwell Castle was still the property of the Oliphants. When Andrew Murray inherited it he became known as Murray of Bothwell.

297–318   Jop becomes Wallace's herald. Although Hary gives him a history, he is otherwise unknown. Grimsby is possibly Gilbert de Grimsby, who carried the banner of St. John of Beverley in Edward's progress through Scotland after Dunbar. McDiarmid notes that a William Grymesby of Grimsby stayed for a while at Linlithgow Palace in 1461, and the poet may well have met him there (2.188n297–318).

302–12   Compare Chaucer's portraits of the merchant and seaman in The General Prologue.

309   A pursuivant was the junior heraldic officer below the rank of herald.

329   His oath of allegiance to Edward must have been made in 1296.

336   *Schir Jhone of Tynto*. The association with Tinto suggests he was a Lanarkshire knight, but he has not been identified.

342   This is fabricated, as is the ensuing Battle of Biggar. Edward did not bring an army to Scotland again until 1298, when the Battle of Falkirk was fought.

363–66   Note the romance motif of disguise in battle. Fehew, or Fitzhugh, is a brother of the Fehew who is later beheaded by Wallace while defending his castle of Ravensworth (8.1010–69). McDiarmid notes that a Fitzhugh fought at Bannockburn and refers to another Fitzhugh who was a prominent contemporary of Hary (2.189n363). The relationship to Edward is a complete fabrication, used to introduce a tale about how a nephew's head was sent to Edward with Wallace's reply to the king's writ.

410   Possibly a reference to the tournaments in which heralds relied on their specialist knowledge of participants' coats of arms.

417–19   Wyntoun memorably likened one of Edward's terrible rages to the writhing effects brought on from eating a spider! (8.11.1773–78).

The Wallace

434–73   McDiarmid notes that the same story is told of Hereward the Wake (2.190n434–75).

444   A mark or merk was worth thirteen shillings and four pence.

506   *Somervaill.* McDiarmid identifies him as Sir Thomas Somerville (2.190n506). The Somervilles owned lands in Linton, Roxburghshire, and Carnwath, Lanarkshire (Barrow [1988], p. 325). Sir Walter and his son David of Newbigging (lines 508–10) were probably Somerville retainers. Sir John Tynto (line 509) was another Lanarkshire knight. See explanatory note to line 336.

517–26   Hary's debt to *The Book of Alexander*, possibly indirectly through Barbour, has been noted by McDiarmid (2.191n516–26) and others.

537   *Jhonstoun* and *Rudyrfurd* are place names, and may refer to Sir John of Johnstone and Sir Nicholas of Rutherford, as McDiarmid suggests. Hary claims they are the sons of Haliday (see explanatory note to 5.720).

540   Members of the Jardine family, associated with Annandale, were active in the wars.

543–765   Battle of Biggar. A fabrication that may very well draw on a variety of sources in which other battles and campaigns are depicted, in particular the accounts by Froissart and Barbour of James Douglas' Weardale campaign, especially the skirmish at Stanhope Park, and details from the Battle of Roslin in 1303 found in Wyntoun and Bower. There are many anachronisms therefore in the account of this fictitious battle and its aftermath. Among Hary's most blatant fabrications is his claim that a number of Edward I's relatives were killed at Biggar (lines 649–54).

561   *erll of Kent.* McDiarmid identifies him as Edmund of Woodstock, uncle of Edward III (2.192n561).

592   *that cheiff chyftayne he slew.* I.e., the earl of Kent. The historical earl was actually executed in 1330.

638–41   Supplies are taken to Rob's Bog while Wallace moves his troops to nearby Devenshaw Hill on the right bank of the Clyde River.

Explanatory Notes to Book 6

645   John's Green is probably Greenfield near Crawfordjohn.

669   *duk of Longcastell*. Duke of Lancaster. McDiarmid (2.194n669) points out this is an anachronism, like the reference to the lord of Westmoreland (line 685). The earl of Lancaster at this time was Edmund, brother of Edward I. In 1298 the son Thomas succeeded.

689–91   *A Pykart lord* as keeper of Calais is another anachronism derived from Edward III's French wars.

694   *Schir Rawff Gray*. Hary makes him warden of Roxburgh Castle (8.496–98, here paraphrased), but when it was surrendered to Edward by the Stewart in 1296 the English knight Sir Robert Hastings became keeper (as well as sheriff of Roxburgh) until 1305 when Edward I's nephew, John of Brittany, was appointed the lieutenant of Scotland and keeper of this militarily vital castle (Watson, p. 216). But according to McDiarmid, the name of the English warden of Roxburgh Castle in 1435–36 was Sir Ralph Gray, so this is another anachronism.

698   *Eduuardis man*. Sir Amer de Valence was Edward I's lieutenant in Scotland and was later created earl of Pembroke (1307). He was not a Scot, as Hary seems to suggest, although the description *fals* may refer to the role he later played in commissioning John Menteith to betray Wallace (Book 12). The influence of Barbour is detectable in the reference to Valence immediately after Loudoun Hill, and the connection with Bothwell (similarly in 6.274).

749   The name of the captain of Berwick in 1297 is not known but, as Watson observes, the majority of appointments do not survive in the official record (p. 33). Both Roxburgh and Berwick were strategically very important, as Hary acknowledges (8.1551–52).

761   *Byrkhill*. Birkhall, near Moffat.

765   *Braidwood*. Braidwood, Lanarkshire.

767   *Forestkyrk*. Forestkirk was the old name for Carluke, Clydesdale.

768   The exact date of Wallace's appointment as Guardian of Scotland is unknown, but Barrow (1988) believes it must have been before March 1298 (p. 96). Hary's use

The Wallace

of Wyntoun here and at lines 784–86 is evident (Wyntoun 8.12.2121–22). See also Bower 11.28.

771 *Schir Wilyham*. Sir William Douglas had been the commander of Berwick Castle when Edward sacked it in 1296. He had certainly joined forces with Wallace by May 1297 when together they attacked William Ormsby, the English justiciary at Scone (of which Hary makes no mention). William Douglas' son, Sir James Douglas, was Bruce's companion in arms.

802 *Adam Gordone*. Adam Gordon, a kinsman of the earls of Dunbar (with Gordon in Berwickshire as his principal estate), was a known Balliol adherent (Barrow [1988], p. 189). By 1300 he was the Scots warden of the West March. He later became a prominent magnate under Robert Bruce.

836 *Towrnbery*. Turnberry was the chief castle of Carrick. Around the same time that Wallace slew the sheriff of Ayr, Robert Bruce led a revolt against Edward I in Carrick.

851–53 Wallace administers justice, in keeping with his duty as a Guardian. Bruce similarly rewards *trew* (line 853) men in Barbour's narrative.

854 *brothir sone*. I.e., Wallace's nephew. McDiarmid (2.197n854) takes this as a reference to his elder brother's son, Malcolm, who would have inherited the patrimony as the eldest son, and on his death (which Hary had said took place at Loudoun Hill) his son would have been heir.

855 *Blak Crag*. Blackcraig Castle in the parish of Cumnock, Ayrshire. "His houshauld" (line 856) suggests (like "his duellyng" in line 940) a reference to Wallace's own castle, which is confirmed in Book 12.937–38. This has fed the belief retained by some that Wallace was born in Ayrshire.

863 *byschope Beik*. Anthony Bek, bishop of Durham and Edward's lieutenant in Scotland until August 1296. In Book 1 (lines 171–72) Hary had said that Glasgow diocese was transferred to the jurisdiction of Durham.

865 *Erll of Stamffurd . . . chanslar*. John Langton was actually chancellor of England at this time. Hary may be confusing him with Sir Thomas Staunford, a member of Sir Henry Percy's retinue (Watson, p. 44), especially as he has referred to Percy in the preceding lines (lines 862–64).

Explanatory Notes to Book 7

869   *Ruglen Kyrk*. Rutherglen Church near Glasgow.

Book 7

1–2   If Hary's chronology were at all consistent, this would refer to February 1298 since in the previous book he had placed the killing of Heselrig some time after April of 1297; but the Battle of Stirling Bridge (11 September 1297) will be described later in this book.

7–9   *In Aperill . . . Into Carleill*. According to the records, after he returned from Flanders on 8 April 1298, Edward summoned his leading commanders in Scotland to a royal council at York. On the same date he also ordered a muster of Welsh foot-soldiers at Carlisle (Watson, p. 61) as part of his campaign to invade Scotland. Hary may be confusing preparations before the Battle of Falkirk with those before Stirling Bridge, the previous year.

16   A very striking image of genocide, as Goldstein (1993) notes (p. 231).

23–29   The plans for the wholly fictitious murder of leading Scots, referred to by Hary as *gret bernys* of Ayr (line 25), are hatched. Hary's respect for Percy leads him to dissociate him from the atrocity (lines 31–36).

38   *his new law*. This relates to the justice-ayre that Bek is to hold in Glasgow. McDiarmid finds corroboration in line 517 (2.199n38).

40–41   Arnulf of Sothampton appears to be fictitious. None of the earls of Southampton had this first name. Later Hary mentions that Arnulf received Ayr castle, presumably as a reward for the executions (lines 507–08).

56   *maistré*. Barbour also uses it in the sense of display of might. It is clearly seen as a provocative act in time of truce.

58   *Monktoun Kyrk*. Monkton Church, near Ayr in the west of Scotland.

61   *Maister Jhone*. Probably another reference to Master John Blair (5.533). McDiarmid takes it as evidence of Blair's Ayrshire origins, saying Adamton, the seat of the Blair family, was in Monkton parish (2.199n62). He attempts to warn

The Wallace

Wallace to stay away from the justice-ayre at Ayr because he knows it is ominous that Lord Percy has left the region (lines 63–64).

68–152 Wallace falls asleep and has a vision in the form of a dream. There are plenty of literary models for this dream-vision, including Chaucer's *Parliament of Fowls* and *House of Fame*. A particular debt to the fourteenth-century poem *The Alliterative Morte Arthure,* in which King Arthur is visited by Lady Fortune in a dream, has been proposed. In his dream, Wallace is visited first by St. Andrew and then by the Virgin Mary. A vision of St. Andrew confirming Wallace's divinely ordained role as governor of Scotland is mentioned in the Coupar Angus MS of Bower's *Scotichronicon* (11.28) and probably derived from traditional tales known to both Bower and Hary (see D. E. R. Watt, Notes to *Scotichronicon* 6.236n35–37).

94 *saffyr*. The sapphire is interpreted at lines 139–40 as everlasting grace.

123 In L there are the following Protestant substitutions: *The stalwart man* instead of *Saynct Androw*, and "Goddis saik" replaces "For Marys saik" in line 291.

178–90 *Jupiter, Mars . . . Saturn*. These allusions recall Chaucer's The Knight's Tale, *CT* I(A)2454–69, as previous readers have noted. The echoes are particularly striking in lines 183 and 185.

190 *heast sper*. In the earth-centered medieval cosmography, Saturn, like the other planets, moved within its own sphere. The moon moved within the sphere closest to the earth, while Saturn moved in the sphere furthest away, or highest in the heavens.

191–92 The death of the Argive hero and seer Amphiorax (*Phiorax*, line 192), or Amphiaraus, is told at the end of Statius's *Thebaid* 7. McDiarmid cites *Troilus and Criseyde* 5.100–05, and Lydgate's *Siege of Thebes* as Hary's more immediate sources (2.202n191–92).

195 *Burdeous*. Bordeaux. McDiarmid (2.202n195) reckons Hary is referring to Charles VII's capture of Bordeaux (1453), in which case this is another anachronism.

197–98 *braid Brytane feill vengeance . . . .* This may be a veiled reference to recent or contemporary history, but it is too vague for more than speculation.

Explanatory Notes to Book 7

202   *towboth*. Tolbooths were prisons and, traditionally, execution sites in Scotland.

205–10   Sir Reginald Crawford and Sir Bryce Blair — who, like Robert Boyd (2.436), was a Cunningham knight — were actually executed much later: Blair was hanged, possibly in a barn in Ayr in 1306, while Crawford was hanged and beheaded at Carlisle in 1307. Hary's source was *Bruce* 4.36–38:

> Off Crauford als Schyr Ranald wes
> And Schyr Bryce als þe Blar
> Hangyt in-till a berne in Ar.

214   *Schir Neill of Mungumry*. Unknown. McDiarmid (2.202n214) suggests Hary may have meant Neil Bruce, Robert Bruce's brother, because his summary execution after a valiant defence of Kildrummy castle is described by Barbour shortly after the lines quoted above (*Bruce* 4.59–61, 314–22).

218–20   The Crawfords, Kennedys, and Campbells came from the southwest (Carrick and Ayrshire), while the Boyds and Stewarts, originally from Renfrewshire, became kinsmen of Robert I through marriage. The Stewarts eventually formed a royal dynasty. McDiarmid may be correct in saying that some are names Hary wished to honor in his own day (pp. xlix, lvii).

229   *curssit Saxons seid*. One of Hary's many disparaging references to the "enemy." The English are first referred to as Saxons in 1.7.

237   Hary's partisan view is in evidence and, as in the opening lines of Book 1, here he makes an appeal to contemporaries.

280–81   There is a possible echo of Suetonius's account of the covering up of the assassinated Julius Caesar (to preserve his dignity), which Hary could have known through Fordun (*Chronica* 2.17).

288   William Crawford, presumably Sir Reginald's son.

331   *deill thar landis*. He refers to the lands of the murdered Scottish barons. See lines 436–37, below.

342   McDiarmid (2.203n342) says Irish ale is whisky, but I have been unable to confirm this.

The Wallace

346–49	Note the emotive language used here to condemn the English. Goldstein (1993) cites this as an example of Hary's "racist discourse" (pp. 224–25).
362	*burges*. A burgess was a citizen of a burgh, a freeman.
380	*Adam . . . lord of Ricardtoun*. Adam Wallace. See explanatory note to 1.144. Riccarton in Kyle, Ayrshire was long associated with the Wallace family as noted earlier (explanatory note to 1.355). See explanatory note to 5.465–66, above, on Auckinleck.
385–86	Wallace's divine mission is thus manifest.
400–01	Compare Chaucer on true nobility in his lyric on *Gentilesse*, and the curtain lecture in The Wife of Bath's Tale (III[D]1109–64).
403	*the Roddis*. The island of Rhodes, possibly a contemporary reference by Hary to the Knights of St. John, as McDiarmid suggests (2.204n403).
408	*der nece*. This is the "trew" woman (line 252) who had warned him to stay away from the barns and advised that the English were drunk.
434–35	The lines are bitterly ironic and allude, of course, to the treachery perpetrated at the barns of Ayr and the revenge about to be taken.
440	A typical example of Hary's grim humor.
450–70	The repetitions and heavy alliterations are particularly effective in conveying the merciless killings described in these lines.
453–54	"Some rushed quickly to reach Ayr, if they could. / Blinded by fire, they could not see properly what they were doing." McDiarmid interprets *thar deidis war full dym* as "their deaths were in utter darkness" (2.204n454), but line 472 makes clear that some did escape.
471	There was a Dominican priory in Ayr, and Drumley was the name of a property not far from Ayr that belonged to the Gilbertine monastery of Dalmulin, according to McDiarmid (2.205n471).
488	*the furd weill*. McDiarmid suggests this is St. Katherine's Well (2.205n488).

Explanatory Notes to Book 7

491–92	Compare the irreverent humor here with lines 546–47, below.
559	Throughout *The Wallace* Hary is generous in his praise of warriors from Northumberland. Their mettle would have been tested in border warfare over many years. See line 585 for corroboration.
579–80	*strang stour . . . the clowdis past.* The dust raised by horses and clashing forces. McDiarmid cites James Scott's comment that such vivid imagery is not to be expected from a man born blind (2.205n579–80).
585	The Percy's men are said to be experienced warriors, just as men of Northumberland are acknowledged as "gud men of wer" (line 559).
595–96	Wallace kills Percy. Factually this is untrue since Henry Percy was alive until 1314. Robert Bruce's attack on Percy and his garrison in Turnberry Castle is described by Barbour (*Bruce* 5.43–116).
607	*that place.* I.e., Bothwell, which is occupied by Valence, as Hary has observed.
609–11	*began of nycht ten houris in Ayr.* "Started from Ayr at ten o'clock at night." Hary reckons it took Wallace fifteen hours altogether to travel from Ayr via Glasgow to Bothwell (Ayr to Glasgow 11 hours, Glasgow to Bothwell 4 hours).
613	The impression of verisimilitude is bolstered by another reference to an authoritative source, *the buk*.
617–954	While disturbances are known to have occurred in the first half of 1297 in the west Highlands, Aberdeenshire and Galloway, Wallace's involvement in any of these is not confirmed by other sources. After he killed the sheriff of Lanark his next recorded strike, with William Douglas, was against the English justice at Scone in May. Hary does not mention this.
620	The recital of names is probably more important than any particular individuals here.
621–23	*Apon Argyll a fellone wer . . . .* John of Lorn is described as "Fals" (line 629), perhaps because, with his father, Alexander MacDougall, lord of the Isles, he submitted to Edward in 1296. He was a Balliol supporter, and was related to John Comyn; after the latter's murder, he became Bruce's implacable enemy.

The Wallace

623	Probably Sir Neil Campbell of Loch Awe, who plays a part as one of Bruce's closest companions in *The Bruce* (2.494; 3.393, 570–74).
626–28	*Makfadyan*. Said to have sworn fealty to Edward, but probably not a historical person. As McDiarmid points out (2.206–07n626), these "events" are modeled on Barbour's account of the Lorn episodes (*Bruce* 10.5–134).
633	Duncan of Lorn was Alexander MacDougall's second son.
643	McDiarmid glosses *Irland* as Hebridean islands (2.207n643). *The Wallace* uses "Irland" to designate northern and western Celtic settlements on the mainland (Highlands) and the Gaelic inhabited islands. See OED, *Irish* adj. 1.
647	*Louchow*. Loch Awe region, near Lorn.
649	*Crage Unyn*. McDiarmid identifies this as Craiganuni (2.207–08n649).
670	This is the second reference to Wallace's schooling in Dundee. Duncan of Lorn is said to have been Wallace's school companion.
673	*Gylmychell*. Possibly a member of the local clan Gillymichael.
679	Sir Richard Lundy is consistently presented as a patriot by Hary, fighting with Wallace at the Battle of Stirling (7.1237). The historical Lundy actually went over to the English when the Scots leaders prepared to surrender at Irvine in 1297. He was with the English at Bannockburn (1314). The Lundy family held estates in Angus.
685	*The Rukbé*. Another anachronism, if the allusion is to Thomas Rokeby, mayor of Stirling Castle in 1336–39, as McDiarmid suggests (2.209n685–86). The sheriff of Stirling, and probably the keeper of Stirling Castle at the time, was Sir Richard Waldergrave.
723	Lennox men were known for their patriotism, and their loyalty to their "lord," Earl Malcolm.
755	*In Brucis wer agayne come in Scotland*. There is no mention of them in *The Bruce*.

Explanatory Notes to Book 7

757–58   *Mencione of Bruce* .... Another reference to the spurious biography by Blair. The claim that Wallace fought for Bruce, *[t]o fend his rycht* (line 758), is incorrect, since the historical Wallace fought for Balliol, not Bruce.

764   *small fute folk*. As McDiarmid notes, these were lightly armed auxiliaries (2.210n764).

776   *westland men*. Warriors from the west country, presumably from Argyll.

798   *Cragmor*. Creag Mhor, facing Loch Awe.

842   *Yrage blud*. The "Irish" here refers to Celtic clansmen, whether from the Highlands, the Hebrides, or Ireland.

849   In other words, native Scots threw themselves on the mercy of Wallace.

880   John was the heir and Duncan was his younger brother, not his uncle. The MacDougalls were related to the Comyns and were Balliol supporters.

890   Sir John Ramsay is briefly mentioned by Barbour as a member of Edward Bruce's retinue bound for Ireland (*Bruce* 14.29).

900–02   Although Barbour describes Ramsay of Auchterhouse as chivalrous (*Bruce* 14.29–30), McDiarmid notes there is no such reference to Sir Alexander Ramsay in *The Bruce* (2.211n901–02).

913   There is no reason to believe that Ramsay held Roxburgh Castle. See explanatory note to 6.694.

917   Hary comments on his own inclination to digress and the criticism it attracts, employing a well-known rhetorical *topos*.

927–32   *a gud prelat*. I.e., Bishop Sinclair. Another anachronism, as he was not made bishop until 1312. Barbour had celebrated his exemplary leadership against an English invasion of Fife in 1317. Hary's wish to honor the "Synclar blude" (line 930), as the Sinclairs were prominent literary patrons in Hary's day, may explain this passage.

The Wallace

938 *Lord Stewart*. Lord James Stewart was hereditary lord of Bute (line 936). He had served as a Guardian during the interregnum and had been given charge of a new sheriffdom of Kyntyre by John Balliol during his short reign. He surrendered to Percy and Clifford in July 1297, but had joined Wallace by the Battle of Stirling Bridge.

980 *The wattir doun . . . to that steid*. I.e., along the Tay River to Perth, or St. John's Town, as it was known.

981 Ramsay is said to be their guide, presumably because he knows the area so well, since he held lands in neighboring Angus.

983–1027 The assault on Perth. Bruce had mounted an attack on Perth in June 1306 and, as in Hary's account of Wallace's assault, he had approached from the west. The Battle of Methven followed. Perth was not won by Wallace, and the installation of Sir William of Ruthven as sheriff in 1297 is another fabrication. See explanatory notes to lines 1017, 1025, and 1281, below.

990 Turret Bridge was on the southwest side of Perth (McDiarmid 2.213n990).

1017 *Jhon Sewart*. Sir John Sewart or Siward. See explanatory note to 5.519. The Siwards were a Fife baronial family. The implication is that Siward was the keeper of the castle or sheriff of the town who was replaced by Ruthven (lines 1025–27), but this seems unlikely.

1025 *Rwan*. McDiarmid identifies him as Sir William de Rothievan (i.e., Ruthven), who swore fealty to Edward in 1291 (2.213n1025–28).

1031 *Cowper*. Coupar Abbey in Angus.

1044 *Dwnottar*. Dunnottar Castle on the east coast of Scotland.

1078 *Lord Bewmound*. Sir Henry Beaumont, a cousin of Edward II, had married Alice Comyn, an heiress to the earldom of Buchan. He fought at Bannockburn.

1079 *Erll he was*. Beaumont was an earl, but not of Buchan as Hary claims (line 1077). John Comyn was earl of Buchan 1289–1308 and died childless (Barrow [1988], p. 271).

Explanatory Notes to Book 7

1082   *Slanys.* Slains Castle was on the coast.

1088   *Lammes evyn.* I.e., July 31. Lammas Day is the first day of August, and traditionally the day on which there was thanksgiving for harvest.

1089   *Stablyt.* In the sense of settled the affairs of the kingdom, i.e., through the appointment of officers and the distribution of lands as rewards.

1090–1127   A number of sources, including Wyntoun (8.8.2147–50) and Bower (11.27), confirm that Wallace was laying siege to Dundee in August 1297 when he heard about the English forces sent by Edward to Stirling.

1102   *Kercyingame.* Sir Hugh de Cressingham, Edward's treasurer in Scotland. He seems to have become a hated figure in Scotland, and his corpse was flayed when discovered after the Scottish victory at Stirling Bridge.

1103   *Waran.* Sir John de Warenne, earl of Surrey, appointed keeper of the kingdom and land of Scotland, had commanded the English army at the siege of Dunbar.

1110–19   These lines refer to the capture of Dunbar that Hary referred to earlier, in Book 1. Although Earl Patrick was an adherent of Edward I, his wife remained a Scottish patriot. As the earl of Warenne prepared to take Dunbar Castle in 1296, the countess tricked her husband's garrison into admitting the Scottish forces to the castle. Some of Hary's details may have come from the Guisborough chronicle (lines 977–78). For a full account, see Barrow (1988), p. 72.

1129   *Angwis men.* Men of Angus.

1144–45   Wallace sends the herald Jop to inform the Scots that the battle will take place on the next Tuesday.

1145–1218   Battle of Stirling Bridge. A number of the details given here are peculiar to Hary, such as the sawing of the bridge in two (line 1151); the use of wooden rollers at one end of the bridge (lines 1155–56); and the use of a carpenter to sit in a cradle under the bridge to release pins on command (lines 1158–60). The Scots were probably outnumbered by the English, but Hary's figures (50,000 English) are fanciful. The number of casualties, including the death of Cressingham at Wallace's hands (lines 1194–99), is also Hary's invention. Some of Hary's details agree with the account in Guisborough, for example, his figure of 50,000 for the

The Wallace

English host (line 1166), although Guisborough says there were also 1,000 cavalry. Various sources agree that Cressingham led the vanguard across the narrow bridge, while Warenne remained with the other main contingent on the south side of the bridge (lines 1171–75). According to the records, the English made their way to Berwick after the defeat at Stirling, not Dunbar as Hary says (lines 1218 and 1227). For another account of the battle, see Barrow (1988), pp. 86–88.

1170   *playne feild*. Wallace was on the Abbey Crag slope.

1174   An ironic allusion to a popular proverb, as McDiarmid points out (2.216n1174), to the effect that the wise man learns by the example of others. Barbour quotes it early in *The Bruce*: "And wys men sayis he is happy / Þat be oþer will him chasty" (1.121–22).

1214   Andrew Murray, father of the regent of the same name. He had been in revolt against Edward in Moray since 1297. See Bower, 29.19 and Watt's note on p. 237. Although Wyntoun (8.13.2178) and an inquest of 1300 say that Andrew Murray was killed at Stirling Bridge (Joseph Bain, ed., *Calendar of Documents Relating to Scotland* [Edinburgh: H. M. General Register House, 1881–88] 2.1178), Barrow (1988) and others believe that he did not die until November, probably from wounds received in the battle (p. 343n1). Bower's statement that he was wounded and died (11.30) bears this construction. Murray and Wallace shared leadership of Scotland during the two months after the Stirling victory.

1222   Dunbar Castle was occupied by Waldergrave at this period, not by the earl of Lennox.

1234   *Hathyntoun*. Haddington, near Edinburgh.

1251   McDiarmid suggests Hary makes this Assumption Day because of Hary's presentation of Wallace as a special protégé of Mary.

1252   *Our Lady*. This Catholic reference is amended to *our Lord* in L.

1255–59   Barrow (1988) points out that the history of the lordship of Arran is obscure at this time, but the association with Menteith, a member of the Stewart family, dates from this period (p. 363n88). It was perhaps conquered by Robert I.

Explanatory Notes to Book 8

Menteith's oath of allegiance to Wallace (lines 1261–62) is richly ironic in view of his later betrayal.

1276   *Cristall of Cetoun.* Sir Christopher Seton, a Yorkshire knight married to Bruce's sister Christian, became one of Bruce's most devoted followers. He was captured at Doon Castle and executed in 1306. See *The Bruce* 2.421–30; 4.16–24.

1281   *Herbottell.* The keeper of Jedburgh Castle bears the name of another border castle. Herbottle and Jedburgh castles were held against the English until October 1298. Wallace put John Pencaitland in as keeper (Watson, p. 50) Whether a Ruwan (Ruthven) was installed as captain (lines 1289–90) is unknown.

1293   For the reference to *The Bruce,* see explanatory note to line 1276 above.

1299–1300   This is historically inaccurate since Edinburgh Castle remained in English hands until 1314.

1302   *Mannuell.* Manuel, in Stirlingshire.

1306–08   Bruce is intended, although Wallace was actually a Balliol supporter.

Book 8

1   *Fyve monethis thus.* Five months after the Battle of Stirling Bridge would be February 1298, but references to the months of October and November at lines 433–34 only serve to highlight the problems with Hary's chronology. Wallace may well have tried unsuccessfully to win Earl Patrick over at this time.

21   *king of Kyll.* An insulting play on the Wallace lands held in Kyle.

23–24   Corspatrick's dismissal of Wallace as a knight bachelor, i.e., a relative novice, is also meant to be insulting. The earl refers to that well-known image of mutability, the wheel of Fortune, to predict that while Wallace may currently enjoy good fortune, this will soon change.

29   Many Scots lords held land in England at this time, e.g., Robert Bruce.

37   *a king.* I.e., King Robert Bruce. See line 146, below.

The Wallace

63–66 Robert Lauder became a powerful Scottish magnate under Robert I, richly rewarded by the king for loyalty with grants of lands and the position of justiciar of Lothian. Hary suggests he is keeper of some castle (line 64), presumably Lauder in Berwickshire.

68 *the Bas*. Bass Rock, off North Berwick.

71 *Lyll*. Unknown, although McDiarmid points out that the Lyles of Renfrewshire obtained property in East Linton in the fifteenth century.

115–21 *Coburns Peth . . . Bonkill Wood . . . Noram . . . Caudstreym . . . on Tweid*. All of these place names are in Berwickshire. Norham was on the north bank of the River Tweed and Coldstream on the south bank.

124–29 *Atrik Forrest . . . Gorkhelm*. Ettrick Forest was in the borders and Gorkhelm has not been identified. McDiarmid suggests that the latter may have been in the vicinity of the Cockhum stream near Galashiels (2.220n129).

139 Bek was sent by Edward I in July 1298 to capture castles in East Lothian. See explanatory note to lines 179–80, below.

158 *Lothyane*. The shire of Lothian in eastern central Scotland.

161 *Yhester*. The Gifford Castle of Yester in east Lothian. Peter Dunwich was the English keeper of this castle in 1296–97.

162 *Hay*. Sir Hugh Hay of Borthwick, near Edinburgh, who later fought with Bruce at Methven, where he was captured.

163 *Duns Forest*. In central Berwickshire.

179–80 *Lammermur*. Bek rides through the Lammermuir hills and north to the Spottssmuir, south of Dunbar. McDiarmid notes that this was the scene of the battle of Dunbar in 1296 (2.220n180), so the battle described in lines 188–324 may well be fictitious or a confused rewriting of the earlier battle.

270 *Mawthland*. Maitland was the name of the person who surrendered Dunbar Castle to the earl of Douglas in 1399. According to David Hume of Godscroft, a Robert Maitland was the son of Agnes Dunbar and John Maitland of Thirlestane (*The*

Explanatory Notes to Book 8

History of the House of Douglas, ed. David Reid. 2 vols. Scottish Text Society fourth ser. 25–26 [Edinburgh: Scottish Text Society, 1996], 1.253 and 2.546n253).

314   Compare *The Bruce* 3.45–54, which in turn is influenced by the account of Alexander's defense of his retreating men in the *Roman d'Alexandre*.

317   *Glaskadane*. Said to be a forest. McDiarmid places it near Doon Hill in Spott parish (2.221n317).

334   *Tavydaill*. Teviotdale, in the borders.

337   *Schir Wilyham Lang*. I.e., long or long-legged William Douglas. The Douglas so known was actually the fifth lord of Douglas (c. 1240–76). Hary is referring to his son, the seventh lord (1288–1302), whose nickname was *le hardi*. See explanatory note to 6.771.

373   *knycht Skelton*. Probably one of the Cumberland Skeltons active in the Borders during the wars.

384   *Noram Hous*. Norham Castle, on the north bank of the River Tweed.

439   *Roslyn Mur*. Roslin, south of Edinburgh, in Midlothian. It was the site of a battle, won by the Scots, in 1303.

513–19   According to Bower, Newcastle seems to have been the furthest south Wallace reached in the 1297 raids. In May 1318, however, Bruce's army raided Yorkshire. Hary's claim that Wallace's army conducted a burn and slash campaign as far as York which he is supposed to have besieged for fifteen days (line 529) is not supported by the historical record, but was probably influenced by Barbour's account of Bruce's raids. On the extent and impact of the historical Wallace's invasion of northern England in 1297, see C. McNamee, "William Wallace's Invasion of Northern England in 1297," *Northern History* 26 (1990), 540–58.

522–25   Hary describes the revenge Wallace vowed at line 442. No prisoners are taken for ransom: all are put to the sword. All these lines reiterate this idea. Note the grim humor.

530   *King Eduuard*. Edward was actually in Flanders at this stage, returning in March 1298.

The Wallace

636	*schawit thaim his entent*. I.e., he revealed to them what Edward intended.
639–72	Hary is at pains to portray Wallace as a loyal vassal with absolutely no ambitions to usurp his rightful king's place.
651	*Cambell*. Sir Neil Campbell of Lochawe. See explanatory note to 7.623.
662	As a *lord of the parlyment*, Malcolm is a hereditary member of the Scottish parliament. The other estates of the clergy and burgesses were also represented.
886–88	*King Arthour . . . Mont Mychell*. See the account of Arthur's victory over the giant of Gene in *The Alliterative Morte Arthure* (lines 886–87; 1015–16).
945	*Mydlam land*. This has been identified as Middleham, ten miles southwest of Richmond (McDiarmid 2.227n945).
946	*Brak parkis doun*. A park might be a grove, an enclosed tract, a woodland, pasture land, or a game preserve.
953–54	The Commons pressure Edward to accept Wallace's *pes* (line 954).
955	*Na herrald thar durst*. The implication is that none dare come because of what he did to the last ones!
961–72	The posing of a question of this kind to the audience or reader is a typical romance convention. The invited comparison with Brutus, Julius Caesar, and Arthur, all well-known from the Nine Worthies tradition in the Middle Ages, is intended to favor the hero.
972	*brak his vow*. I.e., to fight a battle within forty days.
1009	*Ramswaith*. McDiarmid reckons this is Ravensworth Castle, northwest of Richmond (2.228n1009–10).
1010	*Fehew*. Fitzhugh, said to be Edward's nephew when his head is delivered to the king (line 1101).
1024–25	This refers to an incident described in 6.363–405.

Explanatory Notes to Book 8

1031	*lat his service be*. That is, commanded him to refrain.
1047	The bowmen provide the equivalent of covering fire.
1081–83	Wallace's treatment of Fitzhugh's head is deliberately provocative because Edward has reneged on the agreement to offer battle.
1107	*Wodstok*. Woodstock, according to Hary, the earl of Gloucester and captain of Calais (9.675–85). See explanatory notes to line 1494, below; see also 8.1534–37.
1113–36	The role of Edward's queen is invented by Hary. As previous editors have noted, Edward's first queen had died, and he did not marry his second, the sister of Philip IV of France, until 1299. McDiarmid (2.228–29n1113–36) suggests a literary model in Lydgate's Jocasta (*The Siege of Thebes*).
1120	An allusion to the hanging of the Scots nobles in Ayr, described in 7.199–514.
1137	*queyn luffyt Wallace*. Hary plays briefly with a romance motif when he suggests that the queen may have been motivated by love for Wallace, inspired by his noble reputation. Hary's own comments follow and make conscious use of the authority *topos*.
1147	*luff or leiff*. This does seem to be a tag, as McDiarmid suggests, meaning "for love or not for love."
1183–94	Hary normally places such astrological descriptions at the beginning of a new book, for example at the opening to Book 4.
1215–21	The queen's retinue, which is all female with the exception of seven elderly priests, is another literary touch.
1225	*lyoun*. The lion rampant of Scotland emblazoned on Wallace's tent is the central emblem of the Royal Arms of Scotland. The leopard is the corresponding emblem on the English royal arms (6.466).
1237–1462	Wallace's long dialogue with the queen is a remarkably courteous exchange, evincing the nobility of both parties. Wallace's cautiousness about the queen's motives is expressed to his men, whom he warns to be on guard against the treachery of women. He is nevertheless courteous enough to exclude the queen

The Wallace

from his suspicions. The queen in turn strives to allay suspicions by tasting all the food she has brought by way of gift. Her mission, she says, is peace. Wallace resists her overtures by recounting instances of English aggression which have provoked and perpetuated the war, from the arbitration between the competitors for the throne through the injustices done to Scotland and the personal injustice to Wallace, particularly the murder of his wife, to the truce breaking, and the atrocity at Ayr. She hopes to win him over through offering gold as reparation and tries to appeal to his chivalry, but he refuses to play the courtly game. He says he has no faith in a truce which will not necessarily be binding, or honored by the English king. In the end, he is persuaded by her *gentrice* (line 1456) or noble magnanimity when she generously distributes the gold to his men in any case.

1256–62   *Rownsyvaill.* The epic poem, *The Song of Roland*, made the betrayal and death of Roland at Ronceval famous in the Middle Ages. Hary may have used the *Historia Karoli Magni*, copied at Coupar Angus Abbey in the fifteenth century, for this episode as well as for the description of Wallace in Book 10, as McDiarmid suggests (2.230n1251–62).

1281   *marchell.* Here a functionary of the kind appropriate in a royal court.

1286   *byrnand wer.* A reference to Wallace's scorched-earth tactics in England.

1320–21   *pape.* The pope was approached in the late thirteenth century to intercede and stop England's suzerainty claims.

1327–28   These lines echo Barbour (*Bruce* 1.37–40).

1335   This refers to the coronation of John Balliol.

1339   Bower has an account of Julius Caesar's failure to secure tribute from the Scots (*Scotichronicon* 2.14–15).

1341–43   These lines refer to the pledge Edward made to Robert Bruce the Elder to promote him to the throne of Scotland once Balliol was deposed. Bower claims that Edward basically used Bruce to ensure the surrender of the Scottish nobles (*Scotichronicon* 11.18).

1345–47   This derives from Bower, *Scotichronicon* 11.25:

Explanatory Notes to Book 8

> Robert de Bruce the elder approached the king of England and begged him to fulfil faithfully what he had previously promised him as regards his getting the kingdom. That old master of guile with no little indignation answered him thus in French: "N'avons-nous pas autres chose a faire qu'a gagner vos royaumes?", that is to say: "Have we nothing else to do than win kingdoms for you?"
> (vol. 6, trans. Wendy Stevenson)

1368   *woman*. This alludes, of course, to the murder of his wife by Heselrig (6.124–264).

1391   *gold so red*. Red gold was considered the most precious and valuable.

1407   *That ye me luffyt*. A tenet of courtly love was that the loved one should love in return or be considered merciless.

1478   *key of remembrans*. Whereas Chaucer made old books "of remembraunce the keye" (*Legend of Good Women*, Prologue F.26), Hary represents Wallace himself, through the queen's acknowledgment of his qualities, as the key to remembrance.

1494   *thre gret lordys*. Clifford, Beaumont, and Woodstock (lines 1503–04).

1523   *yong Randell*. Sir Thomas Randolph, later earl of Moray and regent of Scotland. He figures prominently in *The Bruce*.

1525   *Erll of Bowchane*. Sir John Comyn was the earl of Buchan and a Balliol supporter. Hary does not indicate that he is the same person as the John Comyn referred to two lines later, perhaps because he thinks of Beaumont as the earl of Buchan. (See explanatory note to 7.1079.)

1527   *Cumyn and Soullis*. All the early Scottish chroniclers claim that Sir John Comyn betrayed Bruce to Edward after making a secret covenant with him. See also *The Bruce* 1.483–568. Comyn was killed by Robert Bruce in 1306 (*Bruce* 12.1185 ff.). Sir William Soules was later executed for conspiracy against Robert I (*Bruce* 19.1–58).

1536   *Glosister*. The earl of Gloucester, Bruce's uncle through marriage.

1539–43   *erll Patrik*. As noted earlier, Earl Patrick in fact remained an adherent of Edward I until his death in 1308.

The Wallace

1573–74 *All Halow Evyn.* Halloween, or the eve of All Saints Day (31 October and 1 November, respectively), so Hary gives their departure date as 21 October, ten days before the feast day, and their arrival at Carham Moor (near Coldstream) as Lammas Day, August 1, the following year, making the raiding campaign in England last over nine months, for which there is no historical confirmation, as noted earlier.

1583–86 The installation of Seton and Ramsay as captains of Berwick and Roxburgh respectively is Hary's invention, as Berwick remained in English hands until 1318 and Roxburgh until 1314.

1597 *gossep.* I.e., Wallace had been godfather to two of Menteith's children.

1602 *March.* The Marches, specifically the border between Scotland and northern England.

1616–18 *Of this sayn my wordis . . . yeit fell.* This should be the last sentence of Book 8, but the scribe errs and continues for another 124 lines.

Book 10

93 *Thar.* I.e., the ancient Perthshire forest of *Blak Irnsid* (lines 92 and 333), Black Earnside, not far from the Benedictine abbey of Lindores where various historical battles were fought. Records show that Wallace was here, but in 1304, where he was attacked by the English several times.

98–99 *Guthré, / And Besat.* Hary thinks of Guthrie and Bisset as local to Perthshire and Fife, probably landowners.

112 *Woodhavyn.* Woodhaven on the Firth of Tay, opposite Dundee.

118–20 Wallace is referring to events described in 5.19–42.

128 The sentiment of *pro patria mori*, more or less.

150 *Jhon Wallang.* Sir John de Valence, Sir Amer's brother. He is referred to as sheriff of Ayr in 12.891.

Explanatory Notes to Book 10

188	*erll of Fyff*. Siward is a leading Fife baron. Of course he soon threatens to hang him high if he refuses the order to remain at Earnside Forest (lines 300–02, below).
292	*Coupar*. In Fife.
310–19	Valence going over to Wallace is a fiction, of course.
835–36	Compare to 1.296–97.
857–75	*Schyr Wilyam Lang, of Douglace Daill*. See earlier explanatory note to 8.337. Hary claims he was married twice and had two sons by each wife, Sir James and Sir Hugh by the sister of Sir Robert Keith, and two others by Lady Eleanor Ferrars. In his *History of the House of Douglas* (1633), David Hume of Godscroft also claims this (p. 59), but he is probably following Hary. William Fraser, on the other hand, says the first wife, and the mother of James Douglas, was Elizabeth Stewart, daughter of Alexander, High Steward, and that Hugh was one of two sons born to the second wife, whom he calls Elizabeth Ferrars, the other son being Archibald Douglas (*The Douglas Book*, 4 vols. [Edinburgh: T. and A. Constable, at the Edinburgh University Press, 1885], pp. 75, 104).
865	*Gud Robert Keth*. Sir Robert Keith, marischel of Scotland, a patriot who supported Wallace until 1300, when he submitted to Edward I.
866–68	Barbour also places James Douglas in Paris during his formative years (*Bruce* 1.330–44).
873	*lady Fers*. Lady Eleanor Ferrars, or Ferriers, a widow.
883	*Sawchar*. Sanquhar Castle, Dumfrieshire, possibly built by the English. It was not won by Wallace as far as is known.
885	*Bewffurd*. Beaufort is otherwise unknown.
896	*Thom Dycson*. The Dickson family was associated with Sanquhar, but the source is probably *The Bruce* (5.255–462), where a Thomas Dickson helps James Douglas capture Douglas Castle. Sir William had been Edward's prisoner since 1297 so could not have been involved in taking Sanquhar at this time.

912	*clewch ner the wattyr of Craw.* Crawick, in the parish of Sanquhar.
962	*Dursder.* Durisdeer Castle at Castlehill.
964–65	*Enoch . . . Tybris.* Enoch and Tibbers castles in Durisdeer parish.
976	*Ravynsdaill.* Ravensdale is said to be the keeper of Kynsith, near Cumbernauld.
978	*Lord Cumyn* (Comyn) held Cumbernauld Castle.
997	*Lithquow.* Linlithgow, which Edward held from 1296.
1017	*Hew the Hay.* See explanatory note to 8.162.
1025	*Ruthirfurd.* See explanatory note to 6.537.
1221–46	*Wallace statur.* Wallace's portrait is drawn from Bower, *Scotichronicon* 11.28, who in turn derived details and phrases from the Pseudo-Turpin description of Charlemagne, and from Fordun.
1242–44	*Alexander the king . . . Ector was he.* Comparisons with the magnanimity of Alexander and the audacity of Hector (line 1244) were conventional. There may also be echoes from Chaucer's portrait of the Knight in The General Prologue to the *Canterbury Tales* (line 1243).
1259	*Scrymiour.* Probably Alexander Scrymgeour, appointed constable of Dundee by Wallace in March 1298 (10.1162).

Book 11

72–438	Battle of Falkirk. The historical battle was indecisive (Barrow [1988], p. 103), but Scheps notes that in some MSS of the fourteenth-century romance, *Thomas of Ercildoun*, the victory is also given to the Scots, so this outcome is not just Hary's invention (Scheps, "Possible Sources," p. 126). Without Wallace, who withdraws from the field in anger (line 158), the Scots are overpowered, but Wallace eventually comes to the rescue and snatches victory from defeat. Hary, like Wyntoun (*Cronykil* 8.15.2245–69) and Bower (*Scotichronicon* 11.34), makes the treachery of Comyn a key factor in the initial Scottish defeat. Wallace could not

Explanatory Notes to Book 11

rely on the cavalry in the end. The issue of rank is highlighted in Hary's invented exchange between Wallace and Stewart (lines 105–19), in which Stewart articulates the fears of the nobles.

101   *Cunttas of Merch*. The countess of Dunbar, wife of Earl Patrick, and sister to Sir John Comyn whose hostility towards Wallace is attributed by Hary to this alliance.

135   *howlat*. The fable of the owl (lines 134–38) derives from Richard Holland's *Book of the Howlat* (c. 1448) in which the owl is presented as a treacherous upstart.

151   *Cumyn*. Like Fordun, Hary uses the name of Comyn as a byword for treachery.

153   *I of danger brocht*. A reference to the release he negotiated with Woodstock in 8.1525.

179   *Erll of Harfurd*. An earl of Hereford is known to have been an English commander who saw action in Scotland and was in Carlisle in September of 1298 (Watson, p. 68), but whether he was at Falkirk is not known.

203   *Bruce*. Whether Bruce was present at Falkirk is a much-debated matter. See Barrow (1988), p. 101. Fordun and Wyntoun say he was; the English chroniclers, including Guisborough (who is the most detailed), do not mention his presence. Hary uses his purported presence to create a confrontation between Bruce and Wallace.

207   *gold of gowlis cler*. The royal Scottish coat of arms. At line 209: "The rycht lyon."

217–40   Hary moves into allegorical mode to represent Wallace's internal debate or struggle.

279   *Rewellyt speris all in a nowmir round*. This is the classic *schiltron* formation in which foot soldiers with long spears were grouped in circular bodies as a first line of defense against advancing cavalry. It has been estimated that some of the *schiltron* formations at Falkirk comprised as many as 1,500 men (Roberts, p. 122). These *schiltrons* were, however, vulnerable to attack by archers, as Falkirk testifies. Cavalry protection to deflect the archers was lacking.

The Wallace

295 *The erll of York.* An anachronism, as this title was not created until the reign of Edward III.

342 Comparison with Alexander again, this time against Gadifer. Barbour, too, uses the analogy to describe Bruce's cover of his men after a skirmish with John of Lorn (*Bruce* 3.72–84)

361 *Quham he hyt rycht.* A tribute paid only to Wallace so far.

378–92 The account of Graham's death owes much to *The Alliterative Morte Arthure*, as previous readers have noted.

434 *Magdaleyn Day.* Wyntoun and Bower also date the Battle of Falkirk on St. Mary Magdalene Day (i.e., 22 July) 1298.

440–527 The Bruce-Wallace dialogue across the Carron owes much to Bower's account of a conversation between the two across a narrow ravine. According to Hary, Wallace considers Bruce as the rightful king of Scots, but the historical Wallace was a Balliol supporter. The dialogue focuses on Wallace's rebuke of Bruce for being *fals* (line 461) and killing his *awn* (line 447) people, especially Stewart and Graham. In Bower, Wallace's accusation that Bruce is effeminate and delinquent in not defending his own country persuades Bruce to change sides (*Scotichronicon* 11.34).

454 *Ra.* McDiarmid notes that a Robert Ra of Stirling occurs in the records (2.261n454).

472 *offspryng.* This implies that Bruce is the (unnatural) father of his people.

492 *Thow renygat devorar of thi blud.* The charge conveyed in this startling image is taken to heart when, after Falkirk, Bruce refuses to wash the blood from his clothes and person and endures at supper the scorn of the English: "Ane said, 'Behald, yon Scot ettis his awn blud'" (line 536).

1085 *Bewmound.* Sir Henry Beaumont. See explanatory note to 7.1078.

1089 Clifford received the Douglas lands in 1297 (Barrow [1988], p. 157). Barbour describes James Douglas's attack on Clifford's garrison there in 1307 (*Bruce* 8.437–87).

Explanatory Notes to Book 12

1093–1111   The debt is to *The Bruce* 1.313–45.

1111   *lord Soullis*. McDiarmid suggests a possible debt to Barbour for the claim that de Soules was given the Merse.

1113   *Olyfant*. Sir William Oliphant, a Perthshire knight, was commander of Stirling Castle when it was heavily attacked by Edward's new siege machines in 1304, despite Oliphant's offer to surrender the castle. In 1299 Gilbert Malherbe was sheriff when John Sampson surrendered. Oliphant was installed by Sir John de Soules.

1114–56   These lines represent the Bruce-Comyn pact. Compare Barbour's *Bruce* 1.483–510.

Book 12

740   *Bowchan Nes*. Literally the nose of Buchan.

743   *Climes of Ross*. Identification is uncertain.

791–95   The role of Menteith in the capture of Wallace is not doubted. He is accused of treachery by Fordun, Wyntoun, and Bower. Barrow (1988) points out that Menteith was a staunch patriot but submitted to Edward in 1304 and so was acting in line with this allegiance in handing Wallace over (p. 136).

835–48   Another homily, this time on covetise (covetousness). The particular allusions to Hector and Alexander suggest a probable debt to Barbour, but of course such analogies were common. Barbour has a similar descant on treason as exemplified in the fates of Alexander the Great, Julius Caesar, and King Arthur, among others (*Bruce* 1.515–60).

885–94   *erll of Fyf*. Duncan, earl of Fife. was not actually active on the patriot side in Wallace's lifetime. He was later a companion-in-arms when Bishop Sinclair repelled an English attack in Fife in 1317 (*Bruce* 16.543–666).

894   *ald thane*. The thane referred to is MacDuff, famous for slaying Macbeth.

918–24   Barbour's mention of Edward Bruce's return to Galloway may be the source here (*Bruce* 9.477–543).

The Wallace

928 *Lowmabane.* Lochmabon Castle was part of the Bruce lordship of Annandale.

937 *Blak Rok.* See earlier reference to the Blackcraig (6.855) and explanatory note.

959–82 Hary has Wallace rescue Scotland three times before he hands over to Bruce. The correspondence between the two is, of course, Hary's invention.

960 McDiarmid suggests *lestand pees* could mean "heaven" (2.273n960).

962 *purpost than to serve God.* I.e., to enter religious orders.

984 *Glaskow.* Bower says Glasgow was where Menteith's men captured Wallace (*Scotichronicon* 12.8).

1062 *byndyng rew.* The binding of captured Wallace ironically parallels the break-up of Scotland.

1075 *thai Menteth.* McDiarmid suggests "these Menteiths," i.e., kinsmen (2.274n1075).

1077 *saiff thar lord.* Hary refers to Sir John Stewart, but Sir James was actually chief. Menteith was Sir John Stewart's uncle.

1081 *eighteen yer.* Falkirk was fought in 1298, so eighteen years makes no sense. Even if eight is meant, this would put Wallace's capture in 1306, which is too late.

1082 Hary presents Comyn's death as in part a payback for his role in bringing about the death of Stewart at Falkirk.

1089–90 *Clyffurd.* See explanatory note to 5.737.

1096 The Scots did not have Berwick at this time.

1109–28 *Allace.* The anaphora on "alas" marks these lines as a formal complaint or lament.

1139 *Longawell.* Thomas Longueville is the French knight (and reformed pirate) who accompanied Wallace from France. His adventures are detailed in Book 9 (omitted from these selections).

1147 *Brucys buk.* An explicit reference to Barbour's *Bruce*, possibly 9.396.

Explanatory Notes to Book 12

1151   The Charteris family was a prominent one in Hary's day and he pays a compliment by making Thomas of Longueville an ancestor.

1163   Possibly an echo of the opening lines of Chaucer's *Troilus and Criseyde*.

1164–76   Edward Bruce's eulogy on Wallace is an interesting exercise in propaganda as once again Hary suggest that Wallace fought to make Robert Bruce's reign possible.

1183–84   The order for Comyn's killing is given because he is seen as responsible for Wallace's death, just as he had earlier been accused by Hary of a part in the death of Stewart (lines 1079–82).

1195   A reference to Barbour's account in *The Bruce*, as line 1212 acknowledges. See also notes above on Berwick as held by the English until 1318 (8.1583–86).

1205   *best chyftayn*. A comparison of James Douglas and Wallace as chieftains, but inevitably to Wallace's advantage.

1226–28   McDiarmid (2.277n1227–28) suggests that this refers to the Black Parliament, held at Scone in 1320 to deal with Soules, Brechin, and the other conspirators, described by Barbour (*Bruce*, 19.46) and Bower (*Scotichronicon*, 13.1).

1239–1301   Bower mentions the vision of a holy man in which he saw the ascent of Wallace's soul to heaven. Hary may be extending this as he draws on other sources, such as traditional tales about Wallace, to which Bower may also have had access.

1260   *fyr brund*. McDiarmid identifies this as the flame of Purgatory (2.279n1260).

1269   *layff*. The monk asks about the brand in his fellow's forehead.

1280   The date is erroneous. Wallace was executed on Monday, 23 August 1305.

1297   *bellys sall ryng*. See McDiarmid for other examples of bell-ringing as witness to virtue (2.279n1297).

1305–09   Wallace as a martyr is compared to the greatest of English saints: Oswald, Edmond, Edward, and Thomas.

The Wallace

1312–37　Edward's prohibition on shriving Wallace and the retort of the bishop of Canterbury who proceeds to hear Wallace's last confession are entirely fanciful. The intention is to blacken Edward's character further.

1384–86　McDiarmid (2.280n1385–86) suggests an echo of Henryson's *Fox and the Wolf* (lines 694–95). Note the contrast to Bruce's deathbed words (Barbour's *Bruce* 20.171–99). Wallace is nevertheless presented as devout, in his reading of the psalter to the last.

1400　*done*. I.e., tortured.

1414　*Blair*. See explanatory note to 5.533–45.

1417　*Byschop Synclar*. This seems to be Hary's invention.

1427–28　McDiarmid omits these lines which contain a contradiction about Wallace's age at death.

1439　McDiarmid translates as, "No one had engaged himself to pay for the writing of this work" (2.281n1437).

1445–46　*Wallas . . . Liddaill*. See my Introduction for a comment on these two patrons.

1451–66　Note the convention employed in this epilogue. Compare with Chaucer's The Franklin's Tale.

Textual Notes

Abbreviations: **C** = *The Lyfe and Actis of the Maist Illvster And Vailzeand Campiovn William Wallace*, ed. Charteris (1594); **F** = Fragments of an edition in the type of Chepman and Myllar (1507/8); **Jamieson** = *Wallace, or, The Life and Acts of Sir William Wallace of Ellerslie* (1869); **L** = *The Actis and Deidis of Schir William Wallace*, ed. Lekpreuik (1570); **McDiarmid** = *Hary's Wallace* (1968–69); **MS** = National Library of Scotland MS Advocates 19.2.2, fols. 79r–194r.

Book 1

26	*of.* MS: *off.* So too in lines 47, 66, 94, 108, 133, 134, 143, 166, 190, 204, 290, 356, 375, 379, 420 and *passim*.
32	*hyr*. L: *heir*. McDiarmid emends to *her*.
37	*as cornyklis*. MS: *as conus cornyklis*. McDiarmid's emendation, based on L.
57	*landis*. McDiarmid notes that *-is* endings in the MS frequently look like *-e*.
64	*croun*. MS: *toun*. L: *Crown*. McDiarmid's emendation.
87	*folowid*. McDiarmid: *followid*.
97	*Eduuard maid*. McDiarmid adds *has*, based on L.
106	*than*. McDiarmid: *then*.
116	*homage*. So L. MS: *ymage*. McDiarmid's emendation.
118	*he send*. MS: *send he*, with caret indicating inversion.
159	*cummyng*. McDiarmid adopts *couth ring* from L.
193	*outhir*. McDiarmid: *othir*.
269	*the*. McDiarmid's addition from L.
278	*Hym disgysyt*. McDiarmid adds *self*, following L.
285	*Landoris*. McDiarmid emends to *Lundoris*, following L.
302	*Welcummyt*. McDiarmid: *Welcwmmyt*. Also at line 329.
336	*Wallas*. McDiarmid: *Wallace*.
352	*thaim*. McDiarmid: *thame*.
407	*ane awkwart straik him gave*. MS: *awkwart he him gawe*. L: *ane akwart straik him gaif*. McDiarmid's emendation.
423	*Lord abide*. McDiarmid adopts L's reading, which omits *lord*.
429	*discumfyst*. McDiarmid: *discwmfyst*.

265

The Wallace

Book 2

8	*mynd*. McDiarmid: *mynde*.
10	*thaim*. McDiarmid: *thame*.
27	*Aboundandely*. McDiarmid emends to *Abandounly*.
31	*thaim*. McDiarmid: *thame*.
34	*On*. So L. McDiarmid follows the MS: *In*.
49	*Upon*. MS: *Vpon*. McDiarmid: *Apon*.
75	*Wallace*. McDiarmid: *Wallas*.
76	*thaim*. McDiarmid: *thame*.
78	*se*. McDiarmid's addition, following L.
83	*bocht*. MS: *thocht bocht*. McDiarmid's emendation.
86	*schirreff*. McDiarmid: *schireff*.
89	*yeid and said*. McDiarmid emends to *ʒeid, said*.
93	*thow*. So L. MS: *the*. McDiarmid's emendation.
100	*sodanlé*. McDiarmid: *sodanli*.
138	*ga*. McDiarmid and Jamieson adopt *ta*, following L.
153	*fell*. McDiarmid: *sell*. L also has *fell*, as McDiarmid notes.
175	*law*. McDiarmid notes this is the MS reading, but emends to *lawe*.
198	*yow*. McDiarmid: *thow*.
216	*Compleyn*. McDiarmid: *Compleyne*.
219	*sellis*. L: *cellis*. McDiarmid: *sell is*.
231	*hym*. McDiarmid: *him*.
234	*Celinus*. McDiarmid: *Celinius*.
244	*thar*. McDiarmid: *that*.
308	*thar presoune*. MS omits *thar*. L: *thair presoun*. McDiarmid's addition.
339	After this line in L a different hand inserts an extra line: "I wald his weilfair and caist into his thocht."
425	*thrang*. So L. MS: *fand*. McDiarmid and Jamieson emend to *fang*.

Book 3

9	*rialye*. McDiarmid: *realye*.
13	*coud*. McDiarmid: *could*.
24	*was*. McDiarmid: *war*.
25	*Thai waryit*. MS: *He trowit*. McDiarmid's emendation, based on L.
35	*thai*. McDiarmid's addition.
97	*trastyt*. MS: *trast*. L: *traistit*. McDiarmid's emendation.

100	*the*. McDiarmid's addition.
101	*thair*. So L. MS: *than*. McDiarmid's emendation (*thar*).
114	*caus*. McDiarmid: *causer*.
135	*tuk*. McDiarmid: *tuke*.
145	*byrney*. McDiarmid: *birny*.
146	*throuch*. L: *Throw out*. McDiarmid: *throuch-out*.
147	*offe*. McDiarmid: *off*.
152	*enveround*. McDiarmid: *enverounid*.
174	*he doune*. MS: *doune he*, but marked to indicate alteration.
176	*The and arsone*. McDiarmid: *The gud arsone*, but *the* means "thigh" here.
182	*payne*. McDiarmid: *playne*, though he notes L: *pane*.
189	*brand*. MS: *hand*. McDiarmid's emendation.
201	*ennymys*. MS: *chewalrye*. L: *enemeis*. McDiarmid's emendation.
203	*hors sum part to*. MS: *On horsis some to strenthis part*. McDiarmid's emendation, following L.

Book 4

10	*hevyn*. McDiarmid adopts *the hycht* from L.
19	*far*. McDiarmid's addition, which has support from L.
26	*that*. McDiarmid and Jamieson adopt *at*.
32	*thou*. McDiarmid: *you*.
60	*der*. So L. MS: *her*. McDiarmid's emendation.
92	*fold*. McDiarmid: *feld*, but *fold* is correct and is used at line 469.
339	*hett*. McDiarmid: *heit*.
340	*wett*. McDiarmid: *weit*.
353	*of*. McDiarmid's addition from L.
372	*fynd*. McDiarmid: *find*.
405	*on*. McDiarmid: *in*.
437	*All*. McDiarmid emends to *Off*.
443	*his*. McDiarmid adopts *thar*, based on L.
444	*feild*. McDiarmid: *field*.
466	*throuout*. McDiarmid's addition (*throu-out*), based on L.
480	*Wallace*. L: *The walls*. McDiarmid changes to *wallis*.
481	*was thar lord*. Needs to be understood as "were their lords" to agree with *flearis*.
498	*his*. McDiarmid: *hys*.
503	*Women*. McDiarmid: *Wemen*.
720	*suour*. McDiarmid: *suor*.

761	*tresoun.* MS: *tresour.* L: *tressoun.* McDiarmid's emendation.
787	*Thai folowit him.* MS: *Him thai folowit.* McDiarmid's emendation, based on L.

Book 5

71	*chyftayne.* McDiarmid: *chyaftyne.*
75	*wycht.* McDiarmid: *wyth.*
77	*maide.* McDiarmid: *maid.*
83	*of.* McDiarmid: *off.*
115	*Als Fawdoun was.* MS: *Als Fawdoun als was.* McDiarmid's emendation, based on L.
116	*haldyn.* McDiarmid: *knawin*, following L; but see 5.817 where *haldyn* is used to mean "reputed."
186	*gret ire.* MS: *the gret Ire.* McDiarmid's emendation, based on L.
187	*that.* MS: *he.* L: *that allane.* McDiarmid emends to *him allayne.*
191	*horn.* McDiarmid: *horne.*
196	*it.* McDiarmid's addition from L.
207	*Faudoun.* McDiarmid: *Fawdoun.*
392	*Goddis saik wyrk.* MS: *Goddis wyrk.* McDiarmid's addition, based on L's reading: *Goddis saik mak.*
409	*wes.* McDiarmid: *was.*
476	*into.* So L. MS: *in.* McDiarmid's emendation.
485	*brynt.* MS: *bryt.* McDiarmid's silent emendation.
501	*Lorde.* McDiarmid: *Lord.*
526	*that.* So L. MS: *than.* McDiarmid's emendation.
528	*of.* McDiarmid: *off.*
564	*was of that.* MS: *that was off that.* McDiarmid's reading, modified from L.
576	*bot.* McDiarmid: *but.*
590	*protectiounne.* McDiarmid: *proteccioune.*
616	*his.* McDiarmid: *hys.*
619	*als.* McDiarmid: *as.*
629	*luff.* McDiarmid's addition from L.
652	*remaynyt.* McDiarmid: *remaynt.*
656	*langour.* McDiarmid: *languor.*
714	*ramaynyt.* McDiarmid: *remaynyt.*
758	*contré.* McDiarmid: *cuntre.*
764	*cheyk.* MS: *cheyff.* L: *cheik.* McDiarmid's emendation.
789	*ar.* McDiarmid: *are.*
800	*thai.* McDiarmid emends to *the*, based on L.

Textual Notes to Book 6

849	*wes*. McDiarmid: *was*.
852	*nayne*. McDiarmid: *nane*.

Book 6

1	*utas*. MS: *wtast*. McDiarmid's correction.
19	*for to*. MS: *to*. McDiarmid's emendation, following L.
24	*sor*. MS: *sar*. McDiarmid's silent emendation.
45	*was maid*. MS omits *was*. McDiarmid's addition from L.
62–63	These two lines are reversed in the MS. McDiarmid's emendation.
73	*gudlye*. McDiarmid: *gudly*.
79	*hym fer mar*. MS: *hyr fer mar*. F and L: *hym mair sair*. McDiarmid's emendation.
80	Line missing from MS, supplied from F. This line is also added by McDiarmid.
83	*now*. MS omits. McDiarmid's emendation, following F.
97	*fortoune*. McDiarmid: *fortune*.
140	*Gude*. McDiarmid: *Gud*.
159	*wapynnys*. McDiarmid: *wappynnys*.
171	*his*. McDiarmid: *hys*.
186	*upon*. MS: *wpon*. McDiarmid: *vpon*.
195	*but*. McDiarmid: *bot*.
219	*nocht*. MS omits. McDiarmid's addition, following L.
226	*Gud ... duelyt*. MS: *Off ... duelt*. McDiarmid's emendations.
307	*Pykarté*. McDiarmid: *Pykearte*.
315	*thai him knew*. McDiarmid emends to *that thai him knew*, based on F and L.
360	*Aganys*. McDiarmid: *Agaynys*.
398	*wes*. McDiarmid: *was*.
413	*thee leid*. MS: *thou*. McDiarmid's emendation (*the*), following L.
416	*falow led him*. MS omits *led*. McDiarmid's addition from L.
432	*tell*. MS: *till*. McDiarmid's emendation, following L.
436	*was sone war*. MS omits *sone*. McDiarmid's addition from L.
437	*to sell*. MS: *he to sell*. McDiarmid's emendation.
441	*sell*. MS omits. McDiarmid's addition from L.
471	*he*. MS: *how*. McDiarmid's emendation, following F and L.
473	*pot*. McDiarmid: *pott*.
485	*thai* MS: *thai thai*. McDiarmid silently emends.
507	*the*. MS omits. McDiarmid's addition from L.
510	*Davi son*. MS: *Dauison*. McDiarmid's emendation, based on L.
516	*for chance*. MS: *for charg*. McDiarmid's emendation, following L.

518	*folk*. MS omits. McDiarmid's addition from L.
525	*that*. McDiarmid's addition, based on L.
	we may in our viage. So F. MS: *may we in sic wiage*, followed by McDiarmid.
528	*fullfill*. McDiarmid: *fulfill*.
537	*Jhonstoun*. So F and L. MS: *Wallas*. McDiarmid's emendation.
547	*rych*. McDiarmid: *ryth*, although he notes variant readings of *richt* (F) and *riche* (L).
559	*how*. McDiarmid emends to *full*, following F and L.
561	*walkand had beyne*. MS: *walkand beyne*. McDiarmid's addition from F and L.
578	*owndir*. McDiarmid: *wndir*.
591	*self*. MS: *saw*. My reading, adopted from F and L.
596	*thocht*. McDiarmid substitutes *rocht* from F and L.
679	*Commaund*. McDiarmid: *Command*.
706	*tald it to*. MS: *tald to*. McDiarmid's addition from L.
742	*thar*. McDiarmid: *that*.
776	*Far*. So L. MS: *For*. McDiarmid emends to *Fer*.
780	*till*. McDiarmid: *til*.
810	*Fra*. The second two letters are smudged in the MS.
825	*enterit*. McDiarmid: *entrit*.
838–41	These lines from L are missing from the MS, probably, as McDiarmid suggests (1.134n838–41), because the scribe was misled by the recurrent rhyme *haill*.
936	*repayr*. McDiarmid: *repair*.

Book 7

65	*to the kyrk*. McDiarmid emends to *in to the kyrk*.
89	*thar descendyt*. McDiarmid adopts the reading from L here, which reverses this word order.
115	*sowdandly*. MS: *sowndly*. McDiarmid's emendation, based on L.
116	*his entent*. MS omits *his*. McDiarmid's addition from L.
126	*thou mon rycht*. MS omits *thou*. McDiarmid's addition (*thow*) from L.
153	*him*. McDiarmid: *hym*.
182	*makis*. McDiarmid: *makes*.
209	*his*. McDiarmid: *hys*.
253	*speryt*. MS: *sparyt*. L: *speirit*. McDiarmid's emendation.
273	*Than*. McDiarmid adopts *That* from L.
290	*me thaim all*. MS omits *thaim*. McDiarmid and Jamieson also emend.
291	*Marys saik*. L: *Goddis saik*.
310	*derffly ded doun*. McDiarmid adopts L's reading, which omits *ded*.

Textual Notes to Book 7

353	*selff*. McDiarmid: *self*.
377	*Lat*. McDiarmid: *Latt*.
406	*breiffly*. McDiarmid: *brieffly*.
420	*to the gett*. MS: *to ʒett*. McDiarmid's addition from L.
424	*evirilk*. MS: *ilk*. Accepting the reading from L, as McDiarmid and Jamieson do.
440	*walkand*. McDiarmid adopts *walkning* from L.
451	*beltles*. L: *belchis*. McDiarmid adopts *belches*, meaning "blazes," but *beltles* meaning "undressed" (literally, "without a belt") makes good sense.
453	*tyll*. McDiarmid: *till*.
454	*thar*. MS: *thai*. McDiarrmid's emendation, based on L.
468	*hand for*. McDiarmid inserts *thaim*, citing L's *thame*.
520	*sum*. McDiarmid's addition from L.
556	*Goddis saik*. MS: *Goddis*. McDiarmid's addition from L.
630	*was a new-maid lord*. MS: *was new maid lord*. My emendation, based on L. McDiarmid emends to: *was new maid a lord*.
651	*that*. MS: *quhar*. McDiarmid's emendation, following L.
713	*haiff beyne full*. MS omits *beyne*. McDiarmid's emendation, based on L.
731	*tayne*. McDiarmid: *tane*.
732	*he*. McDiarmid adopts *thai* from L.
741	*him*. McDiarmid: *hym*.
751	*was*. MS omits. McDiarmid's addition from L.
778	*Lundye*. McDiarmid: *Lundy*.
794	*is*. MS omits. McDiarmid's addition from L.
809	*ay*. MS: *thai*. McDiarmid and Jamieson emend, following L.
850	*wapynnys*. McDiarmid: *wappynnys*.
	fra. MS omits. McDiarmid's addition from L.
878	*Hald in Scotland*. MS: *Hald Scotland*. McDiarmid and Jamieson insert *in* from L.
899	*Weill he eschewit*. MS: *Weill eschewit*. McDiarmid's addition from L.
920	*trow*. McDiarmid: *trew*.
924	*harmyng*. MS: *gret harmyng*. McDiarmid's emendation, following L.
953	*All*. MS: *And*. McDiarmid's emendation, following L.
982	*Rewillyt*. McDiarmid: *Rewllyt*.
992	*that*. MS: *thai*. McDiarmid's emendation, following L.
1037	As McDiarmid notes, this line first appears at 1034 but is scored through and then placed here.
1145	*sent*. MS: *send*. McDiarmid's silent emendation.
1152	*trest*. MS: *streit*. McDiarmid's emendation, following L.
1180	*hyntyt and couth blaw*. McDiarmid adopts reading based on L: *hynt and couth it blaw*.

The Wallace

1202	*quhilk*. MS: *quhill*. McDiarmid's emendation, following L.
1211	*the*. McDiarmid adopts *in* from L.
1218	*haist maid*. MS: *haist thai maid*. McDiarmid's emendation, following L.
1252	*Our Lady*. L: *our Lord*.
1262	*and to*. McDiarmid omits *to*, citing L.
1268	*and fled*. McDiarmid adopts *thai*, citing L's *thay*.
1281	*Jadwort*. McDiarmid: *Jedwort*.

Book 8

46	*schaym*. MS: *schapin*. McDiarmid's emendation, derived from L.
48	*realme*. McDiarmid: *Realm*.
55	*taryit*. So L. MS: *tary*. McDiarmid: *taryt*.
105	*war*. McDiarmid: *were*.
155	*bischope*. McDiarmid: *byschope*.
169	*gyff*. McDiarmid: *giff*.
200	*four*. McDiarmid: *iii*.
213	*but*. McDiarmid: *bot*.
231	*And Adam*. MS omits *And*. McDiarmid's addition from L.
275	*his*. McDiarmid: *hys*.
276	*feill*. MS: *till*. McDiarmid's emendation, following L.
282	*his*. McDiarmid: *hys*.
283	*Gud rowme*. McDiarmid: *And rowme*. L: *Gude*. Compare *large rowme* at line 300.
289	*thai*. McDiarmid: *they*.
303	*feill*. So L. MS: *full feill*, followed by McDiarmid.
305	*horssit*. McDiarmid: *horsit*.
312	*sa*. McDiarmid emends to *and*, following L.
343	*thar*. McDiarmid: *thair*.
360	*ded*. McDiarmid: *dede*.
526	*koffre*. MS: *troffie*. L: *trustrie*. McDiarmid's emendation.
532	*to ces*. McDiarmid inserts *for*, citing L.
564	*harmys*. The MS folio has been ripped and sewn together again. The first letter has been obliterated, but is probably *h* as McDiarmid believes. L: *harmis*.
650	*mony*. McDiarmid: *many*.
864	*and*. MS: *of*. McDiarmid's emendation, derived from L.
867	*fer for to wyn*. McDiarmid drops *for*.
869	*warnysoun*. MS: *warysoun*. McDiarmid's emendation, based on L.
896	*Schir*. McDiarmid: *Schyr*.

Textual Notes to Book 8

922	*remanent*. From L. MS: *Ramayn*.
939	*largely*. MS: *largly*. McDiarmid's emendation, following L.
945	*Mydlam land*. MS: *Mydlem*. McDiarmid's emendation.
973	*ransik*. F and L: *resolve*. McDiarmid: *runsik*.
973–74	These lines are reversed in F and L.
1008	*semely*. So F and L. MS: *sembly*. McDiarmid: *semly*.
1049	*fast*. McDiarmid adopts *loud* from L.
1055	*for the defens*. McDiarmid emends to *for fence*, following L.
1060	*hidduys*. McDiarmid: *hidwys*.
1082	*woman*. MS: *women*. McDiarmid's emendation from L.
1109	*curage*. So L. MS: *curag*. McDiarmid's emendation.
1119	*men*. MS omits. McDiarmid's addition from L.
1136	*giffyn*. MS omits. McDiarmid's addition.
1142	*Sa*. McDiarmid: *So*.
1144	*quhill*. MS: *quhilk*. McDiarmid's emendation.
1156	*the Sotheron*. McDiarmid drops *the*.
1167	*stark*. MS: *stargis*. McDiarmid's emendation, following L.
1170	*Tawbawnys*. In the MS the *t* before *awbawnys* is blurred. See *Tawbane* at 8.1498.
1172	*gud*. McDiarmid adopts *fud*, citing L's *fude*.
1174	*Thai*. MS: *Than*. McDiarmid's emendation, based on L.
1178	*wild*. McDiarmid: *wyld*.
1204	*cast*. MS: *clasp*. McDiarmid's emendation, following L.
1219	*Vaillyt*. MS: *wallyt*. McDiarmid's emendation (*Waillyt*), based on L.
1236	*So*. McDiarmid: *Sa*.
1241	*Suffer*. McDiarmid: *Suffyr*.
1250	*Herfor mon*. McDiarmid inserts *And* from L.
1255	*passit*. MS: *past*, McDiarmid's emendation, following L.
1287	*grant us pees*. MS: *awcht haiff pes*. McDiarmid's emendation.
1300	*us*. So L. McDiarmid's emendation (*ws*).
1314	*helpys*. McDiarmid: *helpis*.
1330	*clemyt*. McDiarmid: *clempt*.
1335	*king*. McDiarmid: *kyng*.
1344	*Undid*. So L. MS: *wnd*. McDiarmid's emendation.
1344–45	These lines are reversed in L.
1358	*dispit*. McDiarmid: *despit*.
1398	*but*. McDiarmid: *bot*.
1417	*Madem*. McDiarmid: *Madam*.
1421	*yow*. McDiarmid: *you*.
1424	*Madeym*. McDiarmid: *Madem*.

1439	*Apon*. McDiarmid: *Vpon*.
1451	*menstraillis, harroldis*. McDiarmid: *menstrallis, harraldis*.
1457	*yow*. MS omits. McDiarmid's emendation, based on L.
1462	*sall*. McDiarmid: *sal*.
1500	*a*. MS omits. McDiarmid's emendation, based on L.
1530	*to ask*. MS: *als till*. McDiarmid's emendation, following L.
1549	*thaim*. McDiarmid has *than*.
1555	*ocht*. MS: *och*. McDiarmid's emendation, following L.
1561	*he*. McDiarmid adopts *thai*, citing L.
1590	*that*. McDiarmid adopts *the* from L.
1601	*byg it*. MS: *byggit*. McDiarmid's emendation, following L.
1616	*sayn my wordis*. McDiarmid adopts a version of L's reading here: *saving me wordis*. The sense seems reasonably clear: "With these words I cease my account of this."
1618	Book 8 should end here (as in L), but the scribe errs and continues for another 124 lines.

Book 10

99	*Besat*. MS: *Beset*; L: *Bissat*. The name of a person, as later references make clear (lines 10, 242, 414).
102	*unbeset*. So L. MS: *wnderset*. McDiarmid adopts *wmbeset*.
113	*cald it*. McDiarmid adopts *awfull* from L.
131	*tak*. McDiarmid: *take*.
132	*ar*. McDiarmid: *are*.
148	*Bot*. McDiarmid: *But*.
246	*metyng*. McDiarmid: *and metyng*.
264	*Wythowt*. McDiarmid: *Withowt*.
312	*hym*. McDiarmid: *him*.
319	*Wytht*. McDiarmid: *Wyth*.
323	*bid*. McDiarmid: *byd*.
850	*was*. MS: *wax*. McDiarmid's emendation.
871	*Till him*. McDiarmid adopts *Quhill tym* from L.
891	*his*. McDiarmid: *hys*.
945	*Dowglace*. McDiarmid: *Douglace*.
973	*Of Lewyhous*. McDiarmid emends to *Off the Lewynhous*.
978	*tribut*. McDiarmid: *trewbut*.
981	*nane*. McDiarmid: *nayn*.
992	*that*. McDiarmid omits.

Textual Notes to Book 11

1002	*Newbottyll.* McDiarmid: *Newbottyl.*
1004	*Berwik.* McDiarmid: *Berweik.*
1222	*dyscrecioun.* McDiarmid: *discrecioun.*
1223	*dischevill.* MS: *dissembill.* McDiarmid's emendation.
1246	*dissayff.* McDiarmid: *dissayf.*
1248	*ane.* From L. MS: *in.* McDiarmid: *a.*
1274	*saraly and in.* MS: *far alyand in.* McDiarmid's emendation.
1276	*north.* McDiarmid inserts *land* to make *northland.*
1278	*rapent.* McDiarmid: *repent.*

Book 11

126	*leyff it.* MS: *leyff on.* McDiarmid's addition, based on L's *tyne it on.*
131	*fairest.* MS: *farrest.* McDiarmid's emendation from L.
146	*Thair I have biddin.* MS: *Thar and I baid.* McDiarmid's emendation, based on L.
151	*consaill.* MS: *conselle.* L: *counsaill.* McDiarmid's emendation,
173	*he.* MS omits. McDiarmid's addition from L.
198	*To God.* McDiarmid adopts L's reading *O god.*
200	*thar.* McDiarmid and Jamieson render as *thir.*
204	*beyn.* McDiarmid: *been.*
227	*na.* McDiarmid: *na the,* following L.
236	*him.* McDiarmid: *hym.*
251	*All.* McDiarmid adopts *Wer* from C.
256	*saw that.* MS: *saw quhen.* McDiarmid's emendation, following L.
342	*of Gawdyfer.* MS: *the Gawdyfer.* McDiarmid's emendation.
352	*thre.* McDiarmid: *three.*
355	*weryt.* McDiarmid adopts *reryt,* citing L's *reirit.*
418	*on.* MS omits. McDiarmid's addition from L.
432	*amange.* McDiarmid: *amang.*
452	*heir.* From L. MS: *eftir.* McDiarmid: *her.*
481	*wagis.* McDiarmid: *wage.*
514	*the orient.* MS omits *the.* McDiarmid's addition from L.
520	*se me.* McDiarmid emends to *me se.*
522	*him.* McDiarmid: *hym.*
528	*Lythqwo.* McDiarmid: *Lythquo.*
529	*a.* McDiarmid adopts *be* from L.
542	McDiarmid drops *that,* following L.
1082	*endyt.* McDiarmid: *endit.*

1088	*Thair to.* MS: *Thair for.* McDiarmid's emendation, following L.
1090	*Marchis.* McDiarmid: *merchis.*
1139	*herto.* MS: *to her.* McDiarmid's emendation (*her-to*), based on L.
1146	*haiff.* MS: *haff.* McDiarmid's emendation, based on L.
1150	*this.* McDiarmid: *his.*
1155	*Fell thar.* MS: *Fayr thai.* McDiarmid's emendation, based on L.
1156	*That we micht get agane Wallace of France.* Like McDiarmid, I insert this line from L.
1169	*Cumyn.* MS: *Eduuard.* McDiarmid's emendation, based on L.

Book 12

781	*thar.* McDiarmid: *thai.* L: *thair.*
787	*Thai.* McDiarmid adopts *He* from L.
799	*this.* MS omits. McDiarmid's addition from L.
802	*thow.* McDiarmid: *thou.*
819	*thai.* MS omits. McDiarmid's addition from L.
820	*fayn haiff had.* MS: *fayn had.* McDiarmid's emendation, based on L.
837	*tuk.* MS: *to.* McDiarmid's emendation, based on L.
841	*Bretan.* McDiarmid: *Bretane.*
842	*had.* McDiarmid adopts *has*, citing L.
843	*covatice.* McDiarmid: *cowatyce.*
854	*yit.* MS omits. McDiarmid's emendation (*ʒeit*), based on L.
855	*sogeyng.* McDiarmid: *segeyng.*
909	*be tak.* McDiarmid: *betak.*
926	*it.* MS omits. McDiarmid's addition from L.
946	*past.* McDiarmid emends to *passit*, following L
990	*Menteth.* MS omits. McDiarmid's addition, based on L.
993	*he.* McDiarmid emends to *thai*, following L.
1023	*handis mycht on him lay.* McDiarmid reads the insertion points under *handis* and *lay* in MS to move *handis* between *him* and *lay.*
1044	*ma.* McDiarmid: *may.*
1064	*Comyns.* MS: *commounis.* L: *Cumyngis.* McDiarmid's emendation.
1065	*awe.* McDiarmid: *aw.*
1075	*thai Menteth.* MS: *that Menteith.* McDiarmid's emendation. He suggests the meaning is "these Menteiths," i.e., kinsmen (2.274n1075).
1081	*eighteen.* MS: *xviii.* McDiarmid adopts *auchtand*, citing L.
1097	*And.* McDiarmid adopts *To* from L.

Textual Notes to Book 12

1103–04   In the MS these lines are reversed, but the scribe indicates that they should be switched.

1112   *best*. McDiarmid notes that in the MS *best* is written faintly above the line. Although I cannot make it out, I accept the emendation, based on L.

1123   *help*. McDiarmid adopts *kepe*, citing L.

1153   *fer*. MS omits. McDiarmid's addition, based on L.

1175   *suld had na*. MS: *suld nocht had na*. McDiarmid's emendation, following L.

1176   *falsnes*. MS: *falnes*. McDiarmid's emendation, following L.

1184   *dreid*. MS: *deid*. McDiarmid's emendation, following L.

1190   *it is*. MS: *it was*. McDiarmid's emendation, following L.

1209   *as*. MS omits. McDiarmid's addition from L.

1220   *haiff*. MS omits. McDiarmid's addition from L.

1255   *so*. McDiarmid: *sa*.

1263   *lang*. McDiarmid: *long*.

1277   *me ken*. MS: *may ken*. McDiarmid's emendation, following L.

1305   *Sotheroun*. McDiarmid: *Sotherun*.

1319   *said*. MS omits. McDiarmid's addition from L.

1331   *thy*. MS omits. McDiarmid's addition (*thi*) from L.

1335   *Inglismen*. McDiarmid adopts *wyse men* from L.

1361   *force*. McDiarmid: *fors*.

1365   *I*. MS omits. McDiarmid's addition from L.

1369   *this*. McDiarmid: *the*.

1382   *sald*. McDiarmid: *suld*.

1384   *smyld a litill*. MS: *smyld litill*. McDiarmid's silent emendation.

1395   *viagis*. McDiarmid: *wiage*.

1396   *dispolyeid*. McDiarmid: *dispulyeid*.

1405   *spreyt*. MS: *preyt*. Damaged folio means some letters are effaced in the following words: *spreyt* (1405), *we* (1406), *spreyt* (1409), *blair* (1414), *compild* (1415), *mair* (1416).

1409   McDiarmid inserts a break after this line so that lines 1410 to the end are presented as an epilogue.

1414   *Blair*. McDiarmid: *Blayr*.

1421   *was till*. MS: *was for till*. McDiarmid's emendation, based on L.

1427–28   McDiarmid rejects these lines "as an intrusion" on the grounds that "45 years as the age of Wallace at his death is grossly at variance with the life-span presented in the poem and illustrated in my Introduction" (2.281n1426f).

1459   *banevolence*. McDiarmid: *beneuolence*.

1461   *burel*. McDiarmid: *burell*.

1463   *of Pernase*. MS: *aspernase*. McDiarmid's emendation.

Glossary

abaid *delay; waited*
aboundandely *boldly*
abown(e) *above*
adeill(e) *at all*
affer, effer *appearance, array*
ald *old*
allane *alone*
ane *one*
anys *once*
apayn *on pain, on penalty of*
apples *please*
argownd *challenged, debated*
art *area, direction*
as(s) *ask* **ast,** *asked*
aspre *fierce*
assay *attack*
atour *around*
attend *expect*
auchtand *eighteen*
aukwart *cross-wise*
availl *advantage*
availyeit *availed*
avance *praise*
avisit *advised, resolved*
awn *own*
ay *ever, always*
ayk *oak*
ayr *heir; justice-ayre; earlier*

bad *ordered*
baid *delay; waited*
band *bond* (feudal)
bandoun(e) *subjection*

bandounly *boldly*
bane *bone*
bargan(e) *battle*
barmkyn *rampart*
barn, barnis, barnys *infant, infants*
barnage *baronage*
barrace *barrier*
barrat *conflict, hostile encounter*
basnat, basnet *helmet*
bauk *beam*
bauldlye *boldly*
bayn(e) *ready*
behuffyd *of necessity*
beild *escape, refuge*
benyng *gracious*
bern *barn*
bertnyt *put to death*
berys *bury*
beseyn(e) *equipped, dressed*
bestials *siege machine*
betaucht *gave*
birney *corslet*
blaw *blow*
blyn *stop, cease*
bolnyt *swelled* (usually with anger)
bost *boast, threat*
boun, boune *ready, prepared*
boustous *strong*
braid *broad, wide*
braithly *vigorously*
brawn, brayn *flesh; brain*
brig *bridge*
bruk *possess*

Glossary

brym(e) *fierce*
brynt *burnt*
burd *board*
buschement *ambush*
buskit, buskyt *prepared, set on*
but *without; except*
but(e) *use*
butlas, butles *useless*
byg *build*
bykkyr *attack, encounter*
byrn *burn*

cald, cauld *cold*
can *does, did*
carle, carll *fellow*
cast *throw*
chapyt, eschapyt *escaped*
cheis, chewys, cheys *choose*
chos *choice*
claith, claithis *cloth, clothes*
cled *clad*
clos *courtyard; tight, shut-in*
condet, condeyt, condyt *safe-conduct*
confusion *destruction*
connand *agreement*
contenance *countenance, appearance, expression*
conteyn, conteyne *continue*
corp *body*
cost *rib, side; coast*
courch *head-dress*
court *court; retinue*
cowart *coward; cover, hiding* (**under cowart**)
crafft *occupation*
crag *rock*
crag(e) *neck*
cruell *fierce, warlike*
cruk, crukis *crook, bend*

crya *proclamation*
cusyng *cousin, kinsman; accusing, accusation*

dang(e) *struck*
de *die*
debate *resistance*
ded(e) *dead; death*
deid *deed, action*
demed *judged*
der *harm*
derff *violent*
dern *concealing, dark*
dik, dyk *wall, ditch*
douchtie, douchty *valiant, strong*
drayff *drove*
dulfulle *painful, doleful*
dulle *grief*
dur(e) *door*
dynt *blow*

eneuch *enough*
entent *intention, mind*
erar *rather, sooner*
erd *earth*
escheiff, eschew *achieve; avoid, escape*
etlyng *object*
etlyt *tried; armed*
everilk *every*
everilkdeill, everedeill *in every part, entirely*
eyn *eyes*

fa *foe*
fair *behavior, bearing, appearance; journey*
fais *foes*
fantase, fantasye *fantasy, whim*
faw *fall, befall*

Glossary

fecht *fight*
fechtaris *fighters*
feill *many*
feill, fell *cruel*
feill(e) *knowledge*
fell *very*
felloun *fierce*
fenyeit *feigned, false*
fer *far*
fer, feyr *array, store*
ferd *frightened; fourth*
feris *companions;* **in fer** *together*
fers *fierce;* **fersast** *fiercest*
fewté *fealty*
fey *doomed [to die]*
flear *retreating person, fugitive*
flem *banish*
flet(t) *floated*
flothis *floods*
flud *river, flood*
fold *field* (esp. of battle); *earth*
ford *ready* (as in **mak ford**)
forlorn *lost*
formast *foremost, first*
fors *force;* **on fors** *of necessity*
forthink *grieved for, repented*
forthward *forward, bold*
forthwart *promise, agreement*
found *go*
fra *from*
fray *frighten, terrify; din, attack*
fresche, freschly *vigorously*
fruschand *breaking*
fruschit *broke, broken*
fruster *useless*
furd *ford*
fusioun *abundance*

ga *go*
gait *way, street*
ganand *fitting, fine*
gang *go*
garth *garden, enclosure*
gaynest *shortest, nearest*
gaynstand *oppose*
gentrice, gentrys *nobility of character or manner*
gert *caused*
gif(f) *if*
gleid *ember*
graith *ready; make ready*
gyrth *sanctuary, refuge*

haboundand *abundant*
haff, haiff *have; reach*
haill *whole, wholly*
hald, hauld *stronghold, building*
hals *neck*
hap *good fortune*
harrold *herald*
hecht *called; summoned*
heich *high*
hicht, hycht *height; hill or highland;* **on hycht** *loudly*
hidwis, hidwys *hideous*
hir *her, herself*
ho, hoo *stop, halt*
hous *castle*
howlat *owl*
humyll *humble*
hy(e) *haste*
hyng *hang*
hynt *taken, laid hold of*

ilk *same*
ilkane *each one, everyone*
inch(e) *island*

Glossary

inew, inewch *enough*
ische *issue, sally forth*

jeperté *surprise attack, dangerous exploit*
jornay *combat, day's feat*
jowell *jewel, treasure*

keipe, kep(e) *keep, protect, defend; care, heed*
ken *know; teach, show the way*
kest *cast, considered*
kynrent *kinsfolk, family*
kynrik *kingdom*
kyrk *church*
kyth *show, shown*

lait(t) *late*
laith *loath, unwilling*
lang *long*
lap *leapt*
lappyt *surrounded*
lasar, laysar *leisure*
lat(t) *allow; leave; hinder*
lauta *loyalty*
law *low*
layff *the rest*
ler *tell, teach*
let(t) *hindrance; hinder; leave off*
lewch *laughed*
loft (as in **on loft**) *on high, above*
low *flame; love*
lugeyng *lodging*
lusty *pleasing*
lychtlynes *scorn, affront*
lyr *flesh*

ma *more; make, may*
magra, magre *in spite of*

mair *more*
maist *most*
maistré *mastery*
matelent *rage, ill-will*
mayn *strength, power; lament*
mekill *much*
melle *melee, battle*
mendis *amends, revenge*
menyhe *company of soldiers, crowd*
mercat, merket *market, trading*
message *messenger*
mocht *might*
mony *many*
mos *moor, moss; bog*
murn *mourning*
murthyr *murder*
myrk *dark*
myrth *bliss, joy*
mys *wrong*
myster *need*

na *no, nor*
nakyn *no kind of*
nan, nane, nayne *none*
nevo *nephew*
none, nowne *noon*
nother *neither*
nowmer *number*
nycht *night*

ocht *ought, anything*
ony *any*
ordinance *provision of necessaries; decree*
ost *army*
ourhyede *overtake*
owtrage *violence; violent*
oys *use, practice*

Glossary

pais *pace, step*
palyon(e) *pavilion*
perance *appearance, sign*
persew *follow, attack*
persone *person; parson*
pes *peace; truce*
pisan, pyssan, pissand *neck armor*
plait, playt *plate of steel*
playn *plain;* **in playn** *openly, completely*
port *gate*
pow *pull*
power *force of men, main body of an army*
preiff *try, prove, experience*
pres *press of battle*
preva *private, secret*
prys *praise*
purchas, purches *obtain, solicit*

quha *who*
quhar *where*
quhat *what*
quhen *when*
quhi, quhy *why*
quhilk *which*
quhill *while*

rahers *rehearsal, speech; relate, recite*
rais *rose*
rakles *heedless*
ramede *help*
ramuff *remove*
rang(e) *array; reigned, held sway*
raw *row, line of battle*
ray *array*
rede *counsel; read; red*
reiff, reyff *plunder*
reik *smoke*
relevyt *rally, rallied*

remord *cause remorse*
rewll(e) *rule*
rewme *realm*
rewmour *alarm*
rial, ryall *royal*
ribald *rebel*
rout *army, throng*
rowme *room, space*
ryng *rule*

sa *so*
sad *grave, resolute*
saikles, saklace *innocent*
sailye *assail, assault*
sammyn, samyn *same*
sar, sayr, sor *sore, sorely*
scaith, skaith *harm*
schaw *wood; show*
schenand *shining*
schent *destroyed*
scherand *cutting*
scheyne *fair, gleaming*
schirrais, schyrray, schirreff *sheriff*
scho *she*
scor, scoyr *twenty*
scry *cry*
scurrour, skouriouris, skowrrouris *scout, scouts*
seir *several, different*
seker, sekyr *sure*
sell *self* (as in **him sell**)
semblay, sembly *assembly, meeting*
sen(e) *since*
sen syne *since that time*
sic *such*
sicht *sight*
skill *reason*
slaid *valley* (as in **slonk and slaid**); *slid*
slonk *hollow*

Glossary

slop *gap, breach*
slycht *cunning, pretence*
socht *sought, went*
son *soon; son; sun*
Soth(e)ren, Soth(e)ron *the English*
sover *sure*
soverance *assurance, safety*
sper *spear; ask*
spill *destroy*
spoilye, spulye *spoil, sack*
spreit *spirit*
stad *placed*
staill *main body of army*
stark *strong*
statut *rule; establish, decreed*
steik *stab*
ster *stir, move*
stroy *destroy*
stryff *strife*
stuart *steward*
stuff *provisions; reinforcements, garrison; furnish with men*
stynt *stop*
suld *should*
sumdeill *somewhat*
sum part *to some extent*
sune *soon*
supplé *reinforcements*
sutaill(e), sutell *cunning*
suth *truth; true*
suthfast *true*
swa *so*
swar *snare*
swyth *quickly; soon*
syne *since, then, after*
syng *sign, mark*

ta *take*
ta, tayne *the one*

tary *delay*
temer, temyr *timber*
tent *care, attention* (as in **tak tent**)
terand *tyrant*
teyne *rage, harm, vexation; angry*
thai *they*
thaim, thame *them*
thair, thar *their; there*
than *then*
the *thigh*
thedyr *thither*
thine *thence*
thir *these*
tho, thocht, thoucht *though*
thoill *endure*
thrang *press of battle*
throch, throuch *through*
thuortour *transverse, crosswise*
tithand *tiding*
torment *pain*
travaill *hard undertaking, trouble; labor*
trewage *tribute*
trewbut(e) *tribute*
trow *trust, believe*
tryst *appointed meeting time*
turs *truss, pack up*
twa *two*
tyd *time*
tynt *lost*

unes *unease, difficulty*
unrycht *wrong, offense*
us *use, service*

vaill(e) *worth, advantage, power, help, avail; valley*
vaillit, vaillyt *distinguished*

Glossary

vallyt *specially picked*
vantgard *vanguard*
variance *fickleness, variance*
vaslage *vassalage, prowess*
vayne *vain* (**in vayne**)*; vein*
venge *avenge*
verray *very*
vesy *reconnoiter; inspect*
viage *traveling, journey*

wa *woe, pain; grieved*
wach(e) *watch, guard*
wage *hire, fee, reward*
waik *weak; weaken*
waill *good standing, wealth; bulwark*
waill(e) *choose, chose; best*
waillyt *well-chosen*
wald *would*
walk *keep watch; wake*
walkand *walking; watching*
wan *won, got*
wanys *dwellings*
wareide, waryed, waryt *accursed*

warisoun, warysoun *reward*
waverand *changeable*
wayne *quantity*
waynys *carts*
wedder *weather*
weid *clothing;* **weidis** *armor*
weile, weill *well, fine*
wend *go, went*
wer *spring; war; were*
wicht, wycht *brave, strong*
wiff *woman*
wit(t) *knowledge*
worschip *honor, bravery*
worthis *becomes; must, behooves*
wraith *wrath*
wrek *wreak, revenge*
wrocht *wrought*
wryt *writing, letter, document*
wys *way; wise*

yeit *yet*
yemen *yeomen*
yneuch, ynewch *enough*

Volumes in the Middle English Texts Series

The Floure and the Leafe, *The Assembly of Ladies*, and *The Isle of Ladies*, ed. Derek Pearsall (1990)

Three Middle English Charlemagne Romances, ed. Alan Lupack (1990)

Six Ecclesiastical Satires, ed. James M. Dean (1991)

Heroic Women from the Old Testament in Middle English Verse, ed. Russell A. Peck (1991)

The Canterbury Tales: Fifteenth-Century Continuations and Additions, ed. John M. Bowers (1992)

Gavin Douglas, *The Palis of Honoure*, ed. David Parkinson (1992)

Wynnere and Wastoure and The Parlement of the Thre Ages, ed. Warren Ginsberg (1992)

The Shewings of Julian of Norwich, ed. Georgia Ronan Crampton (1993)

King Arthur's Death: The Middle English Stanzaic Morte Arthur and Alliterative Morte Arthure, ed. Larry D. Benson and Edward E. Foster (1994)

Lancelot of the Laik and Sir Tristrem, ed. Alan Lupack (1994)

Sir Gawain: Eleven Romances and Tales, ed. Thomas Hahn (1995)

The Middle English Breton Lays, ed. Anne Laskaya and Eve Salisbury (1995)

Sir Perceval of Galles and Ywain and Gawain, ed. Mary Flowers Braswell (1995)

Four Middle English Romances: Sir Isumbras, Octavian, Sir Eglamour of Artois, Sir Tryamour, ed. Harriet Hudson (1996)

The Poems of Laurence Minot (1333–1352), ed. Richard H. Osberg (1996)

Medieval English Political Writings, ed. James M. Dean (1996)

The Book of Margery Kempe, ed. Lynn Staley (1996)

Amis and Amiloun, Robert of Cisyle, and Sir Amadace, ed. Edward E. Foster (1997)

The Cloud of Unknowing, ed. Patrick J. Gallacher (1997)

Robin Hood and Other Outlaw Tales, ed. Stephen Knight and Thomas Ohlgren (1997)

The Poems of Robert Henryson, ed. Robert L. Kindrick (1997)

Moral Love Songs and Laments, ed. Susanna Greer Fein (1998)

John Lydgate, *Troy Book: Selections*, ed. Robert R. Edwards (1998)

Thomas Usk, *The Testament of Love*, ed. R. Allen Shoaf (1998)

Prose Merlin, ed. John Conlee (1998)

Middle English Marian Lyrics, ed. Karen Saupe (1998)

John Metham, *Amoryus and Cleopes*, ed. Stephen F. Page (1999)

Four Romances of England: King Horn, Havelok the Dane, Bevis of Hampton, Athelston, ed. Ronald B. Herzman, Graham Drake, Eve Salisbury (1999)

The Assembly of Gods: Le Assemble de Dyeus, or Banquet of Gods and Goddesses, with the Discourse of Reason and Sensuality, ed. Jane Chance (1999)

Thomas Hoccleve, *The Regiment of Princes*, ed. Charles R. Blyth (1999)

John Capgrave, *The Life of St. Katherine*, ed. Karen Winstead (1999)

John Gower, *Confessio Amantis*, Vol. 1, ed. Russell A. Peck (2000); Vol. 2 (2003)

Richard the Redeless and *Mum and the Sothsegger*, ed. James Dean (2000)

Ancrene Wisse, ed. Robert Hasenfratz (2000)

Walter Hilton, *The Scale of Perfection*, ed. Thomas Bestul (2000)

John Lydgate, *The Siege of Thebes*, ed. Robert Edwards (2001)

Pearl, ed. Sarah Stanbury (2001)

The Trials and Joys of Marriage, ed. Eve Salisbury (2002)

Middle English Legends of Women Saints, ed. Sherry L. Reames (2003)

Other TEAMS Publications

Documents of Practice Series:

Love and Marriage in Late Medieval London, selected, translated, and introduced by Shannon McSheffrey (1995)

Sources for the History of Medicine in Late Medieval England, selected, introduced, and translated by Carole Rawcliffe (1995)

A Slice of Life: Selected Documents of Medieval English Peasant Experience, edited, translated, and with an introduction by Edwin Brezette DeWindt (1996)

Regular Life: Monastic, Canonical, and Mendicant Rules, selected with an introduction by Douglas J. McMillan and Kathryn Smith Fladenmuller (1997)

Women and Monasticism in Medieval Europe: Sisters and Patrons of the Cistercian Reform, selected, translated, and with an introduction by Constance H. Berman (2002)

Commentary Series:

Commentary on the Book of Jonah, Haimo of Auxerre, translated with an introduction by Deborah Everhart (1993)

Medieval Exegesis in Translation: Commentaries on the Book of Ruth, translated with an introduction by Lesley Smith (1996)

Nicholas of Lyra's Apocalypse Commentary, translated with an introduction and notes by Philip D. W. Krey (1997)

Rabbi Ezra Ben Solomon of Gerona: Commentary on the Song of Songs and Other Kabbalistic Commentaries, selected, translated, and annotated by Seth Brody (1999)

John Wyclif: On the Truth of Holy Scripture, translated with an introduction and notes by Ian Christopher Levy (2001)

Second Thessalonians: Two Early Medieval Apocalyptic Commentaries, translated with an introduction by Steven R. Cartwright and Kevin L. Hughes (2001)

Medieval German Texts in Bilingual Editions Series:

I. *Sovereignty and Salvation in the Vernacular, 1050–1150*, introduction, translation, and notes by James A. Schultz (2000)

II. *Ava's New Testament Narratives: "When the Old Law Passed Away,"* introduction, translations, and notes by James A. Rushing, Jr. (2003)

III. *History as Literature: German World Chronicles of the Thirteenth Century in Verse*, introduction, translations, and notes by R. Graeme Dunphy (2003)

To order please contact: MEDIEVAL INSTITUTE PUBLICATIONS
Western Michigan University
Kalamazoo, MI 49008–5432
Phone (269) 387–8755
FAX (269) 387–8750

http://www.wmich.edu/medieval/mip/index.html

Medieval Institute Publications is a program
of The Medieval Institute, College of Arts
and Sciences, Western Michigan University

Typeset in 10.5 pt. Times New Roman
with Times New Roman display
Manufactured by Cushing-Malloy, Inc.—Ann Arbor, Michigan

Medieval Institute Publications
College of Arts and Sciences
Western Michigan University
1903 W. Michigan Avenue
Kalamazoo, Michigan 49008-5432
www.wmich.edu/medieval/mip/

WESTERN MICHIGAN UNIVERSITY